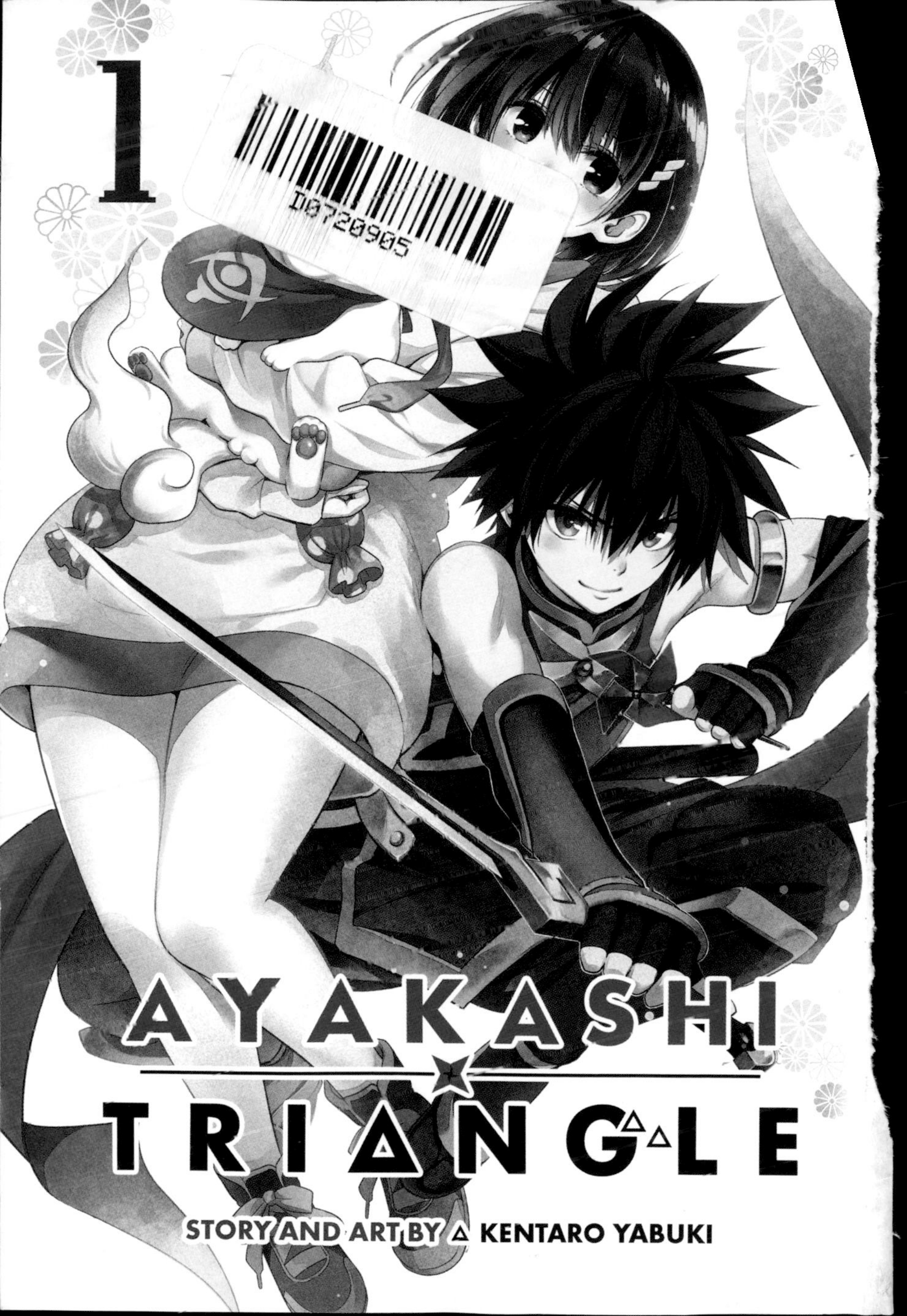
1
AYAKASHI
TRIANGLE
STORY AND ART BY KENTARO YABUKI

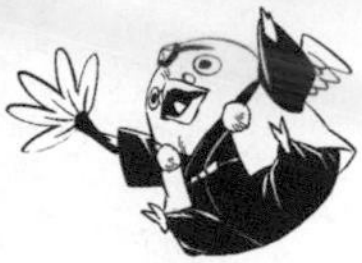

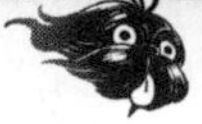

# 1

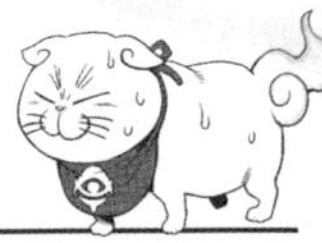

## AYAKASHI TRIANGLE

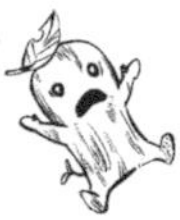

### Table of Contents

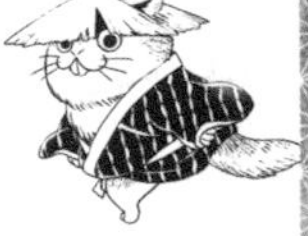



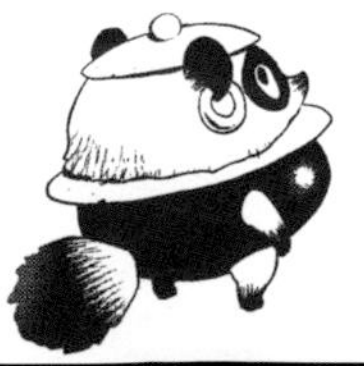

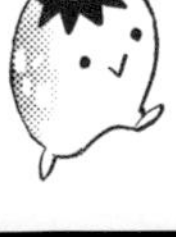

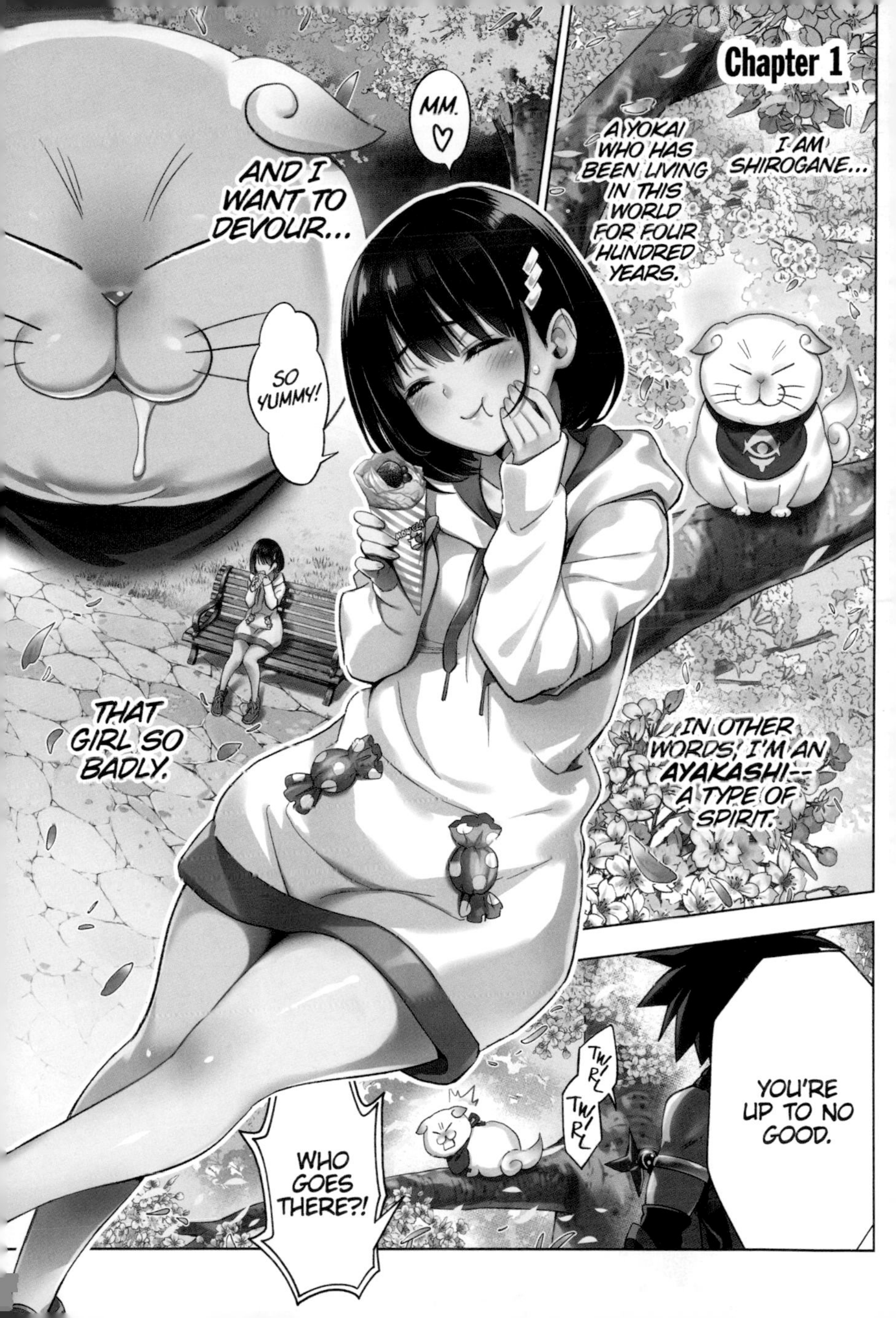
Chapter 1
I AM SHIROGANE...
A YOKAI WHO HAS BEEN LIVING IN THIS WORLD FOR FOUR HUNDRED YEARS.
MM. ♡
AND I WANT TO DEVOUR...
SO YUMMY!
IN OTHER WORDS, I'M AN AYAKASHI-- A TYPE OF SPIRIT.
THAT GIRL SO BADLY.
YOU'RE UP TO NO GOOD.
TWIRL TWIRL
WHO GOES THERE?!

## Chapter 1 Matsuri, Suzu, and the Ayakashi

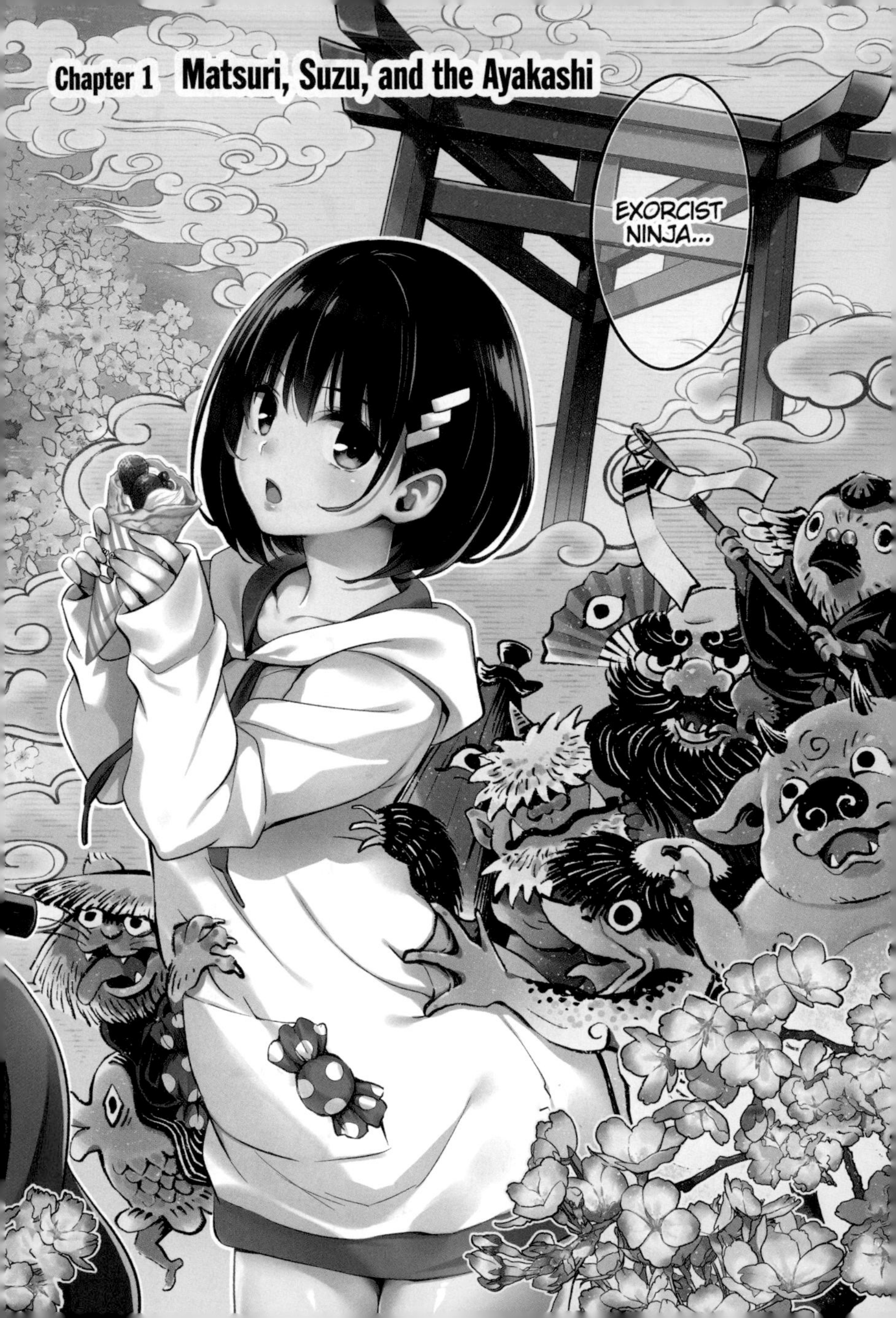
EXORCIST NINJA...

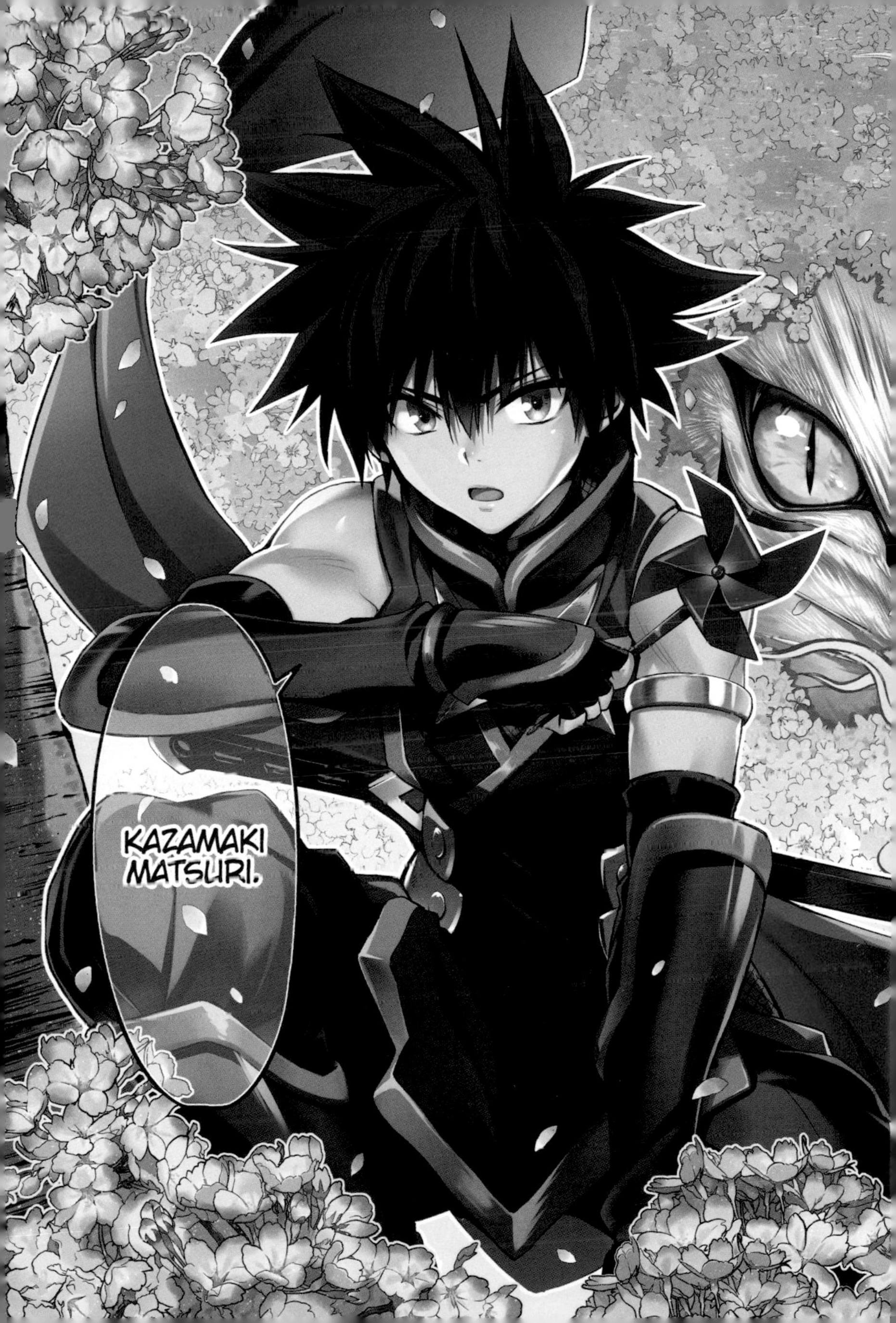
KAZAMAKI MATSURI.

AYAKASHI
TRIANGLE

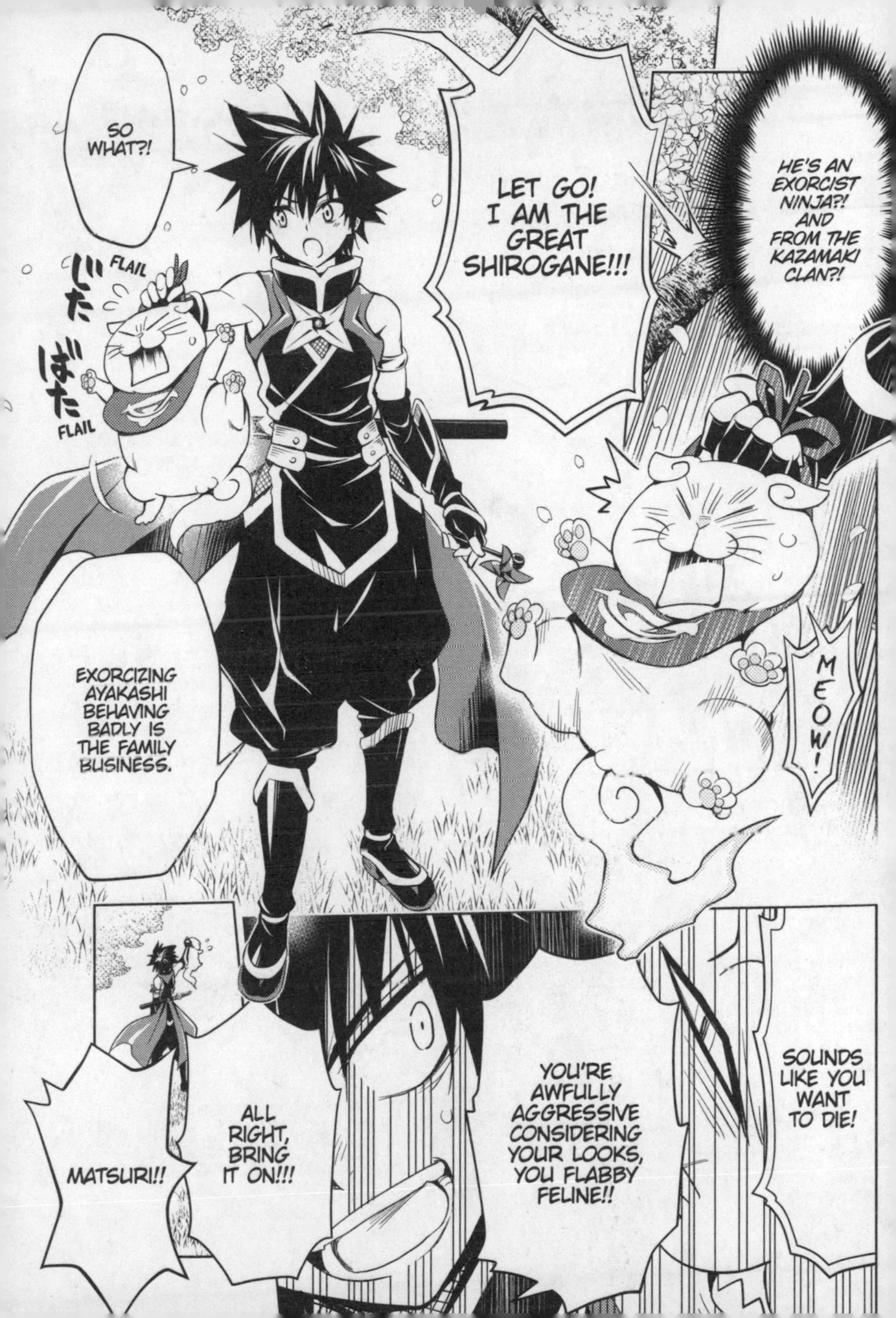
HE'S AN EXORCIST NINJA?! AND FROM THE KAZAMAKI CLAN?!
LET GO! I AM THE GREAT SHIROGANE!!!
SO WHAT?!
じた FLAIL
ばた FLAIL
MEOW!
EXORCIZING AYAKASHI BEHAVING BADLY IS THE FAMILY BUSINESS.
SOUNDS LIKE YOU WANT TO DIE!
YOU'RE AWFULLY AGGRESSIVE CONSIDERING YOUR LOOKS, YOU FLABBY FELINE!!
ALL RIGHT, BRING IT ON!!!
MATSURI!!

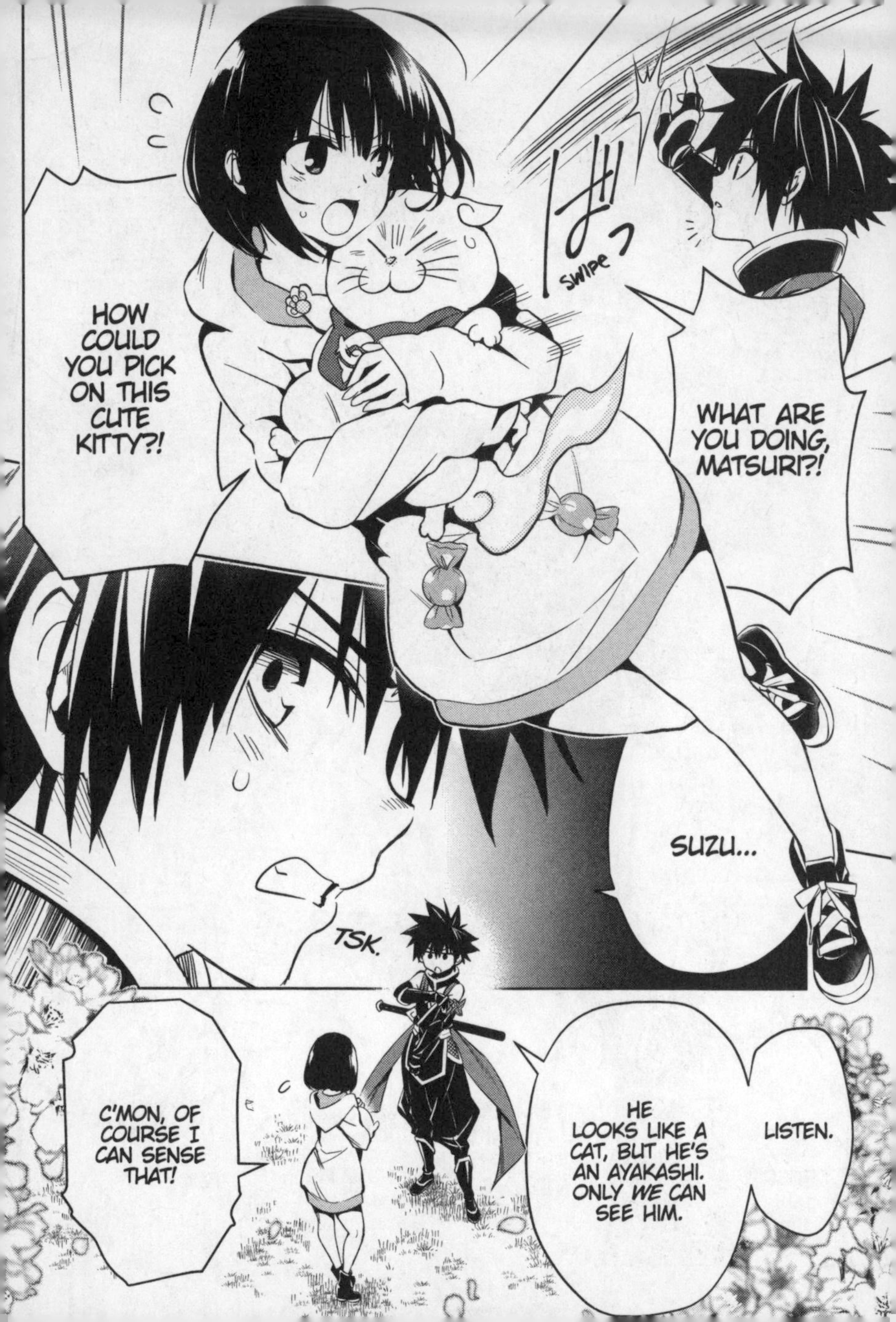
SWIPE
WHAT ARE YOU DOING, MATSURI?!
HOW COULD YOU PICK ON THIS CUTE KITTY?!
SUZU...
TSK.
LISTEN.
HE LOOKS LIKE A CAT, BUT HE'S AN AYAKASHI. ONLY WE CAN SEE HIM.
C'MON, OF COURSE I CAN SENSE THAT!

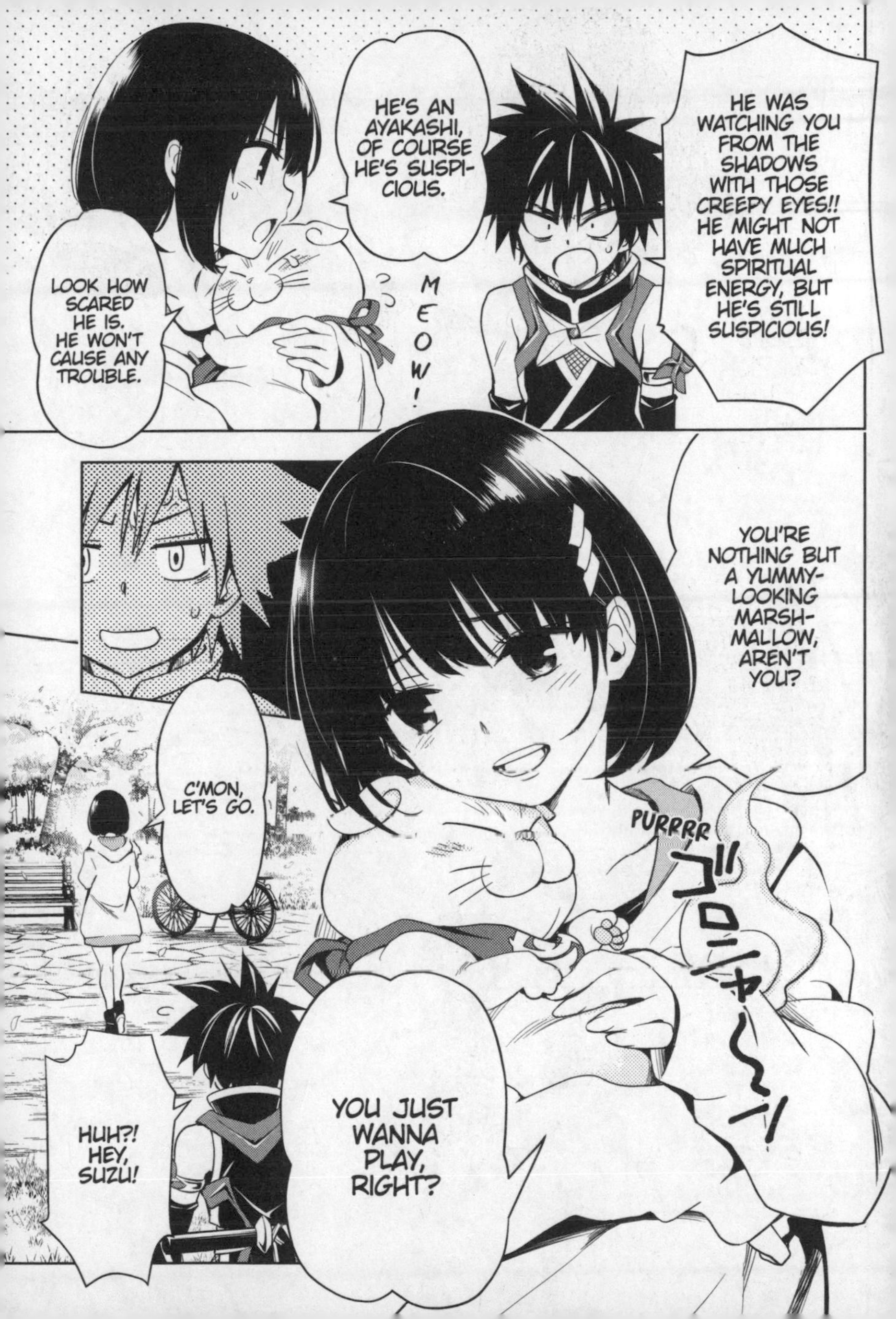
HE WAS WATCHING YOU FROM THE SHADOWS WITH THOSE CREEPY EYES!! HE MIGHT NOT HAVE MUCH SPIRITUAL ENERGY, BUT HE'S STILL SUSPICIOUS!
HE'S AN AYAKASHI, OF COURSE HE'S SUSPICIOUS.
MEOW!
LOOK HOW SCARED HE IS. HE WON'T CAUSE ANY TROUBLE.
YOU'RE NOTHING BUT A YUMMY-LOOKING MARSHMALLOW, AREN'T YOU?
PURRRR
ゴロニャ〜〜!
YOU JUST WANNA PLAY, RIGHT?
C'MON, LET'S GO.
HUH?! HEY, SUZU!

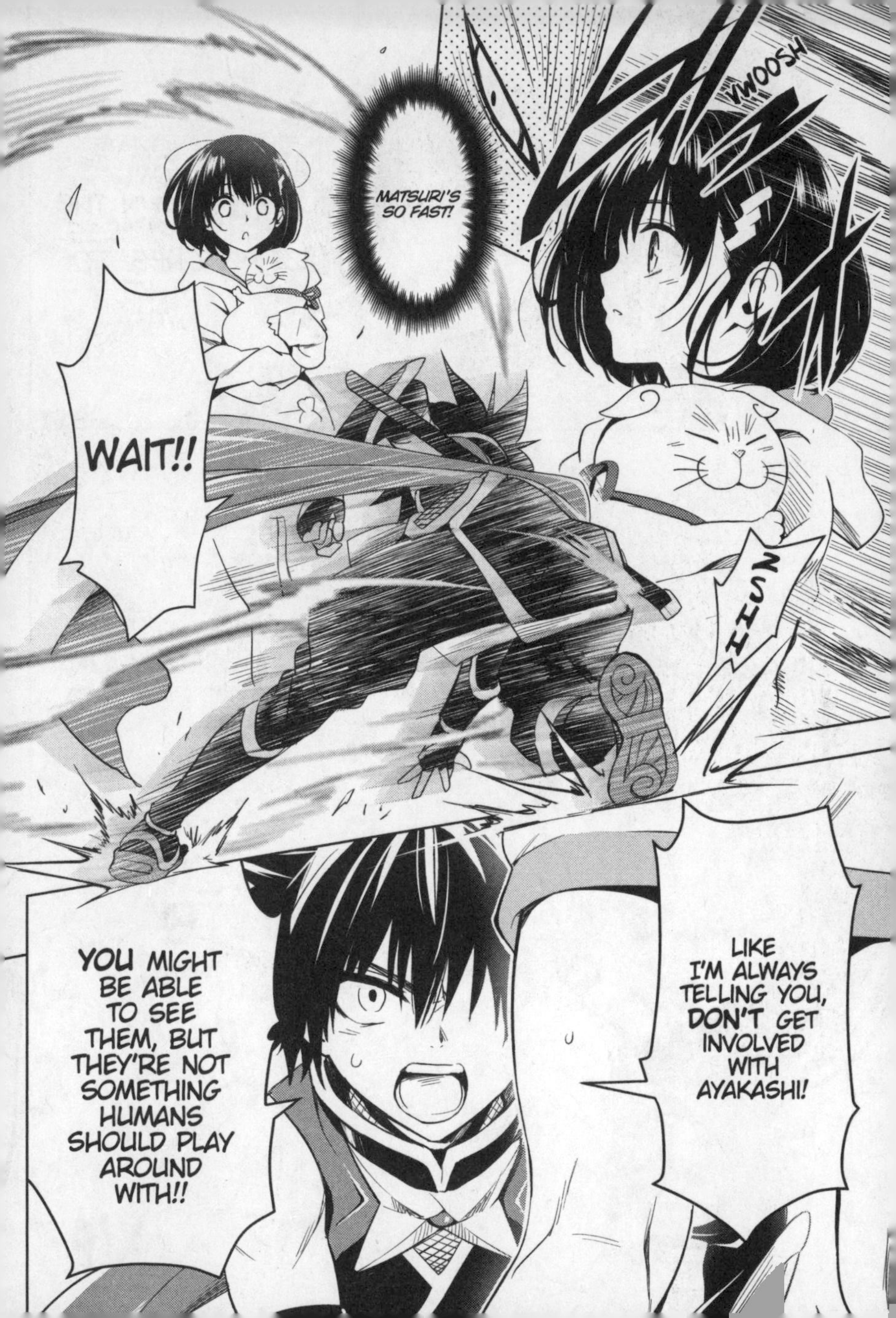
VWOOSH
MATSURI'S SO FAST!
SHHUN
WAIT!!
LIKE I'M ALWAYS TELLING YOU, DON'T GET INVOLVED WITH AYAKASHI!
YOU MIGHT BE ABLE TO SEE THEM, BUT THEY'RE NOT SOMETHING HUMANS SHOULD PLAY AROUND WITH!!

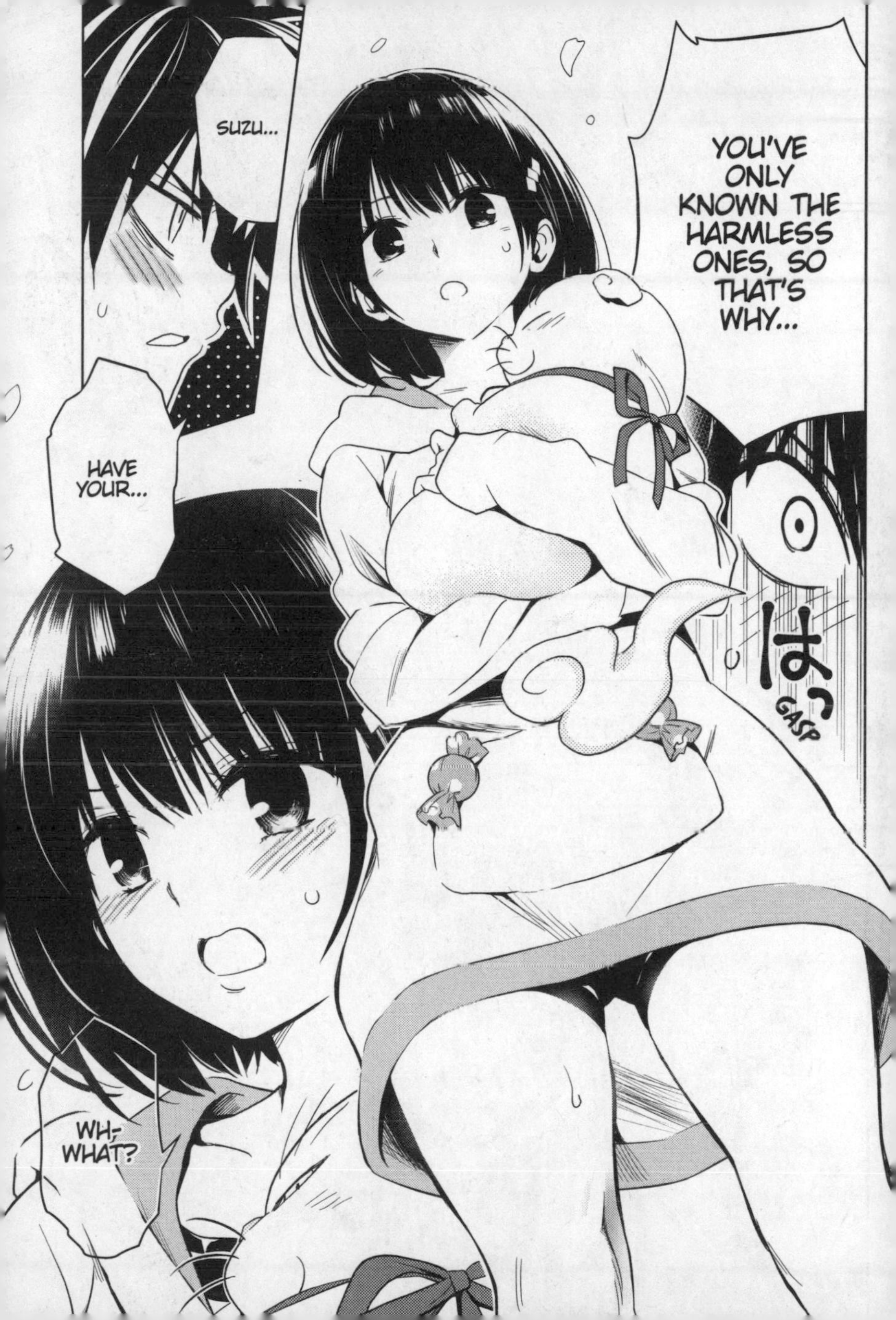
YOU'VE ONLY KNOWN THE HARMLESS ONES, SO THAT'S WHY...
SUZU...
HAVE YOUR...
はっ
GASP
WH-, WHAT?

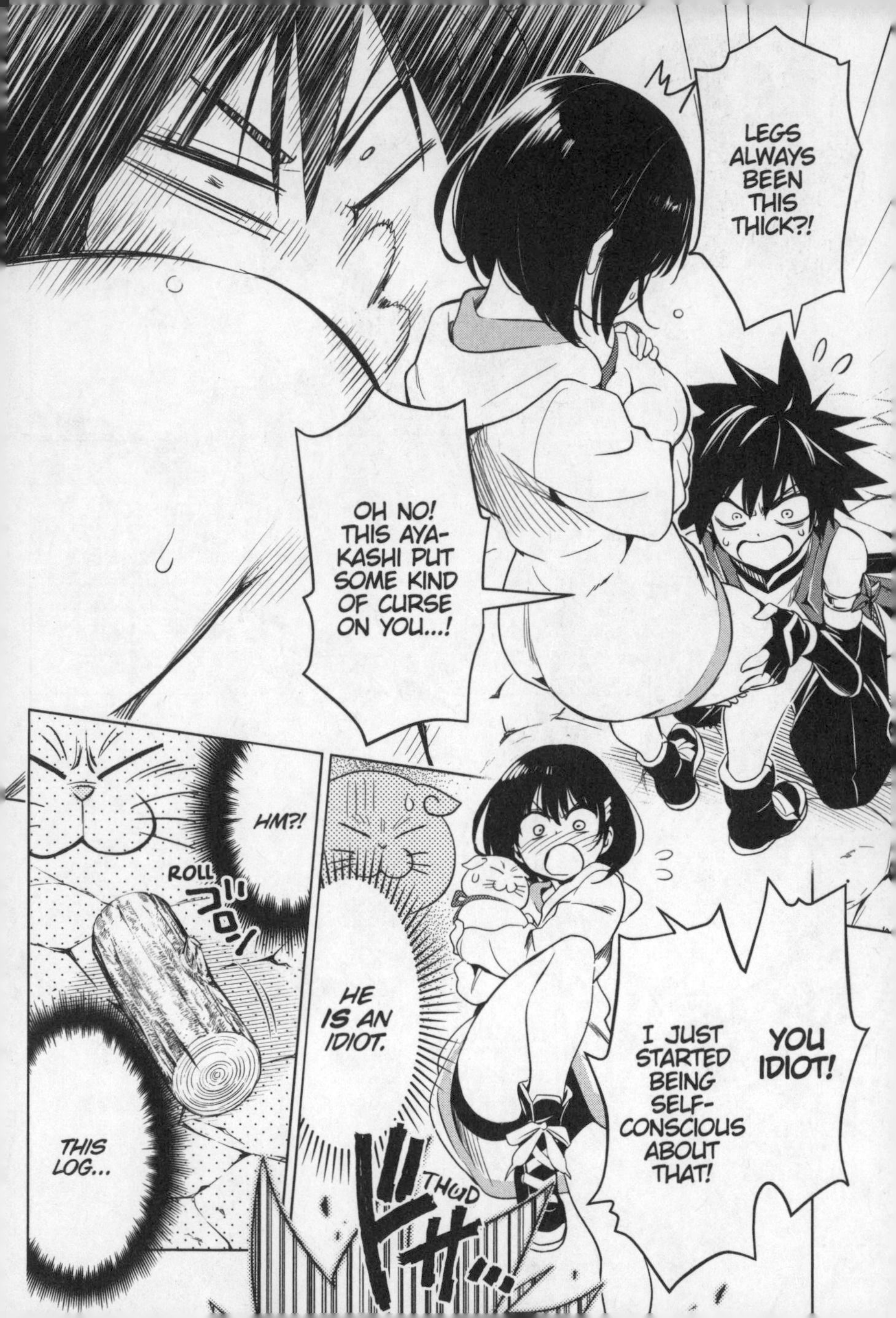
LEGS ALWAYS BEEN THIS THICK?!
OH NO! THIS AYA-KASHI PUT SOME KIND OF CURSE ON YOU...!
YOU IDIOT!
I JUST STARTED BEING SELF-CONSCIOUS ABOUT THAT!
THUD
HE IS AN IDIOT.
HM?!
ROLL
THIS LOG...

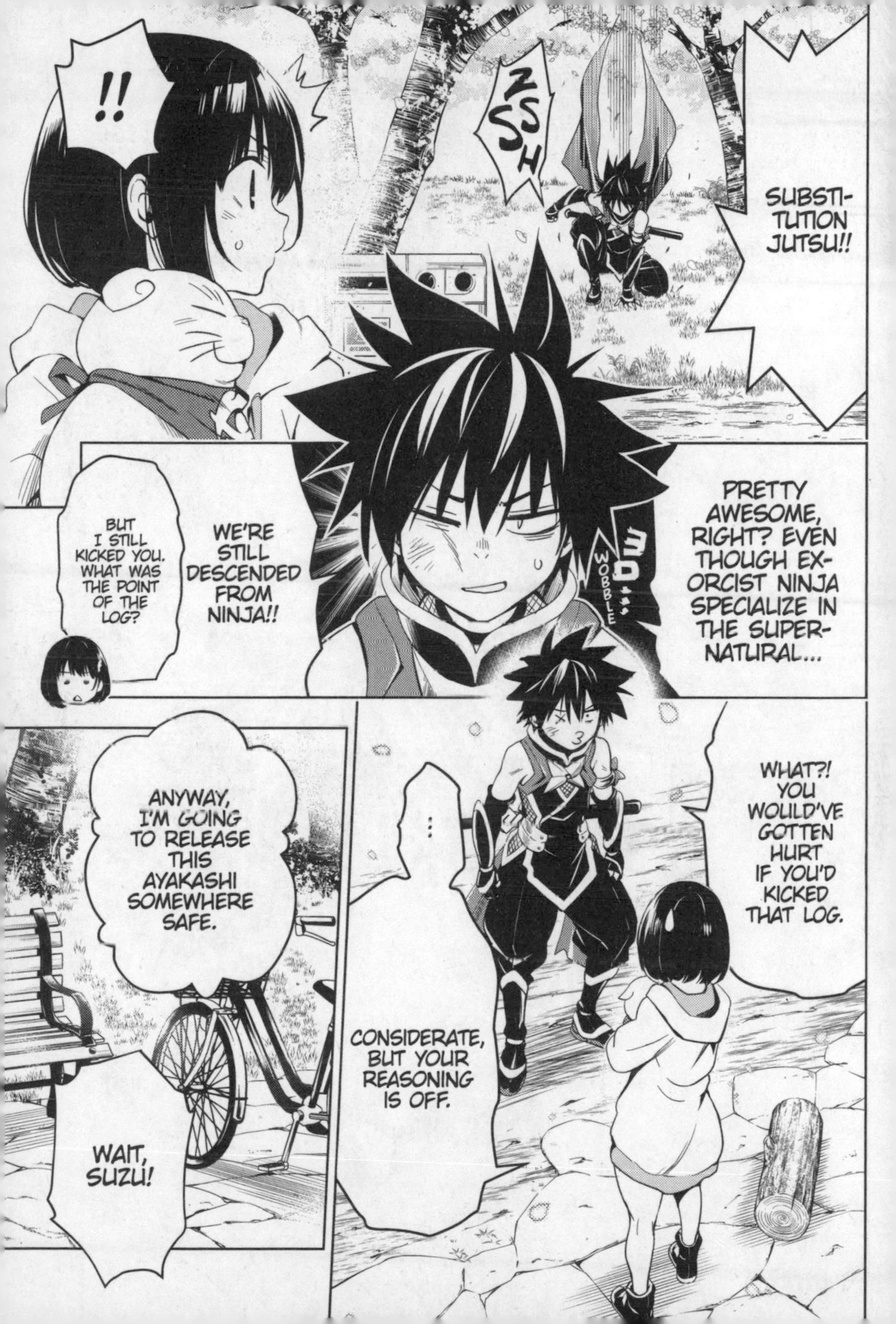
ZSSH
SUBSTI-TUTION JUTSU!!
!!
PRETTY AWESOME, RIGHT? EVEN THOUGH EX-ORCIST NINJA SPECIALIZE IN THE SUPER-NATURAL...
WOBBLE
WE'RE STILL DESCENDED FROM NINJA!!
BUT I STILL KICKED YOU. WHAT WAS THE POINT OF THE LOG?
WHAT?! YOU WOULD'VE GOTTEN HURT IF YOU'D KICKED THAT LOG.
...
CONSIDERATE, BUT YOUR REASONING IS OFF.
ANYWAY, I'M GOING TO RELEASE THIS AYAKASHI SOMEWHERE SAFE.
WAIT, SUZU!

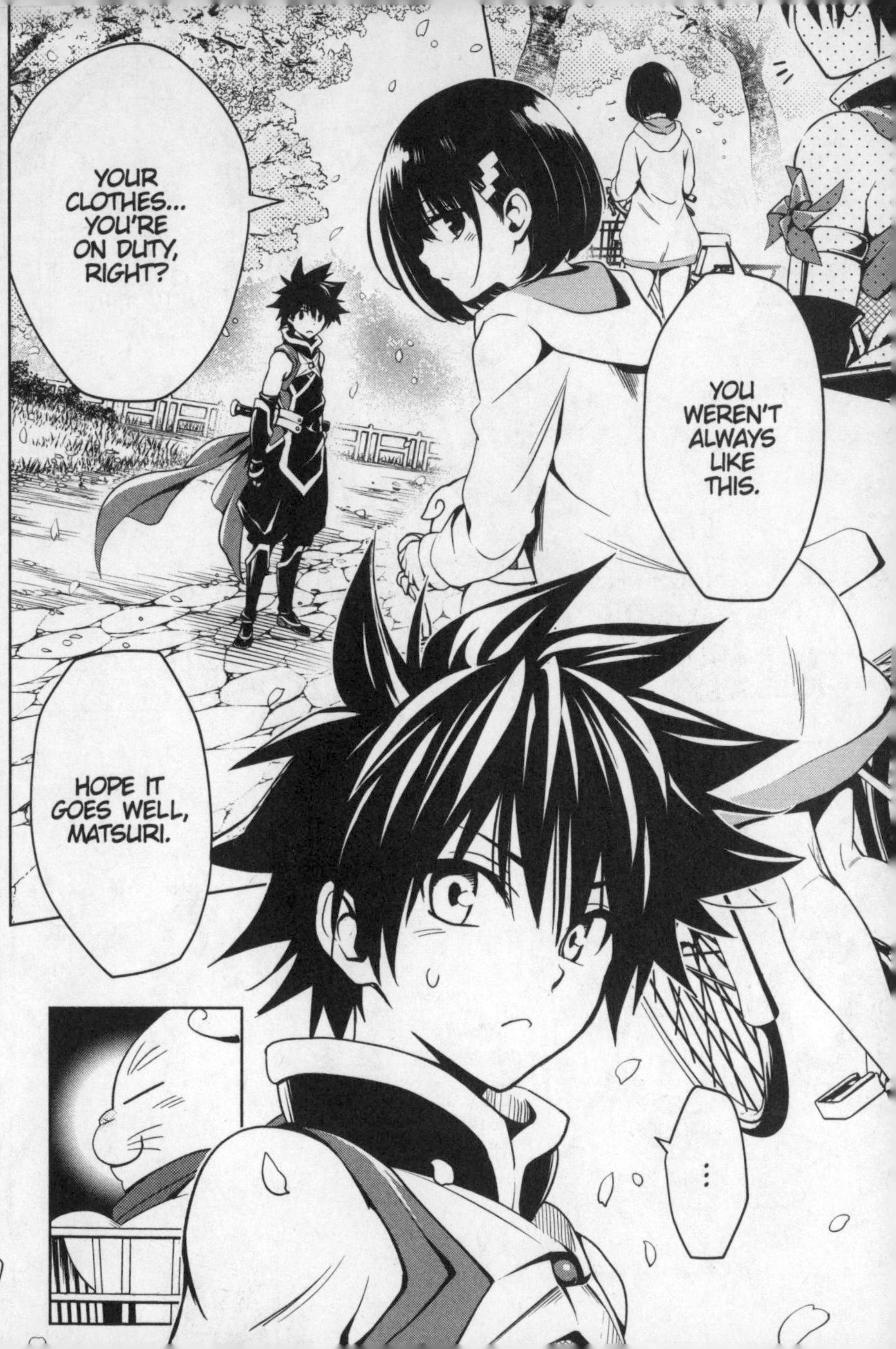
YOUR CLOTHES... YOU'RE ON DUTY, RIGHT?
YOU WEREN'T ALWAYS LIKE THIS.
HOPE IT GOES WELL, MATSURI.
...

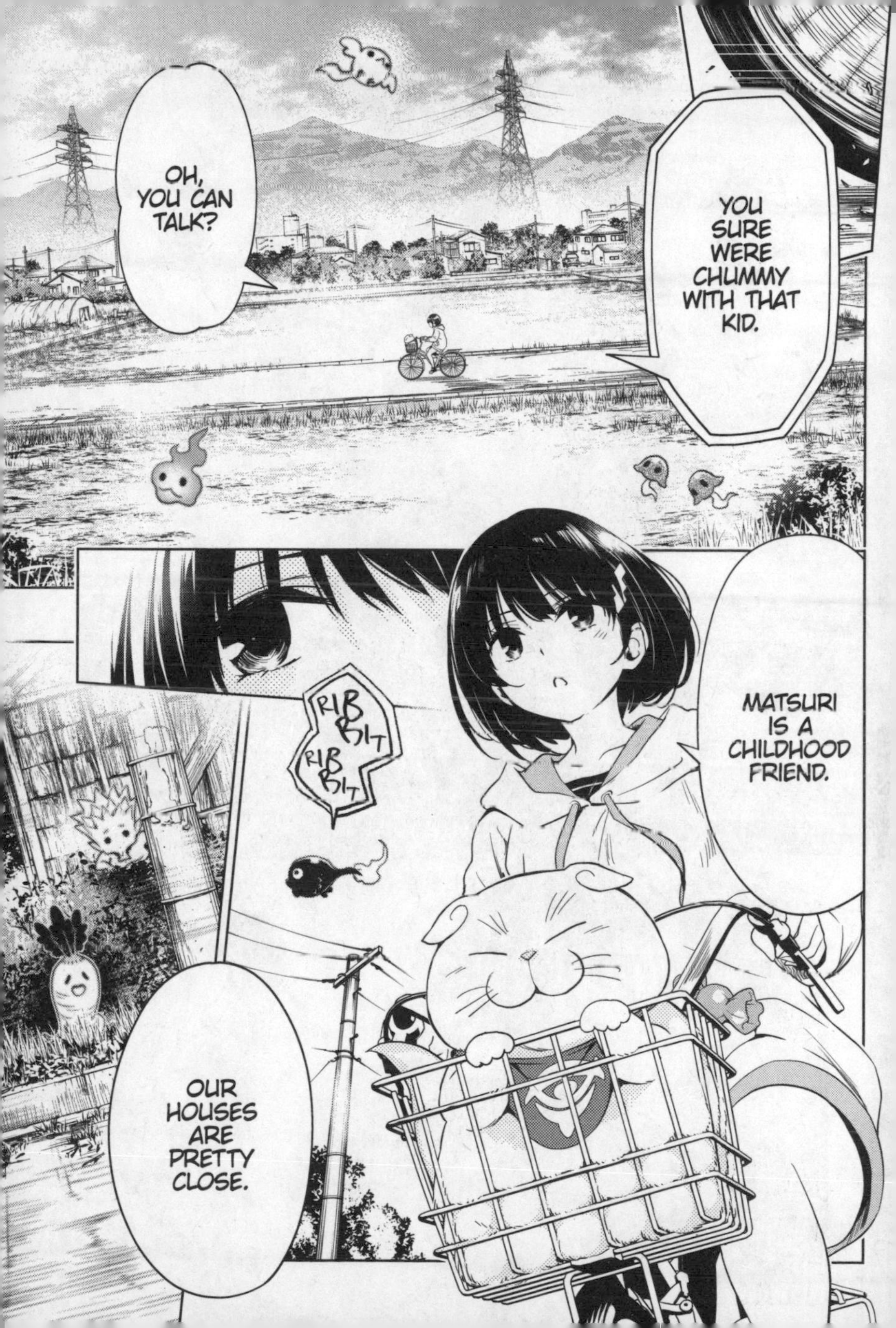
YOU SURE WERE CHUMMY WITH THAT KID.
OH, YOU CAN TALK?
MATSURI IS A CHILDHOOD FRIEND.
RIBBIT RIBBIT
OUR HOUSES ARE PRETTY CLOSE.

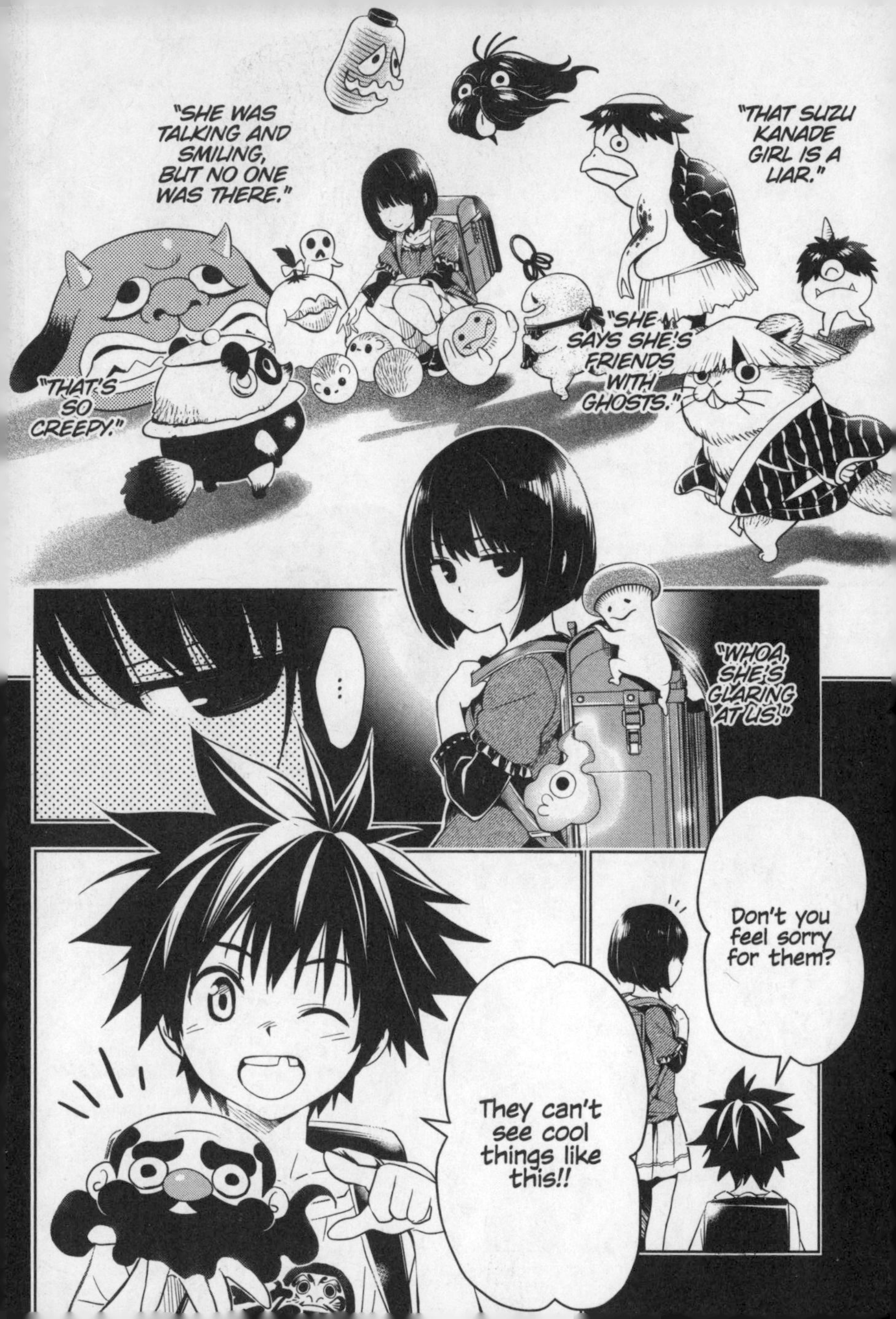
"THAT SUZU KANADE GIRL IS A LIAR."
"SHE WAS TALKING AND SMILING, BUT NO ONE WAS THERE."
"SHE SAYS SHE'S FRIENDS WITH GHOSTS."
"THAT'S SO CREEPY."
"WHOA, SHE'S GLARING AT US."
...
Don't you feel sorry for them?
They can't see cool things like this!!

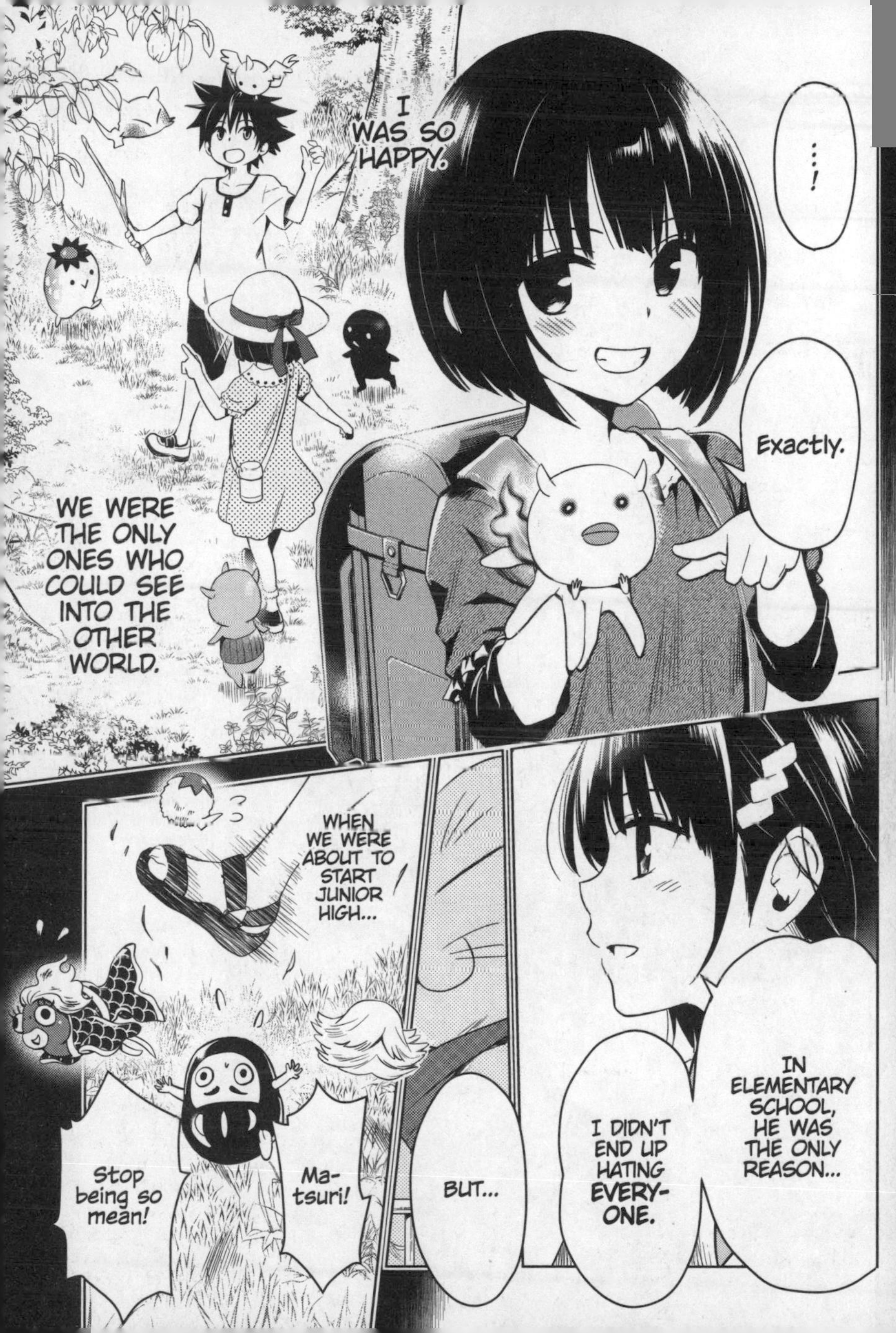

...!
Exactly.
I WAS SO HAPPY.
WE WERE THE ONLY ONES WHO COULD SEE INTO THE OTHER WORLD.
IN ELEMENTARY SCHOOL, HE WAS THE ONLY REASON...
I DIDN'T END UP HATING EVERY-ONE.
BUT...
WHEN WE WERE ABOUT TO START JUNIOR HIGH...
Ma-tsuri!
Stop being so mean!

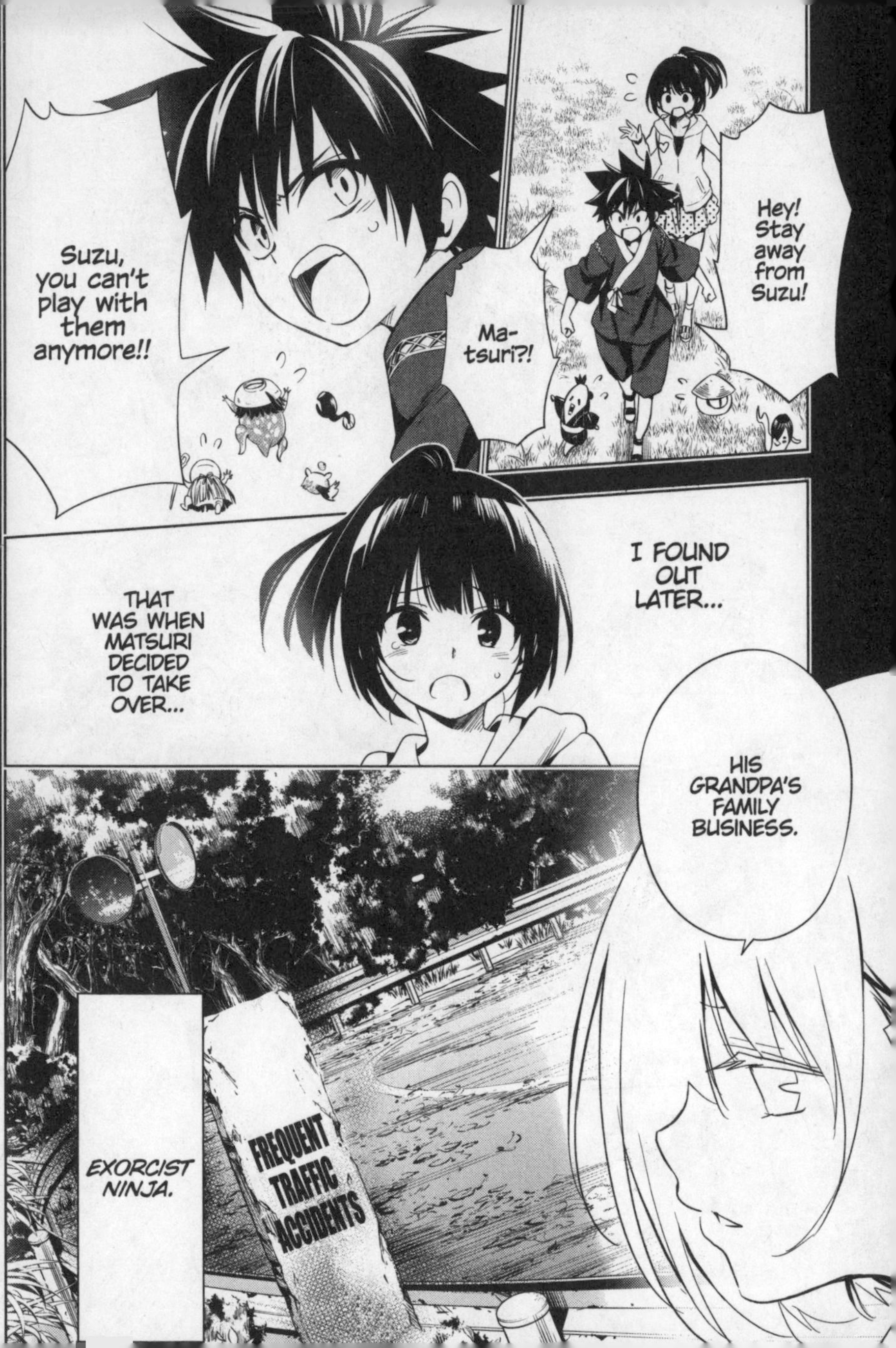
Hey! Stay away from Suzu!
Ma-tsuri?!
Suzu, you can't play with them anymore!!
I FOUND OUT LATER...
THAT WAS WHEN MATSURI DECIDED TO TAKE OVER...
HIS GRANDPA'S FAMILY BUSINESS.
FREQUENT TRAFFIC ACCIDENTS
EXORCIST NINJA.

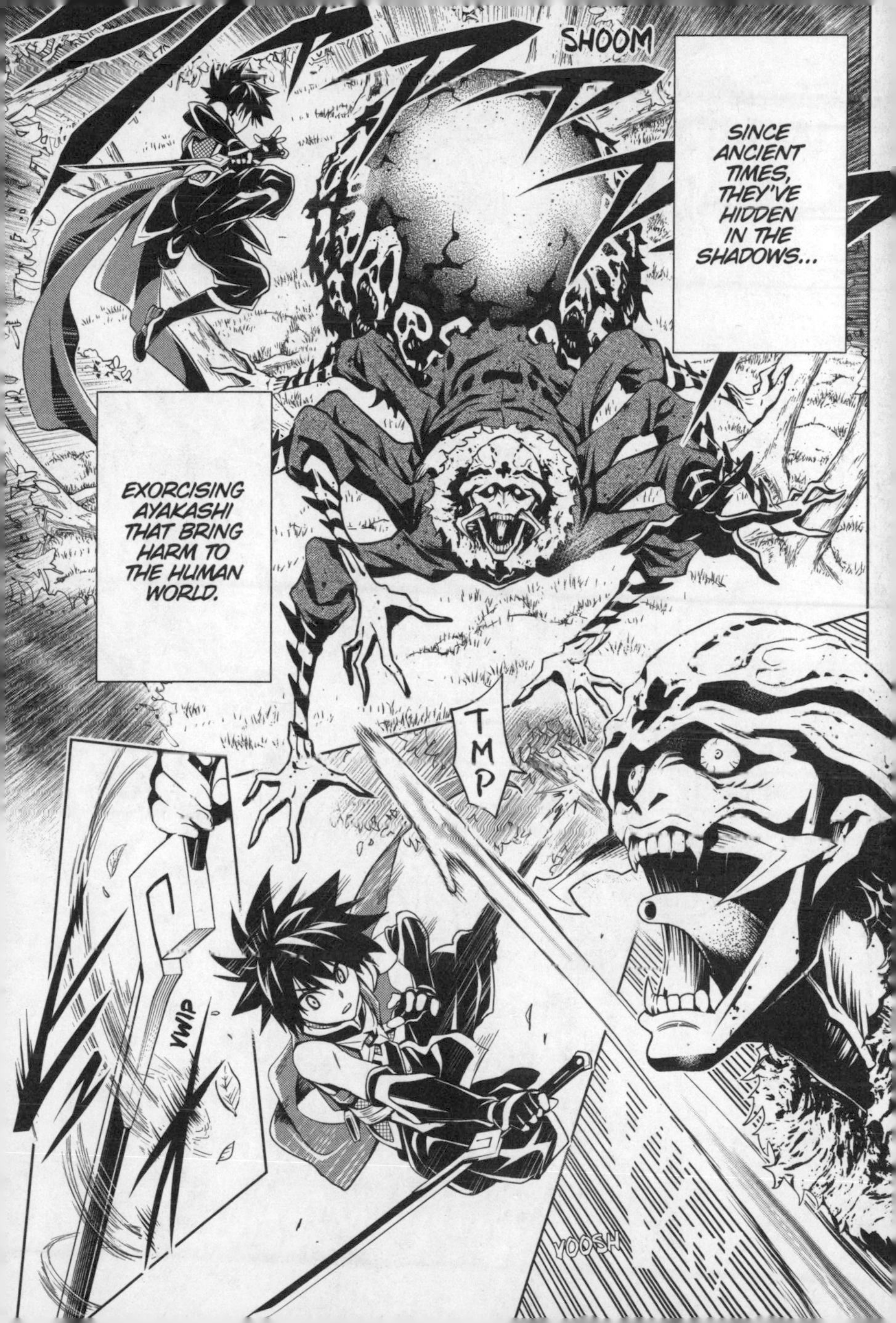
SHOOM
SINCE ANCIENT TIMES, THEY'VE HIDDEN IN THE SHADOWS...
EXORCISING AYAKASHI THAT BRING HARM TO THE HUMAN WORLD.
TMP
YOOSH
VWIP

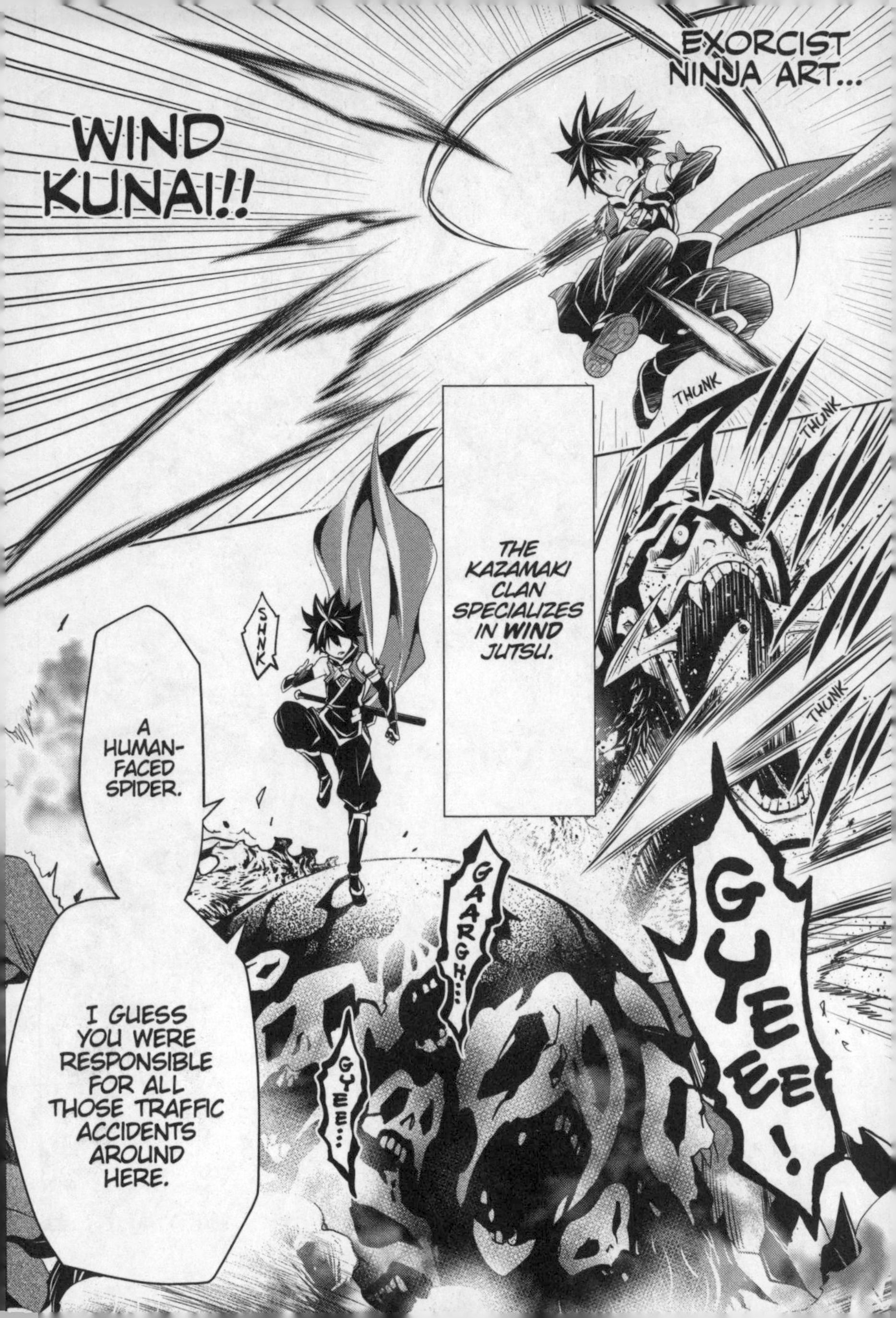
EXORCIST NINJA ART...
WIND KUNAI!!
THUNK
THUNK
THE KAZAMAKI CLAN SPECIALIZES IN WIND JUTSU.
THUNK
GYEEE!
SHNK
GAARGH...
GYEEE...
A HUMAN-FACED SPIDER.
I GUESS YOU WERE RESPONSIBLE FOR ALL THOSE TRAFFIC ACCIDENTS AROUND HERE.

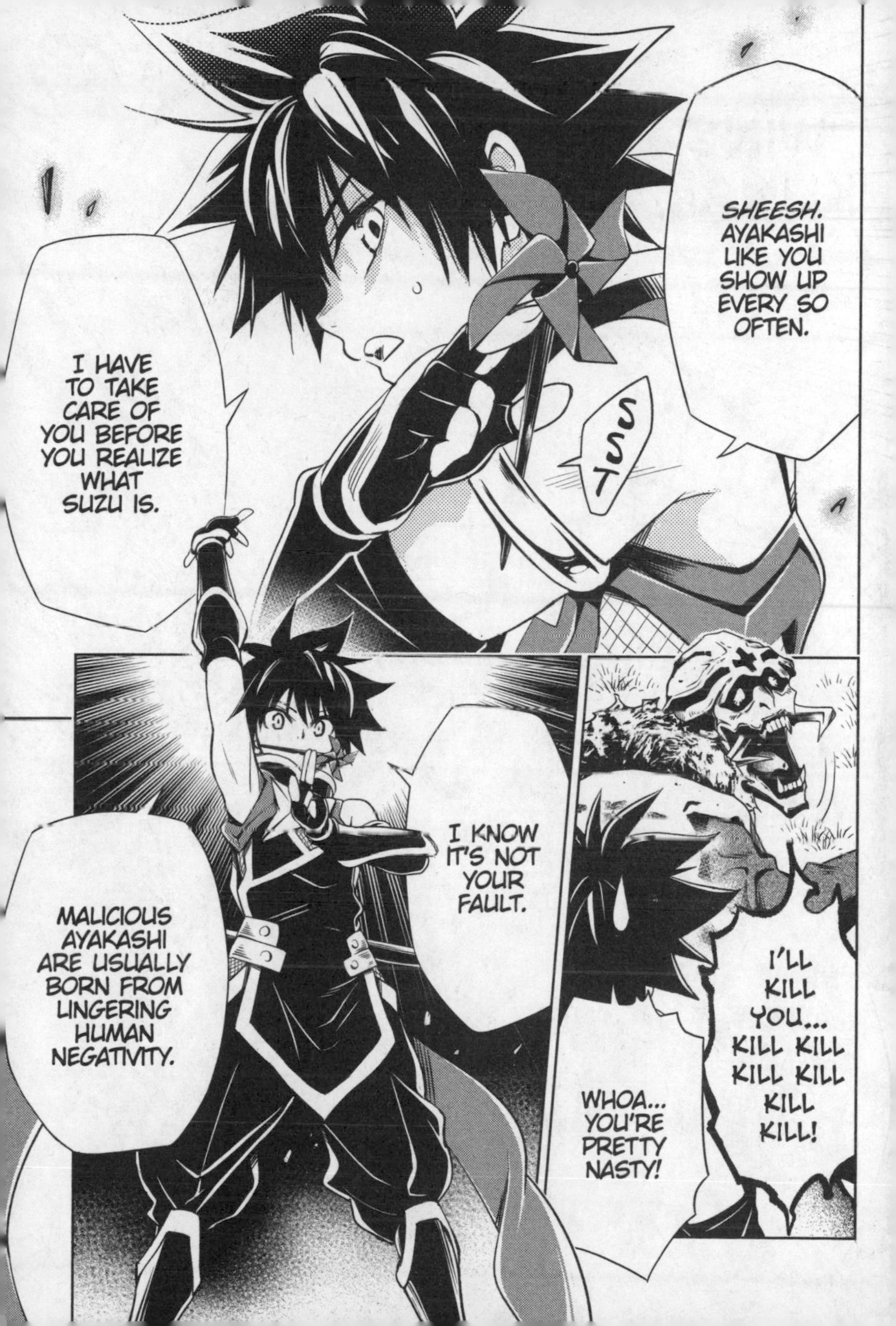
SHEESH. AYAKASHI LIKE YOU SHOW UP EVERY SO OFTEN.
SST
I HAVE TO TAKE CARE OF YOU BEFORE YOU REALIZE WHAT SUZU IS.
I'LL KILL YOU... KILL KILL KILL KILL KILL KILL!
WHOA... YOU'RE PRETTY NASTY!
I KNOW IT'S NOT YOUR FAULT.
MALICIOUS AYAKASHI ARE USUALLY BORN FROM LINGERING HUMAN NEGATIVITY.

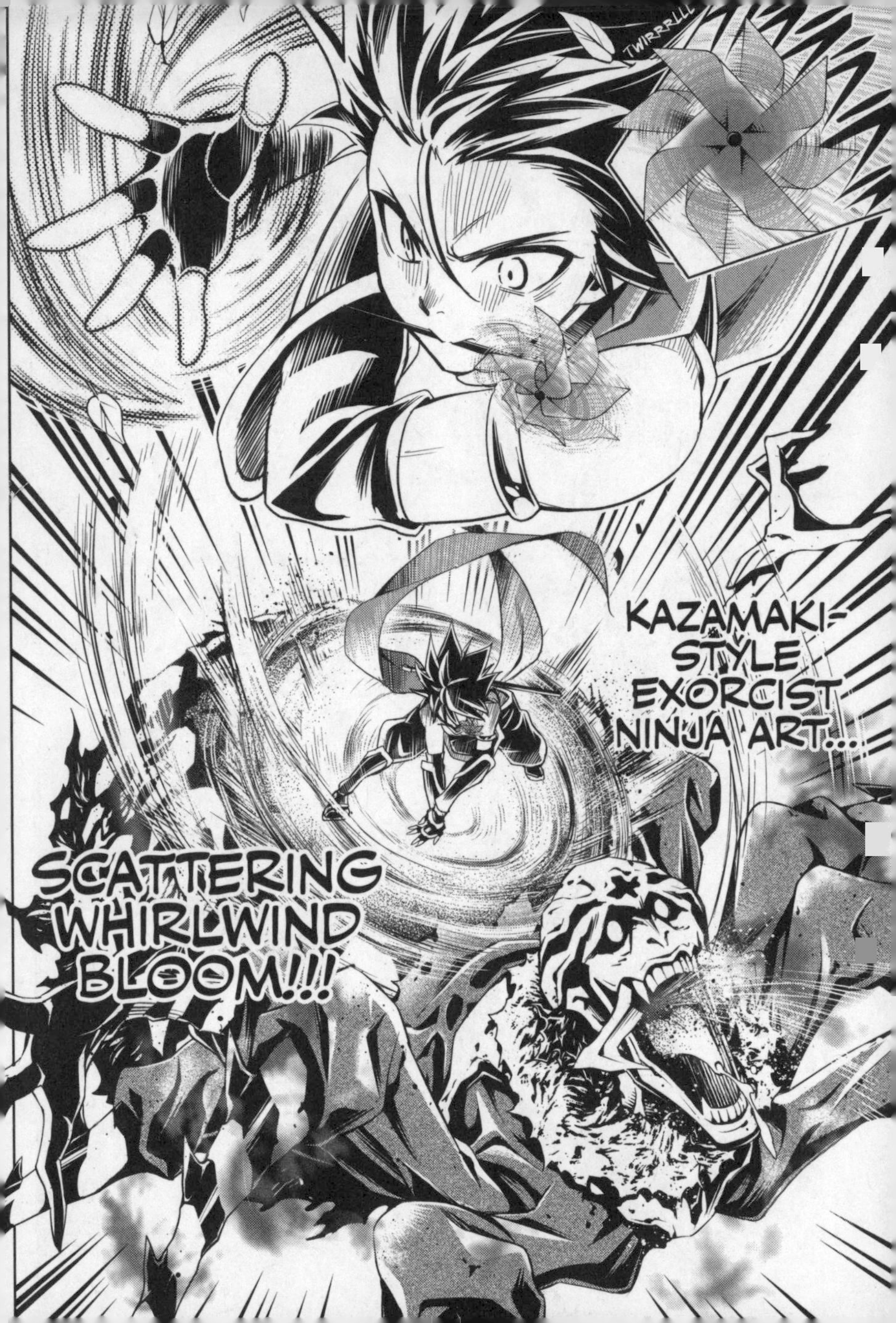
TWIRRRLLL
KAZAMAKI-STYLE EXORCIST NINJA ART...
SCATTERING WHIRLWIND BLOOM!!!

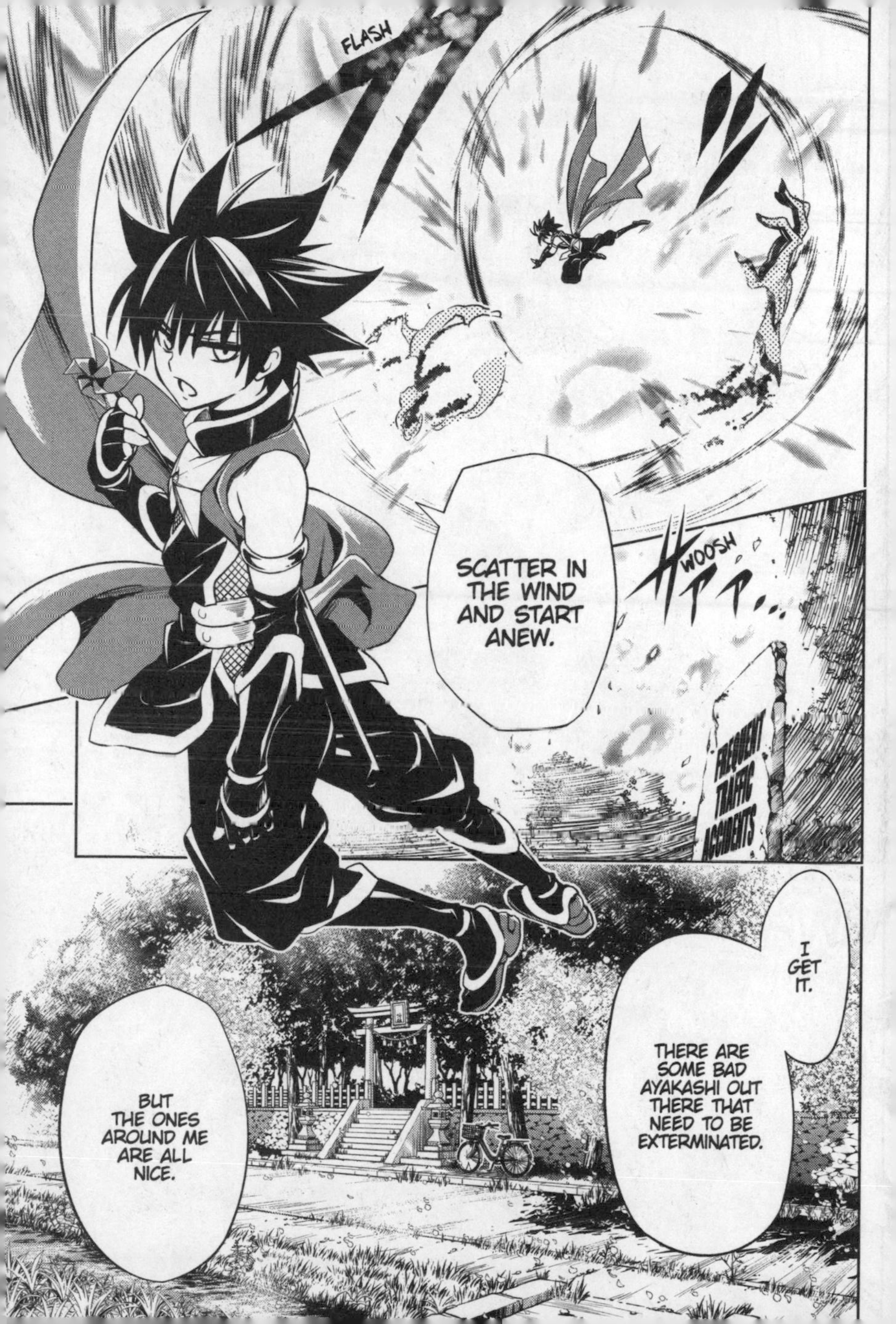
FLASH
SCATTER IN THE WIND AND START ANEW.
WOOSH
FREQUENT TRAFFIC ACCIDENTS
I GET IT.
THERE ARE SOME BAD AYAKASHI OUT THERE THAT NEED TO BE EXTERMINATED.
BUT THE ONES AROUND ME ARE ALL NICE.

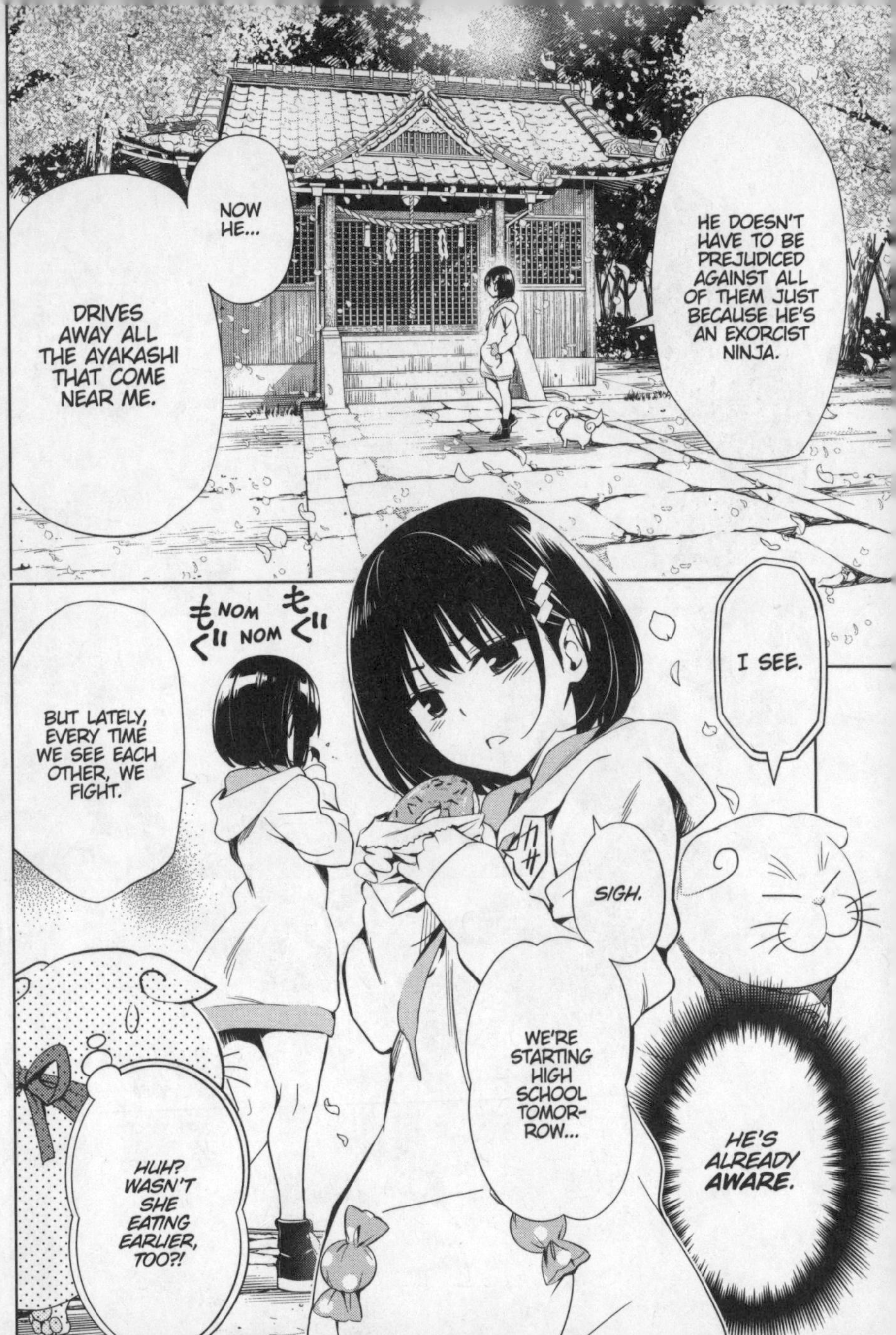
HE DOESN'T HAVE TO BE PREJUDICED AGAINST ALL OF THEM JUST BECAUSE HE'S AN EXORCIST NINJA.
NOW HE...
DRIVES AWAY ALL THE AYAKASHI THAT COME NEAR ME.
I SEE.
もぐ もぐ NOM NOM
BUT LATELY, EVERY TIME WE SEE EACH OTHER, WE FIGHT.
SIGH.
WE'RE STARTING HIGH SCHOOL TOMORROW...
HE'S ALREADY AWARE.
HUH? WASN'T SHE EATING EARLIER, TOO?!

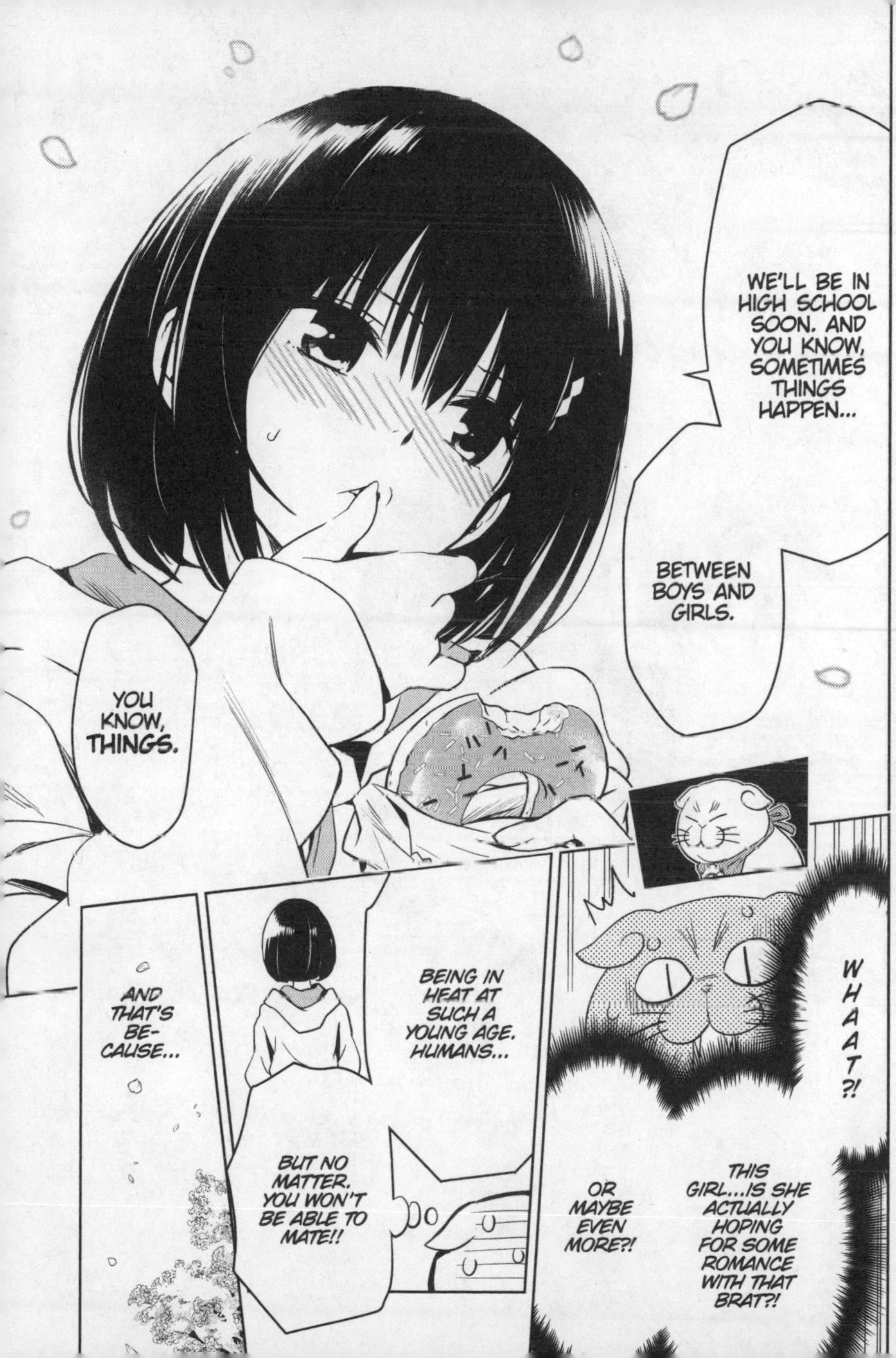
WE'LL BE IN HIGH SCHOOL SOON. AND YOU KNOW, SOMETIMES THINGS HAPPEN...
BETWEEN BOYS AND GIRLS.
YOU KNOW, THINGS.
WHAAAT?!
THIS GIRL...IS SHE ACTUALLY HOPING FOR SOME ROMANCE WITH THAT BRAT?!
OR MAYBE EVEN MORE?!
BEING IN HEAT AT SUCH A YOUNG AGE. HUMANS...
BUT NO MATTER. YOU WON'T BE ABLE TO MATE!!
AND THAT'S BE-CAUSE...

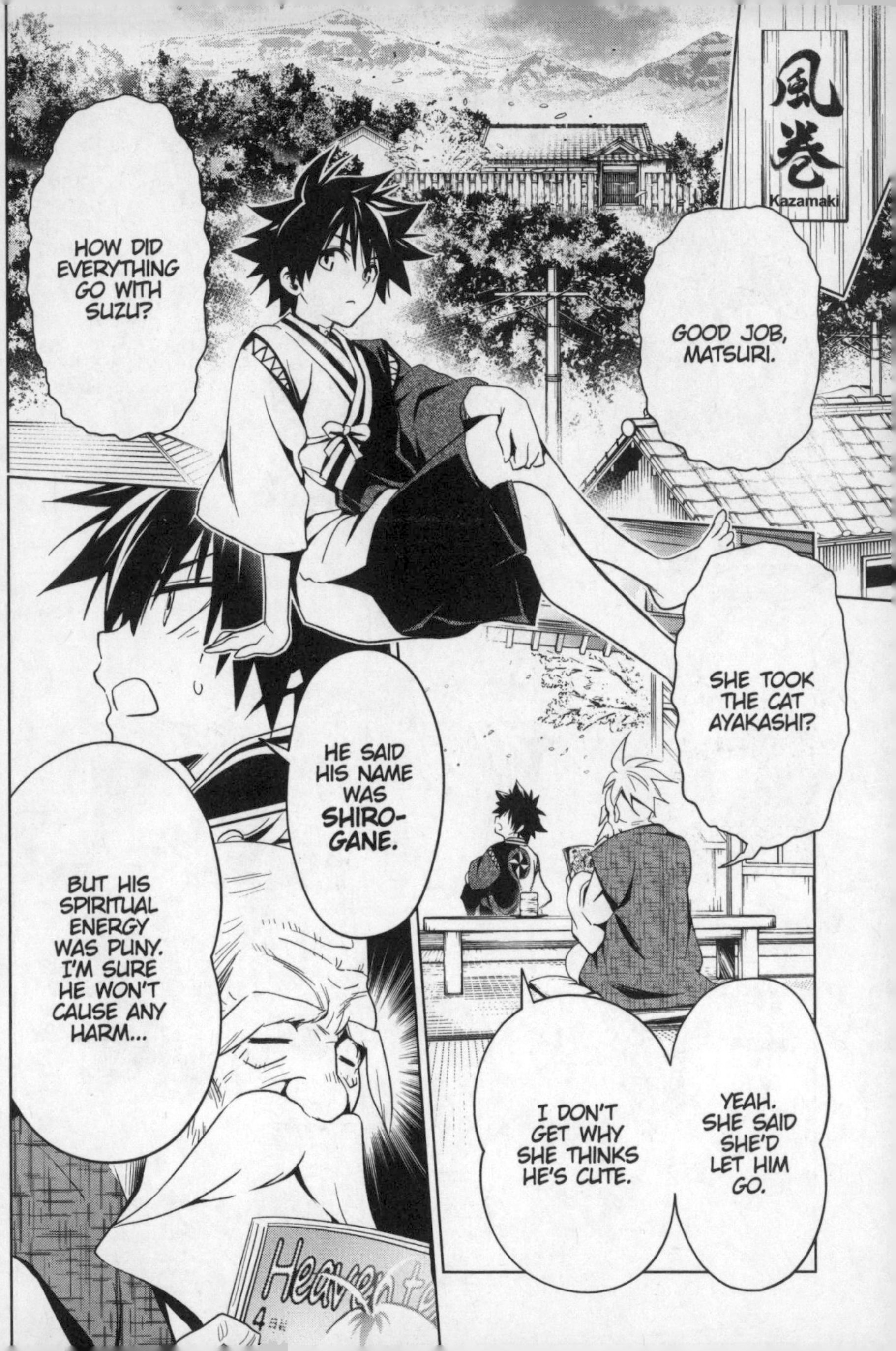
風巻
Kazamaki
GOOD JOB, MATSURI.
HOW DID EVERYTHING GO WITH SUZU?
SHE TOOK THE CAT AYAKASHI?
YEAH. SHE SAID SHE'D LET HIM GO.
I DON'T GET WHY SHE THINKS HE'S CUTE.
HE SAID HIS NAME WAS SHIRO-GANE.
BUT HIS SPIRITUAL ENERGY WAS PUNY. I'M SURE HE WON'T CAUSE ANY HARM...

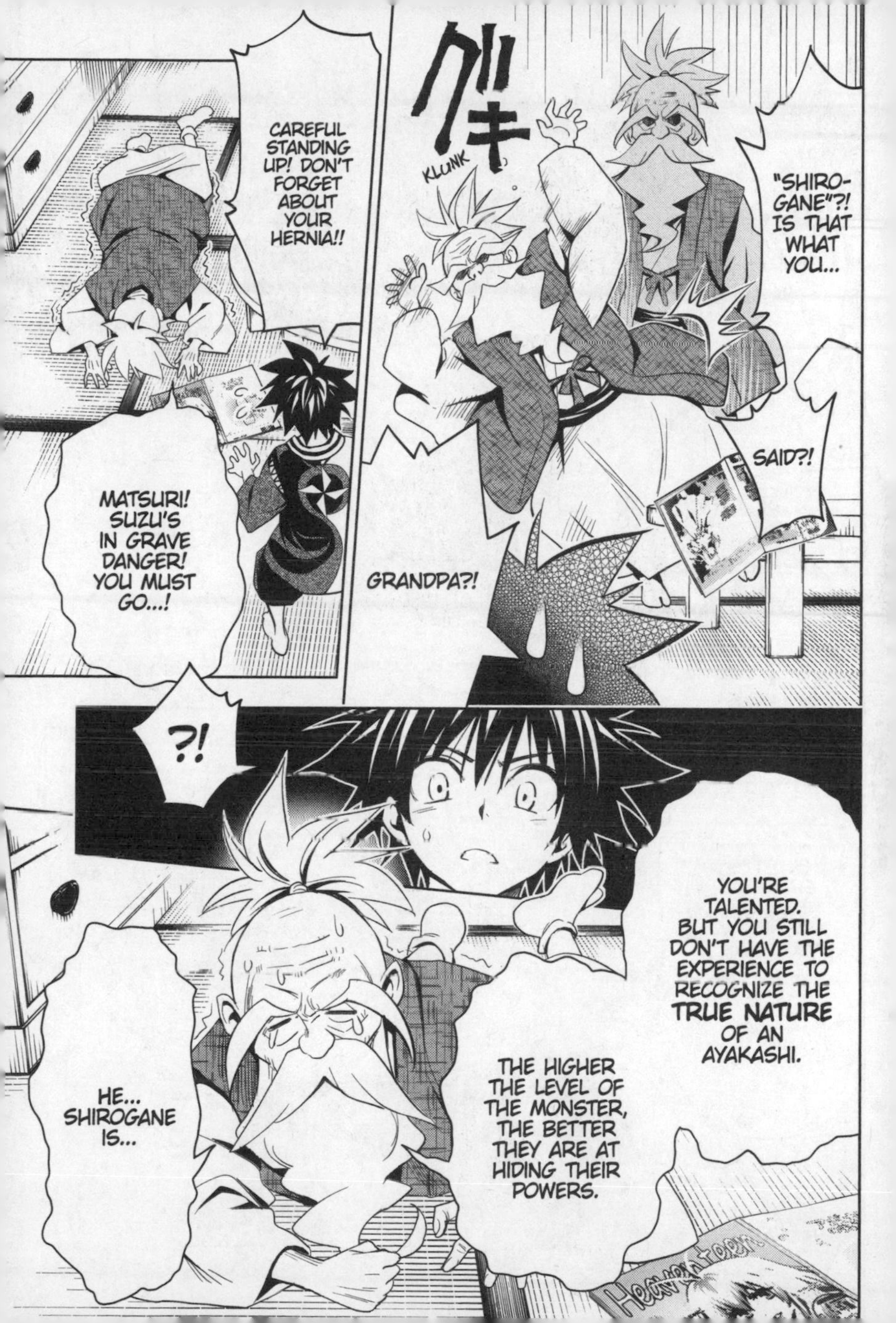
"SHIRO-GANE"?! IS THAT WHAT YOU...
グキ
KLUNK
SAID?!
GRANDPA?!
CAREFUL STANDING UP! DON'T FORGET ABOUT YOUR HERNIA!!
MATSURI! SUZU'S IN GRAVE DANGER! YOU MUST GO...!
?!
YOU'RE TALENTED. BUT YOU STILL DON'T HAVE THE EXPERIENCE TO RECOGNIZE THE TRUE NATURE OF AN AYAKASHI.
THE HIGHER THE LEVEL OF THE MONSTER, THE BETTER THEY ARE AT HIDING THEIR POWERS.
HE... SHIROGANE IS...

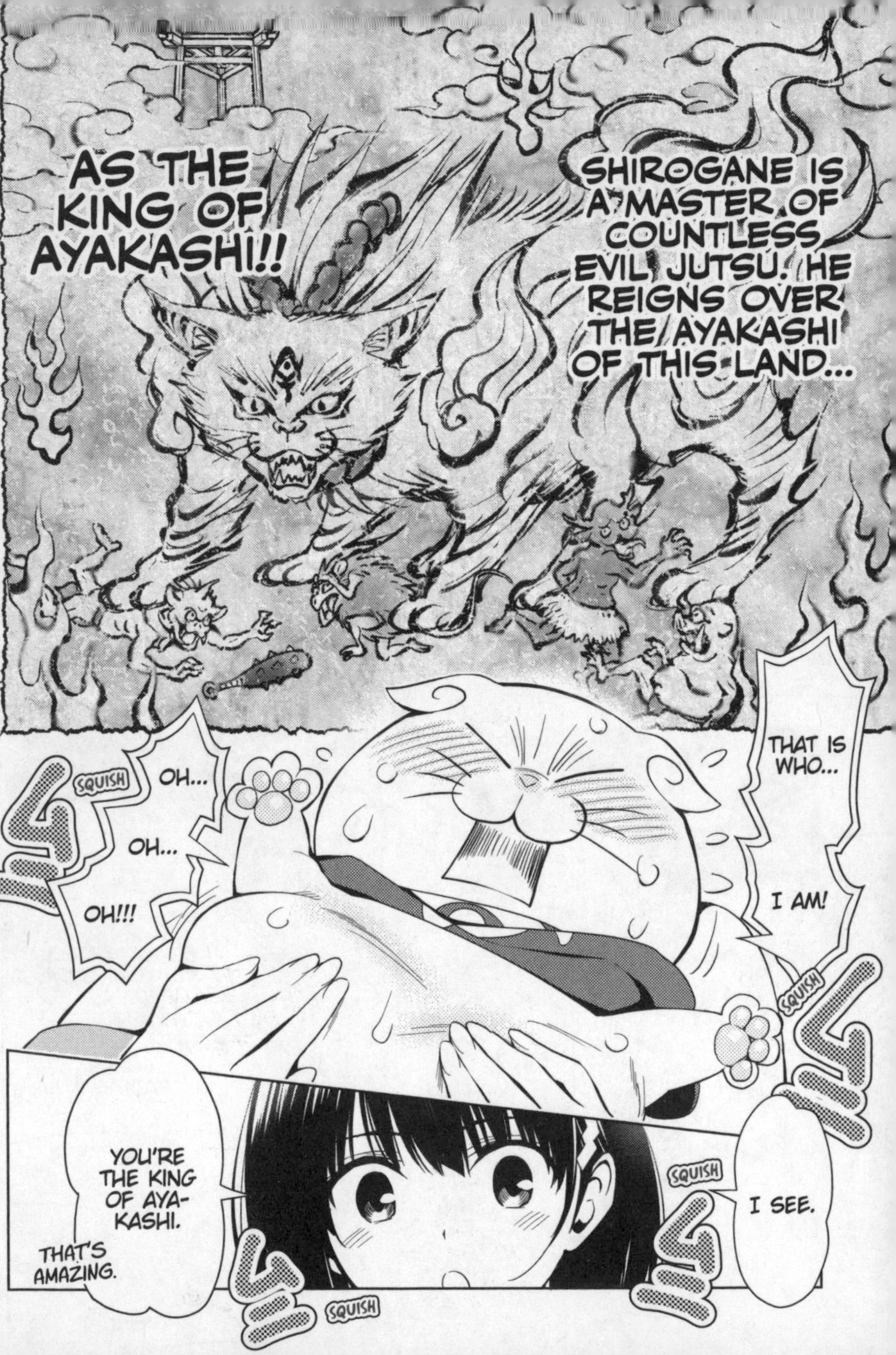
SHIROGANE IS A MASTER OF COUNTLESS EVIL JUTSU. HE REIGNS OVER THE AYAKASHI OF THIS LAND...
AS THE KING OF AYAKASHI!!
THAT IS WHO...
I AM!
SQUISH
SQUISH
OH...
OH...
OH!!!
SQUISH
I SEE.
YOU'RE THE KING OF AYA-KASHI.
THAT'S AMAZING.
SQUISH

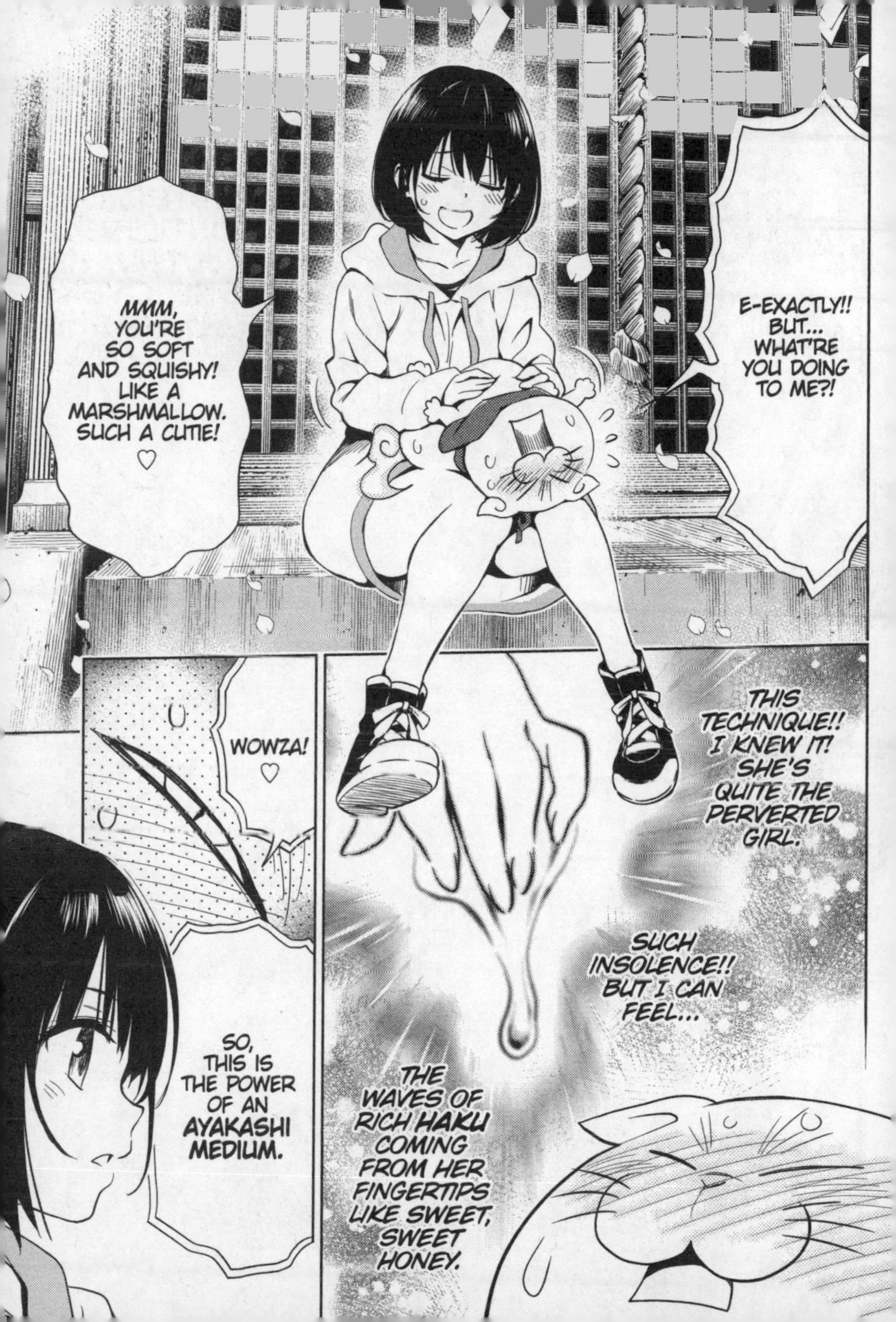
E-EXACTLY!! BUT... WHAT'RE YOU DOING TO ME?!
MMM, YOU'RE SO SOFT AND SQUISHY! LIKE A MARSHMALLOW. SUCH A CUTIE! ♡
THIS TECHNIQUE!! I KNEW IT! SHE'S QUITE THE PERVERTED GIRL.
SUCH INSOLENCE!! BUT I CAN FEEL...
THE WAVES OF RICH HAKU COMING FROM HER FINGERTIPS LIKE SWEET, SWEET HONEY.
WOWZA! ♡
SO, THIS IS THE POWER OF AN AYAKASHI MEDIUM.

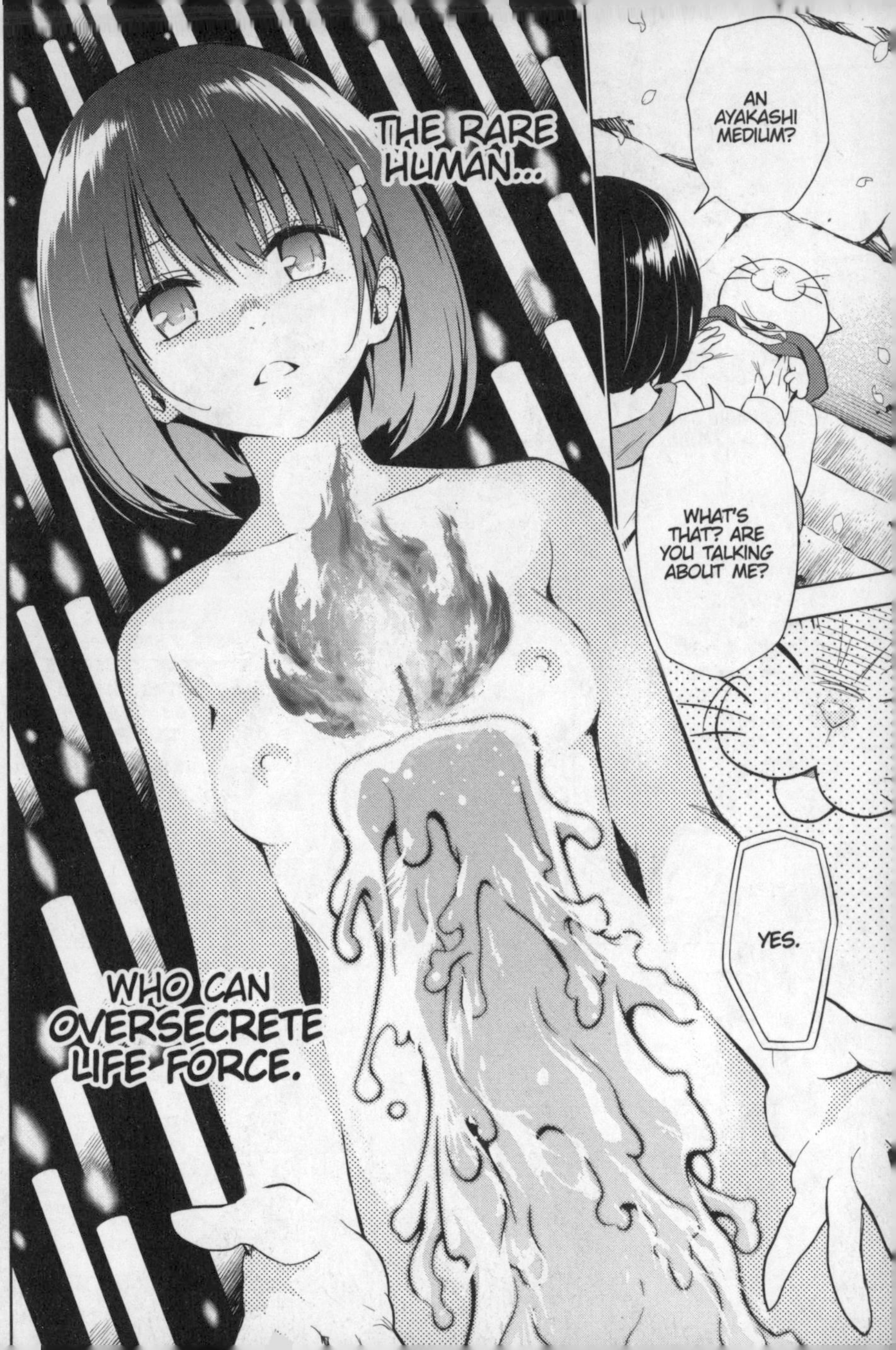
AN AYAKASHI MEDIUM?
WHAT'S THAT? ARE YOU TALKING ABOUT ME?
YES.
THE RARE HUMAN...
WHO CAN OVERSECRETE LIFE FORCE.

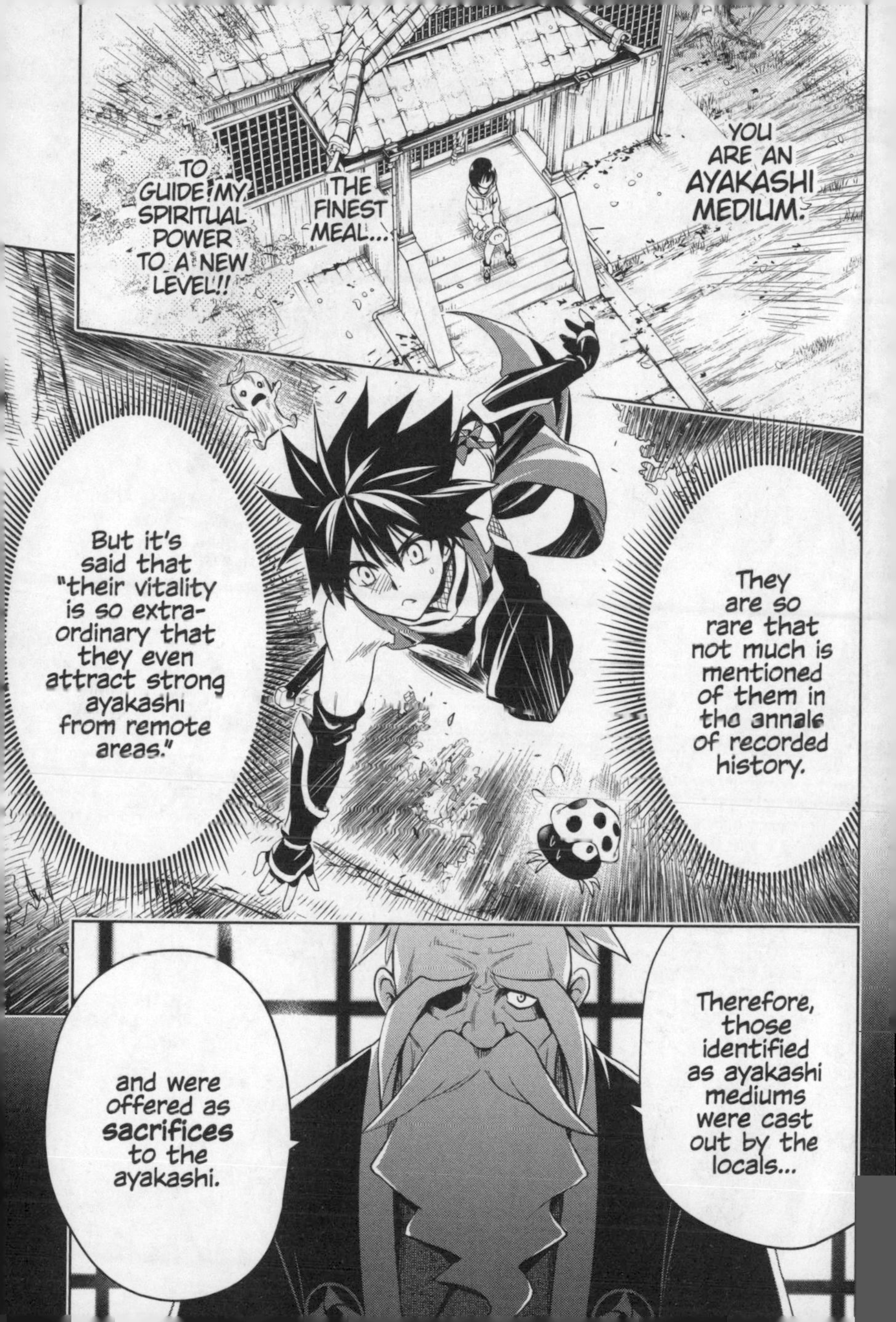
YOU ARE AN AYAKASHI MEDIUM.
THE FINEST MEAL...
TO GUIDE MY SPIRITUAL POWER TO A NEW LEVEL!!
They are so rare that not much is mentioned of them in the annals of recorded history.
But it's said that "their vitality is so extra-ordinary that they even attract strong ayakashi from remote areas."
Therefore, those identified as ayakashi mediums were cast out by the locals...
and were offered as sacrifices to the ayakashi.

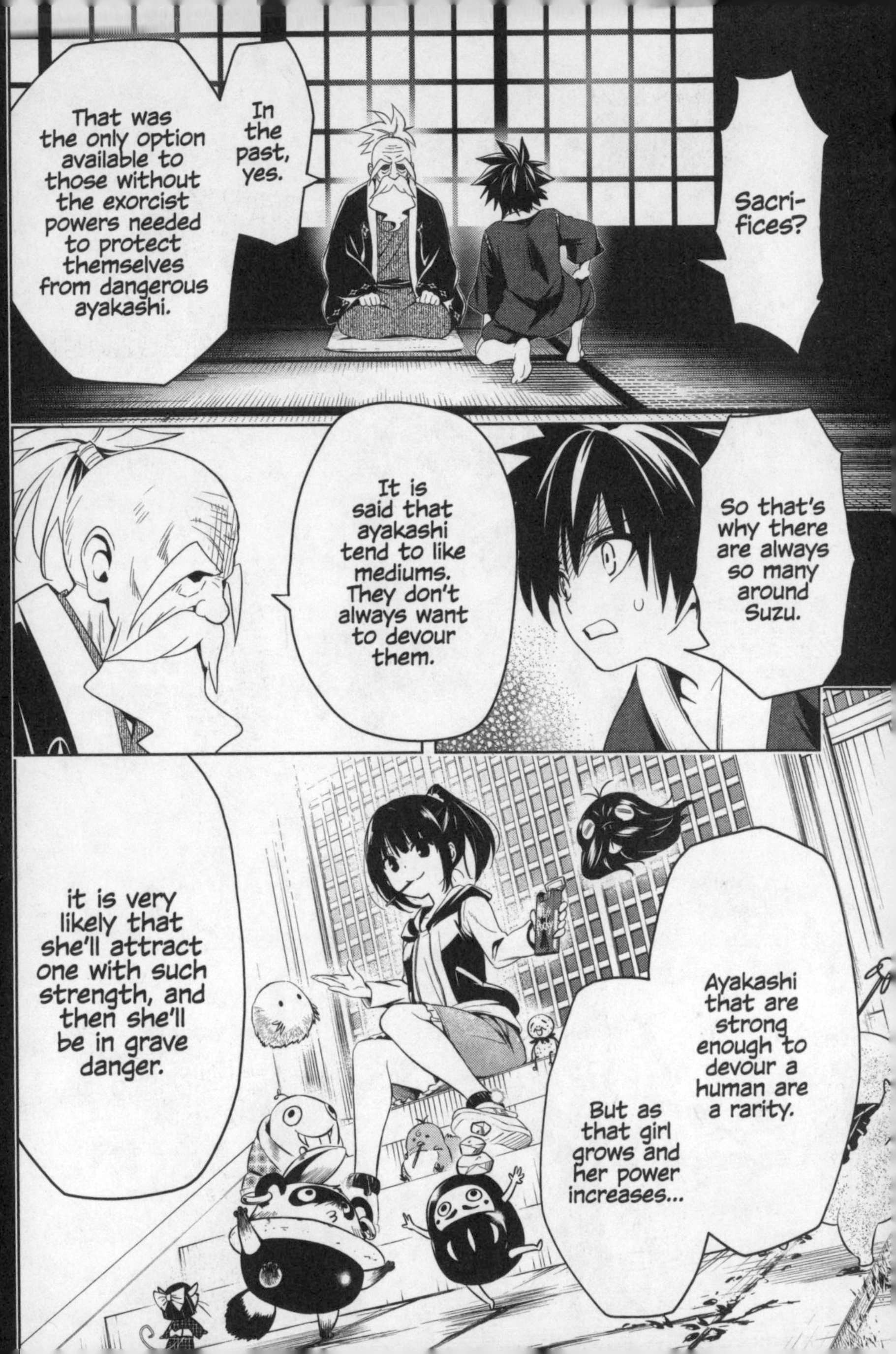
Sacrifices?
In the past, yes.
That was the only option available to those without the exorcist powers needed to protect themselves from dangerous ayakashi.
So that's why there are always so many around Suzu.
It is said that ayakashi tend to like mediums. They don't always want to devour them.
Ayakashi that are strong enough to devour a human are a rarity.
But as that girl grows and her power increases...
it is very likely that she'll attract one with such strength, and then she'll be in grave danger.

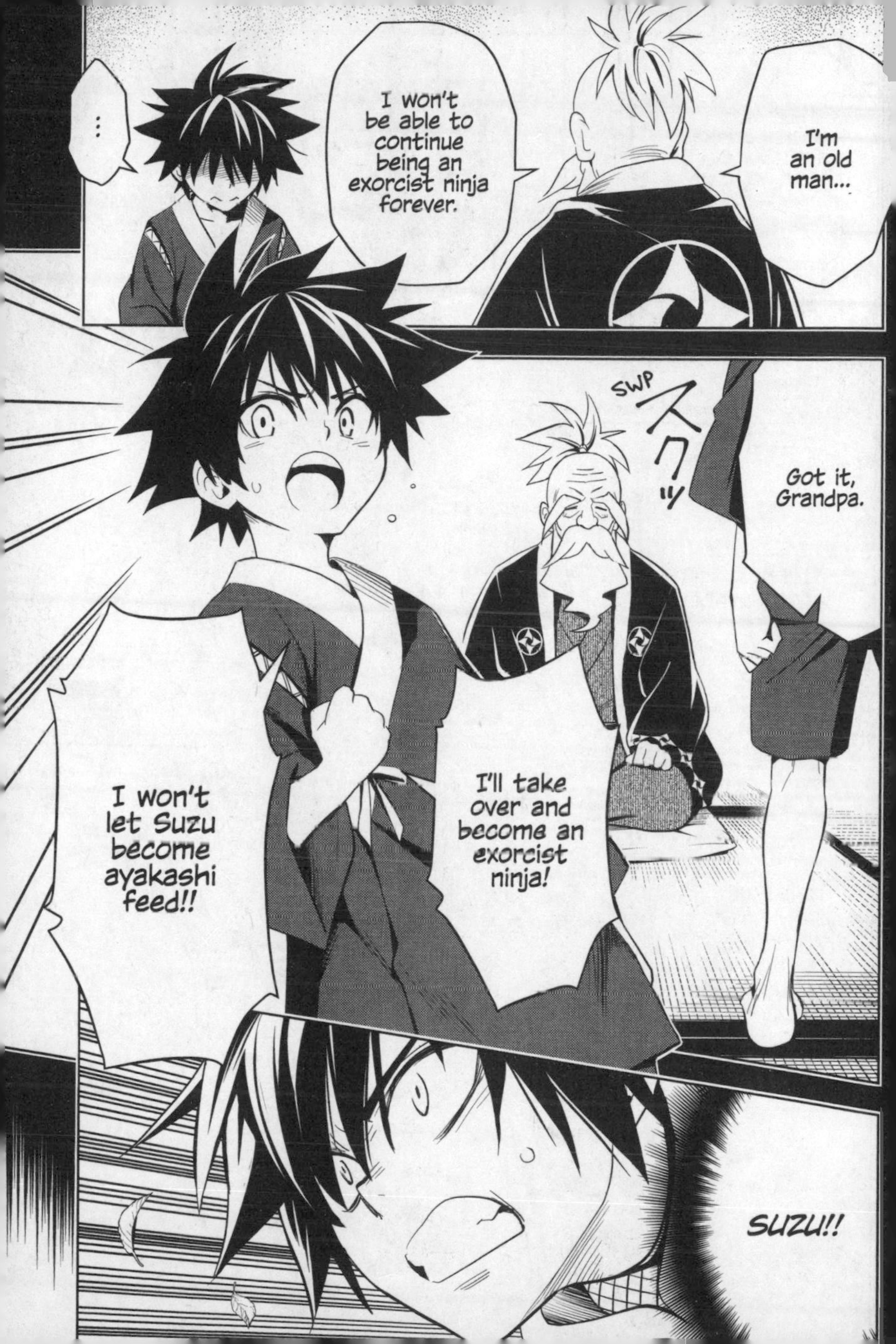
I'm an old man...
I won't be able to continue being an exorcist ninja forever.
...
SWP
スクッ
Got it, Grandpa.
I'll take over and become an exorcist ninja!
I won't let Suzu become ayakashi feed!!
SUZU!!

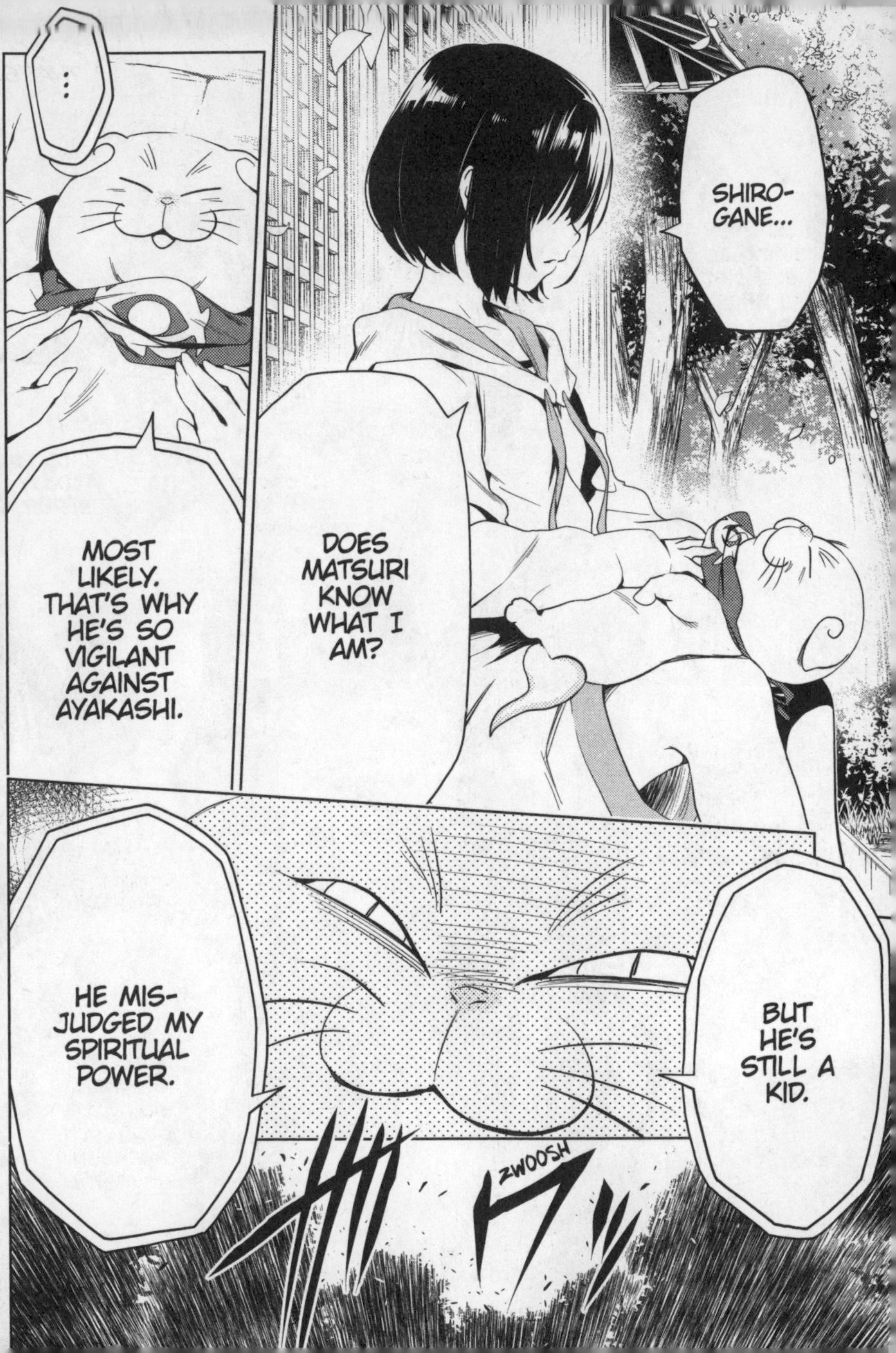
SHIRO-GANE...
DOES MATSURI KNOW WHAT I AM?
...
MOST LIKELY. THAT'S WHY HE'S SO VIGILANT AGAINST AYAKASHI.
BUT HE'S STILL A KID.
HE MIS-JUDGED MY SPIRITUAL POWER.
ZWOOSH

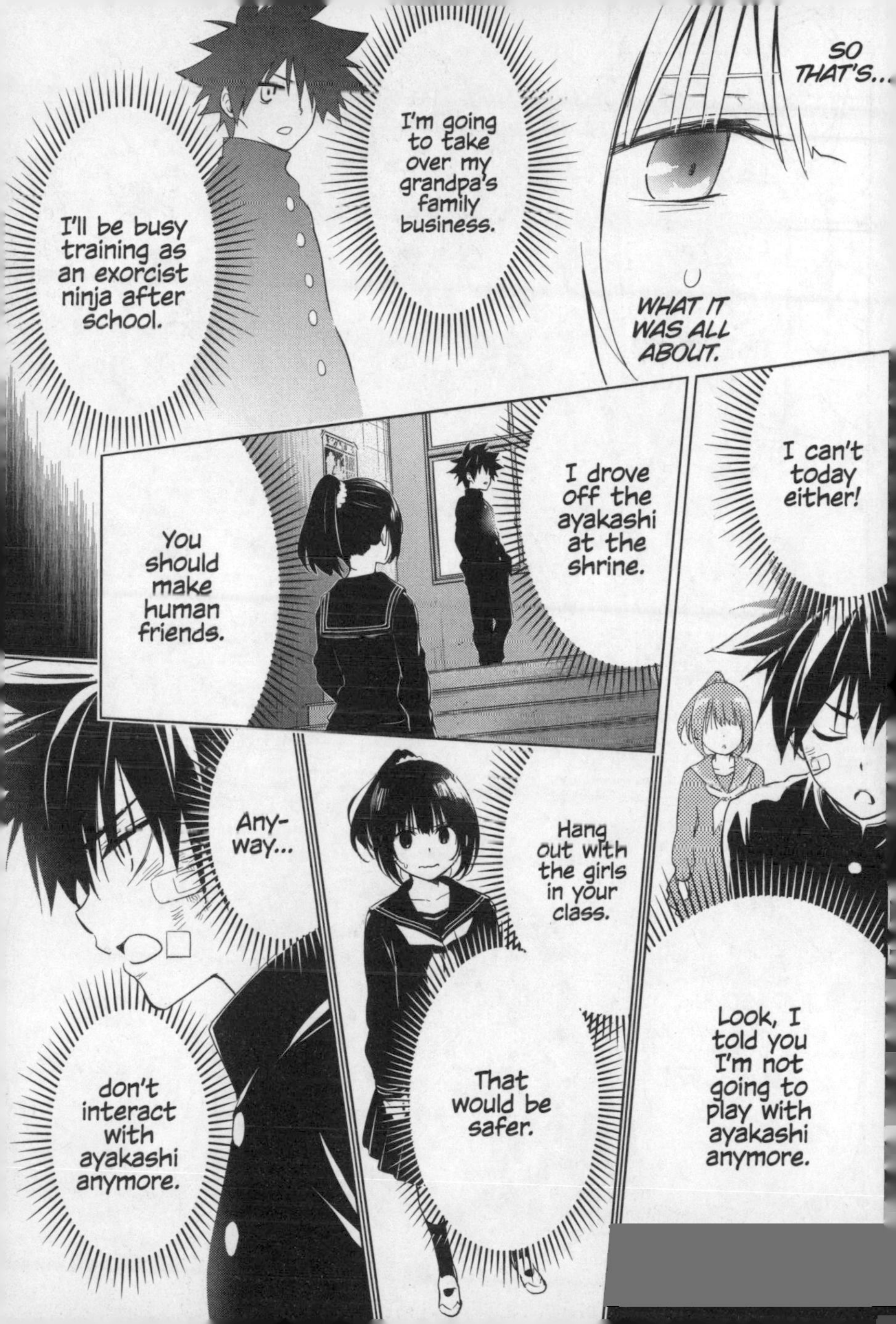
SO THAT'S...
WHAT IT WAS ALL ABOUT.
I'm going to take over my grandpa's family business.
I'll be busy training as an exorcist ninja after school.
I can't today either!
Look, I told you I'm not going to play with ayakashi anymore.
I drove off the ayakashi at the shrine.
You should make human friends.
Hang out with the girls in your class.
That would be safer.
Any-way...
don't interact with ayakashi anymore.

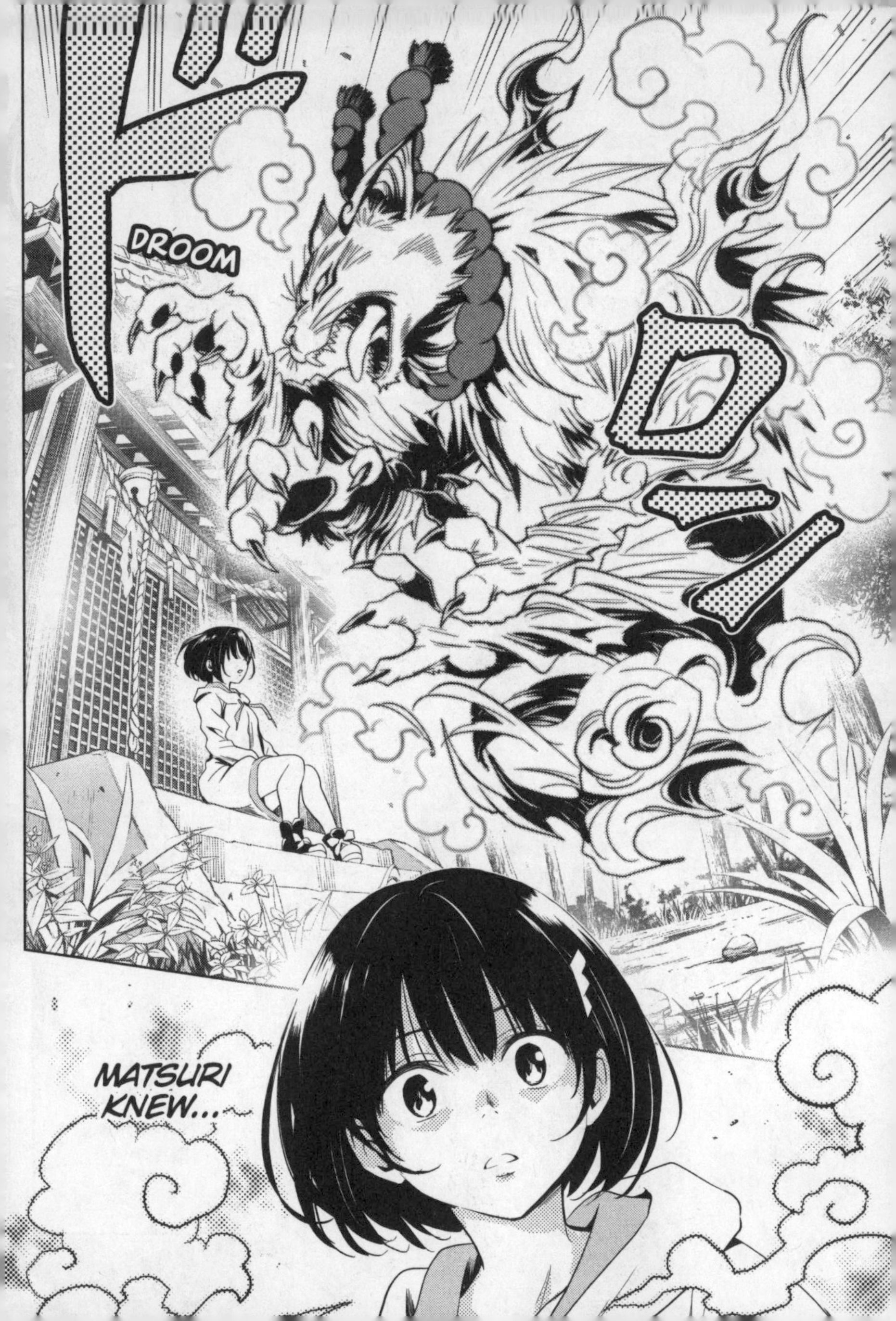

DROOM
MATSURI KNEW...

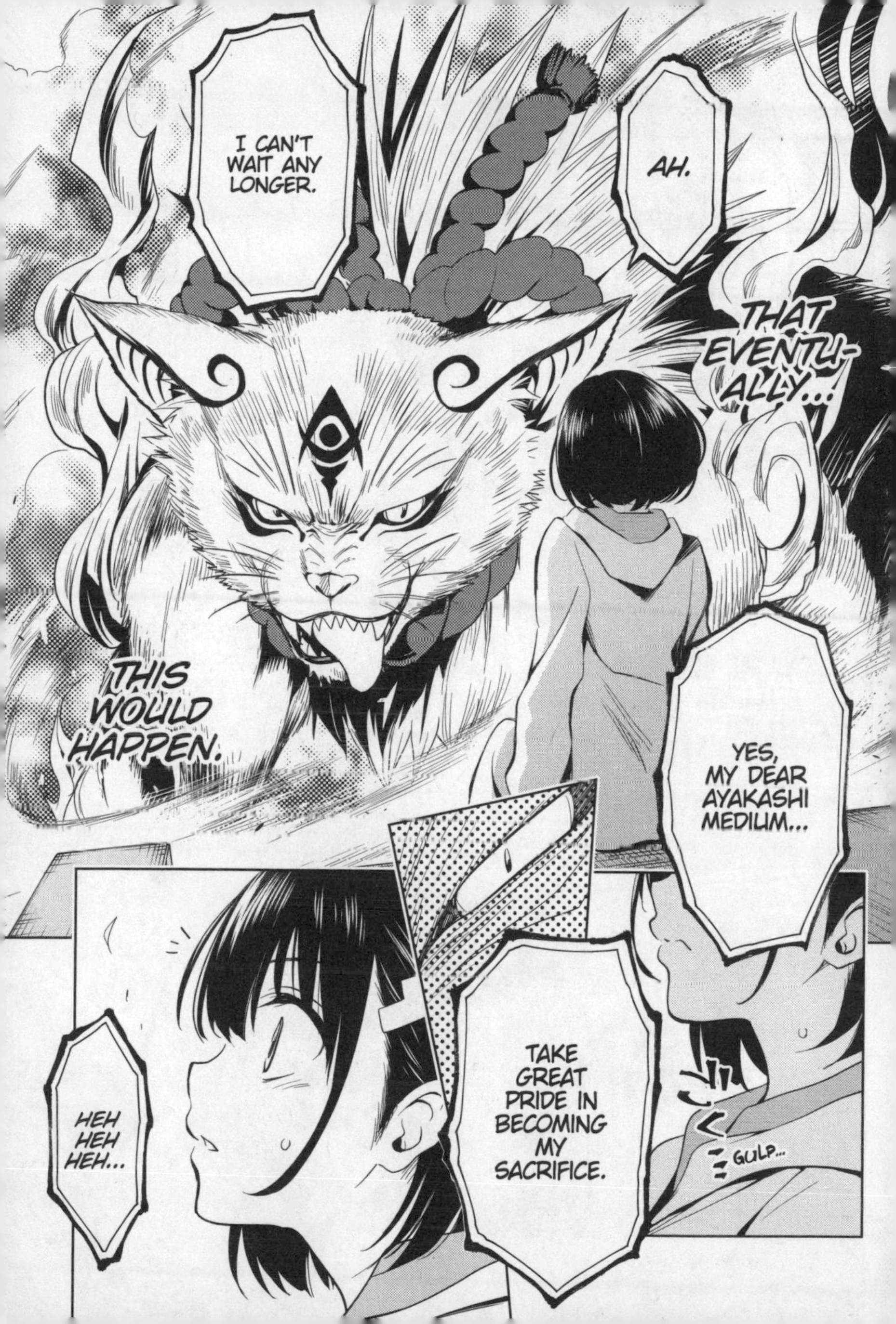
AH.
THAT EVENTU-ALLY...
THIS WOULD HAPPEN.
I CAN'T WAIT ANY LONGER.
YES, MY DEAR AYAKASHI MEDIUM...
TAKE GREAT PRIDE IN BECOMING MY SACRIFICE.
GULP...
HEH HEH HEH...

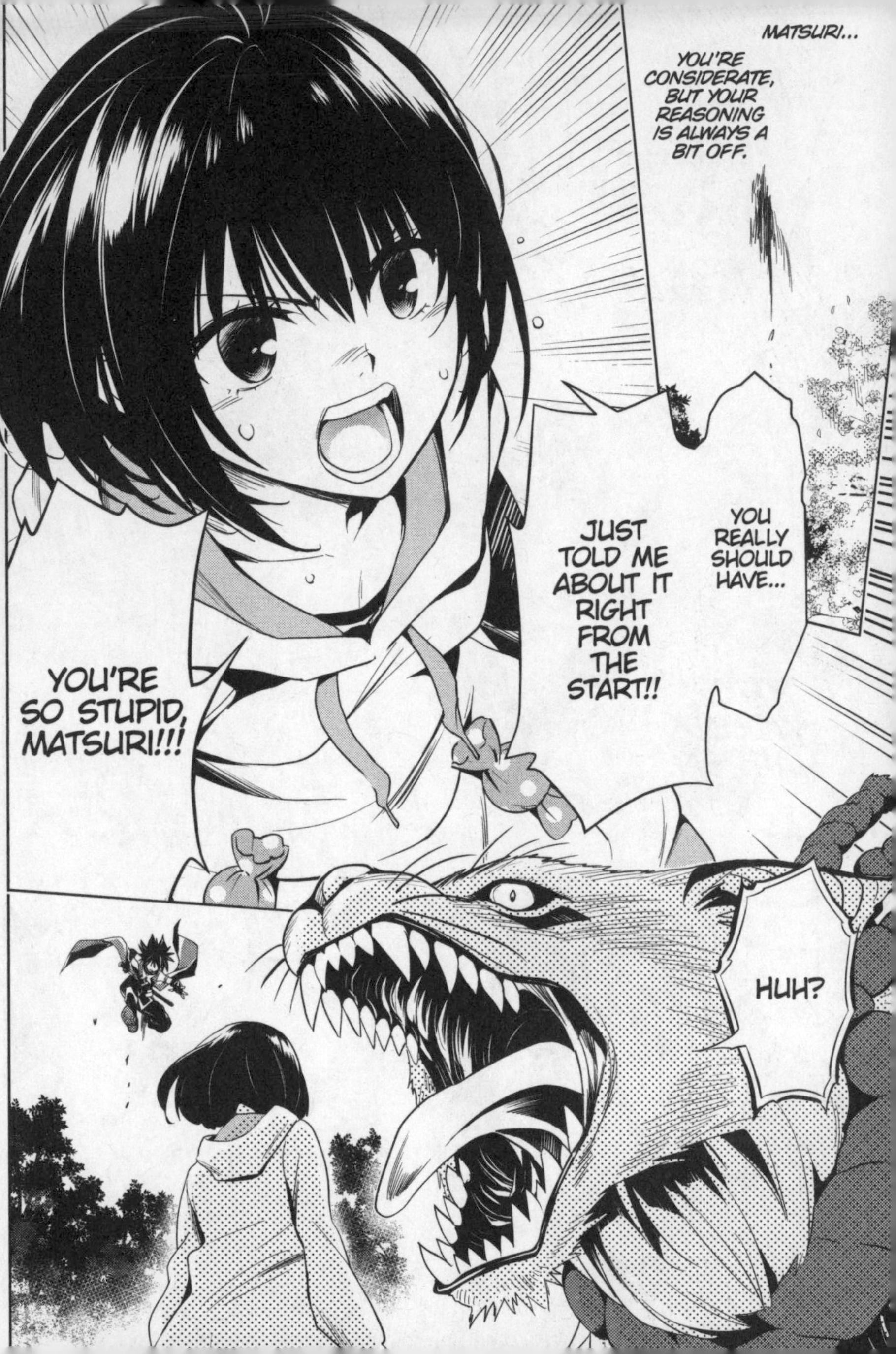
MATSURI...
YOU'RE CONSIDERATE, BUT YOUR REASONING IS ALWAYS A BIT OFF.
YOU REALLY SHOULD HAVE...
JUST TOLD ME ABOUT IT RIGHT FROM THE START!!
YOU'RE SO STUPID, MATSURI!!!
HUH?

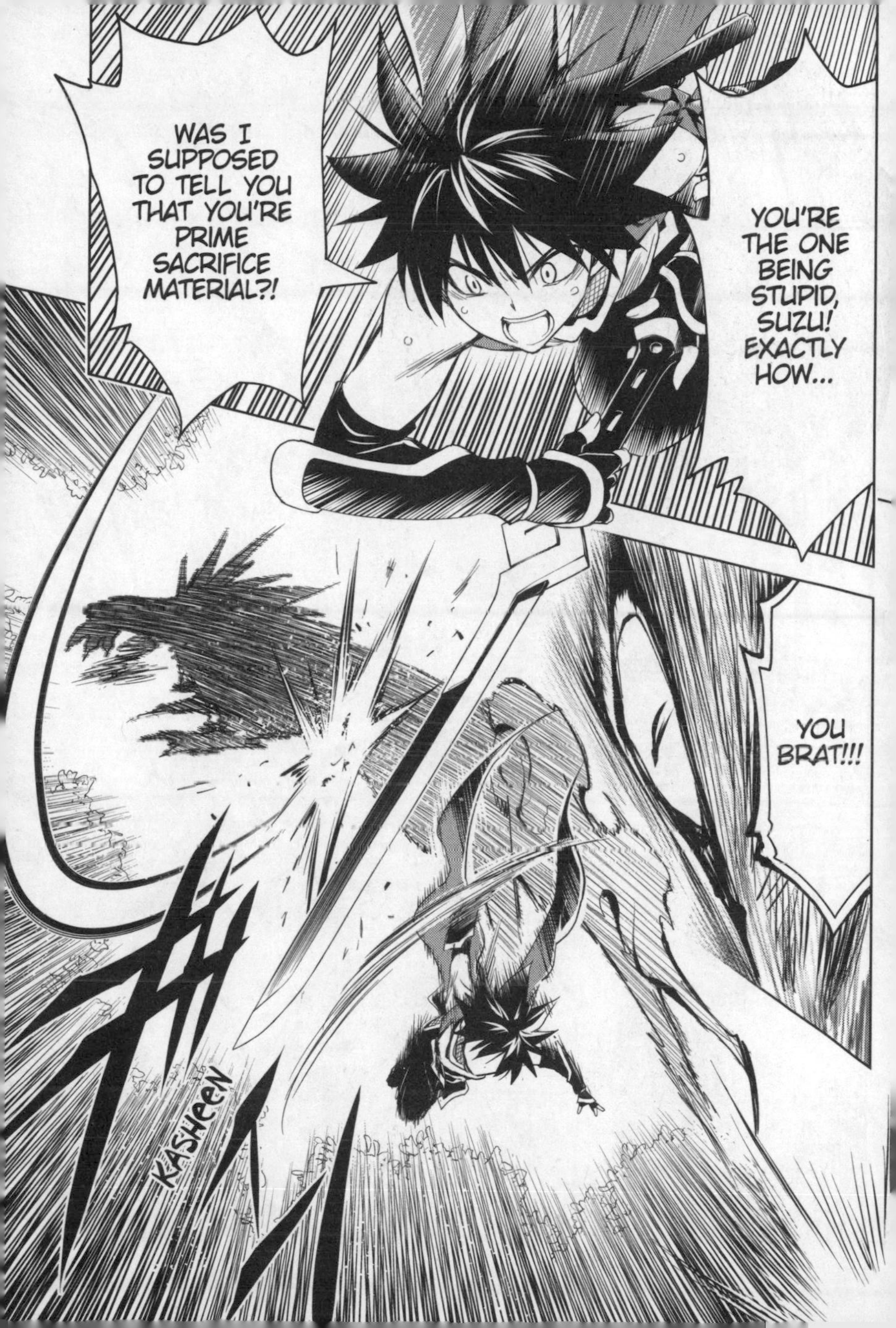
YOU'RE THE ONE BEING STUPID, SUZU! EXACTLY HOW...
WAS I SUPPOSED TO TELL YOU THAT YOU'RE PRIME SACRIFICE MATERIAL?!
YOU BRAT!!!
KASHEEN

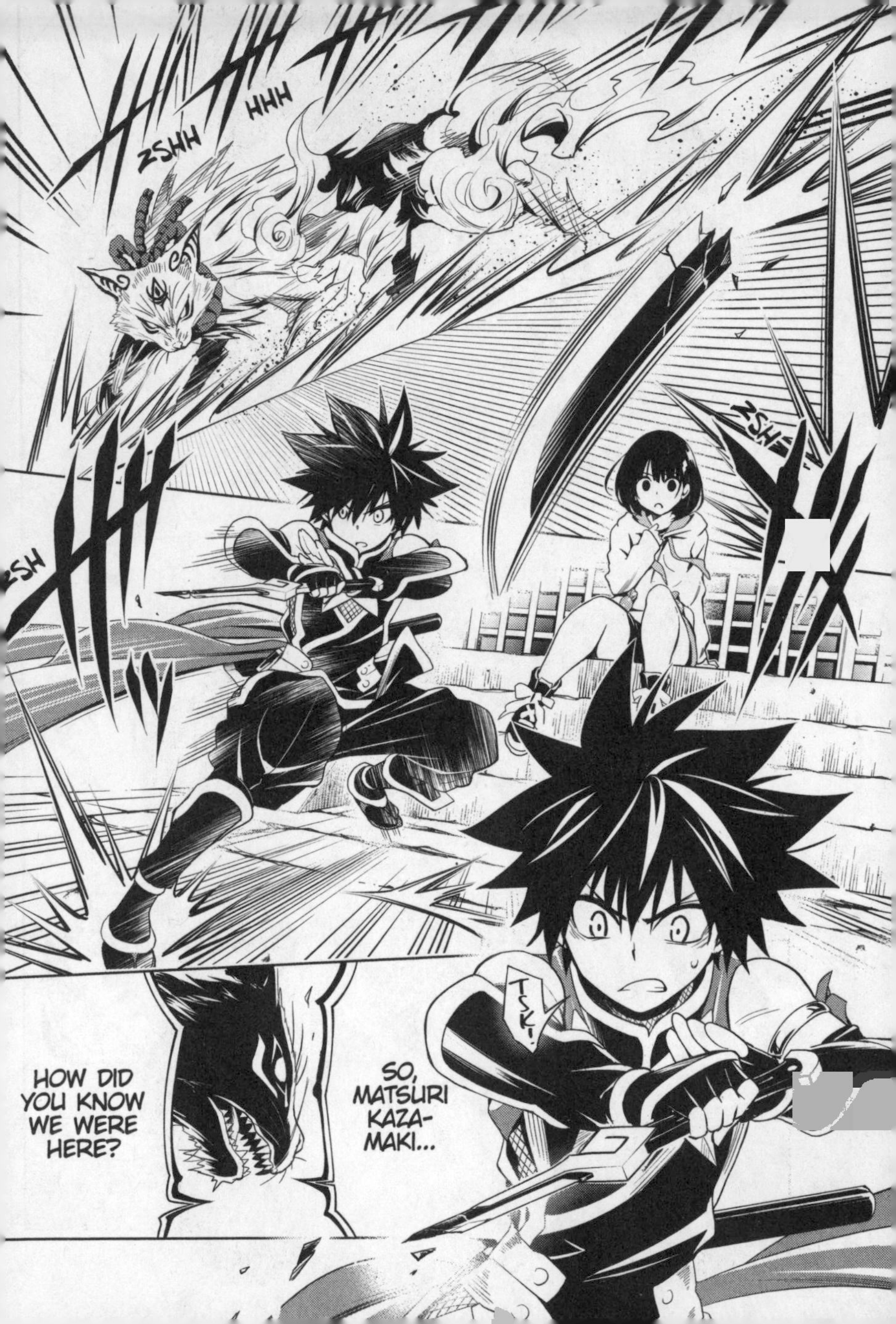
ZSHH
HHH
ZSH
ZSH
TSK!
SO, MATSURI KAZAMAKI...
HOW DID YOU KNOW WE WERE HERE?

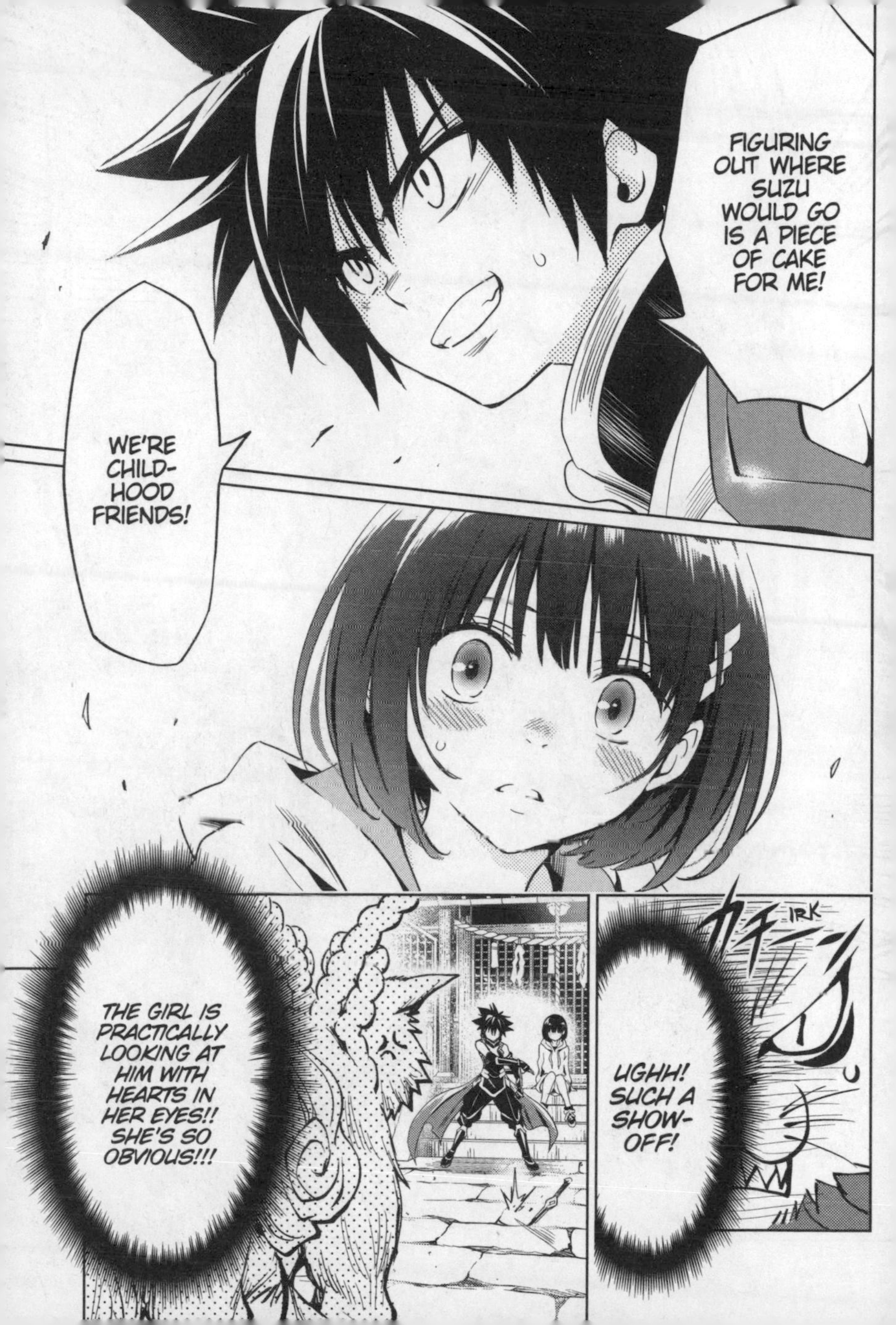
FIGURING OUT WHERE SUZU WOULD GO IS A PIECE OF CAKE FOR ME!
WE'RE CHILD-HOOD FRIENDS!
IRK
UGHH! SUCH A SHOW-OFF!
THE GIRL IS PRACTICALLY LOOKING AT HIM WITH HEARTS IN HER EYES!! SHE'S SO OBVIOUS!!!

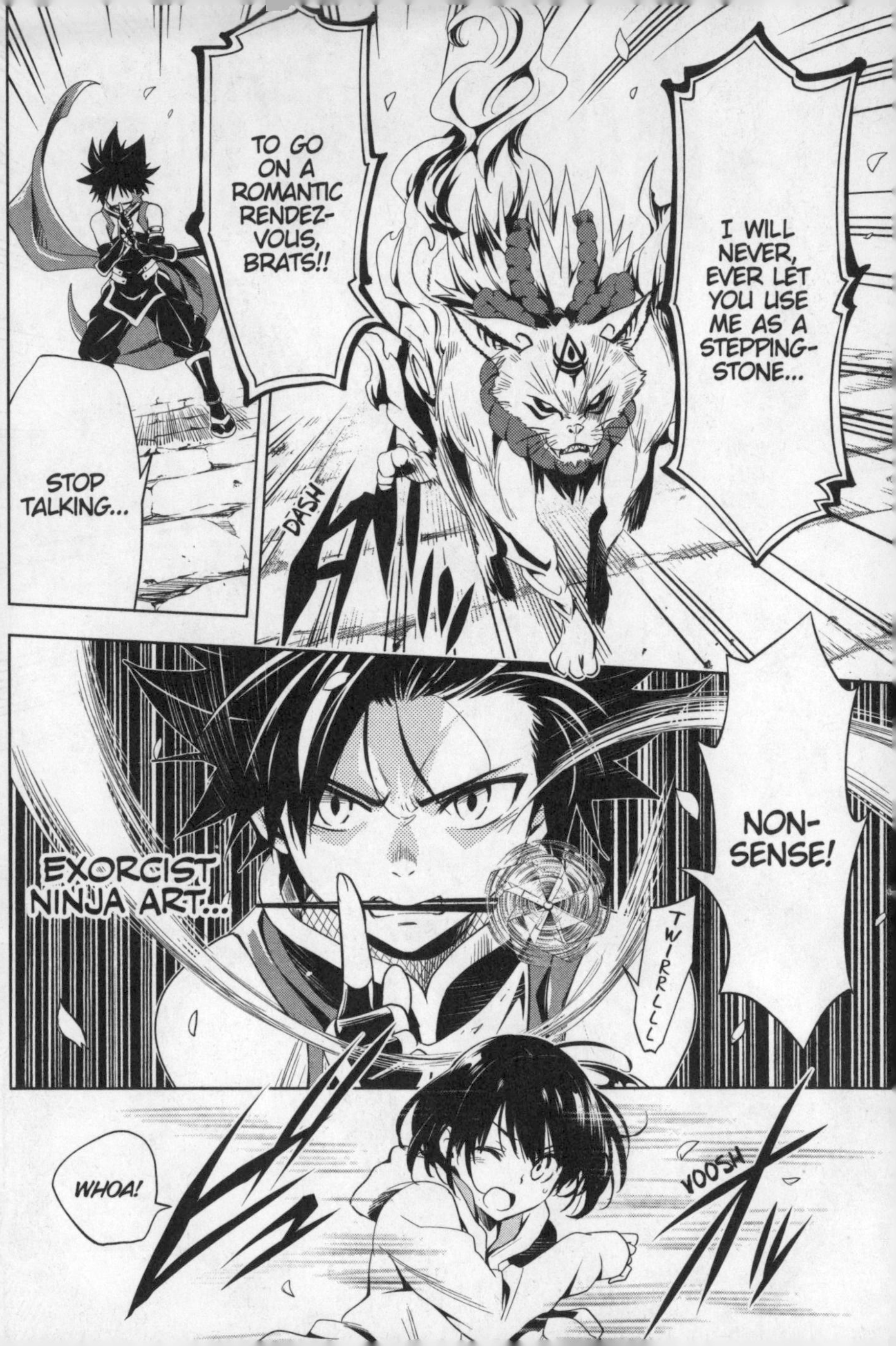
I WILL NEVER, EVER LET YOU USE ME AS A STEPPING-STONE...
TO GO ON A ROMANTIC RENDEZ-VOUS, BRATS!!
DASH
STOP TALKING...
NON-SENSE!
EXORCIST NINJA ART...
TWIRRLLL
VOOSH
WHOA!

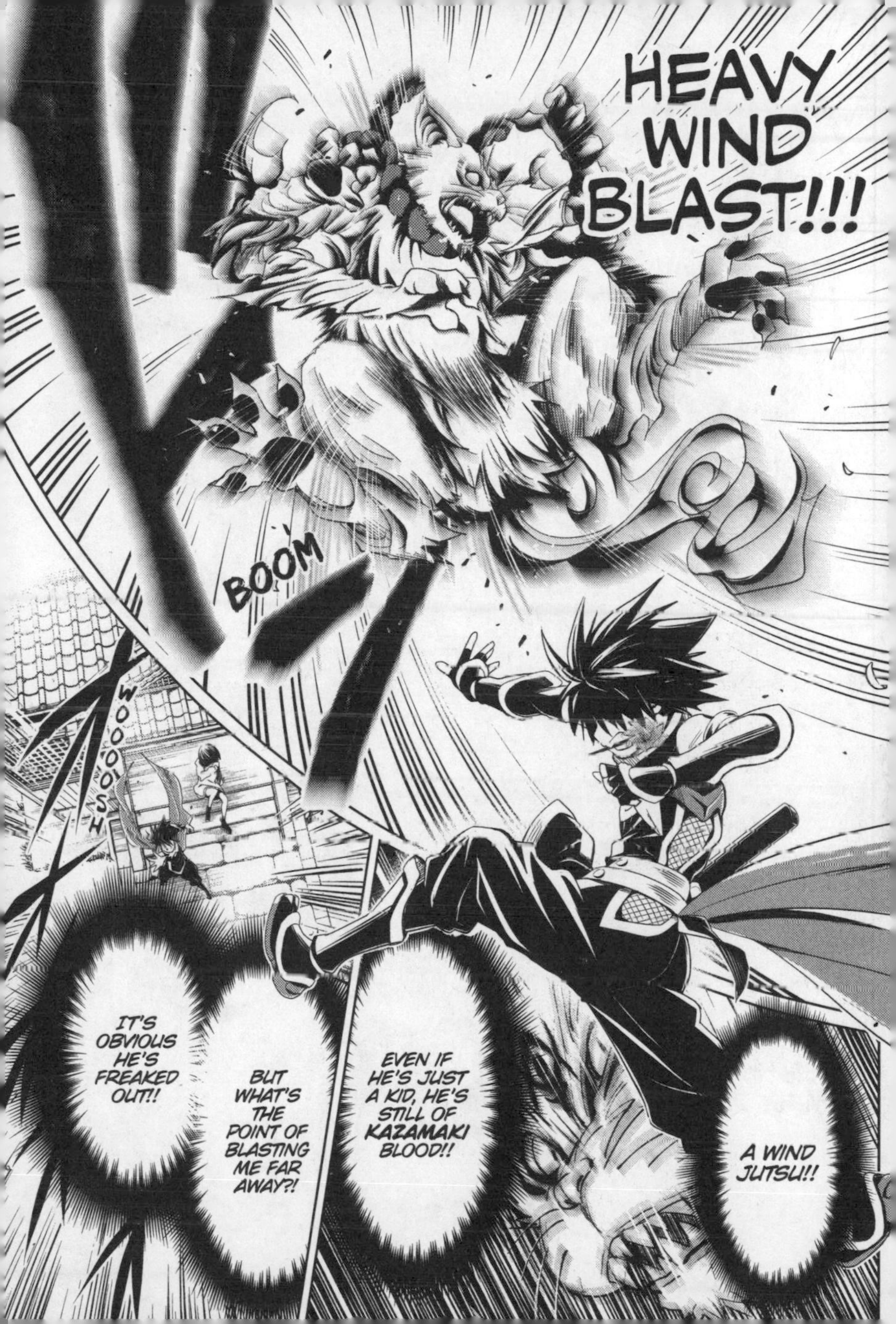
HEAVY WIND BLAST!!!
BOOM
WOOOOSH
A WIND JUTSU!!
EVEN IF HE'S JUST A KID, HE'S STILL OF KAZAMAKI BLOOD!!
BUT WHAT'S THE POINT OF BLASTING ME FAR AWAY?!
IT'S OBVIOUS HE'S FREAKED OUT!!

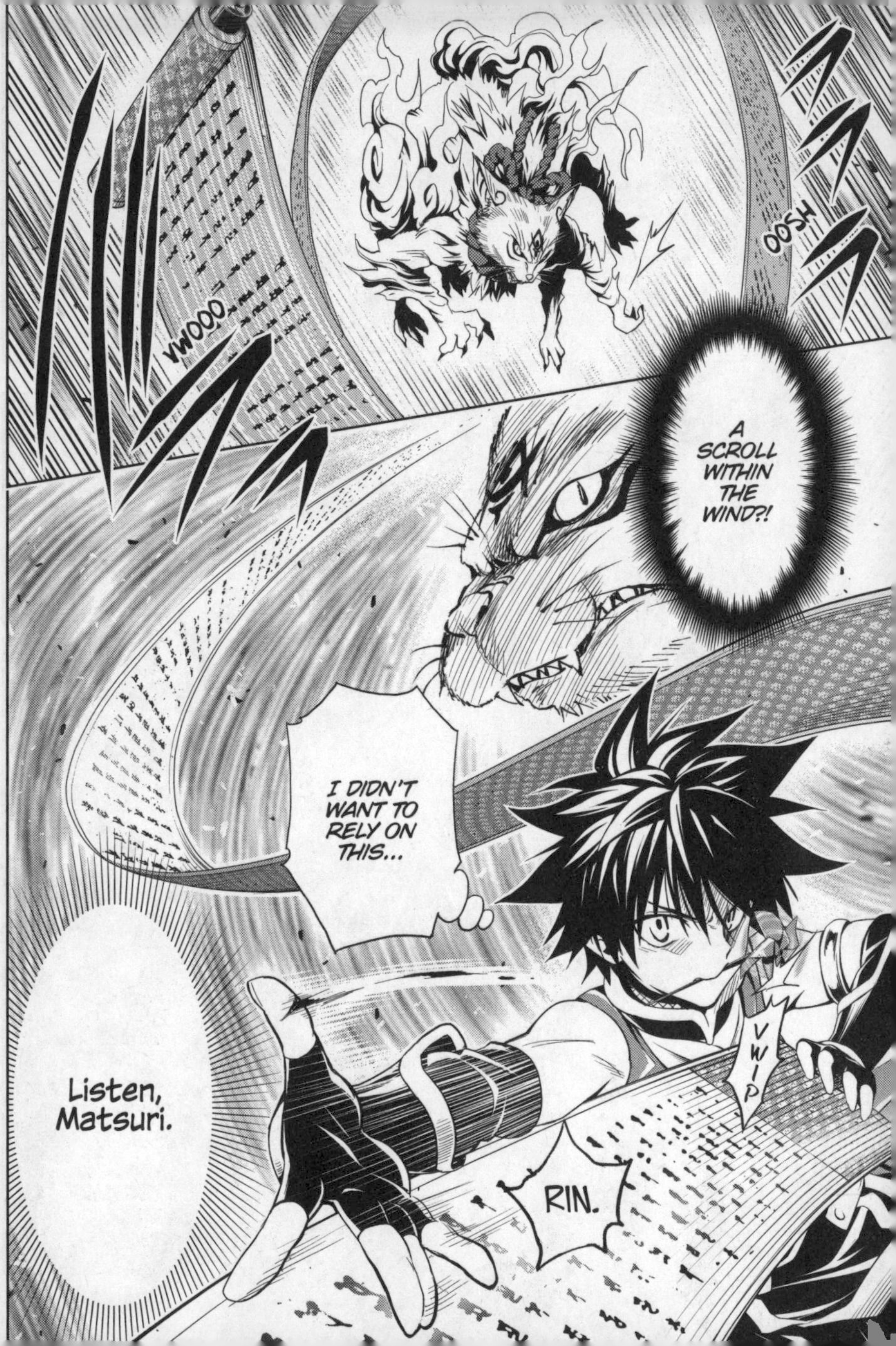
OOSH
YWOOO
A SCROLL WITHIN THE WIND?!
I DIDN'T WANT TO RELY ON THIS...
VWIP
RIN.
Listen, Matsuri.

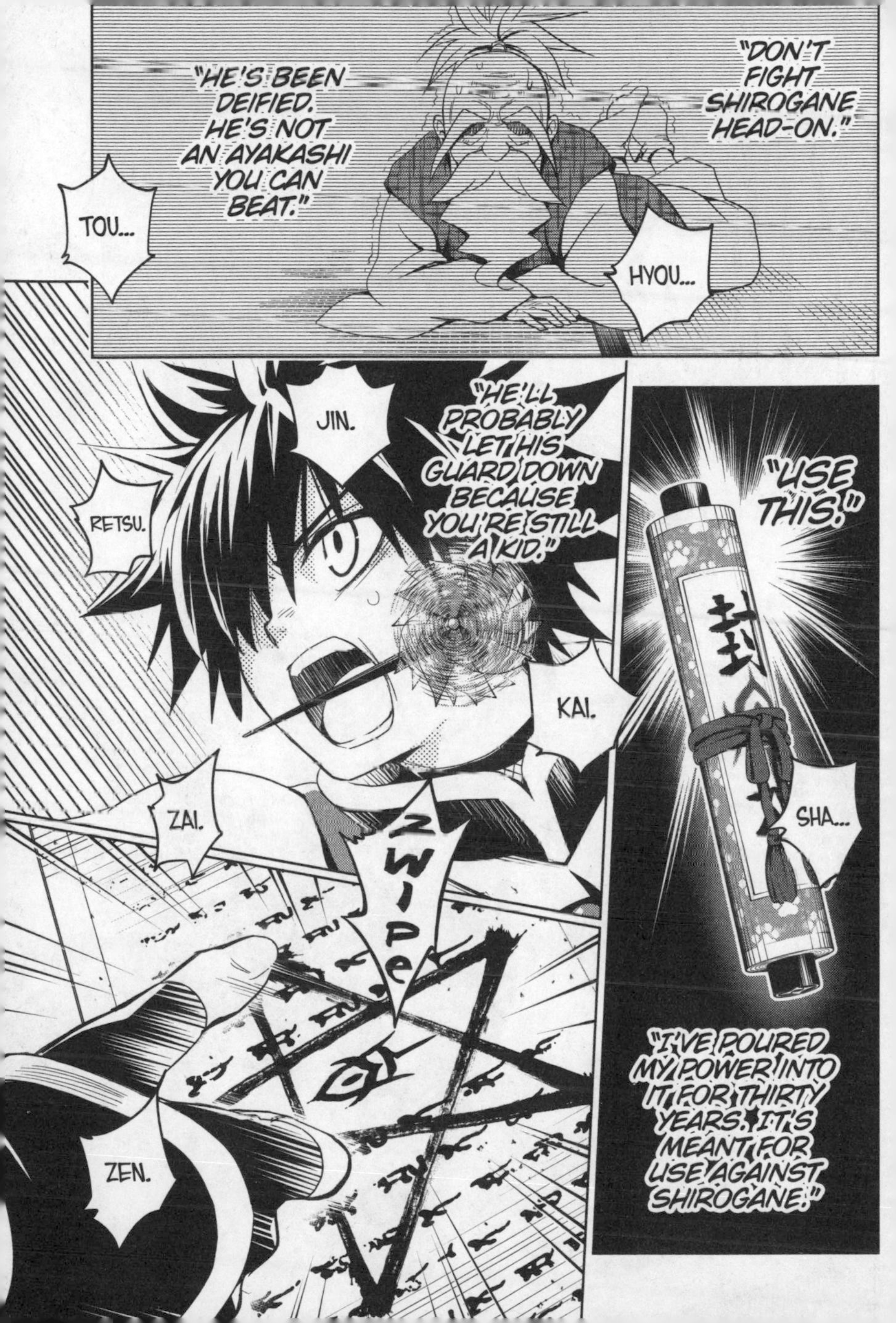
"DON'T FIGHT SHIROGANE HEAD-ON."
HYOU...
"HE'S BEEN DEIFIED. HE'S NOT AN AYAKASHI YOU CAN BEAT."
TOU...
"USE THIS."
SHA...
"I'VE POURED MY POWER INTO IT FOR THIRTY YEARS. IT'S MEANT FOR USE AGAINST SHIROGANE."
KAI.
"HE'LL PROBABLY LET HIS GUARD DOWN BECAUSE YOU'RE STILL A KID."
JIN.
RETSU.
ZWIPE
ZAI.
ZEN.

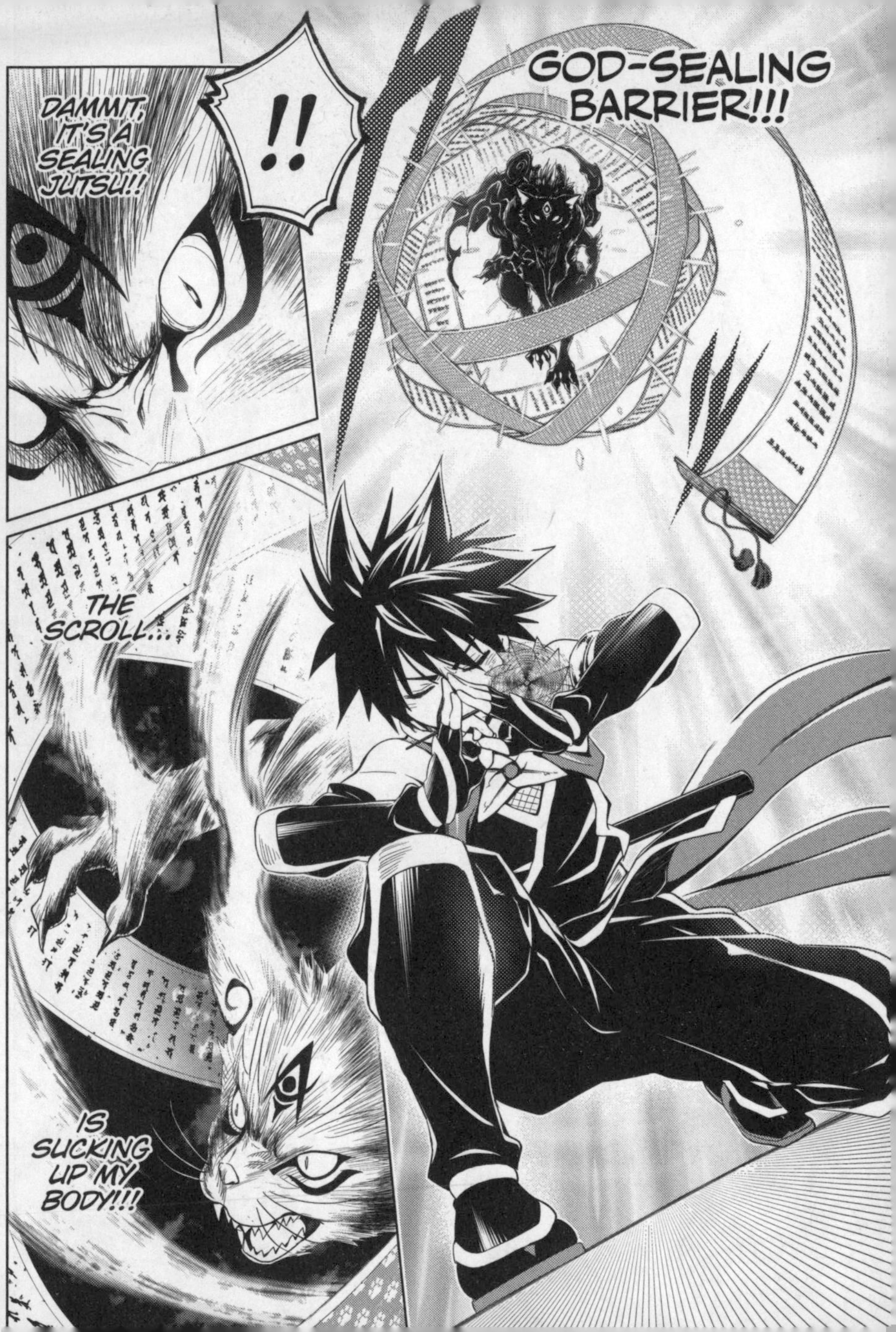
GOD-SEALING BARRIER!!!
!!
DAMMIT, IT'S A SEALING JUTSU!!
THE SCROLL...
IS SUCKING UP MY BODY!!!

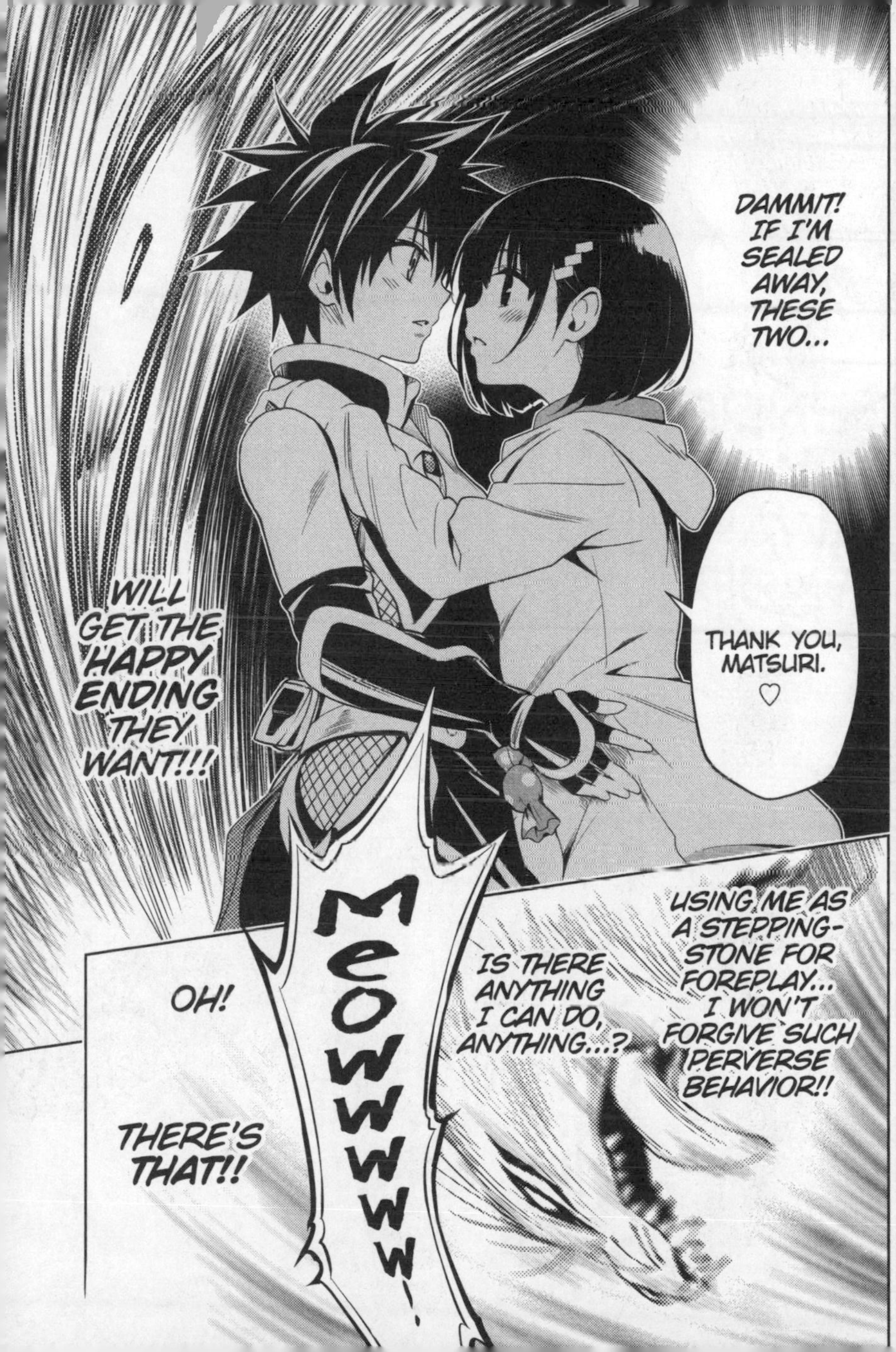
DAMMIT! IF I'M SEALED AWAY, THESE TWO...
THANK YOU, MATSURI. ♡
WILL GET THE HAPPY ENDING THEY WANT!!!
USING ME AS A STEPPING-STONE FOR FOREPLAY... I WON'T FORGIVE SUCH PERVERSE BEHAVIOR!!
IS THERE ANYTHING I CAN DO, ANYTHING...?
MEOWWWWW!
OH!
THERE'S THAT!!

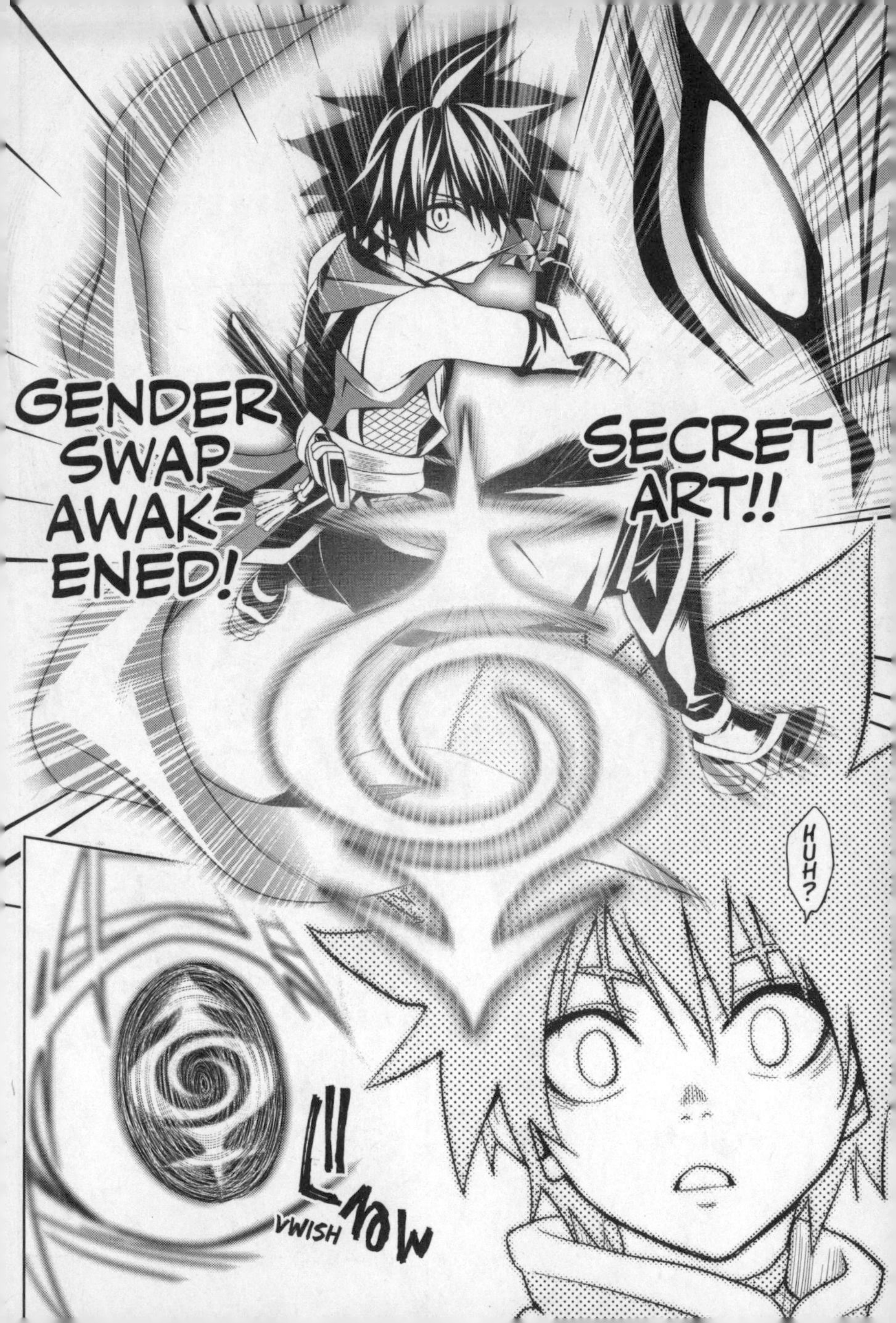
SECRET ART!!
GENDER SWAP AWAK-ENED!
HUH?
VWISH

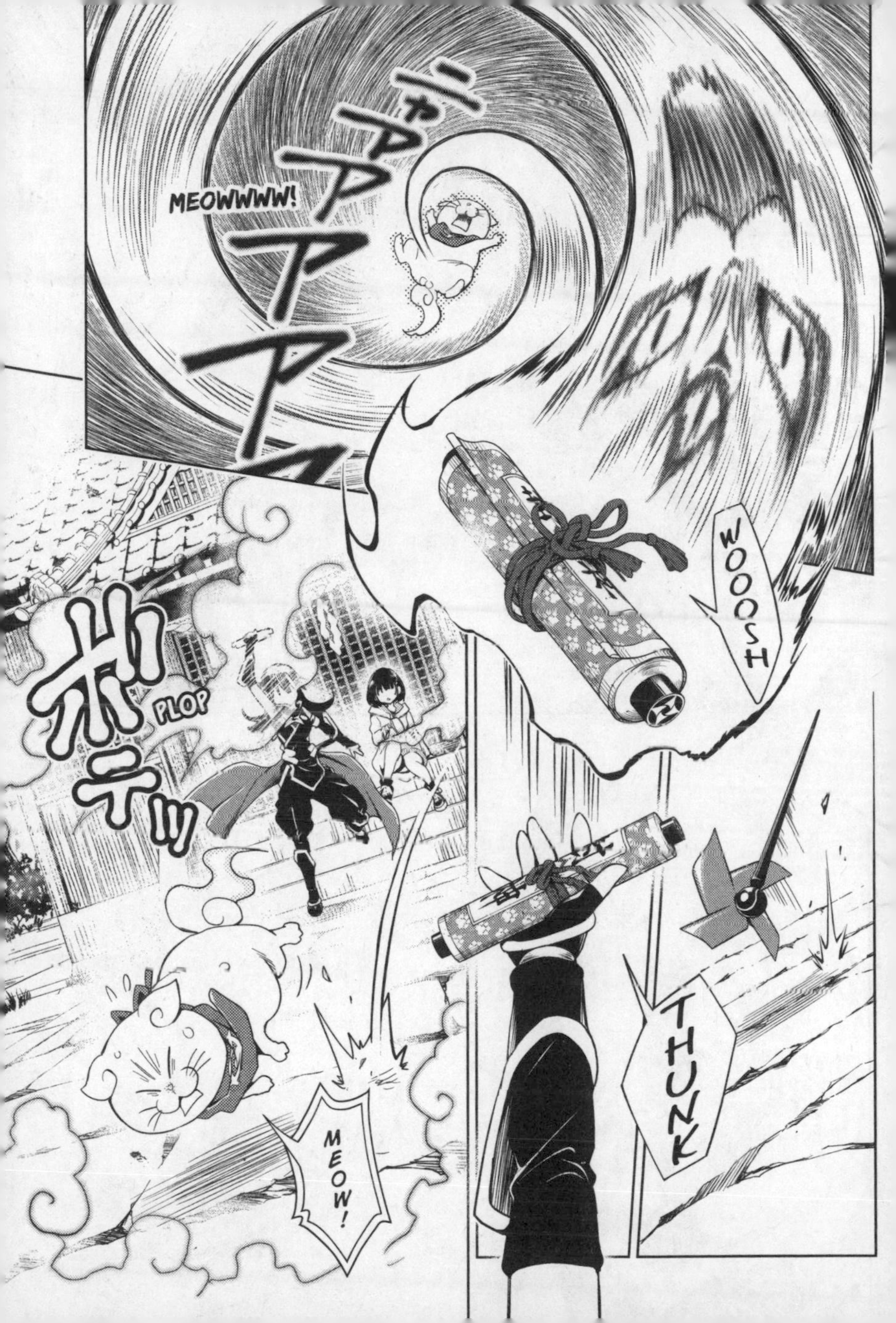
ニャアアアアア
MEOWWWW!
WOOOSH
THUNK
ポテッ
PLOP
MEOW!

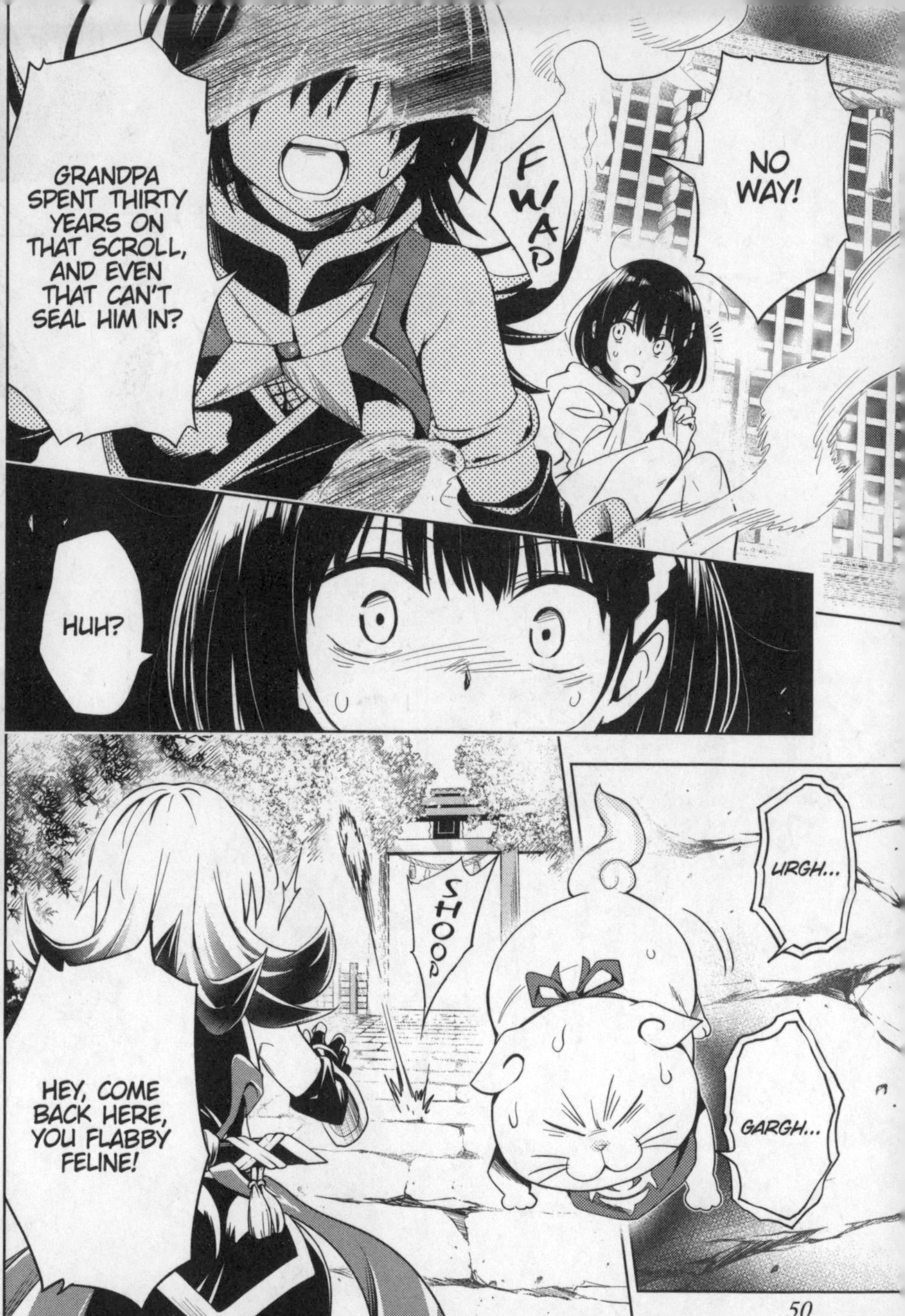
NO WAY!
FWAP
GRANDPA SPENT THIRTY YEARS ON THAT SCROLL, AND EVEN THAT CAN'T SEAL HIM IN?
HUH?
URGH...
GARGH...
SHOOP
HEY, COME BACK HERE, YOU FLABBY FELINE!

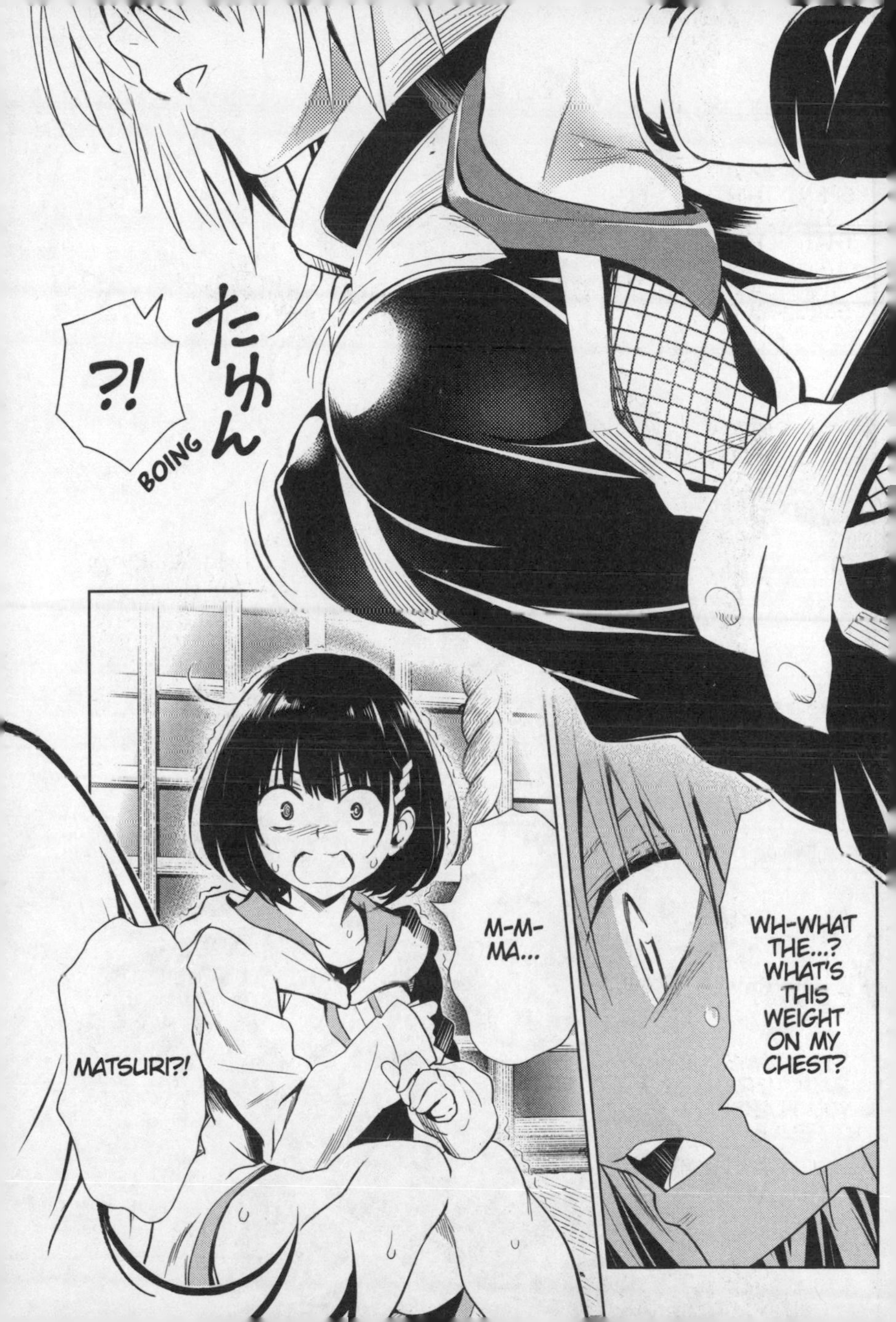
たゆん
BOING
?!
WH-WHAT THE...? WHAT'S THIS WEIGHT ON MY CHEST?
M-M-MA...
MATSURI?!

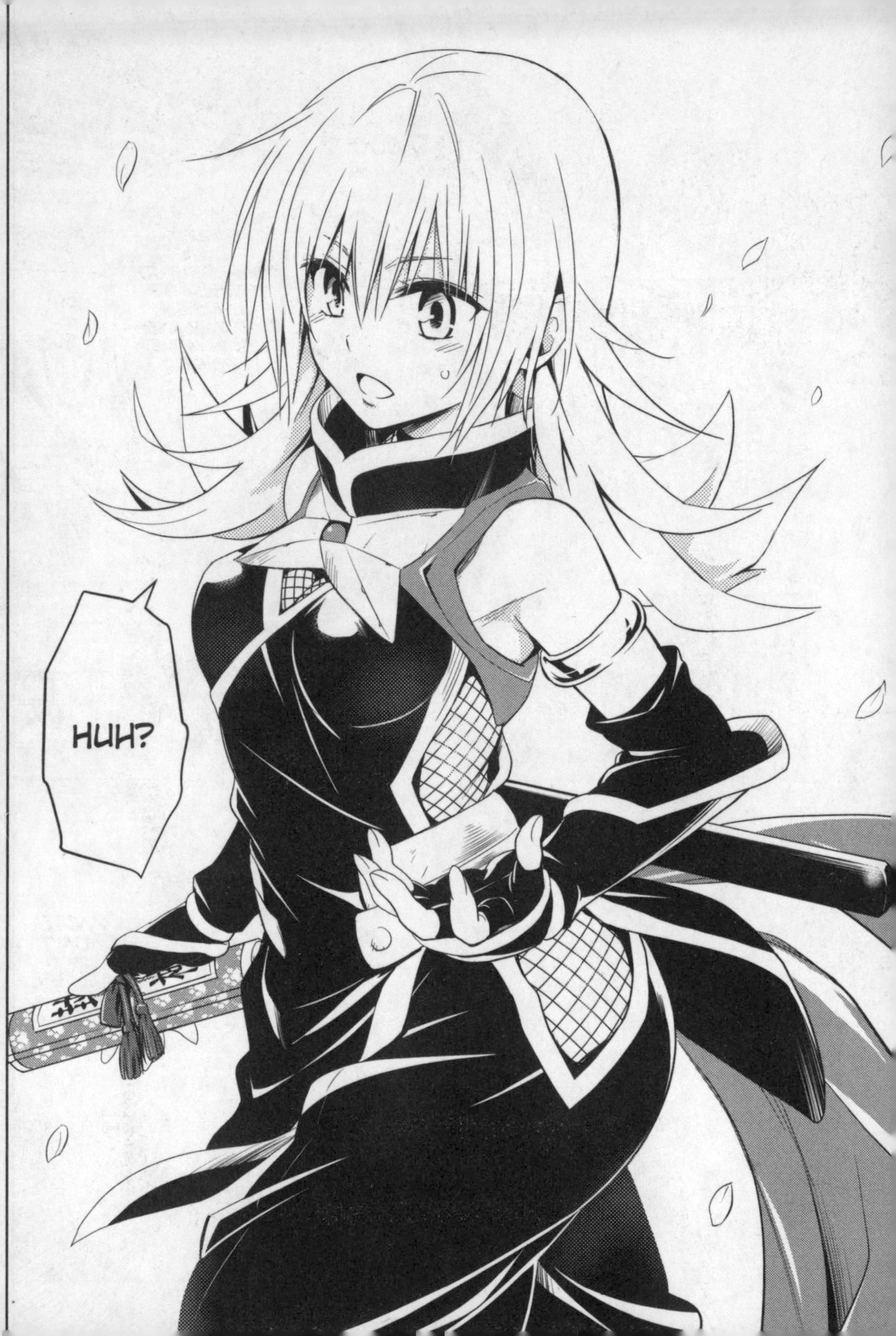
HUH?

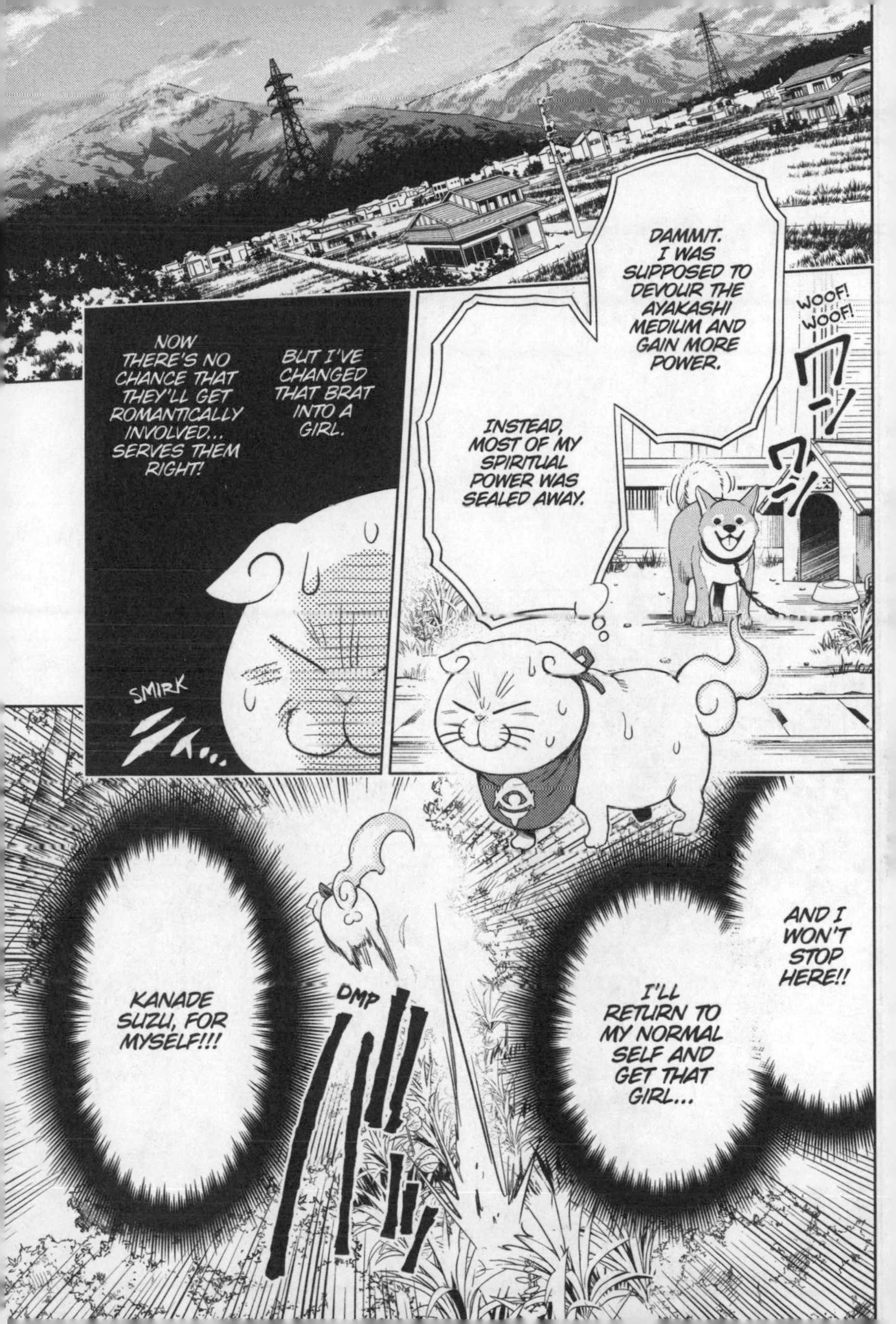
DAMMIT. I WAS SUPPOSED TO DEVOUR THE AYAKASHI MEDIUM AND GAIN MORE POWER.
INSTEAD, MOST OF MY SPIRITUAL POWER WAS SEALED AWAY.
WOOF! WOOF!
BUT I'VE CHANGED THAT BRAT INTO A GIRL.
NOW THERE'S NO CHANCE THAT THEY'LL GET ROMANTICALLY INVOLVED... SERVES THEM RIGHT!
SMIRK
AND I WON'T STOP HERE!!
I'LL RETURN TO MY NORMAL SELF AND GET THAT GIRL...
KANADE SUZU, FOR MYSELF!!!
DMP

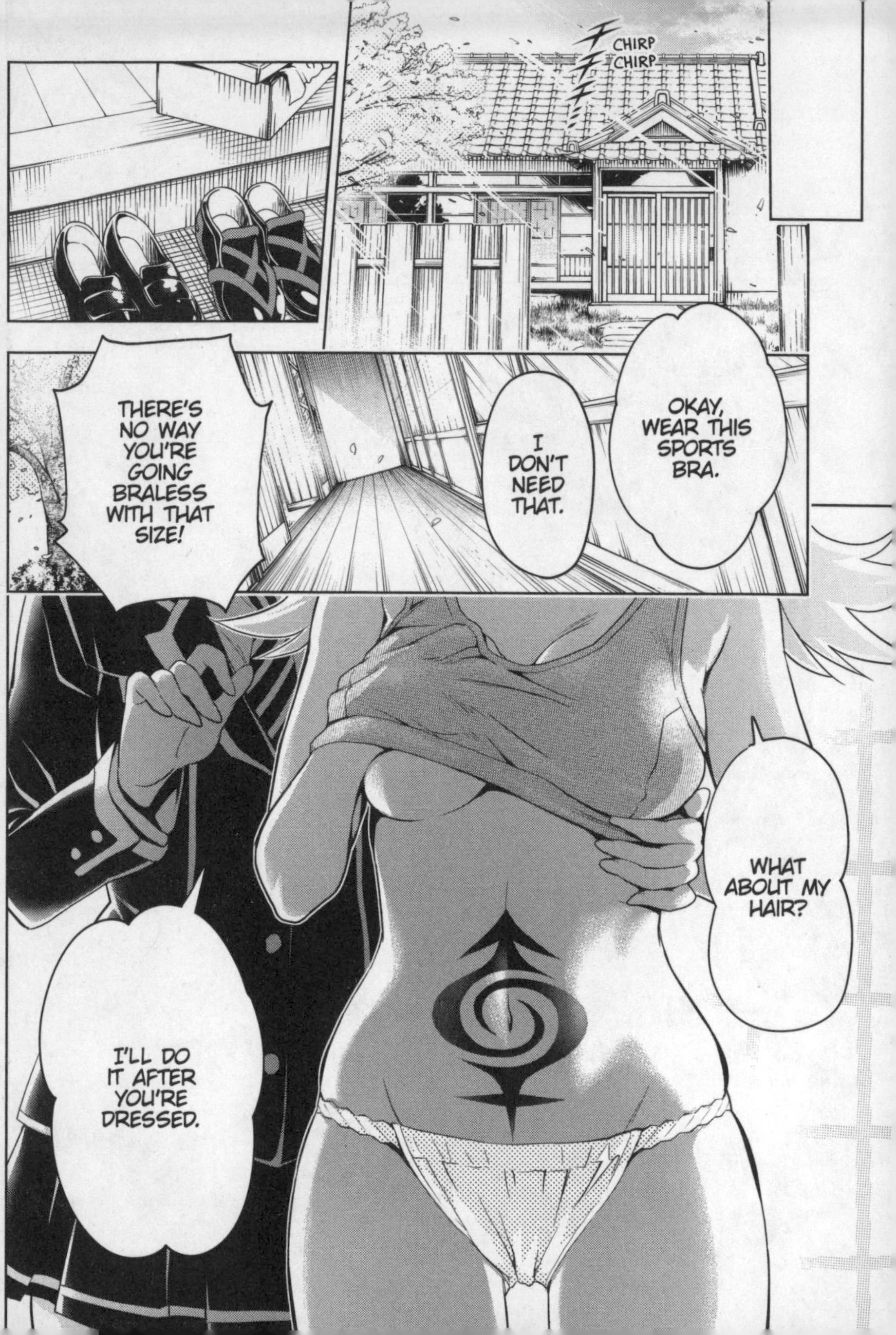
CHIRP CHIRP
OKAY, WEAR THIS SPORTS BRA.
I DON'T NEED THAT.
THERE'S NO WAY YOU'RE GOING BRALESS WITH THAT SIZE!
WHAT ABOUT MY HAIR?
I'LL DO IT AFTER YOU'RE DRESSED.

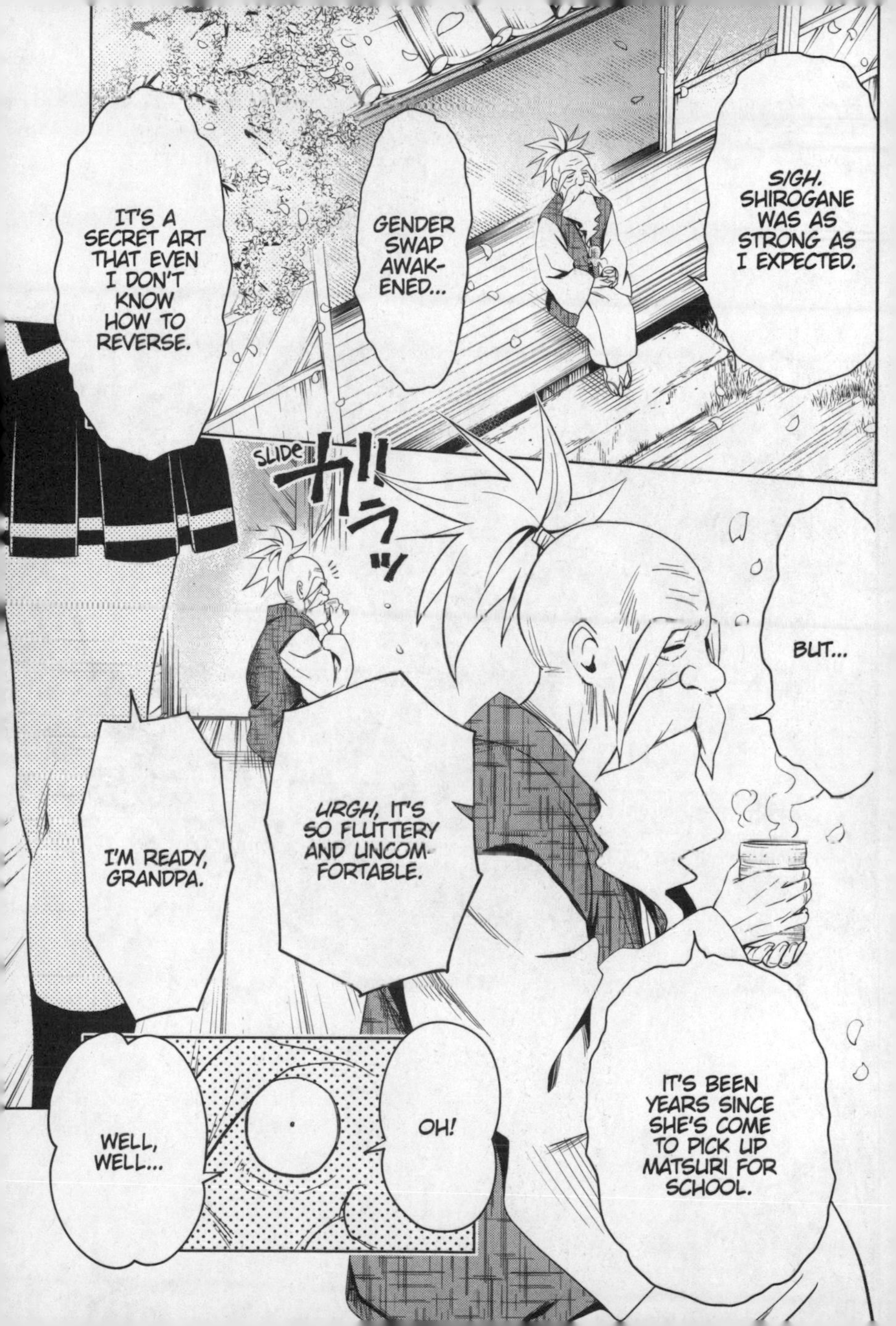
SIGH. SHIROGANE WAS AS STRONG AS I EXPECTED.
GENDER SWAP AWAK-ENED...
IT'S A SECRET ART THAT EVEN I DON'T KNOW HOW TO REVERSE.
BUT...
SLIDE
URGH, IT'S SO FLUTTERY AND UNCOM-FORTABLE.
I'M READY, GRANDPA.
IT'S BEEN YEARS SINCE SHE'S COME TO PICK UP MATSURI FOR SCHOOL.
OH!
WELL, WELL...

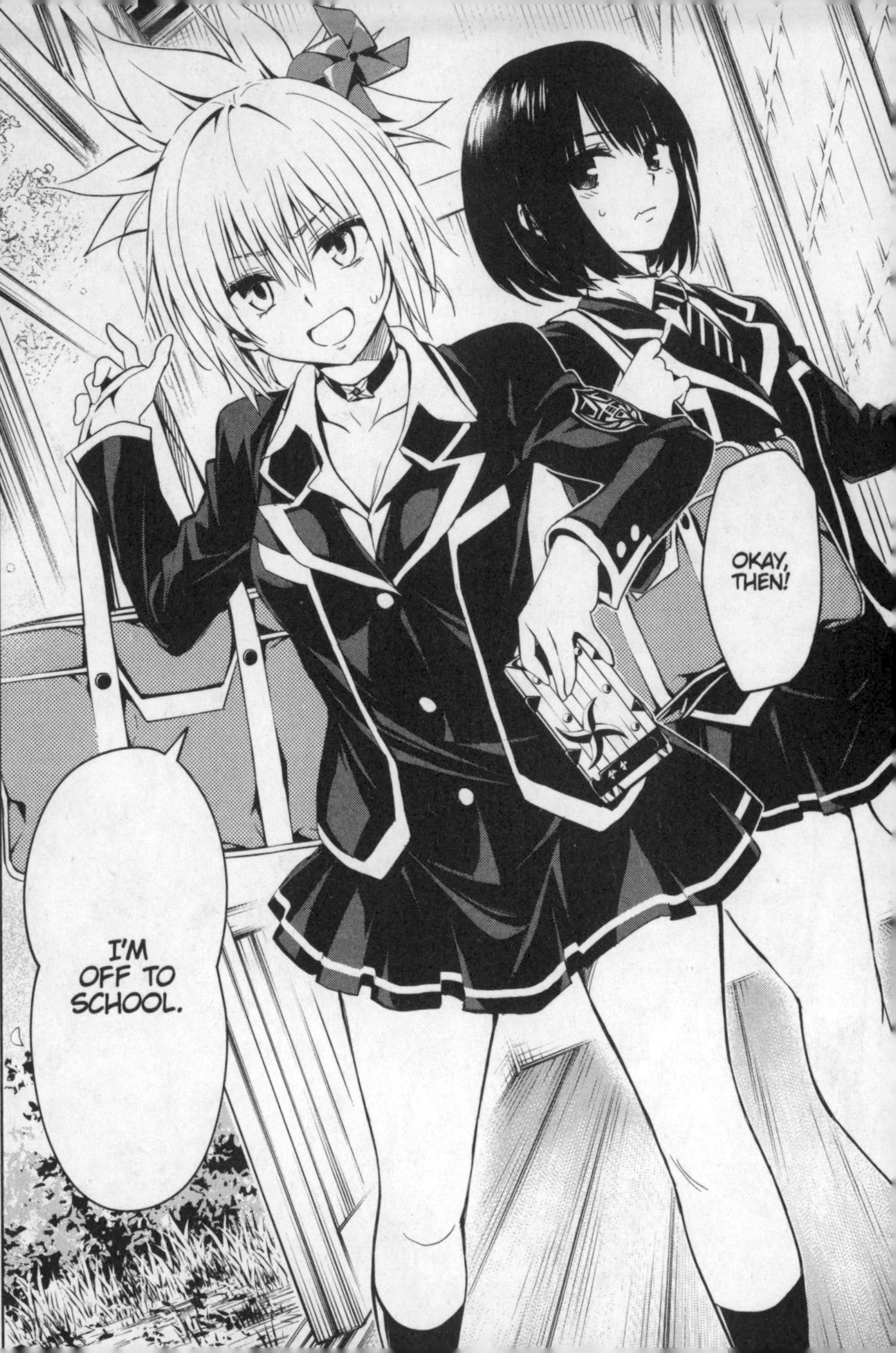
OKAY, THEN!
I'M OFF TO SCHOOL.

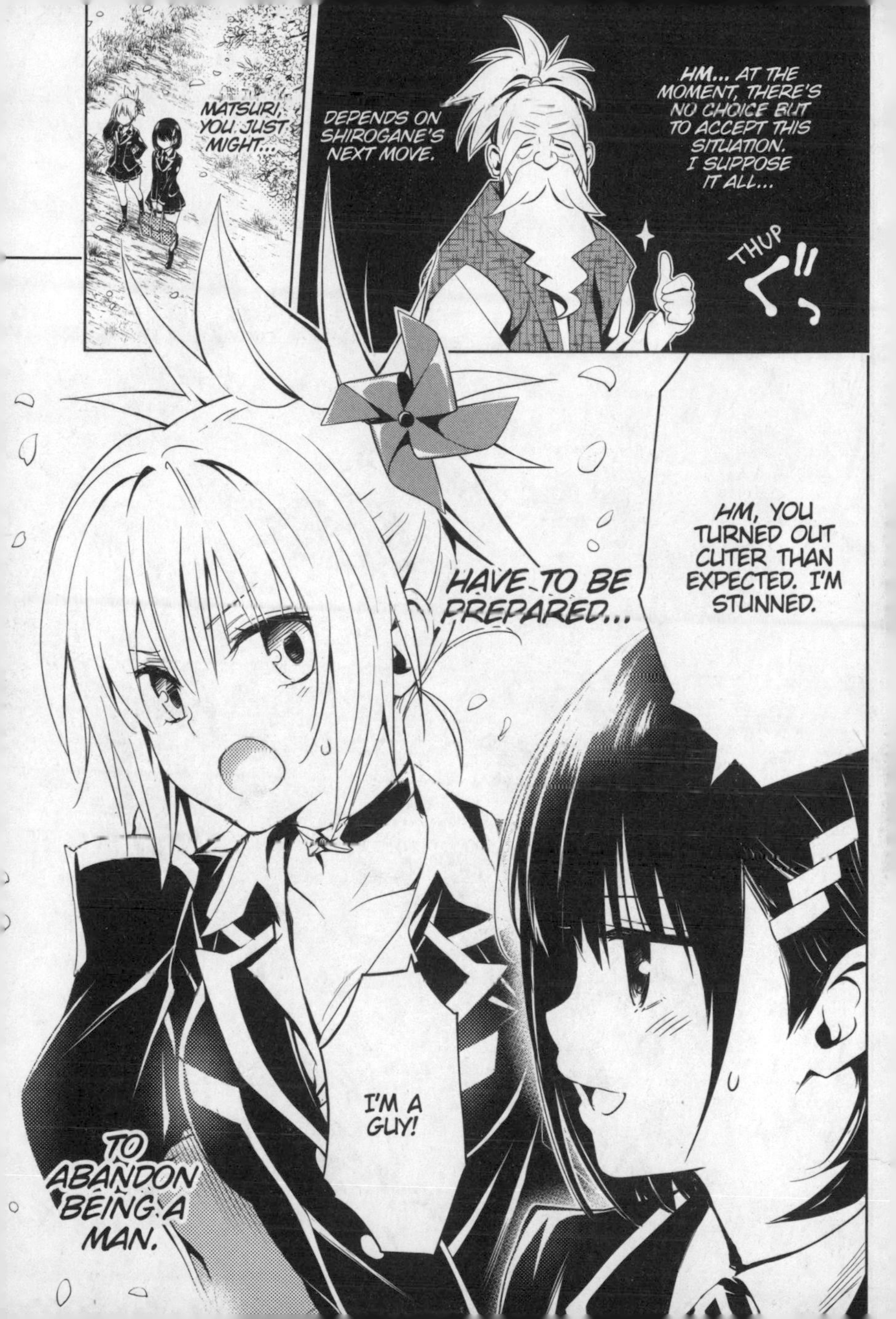
HM... AT THE MOMENT, THERE'S NO CHOICE BUT TO ACCEPT THIS SITUATION. I SUPPOSE IT ALL...
DEPENDS ON SHIROGANE'S NEXT MOVE.
THUP
MATSURI, YOU JUST MIGHT...
HM, YOU TURNED OUT CUTER THAN EXPECTED. I'M STUNNED.
HAVE TO BE PREPARED...
I'M A GUY!
TO ABANDON BEING A MAN.

# Shirogane, the King of Ayakashi

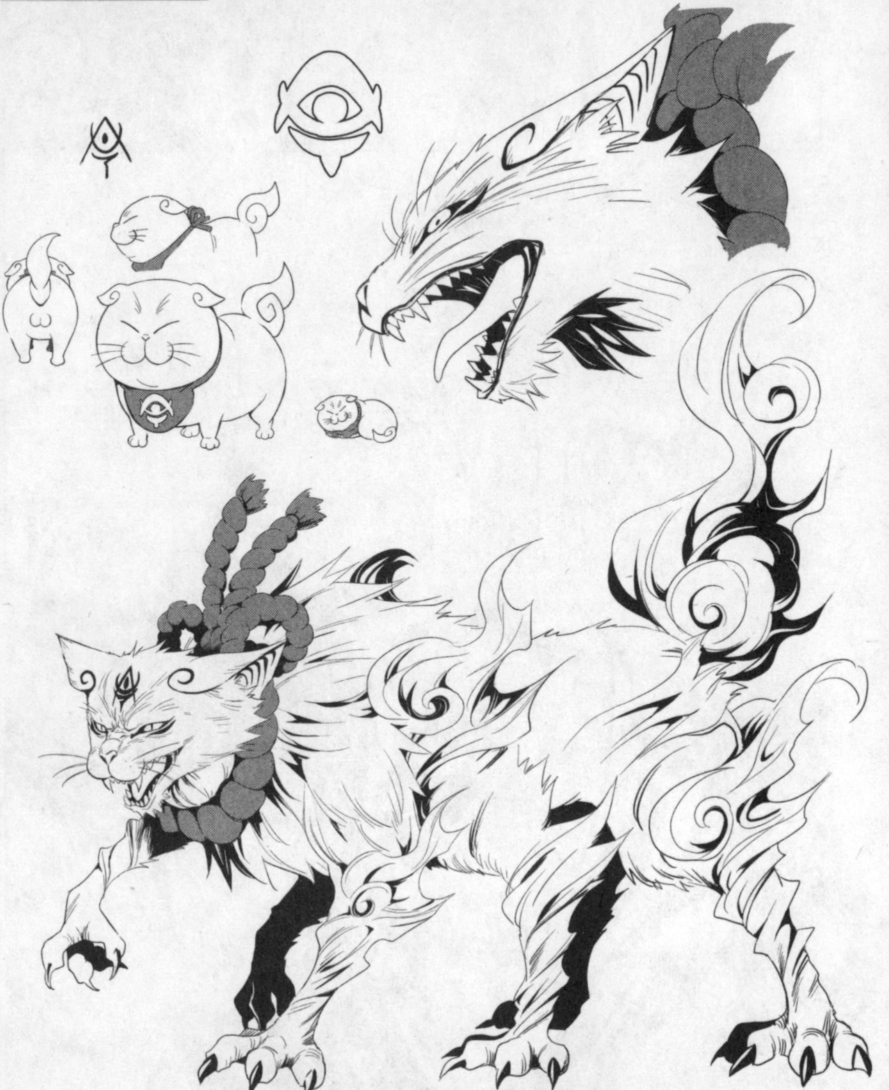

# Chapter 2 Girl Friend

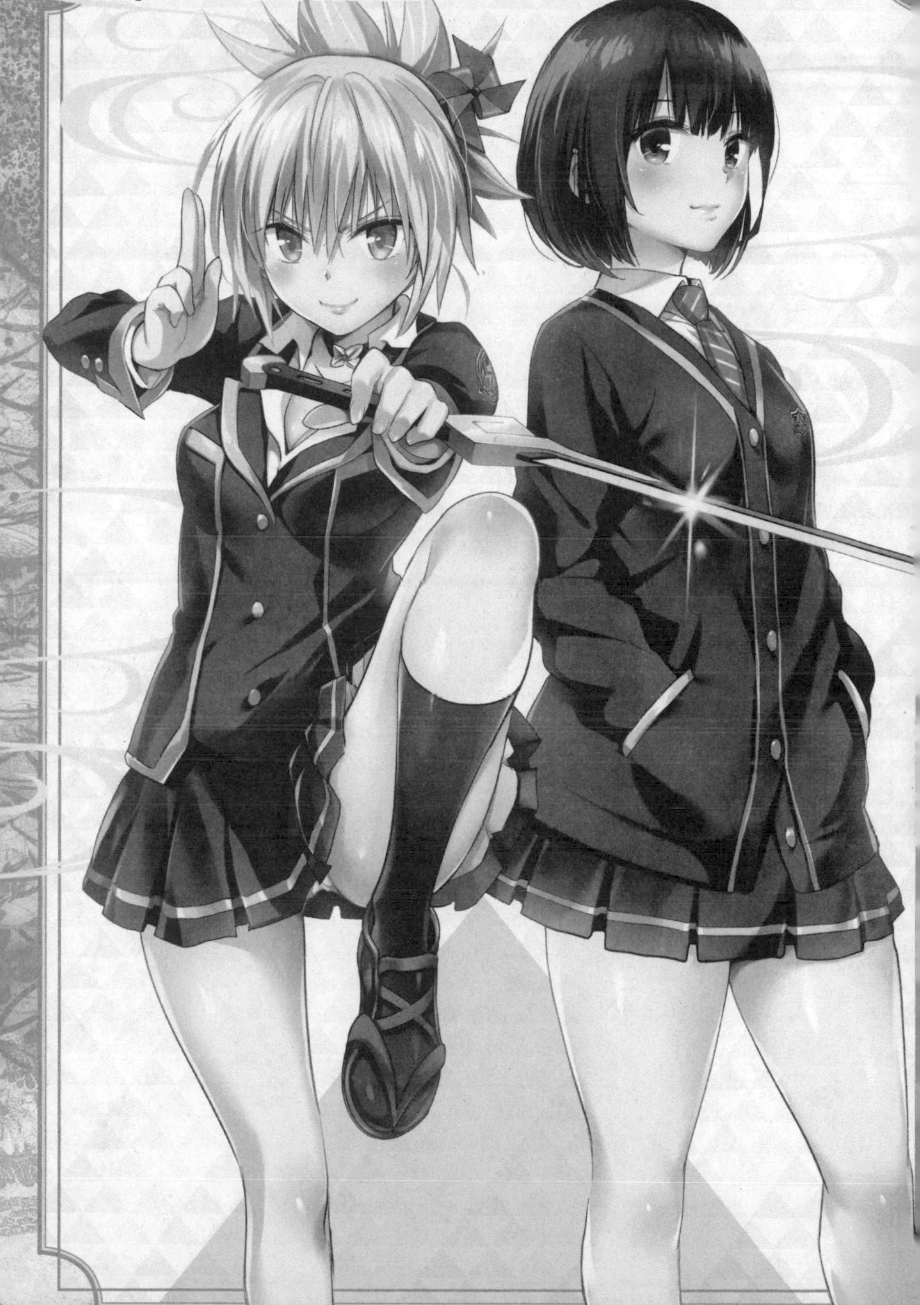

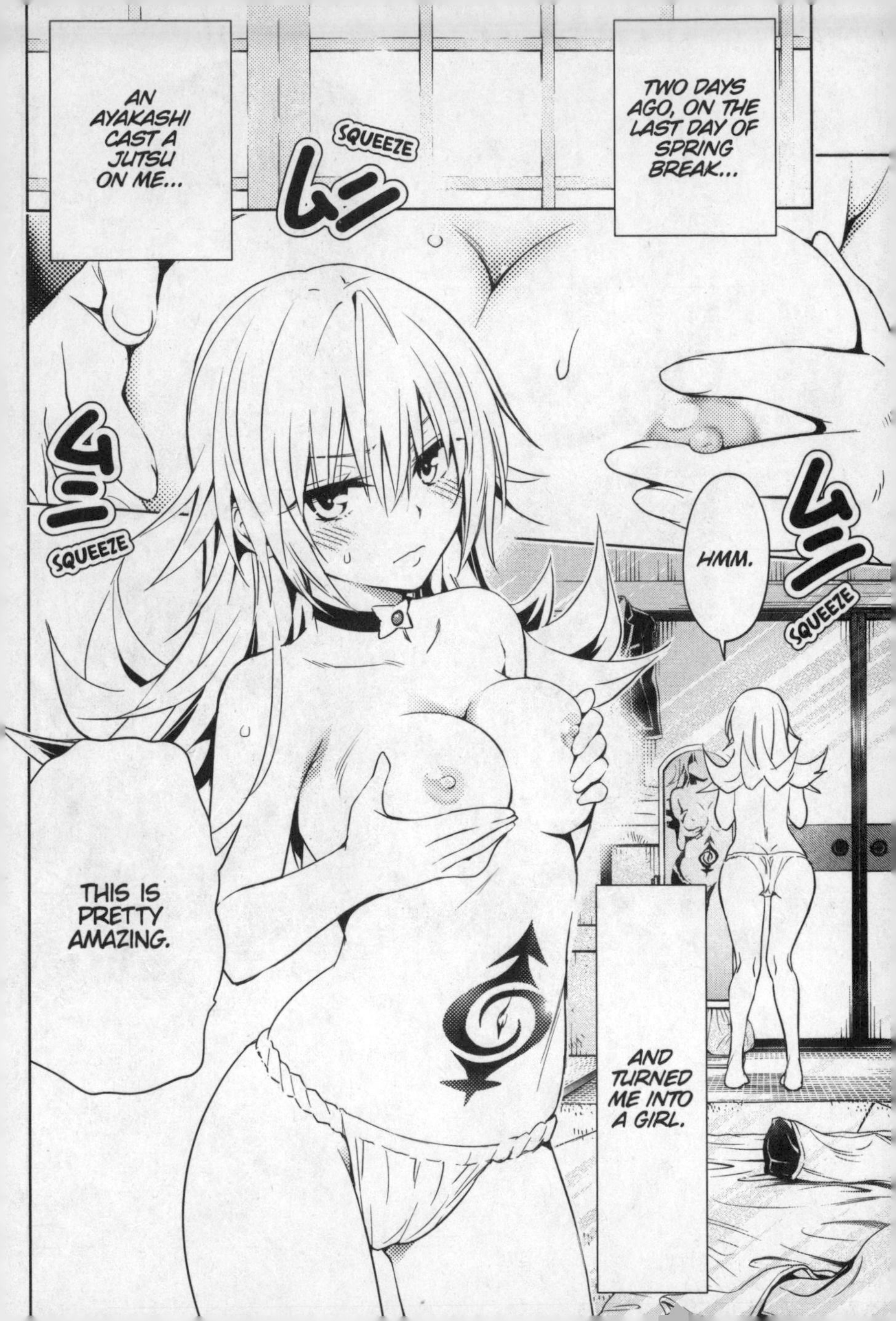
TWO DAYS AGO, ON THE LAST DAY OF SPRING BREAK...
SQUEEZE
AN AYAKASHI CAST A JUTSU ON ME...
SQUEEZE
HMM.
SQUEEZE
AND TURNED ME INTO A GIRL.
THIS IS PRETTY AMAZING.

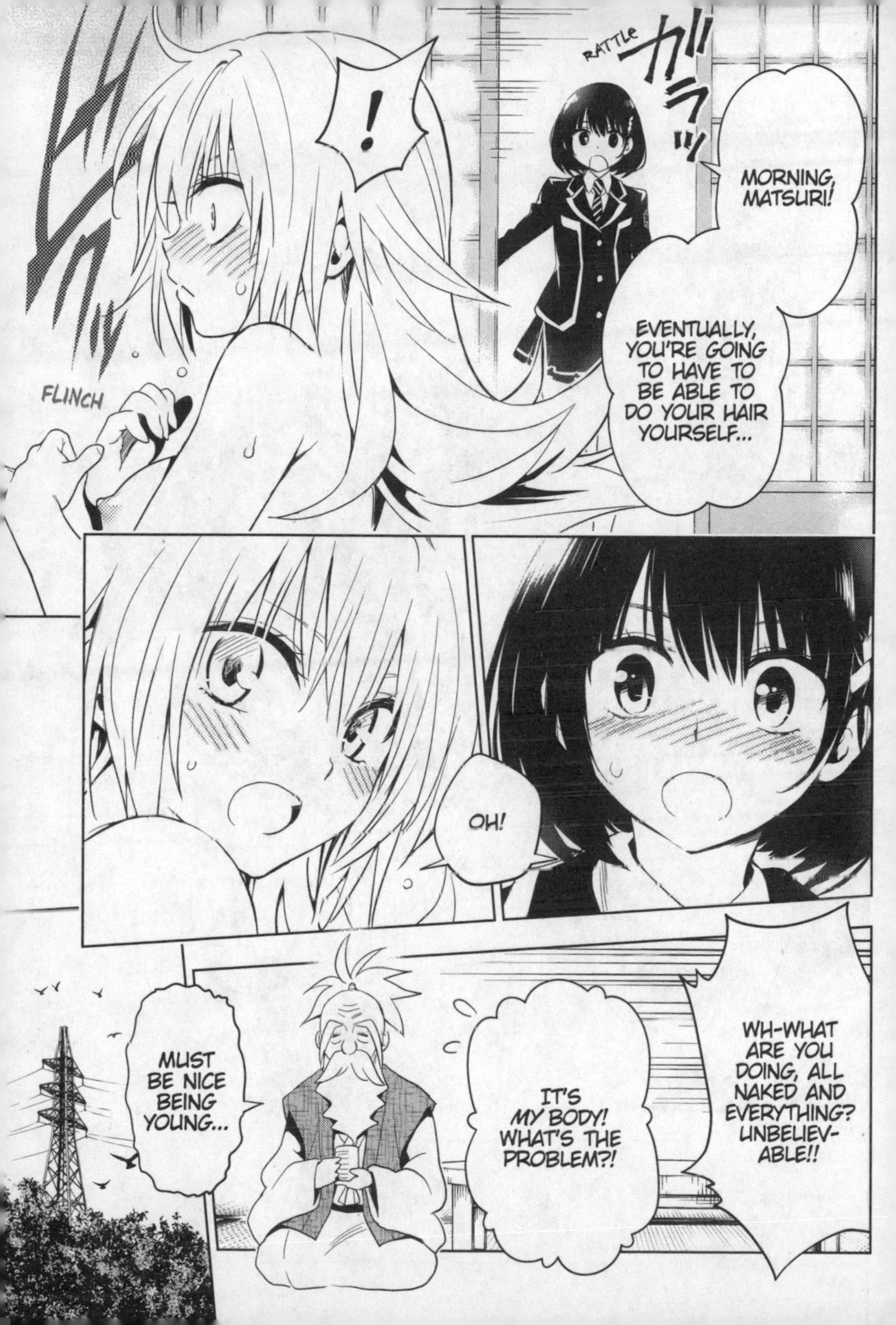
RATTLE
ガラッ
MORNING, MATSURI!
EVENTUALLY, YOU'RE GOING TO HAVE TO BE ABLE TO DO YOUR HAIR YOURSELF...
!
FLINCH
OH!
WH-WHAT ARE YOU DOING, ALL NAKED AND EVERYTHING? UNBELIEVABLE!!
IT'S MY BODY! WHAT'S THE PROBLEM?!
MUST BE NICE BEING YOUNG...

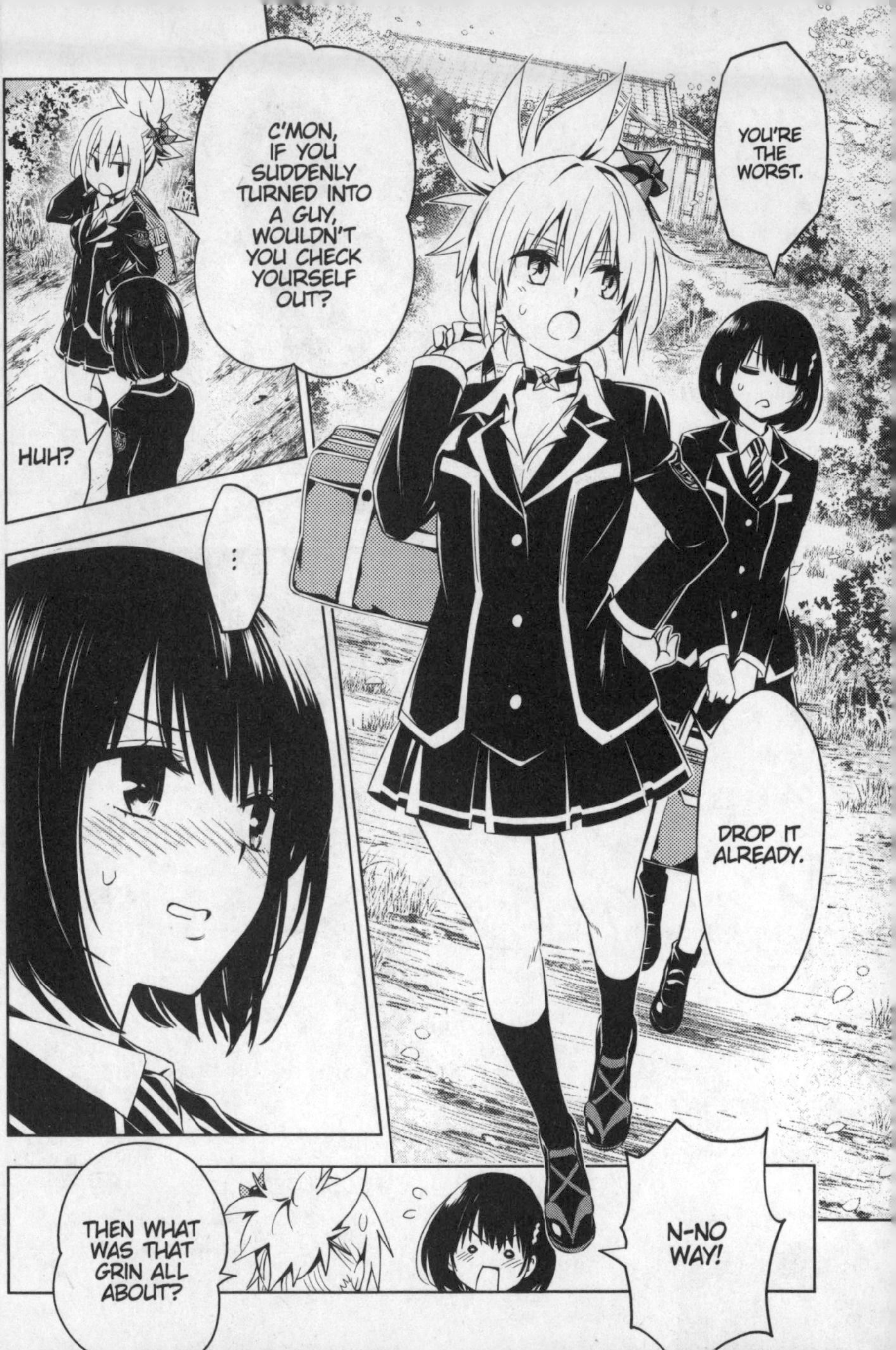
YOU'RE THE WORST.
DROP IT ALREADY.
C'MON, IF YOU SUDDENLY TURNED INTO A GUY, WOULDN'T YOU CHECK YOURSELF OUT?
HUH?
...
N-NO WAY!
THEN WHAT WAS THAT GRIN ALL ABOUT?

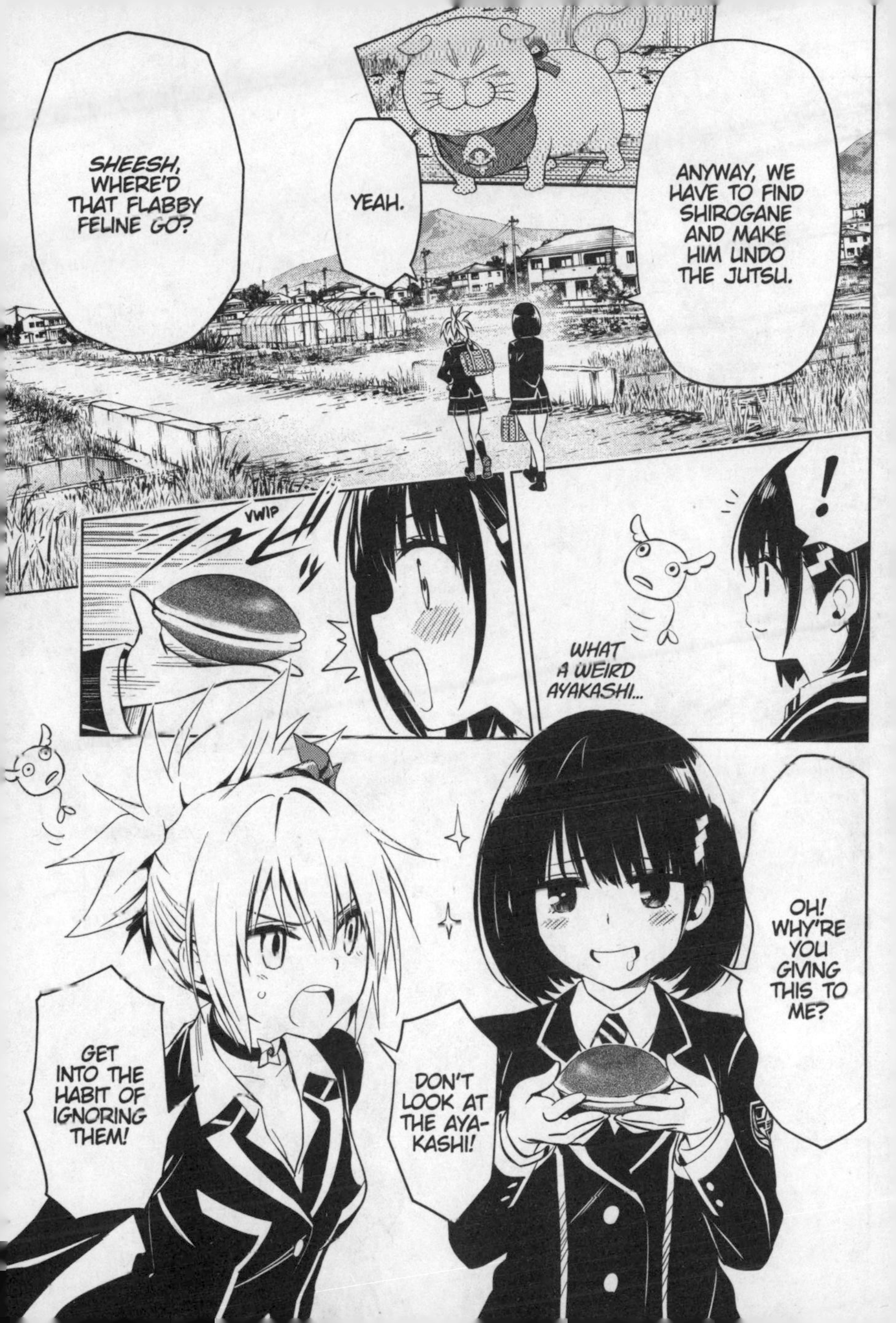
ANYWAY, WE HAVE TO FIND SHIROGANE AND MAKE HIM UNDO THE JUTSU.
YEAH.
SHEESH, WHERE'D THAT FLABBY FELINE GO?
!
WHAT A WEIRD AYAKASHI...
VWIP
OH! WHY'RE YOU GIVING THIS TO ME?
DON'T LOOK AT THE AYA-KASHI!
GET INTO THE HABIT OF IGNORING THEM!

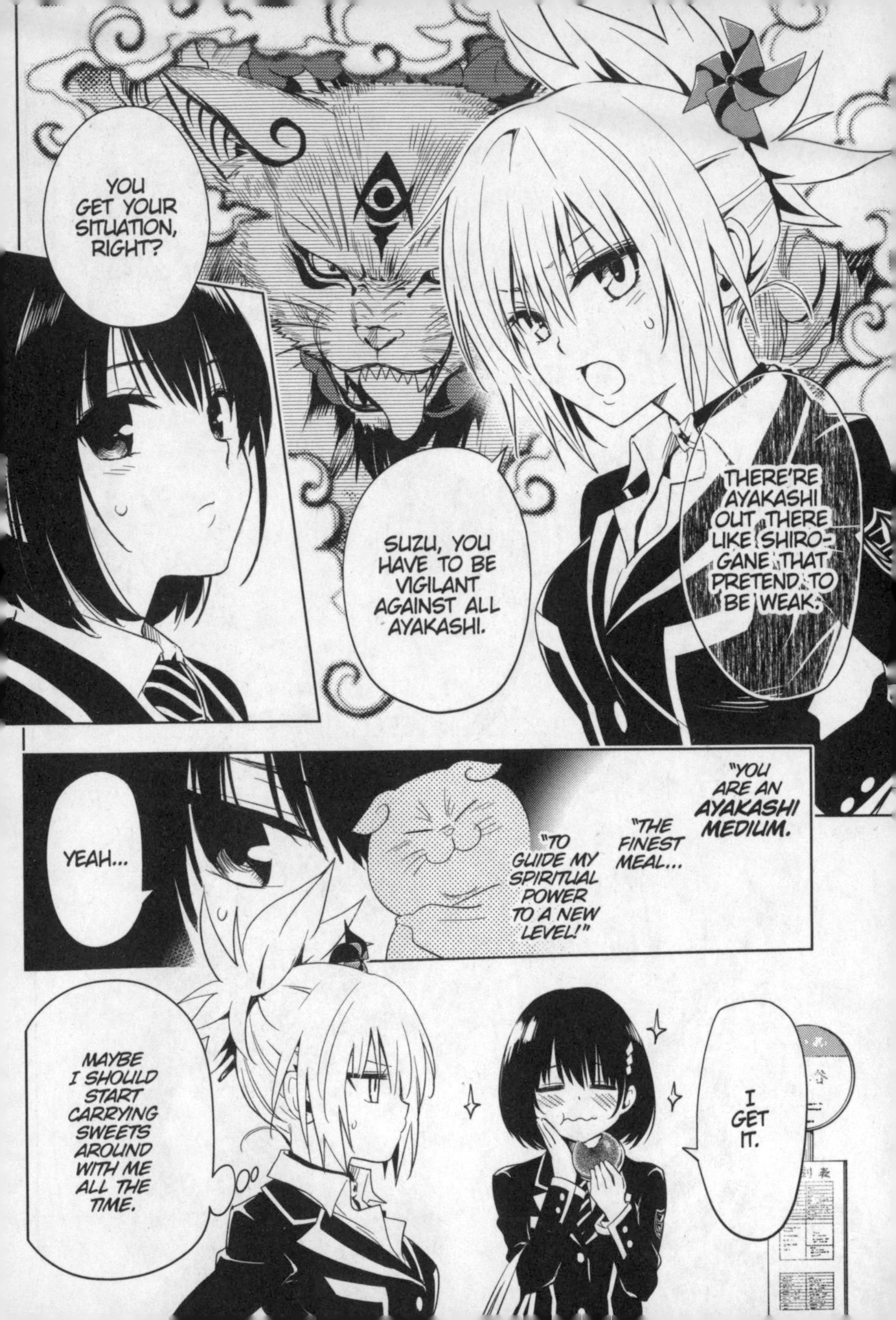
THERE'RE AYAKASHI OUT THERE LIKE SHIROGANE THAT PRETEND TO BE WEAK.
SUZU, YOU HAVE TO BE VIGILANT AGAINST ALL AYAKASHI.
YOU GET YOUR SITUATION, RIGHT?
"YOU ARE AN AYAKASHI MEDIUM.
"THE FINEST MEAL...
"TO GUIDE MY SPIRITUAL POWER TO A NEW LEVEL!"
YEAH...
I GET IT.
MAYBE I SHOULD START CARRYING SWEETS AROUND WITH ME ALL THE TIME.

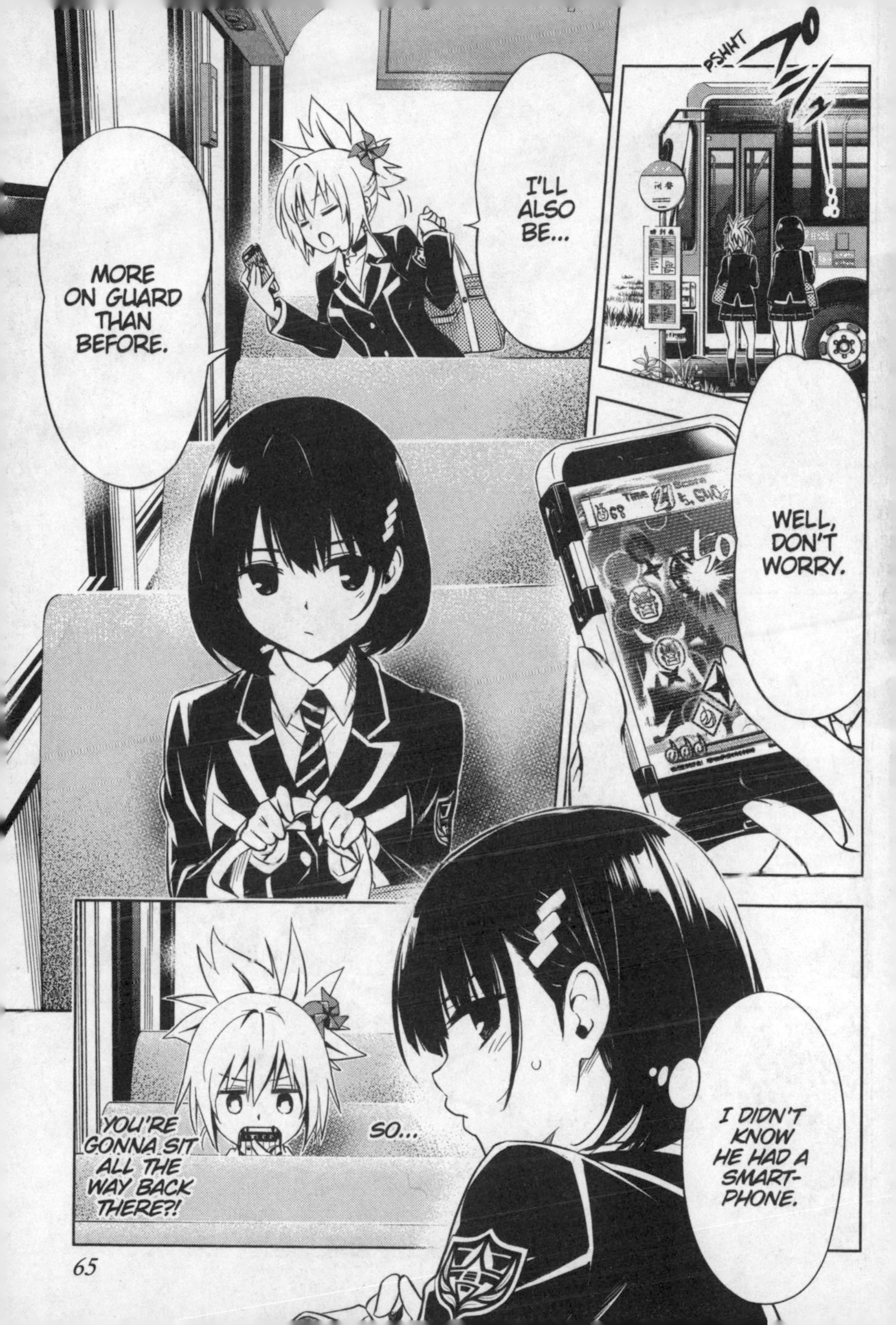
PSHHT
I'LL ALSO BE...
MORE ON GUARD THAN BEFORE.
WELL, DON'T WORRY.
I DIDN'T KNOW HE HAD A SMART-PHONE.
SO...
YOU'RE GONNA SIT ALL THE WAY BACK THERE?!

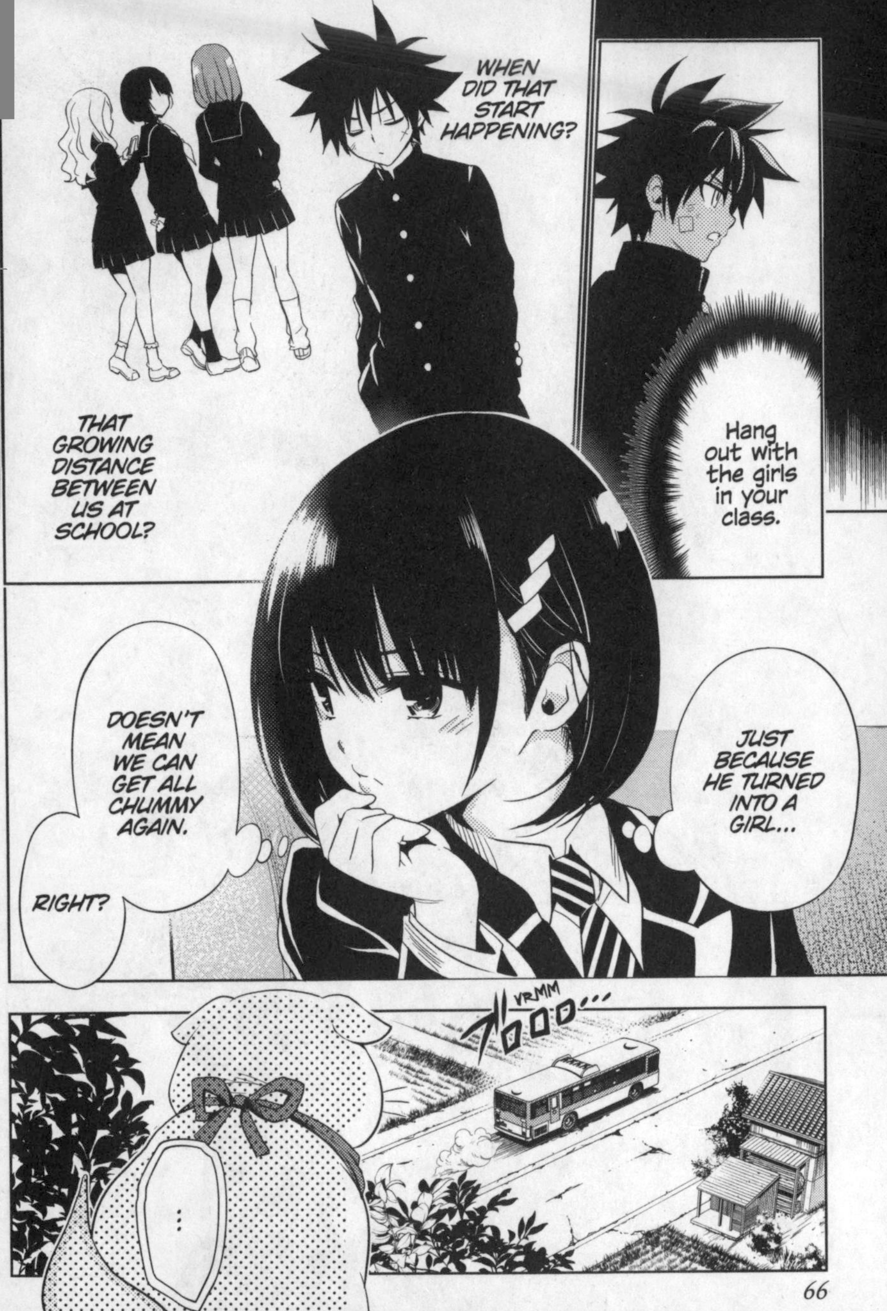
Hang out with the girls in your class.
WHEN DID THAT START HAPPENING?
THAT GROWING DISTANCE BETWEEN US AT SCHOOL?
JUST BECAUSE HE TURNED INTO A GIRL...
DOESN'T MEAN WE CAN GET ALL CHUMMY AGAIN.
RIGHT?
VRMM
...

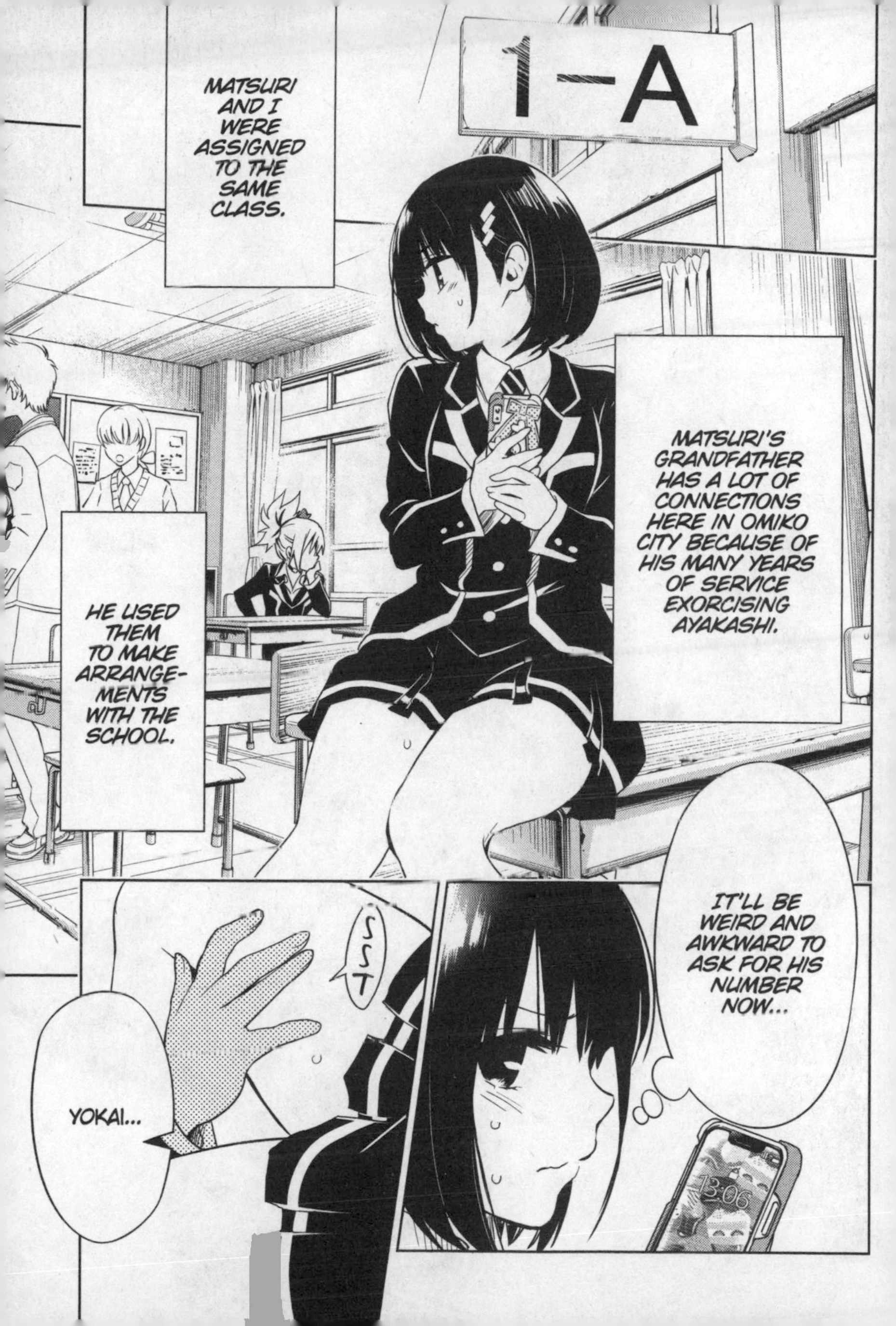
1-A
MATSURI AND I WERE ASSIGNED TO THE SAME CLASS.
MATSURI'S GRANDFATHER HAS A LOT OF CONNECTIONS HERE IN OMIKO CITY BECAUSE OF HIS MANY YEARS OF SERVICE EXORCISING AYAKASHI.
HE USED THEM TO MAKE ARRANGE-MENTS WITH THE SCHOOL.
IT'LL BE WEIRD AND AWKWARD TO ASK FOR HIS NUMBER NOW...
SST
YOKAI...

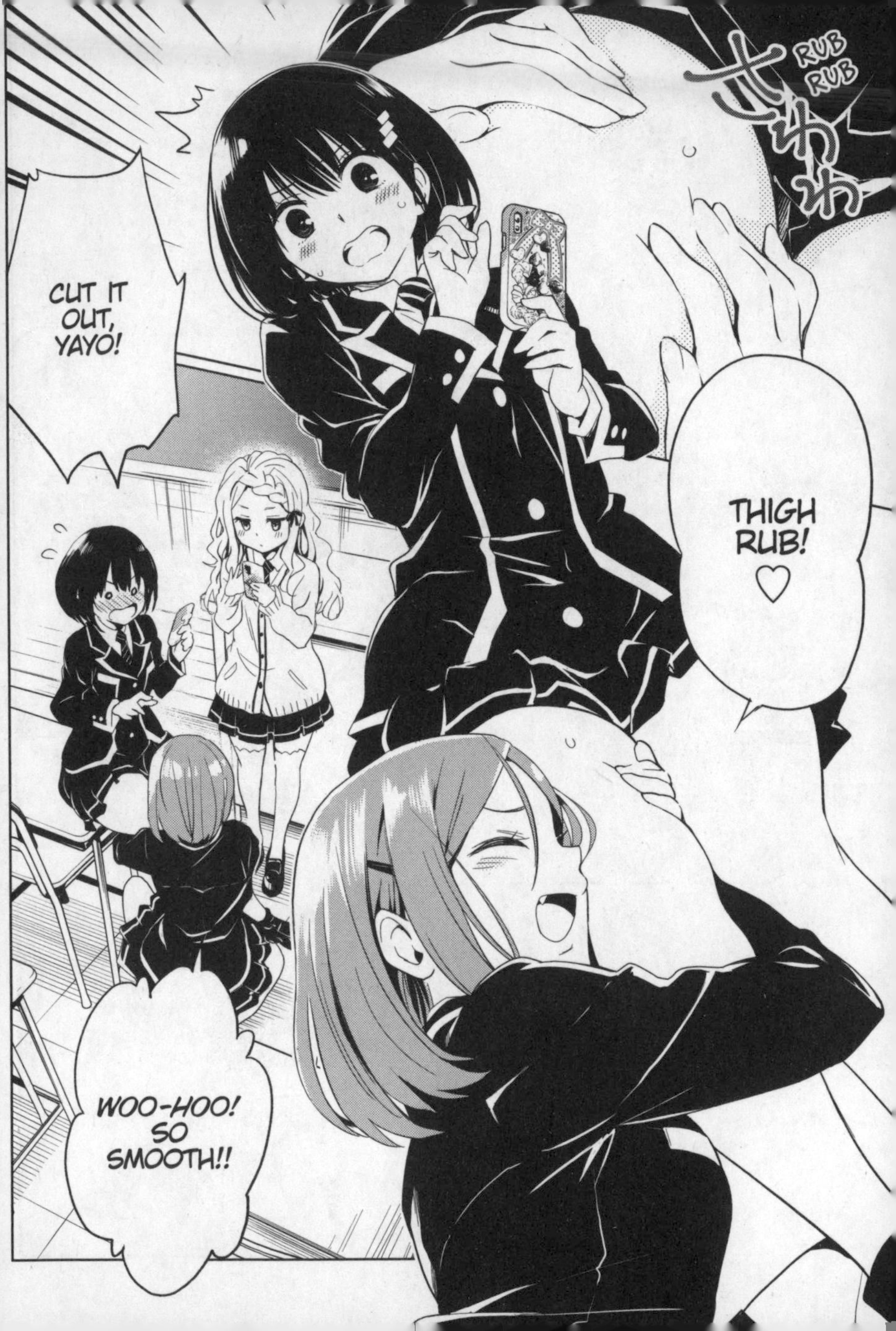
RUB RUB
THIGH RUB! ♡
CUT IT OUT, YAYO!
WOO-HOO! SO SMOOTH!!

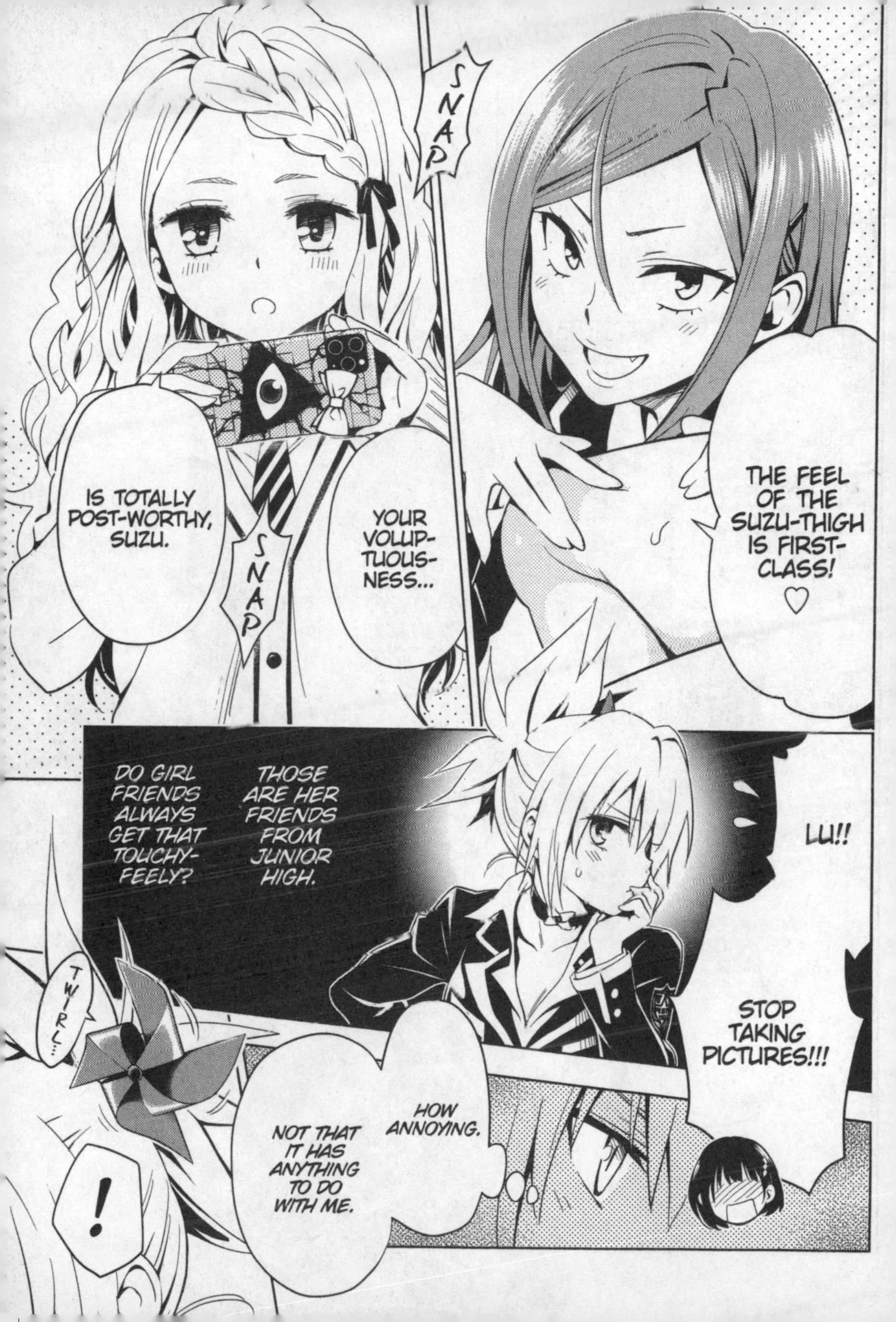
THE FEEL OF THE SUZU-THIGH IS FIRST-CLASS! ♡
SNAP
YOUR VOLUP-TUOUS-NESS...
SNAP
IS TOTALLY POST-WORTHY, SUZU.
LU!!
STOP TAKING PICTURES!!!
THOSE ARE HER FRIENDS FROM JUNIOR HIGH.
DO GIRL FRIENDS ALWAYS GET THAT TOUCHY-FEELY?
HOW ANNOYING.
NOT THAT IT HAS ANYTHING TO DO WITH ME.
TWIRL...
!

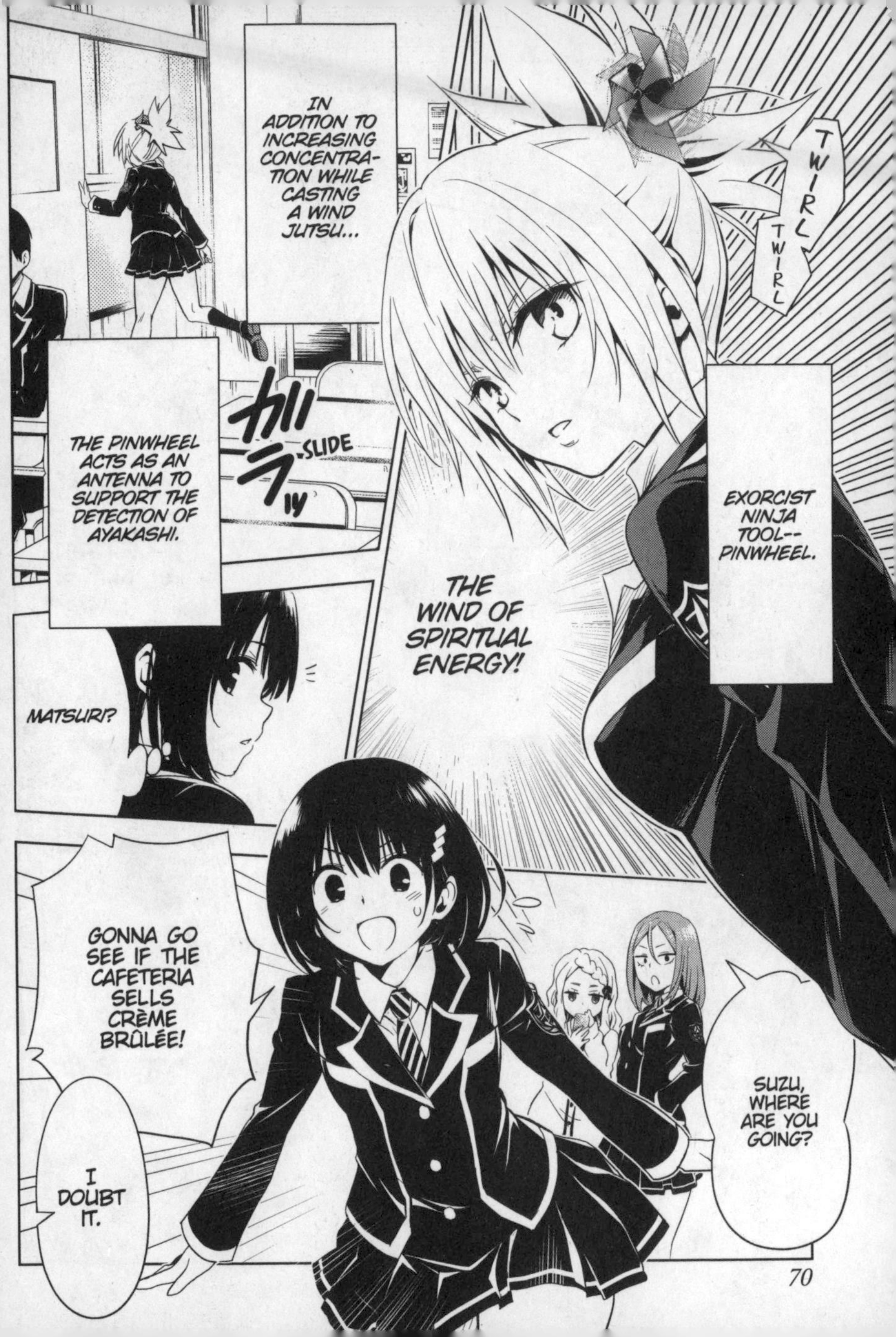
TWIRL TWIRL
EXORCIST NINJA TOOL-- PINWHEEL.
THE WIND OF SPIRITUAL ENERGY!
IN ADDITION TO INCREASING CONCENTRATION WHILE CASTING A WIND JUTSU...
SLIDE
THE PINWHEEL ACTS AS AN ANTENNA TO SUPPORT THE DETECTION OF AYAKASHI.
MATSURI?
SUZU, WHERE ARE YOU GOING?
GONNA GO SEE IF THE CAFETERIA SELLS CRÈME BRÛLÉE!
I DOUBT IT.

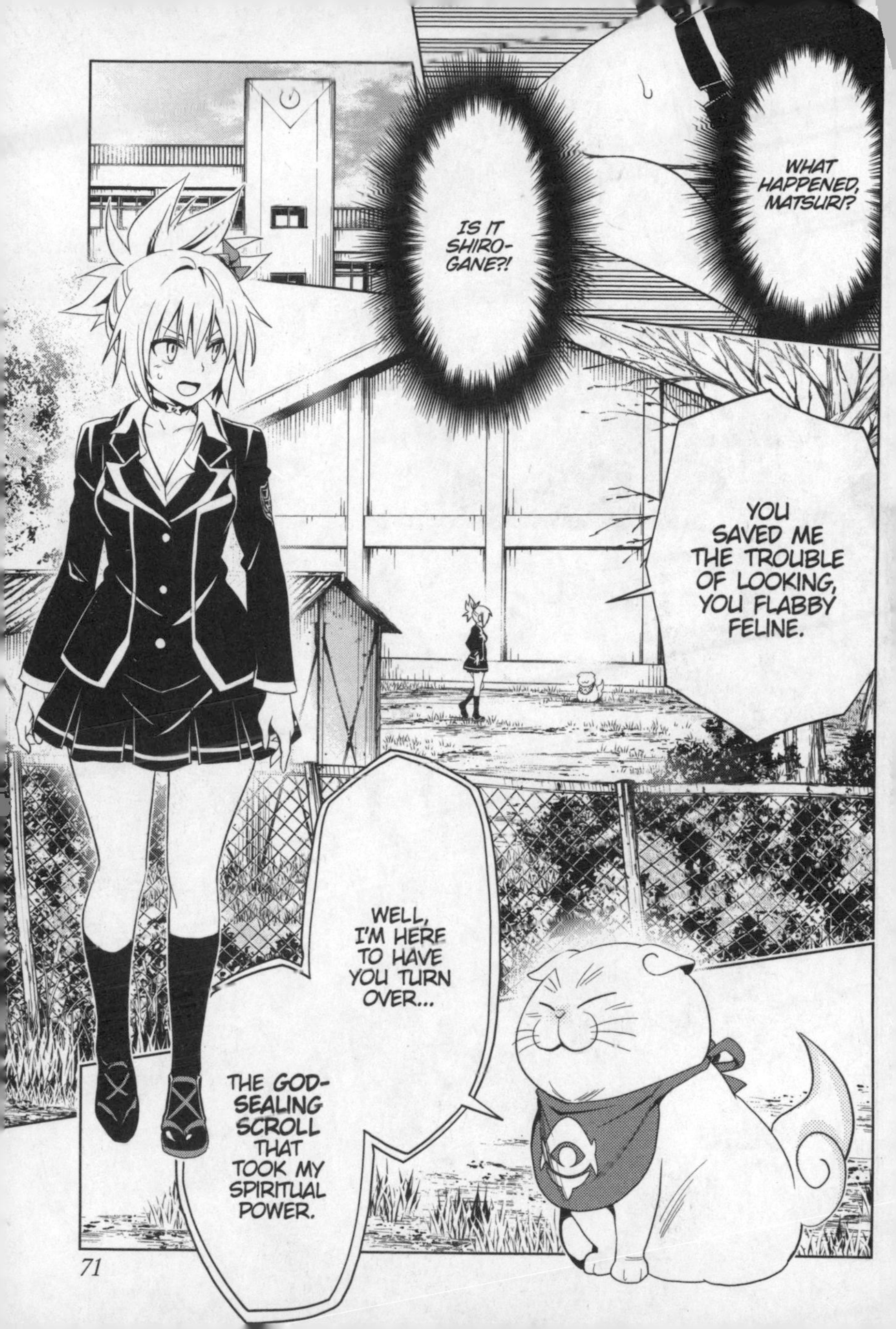
WHAT HAPPENED, MATSURI!?
IS IT SHIRO-GANE?!
YOU SAVED ME THE TROUBLE OF LOOKING, YOU FLABBY FELINE.
WELL, I'M HERE TO HAVE YOU TURN OVER...
THE GOD-SEALING SCROLL THAT TOOK MY SPIRITUAL POWER.

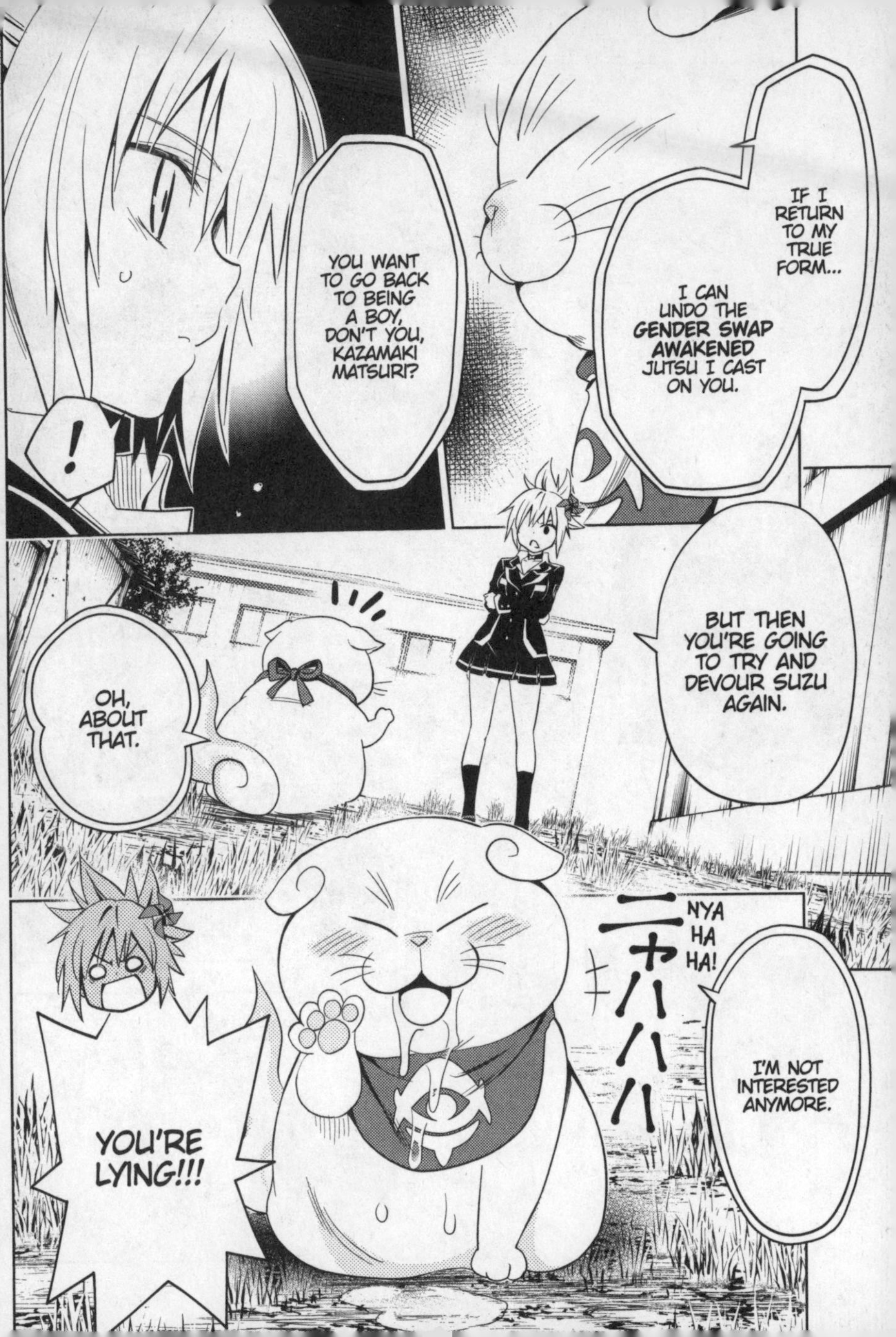
IF I RETURN TO MY TRUE FORM...
I CAN UNDO THE GENDER SWAP AWAKENED JUTSU I CAST ON YOU.
YOU WANT TO GO BACK TO BEING A BOY, DON'T YOU, KAZAMAKI MATSURI?
!
BUT THEN YOU'RE GOING TO TRY AND DEVOUR SUZU AGAIN.
OH, ABOUT THAT.
I'M NOT INTERESTED ANYMORE.
ニャハハハ
NYA HA HA!
YOU'RE LYING!!!

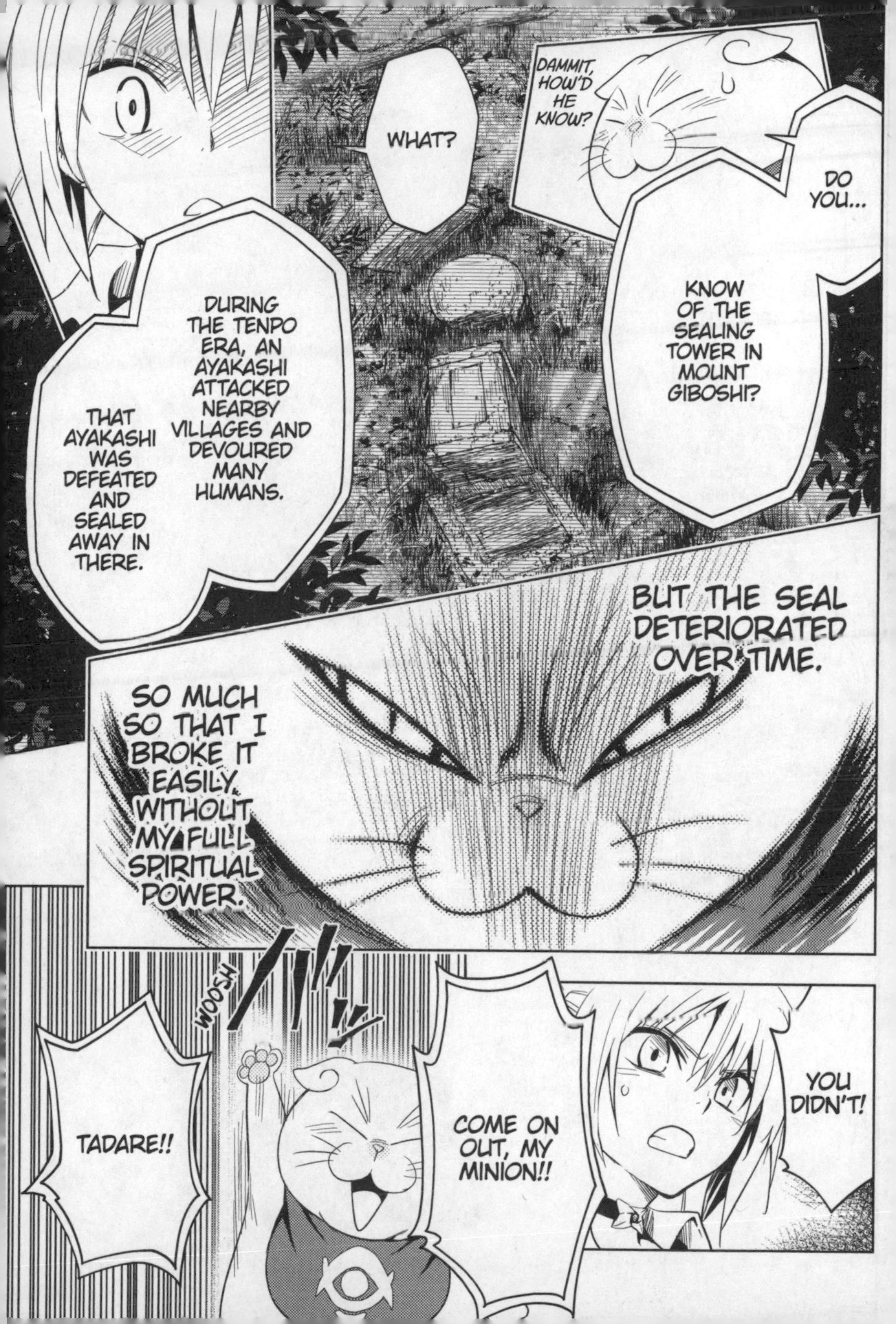
DO YOU...
KNOW OF THE SEALING TOWER IN MOUNT GIBOSHI?
WHAT?
DAMMIT, HOW'D HE KNOW?
DURING THE TENPO ERA, AN AYAKASHI ATTACKED NEARBY VILLAGES AND DEVOURED MANY HUMANS.
THAT AYAKASHI WAS DEFEATED AND SEALED AWAY IN THERE.
BUT THE SEAL DETERIORATED OVER TIME.
SO MUCH SO THAT I BROKE IT EASILY, WITHOUT MY FULL SPIRITUAL POWER.
YOU DIDN'T!
COME ON OUT, MY MINION!!
WOOSH
TADARE!!

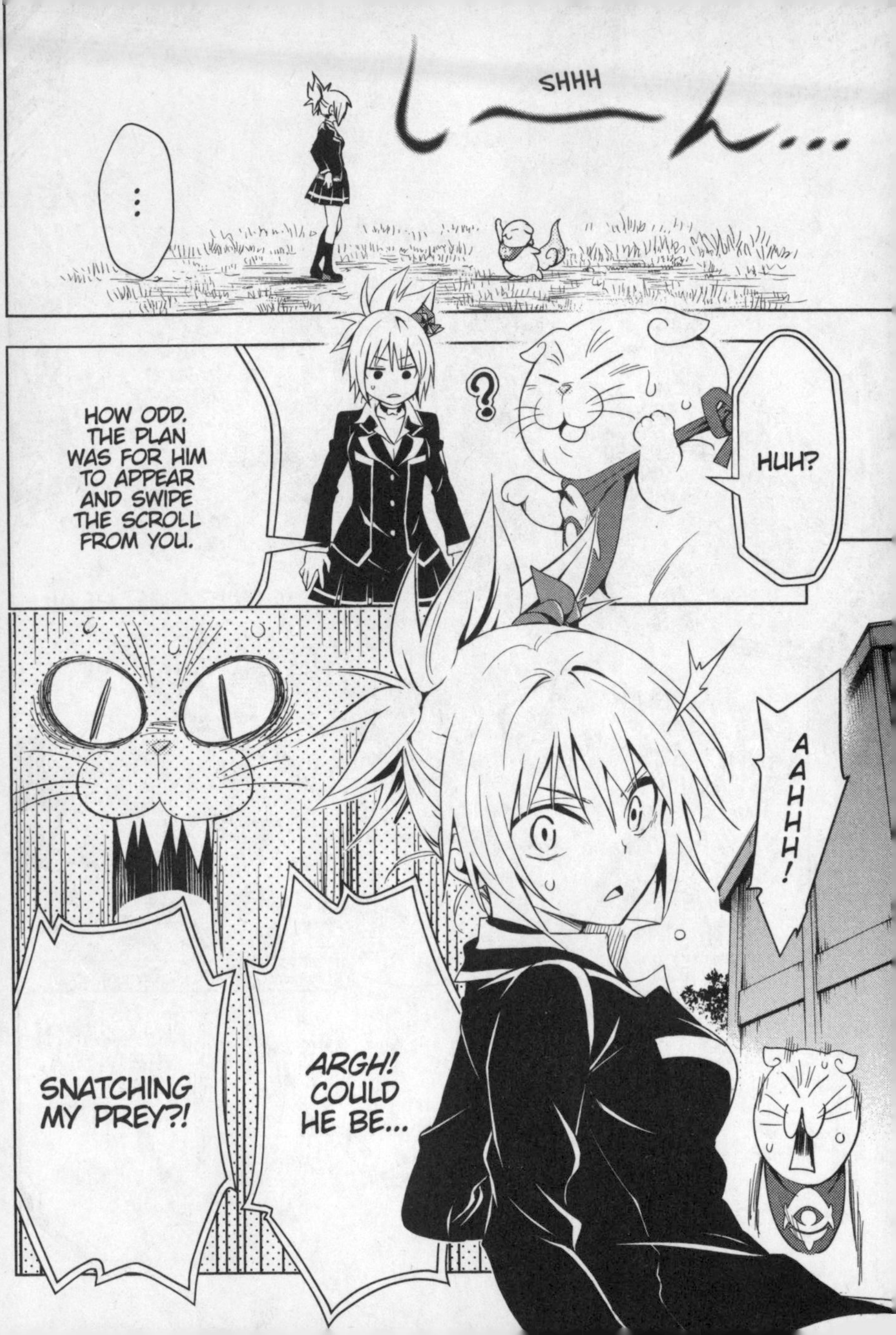
しーん…
SHHH
…
HUH?
HOW ODD. THE PLAN WAS FOR HIM TO APPEAR AND SWIPE THE SCROLL FROM YOU.
AAHHH!
ARGH! COULD HE BE...
SNATCHING MY PREY?!

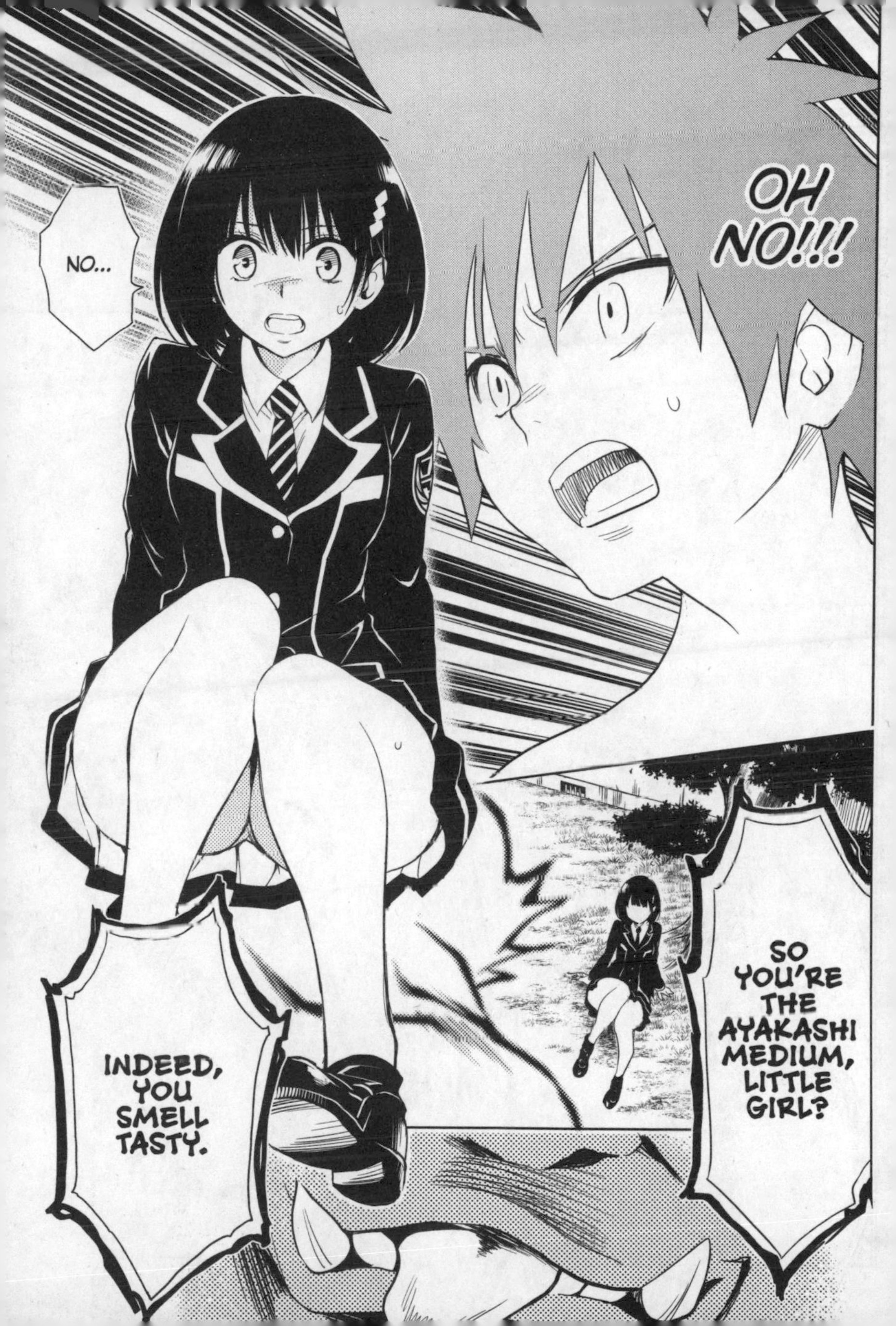
OH NO!!!
SO YOU'RE THE AYAKASHI MEDIUM, LITTLE GIRL?
NO...
INDEED, YOU SMELL TASTY.

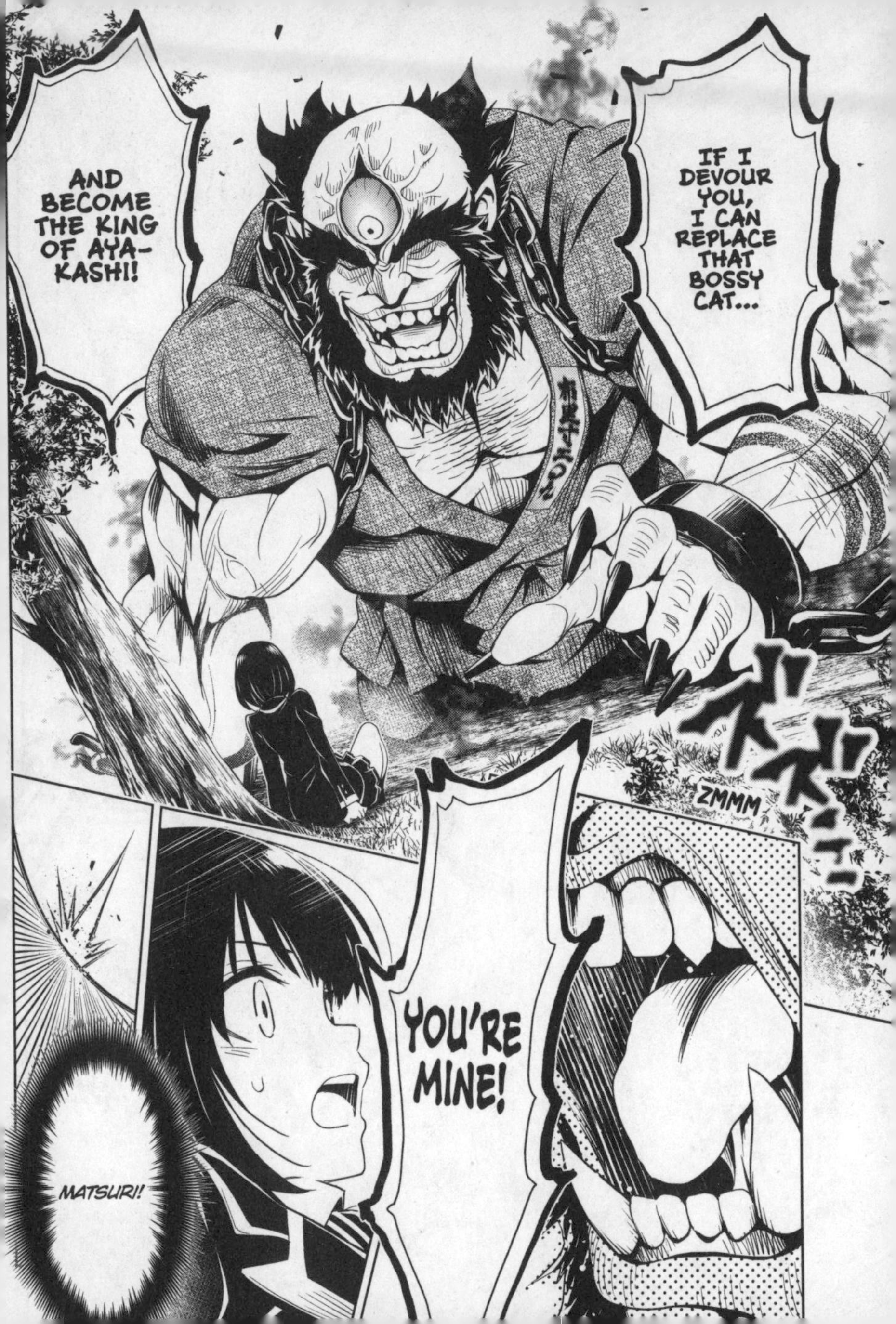
IF I DEVOUR YOU, I CAN REPLACE THAT BOSSY CAT...
AND BECOME THE KING OF AYA-KASHI!
ZMMM
YOU'RE MINE!
MATSURI!

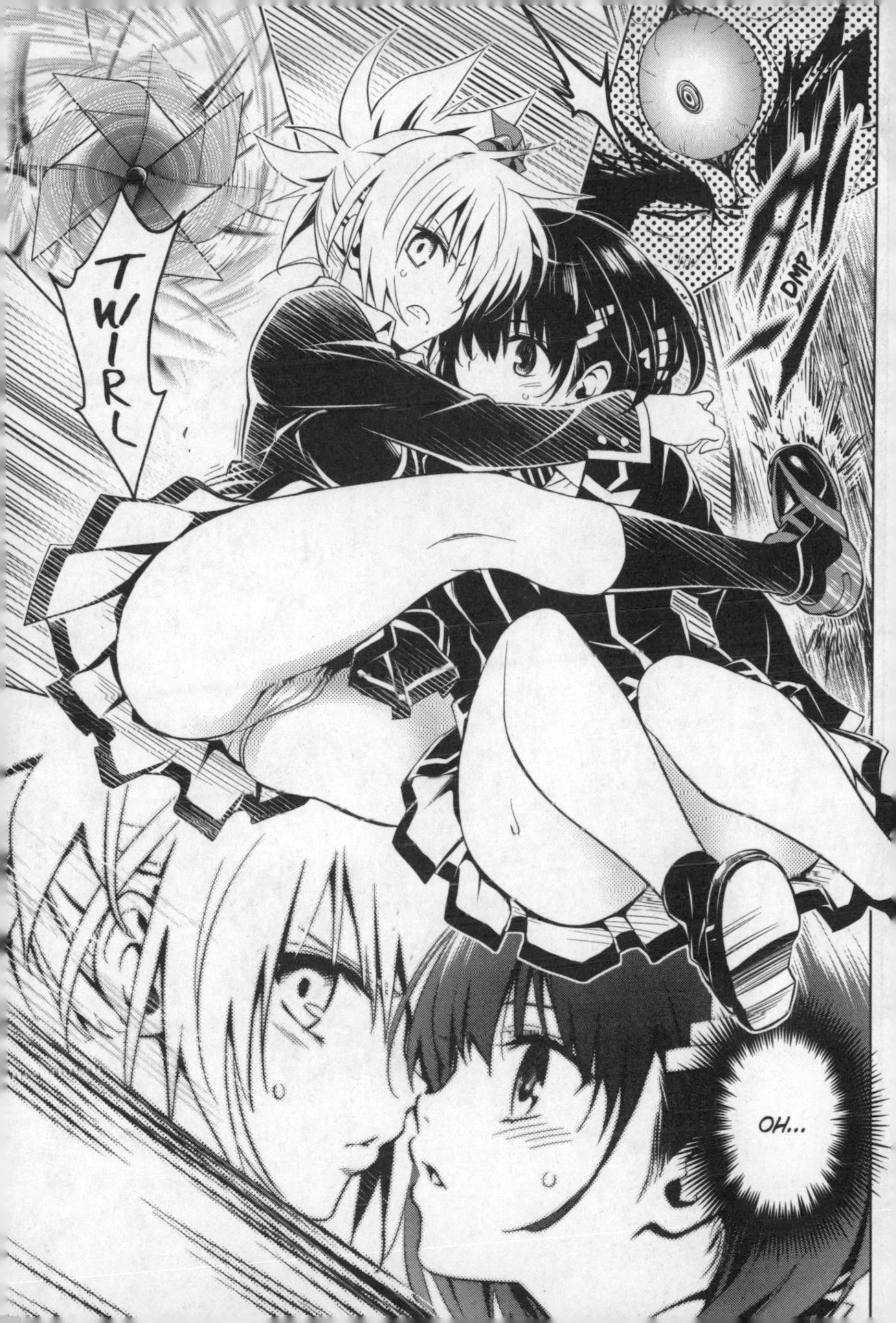
DMP
TWIRL
OH...

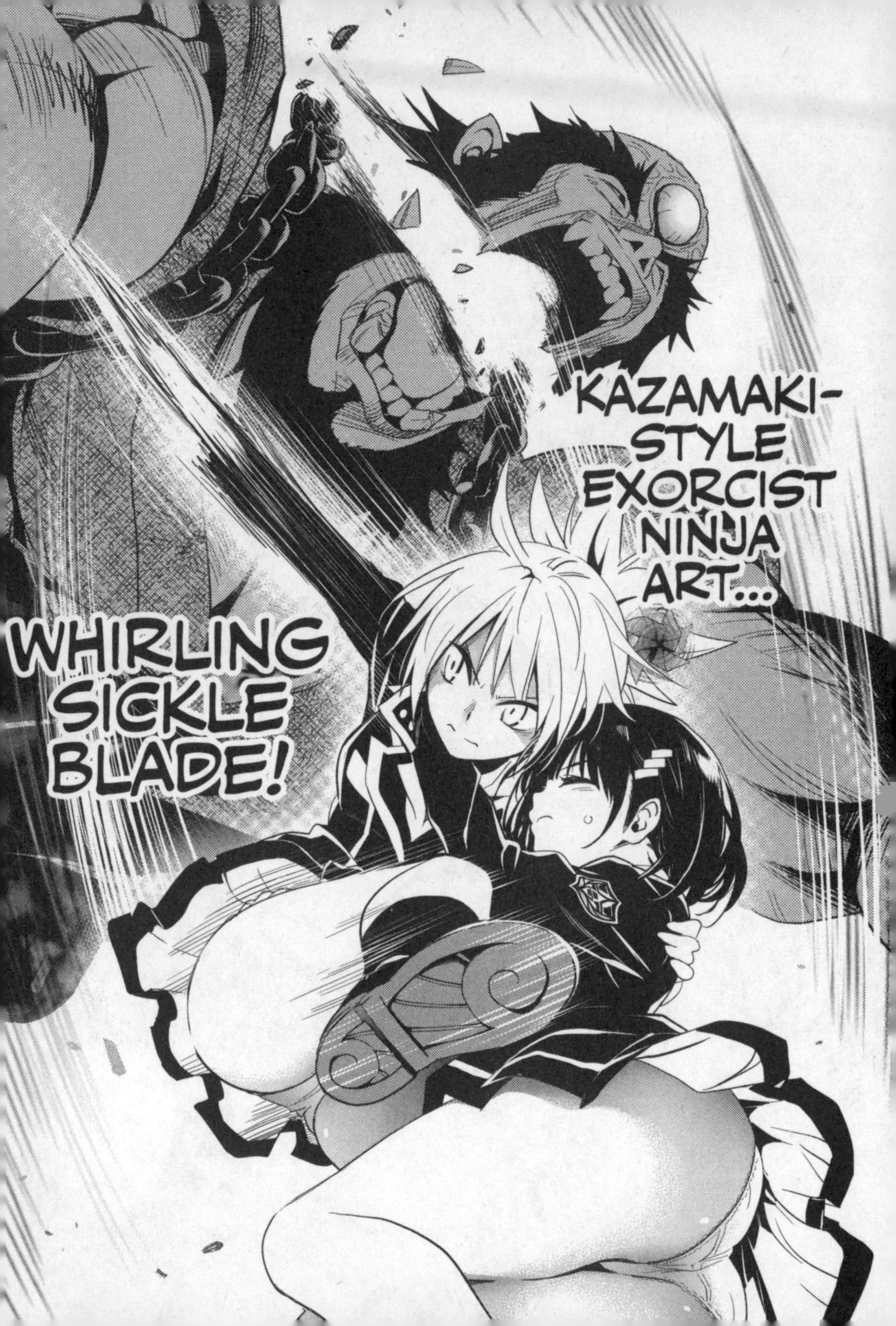
KAZAMAKI-STYLE EXORCIST NINJA ART...
WHIRLING SICKLE BLADE!

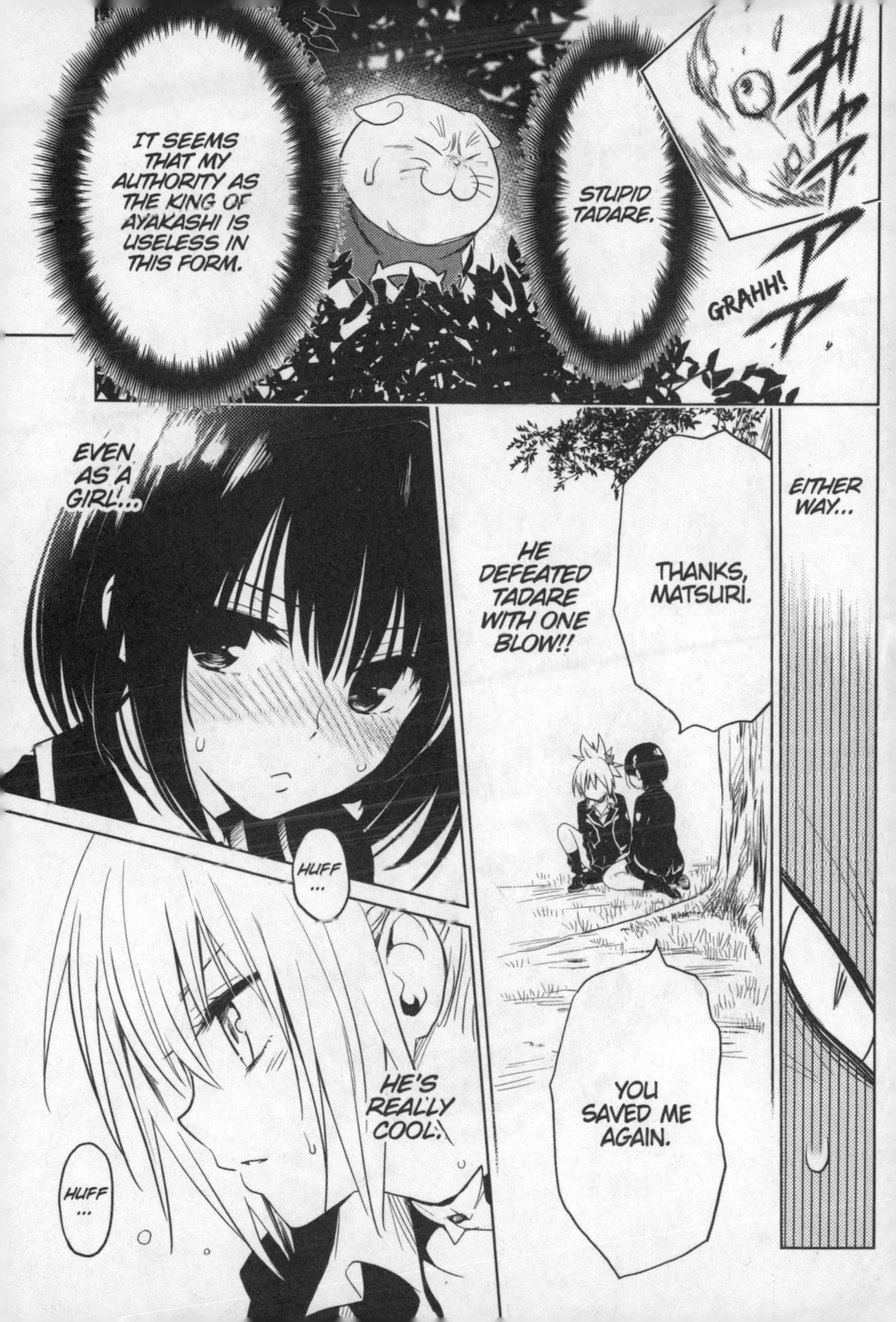
GRAHH!
STUPID TADARE.
IT SEEMS THAT MY AUTHORITY AS THE KING OF AYAKASHI IS USELESS IN THIS FORM.
EITHER WAY...
THANKS, MATSURI.
HE DEFEATED TADARE WITH ONE BLOW!!
YOU SAVED ME AGAIN.
EVEN AS A GIRL...
HUFF...
HE'S REALLY COOL.
HUFF...

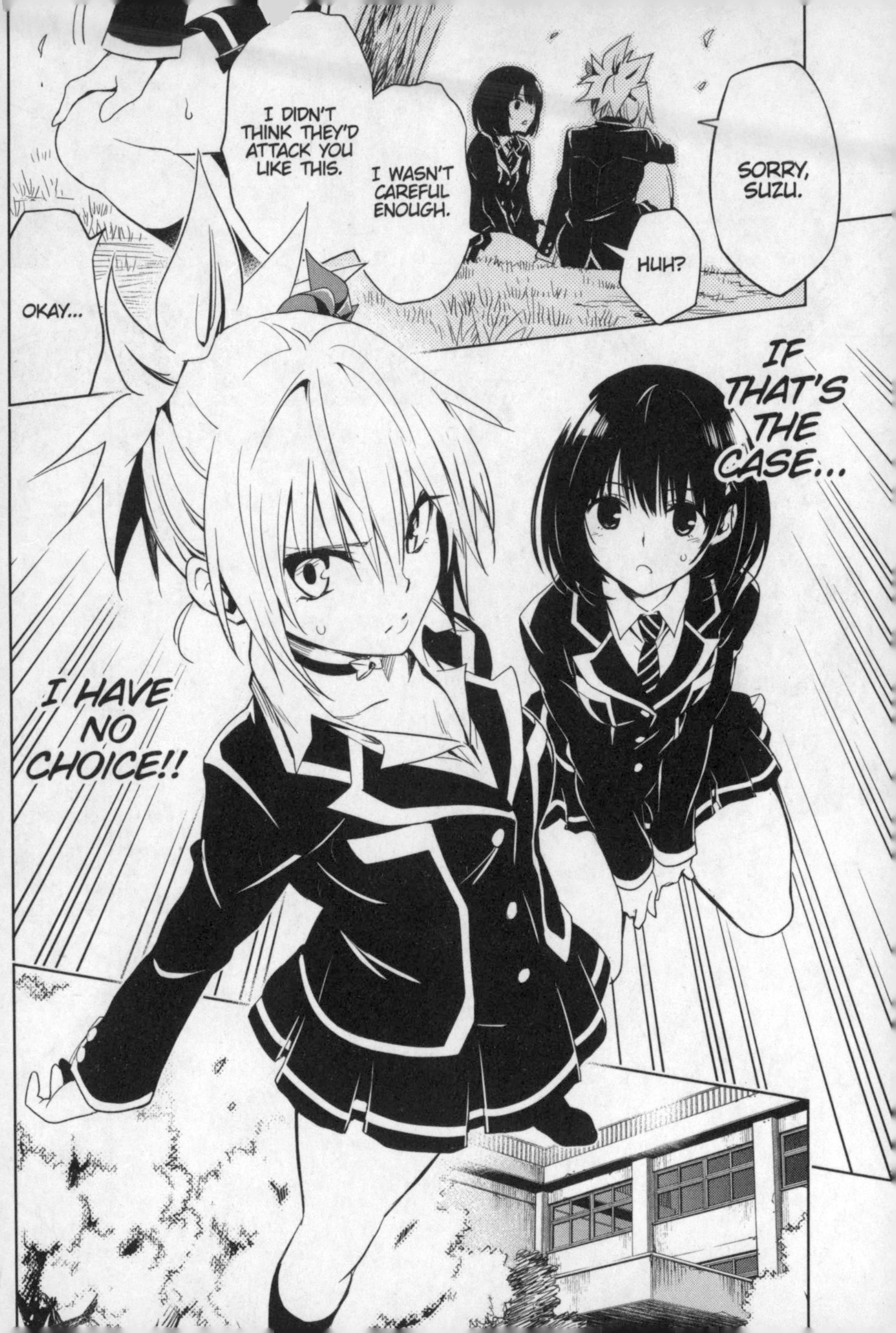
SORRY, SUZU.
HUH?
I WASN'T CAREFUL ENOUGH.
I DIDN'T THINK THEY'D ATTACK YOU LIKE THIS.
OKAY...
IF THAT'S THE CASE...
I HAVE NO CHOICE!!

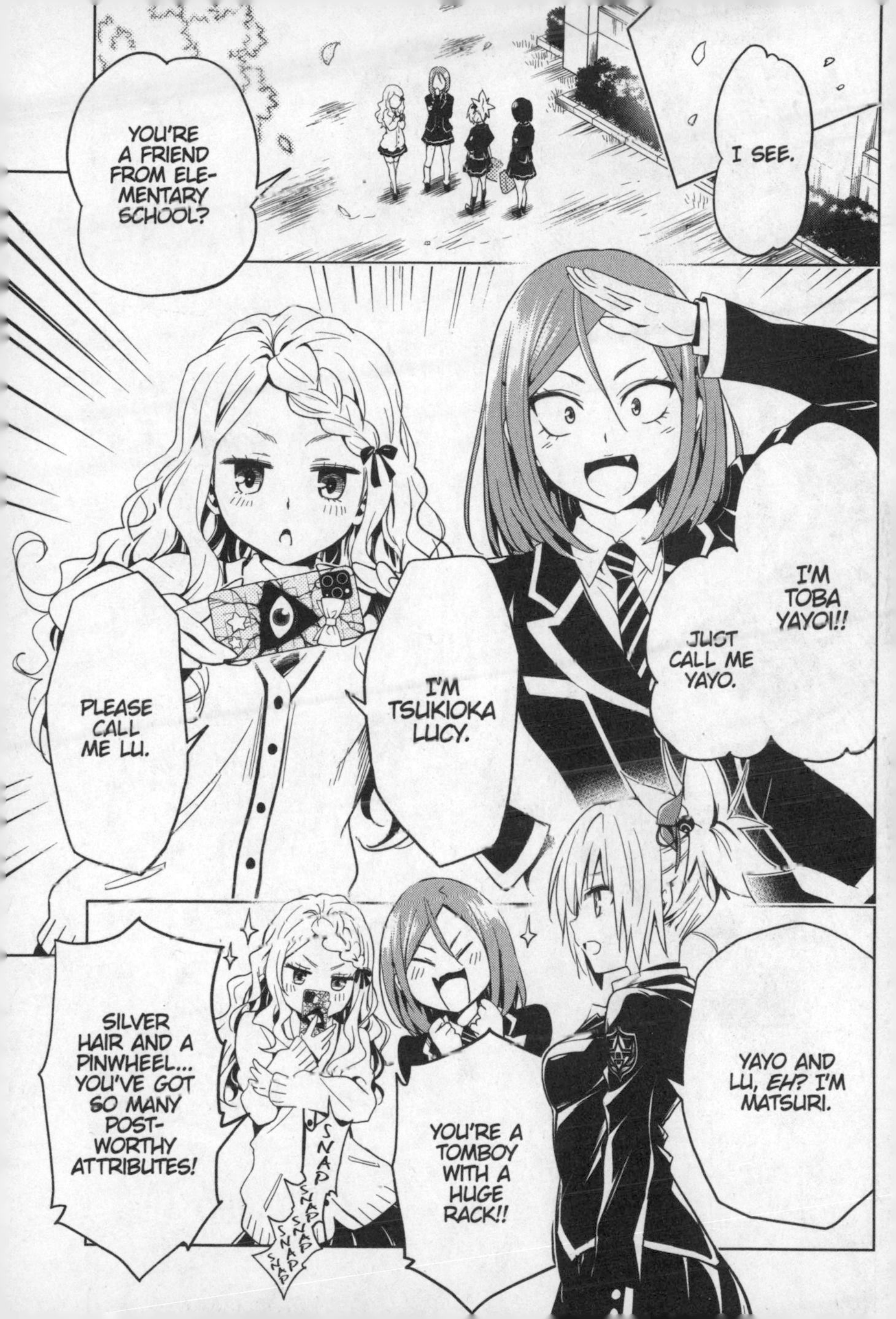
I SEE.
YOU'RE A FRIEND FROM ELE-MENTARY SCHOOL?
I'M TOBA YAYOI!!
JUST CALL ME YAYO.
I'M TSUKIOKA LUCY.
PLEASE CALL ME LU.
YAYO AND LU, *EH*? I'M MATSURI.
YOU'RE A TOMBOY WITH A HUGE RACK!!
SNAP SNAP SNAP SNAP
SILVER HAIR AND A PINWHEEL... YOU'VE GOT SO MANY POST-WORTHY ATTRIBUTES!

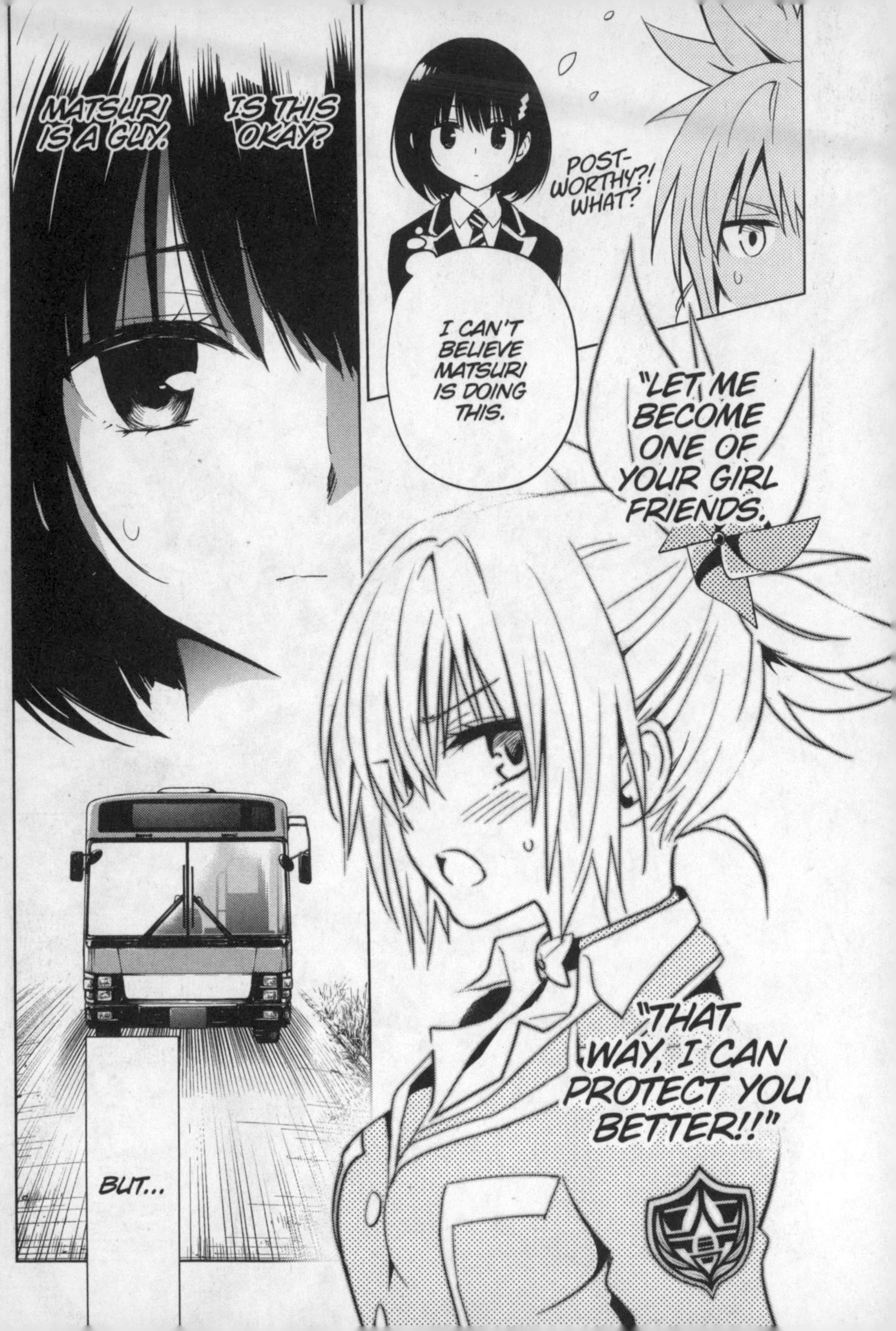
POST-WORTHY?! WHAT?
I CAN'T BELIEVE MATSURI IS DOING THIS.
"LET ME BECOME ONE OF YOUR GIRL FRIENDS.
"THAT WAY, I CAN PROTECT YOU BETTER!!"
IS THIS OKAY?
MATSURI IS A GUY.
BUT...

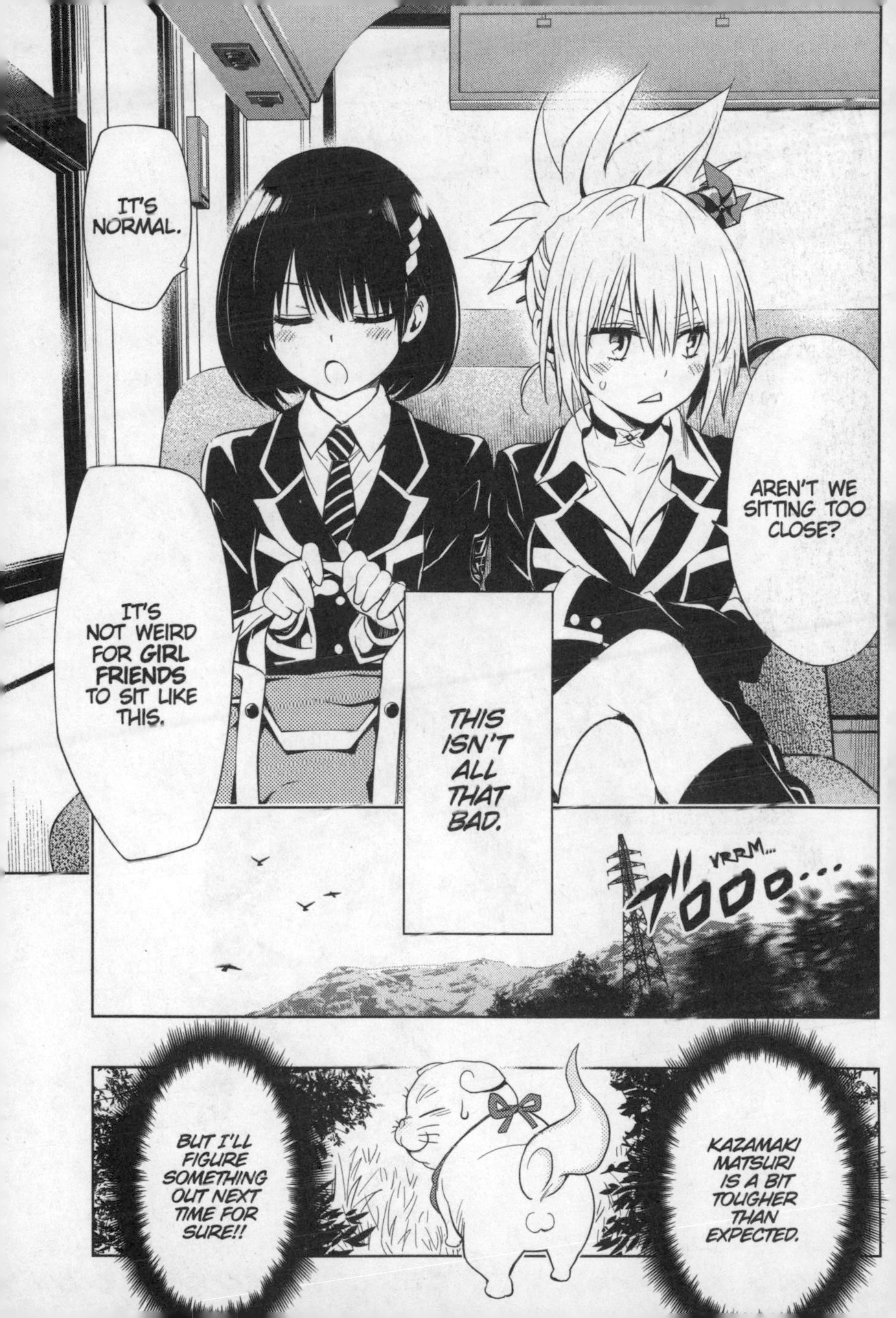
AREN'T WE SITTING TOO CLOSE?
IT'S NORMAL.
IT'S NOT WEIRD FOR GIRL FRIENDS TO SIT LIKE THIS.
THIS ISN'T ALL THAT BAD.
VRRM...
ブロロロ…
KAZAMAKI MATSURI IS A BIT TOUGHER THAN EXPECTED.
BUT I'LL FIGURE SOMETHING OUT NEXT TIME FOR SURE!!

## Series Preview Illustration

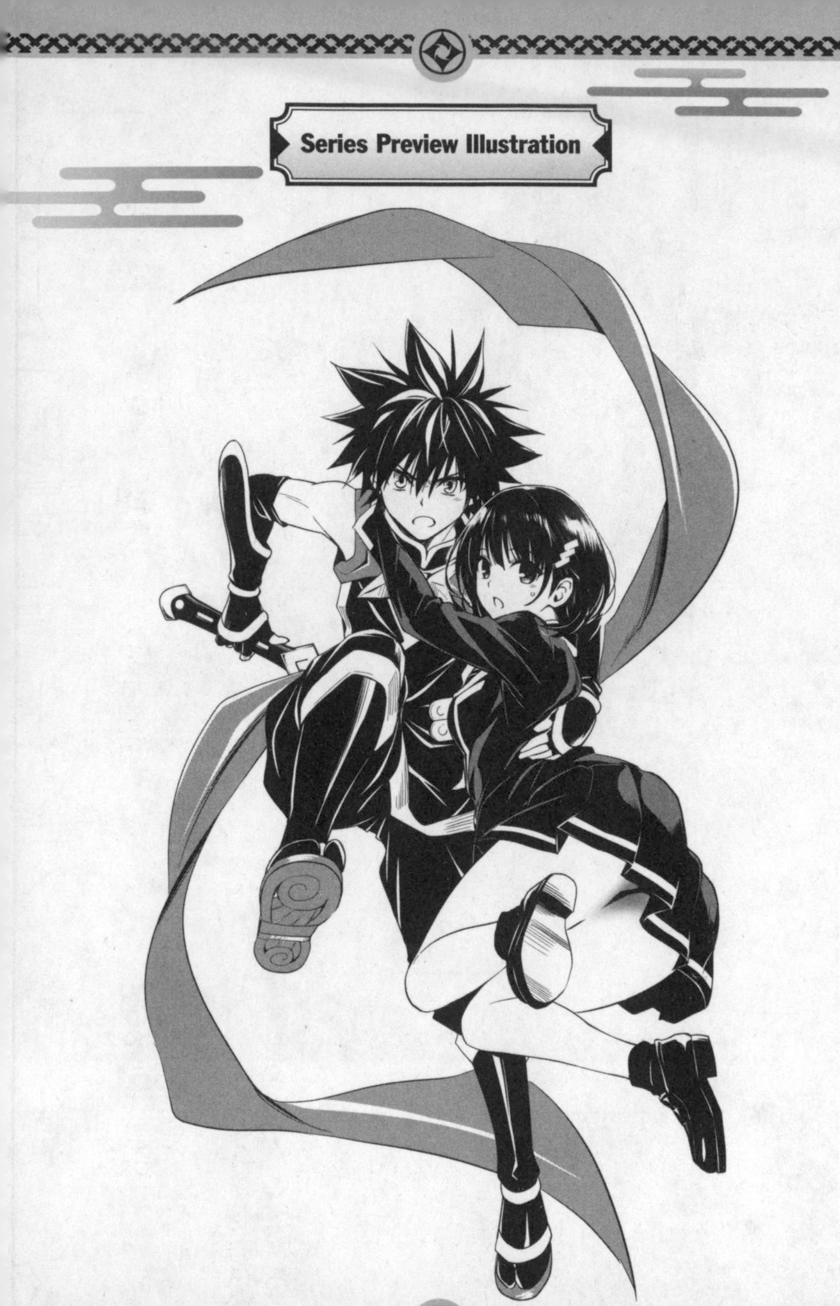

# Chapter 3

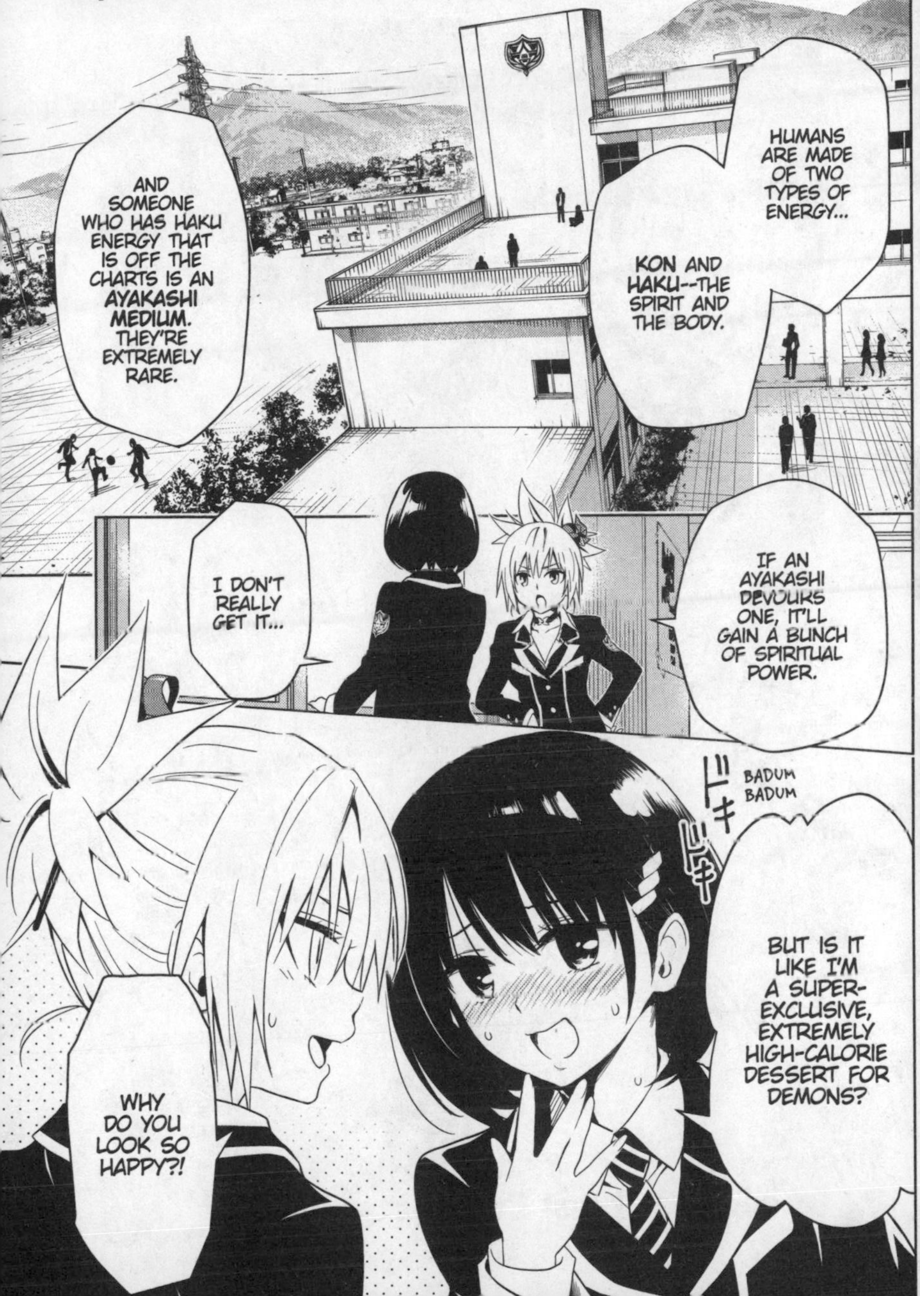
HUMANS ARE MADE OF TWO TYPES OF ENERGY...
KON AND HAKU--THE SPIRIT AND THE BODY.
AND SOMEONE WHO HAS HAKU ENERGY THAT IS OFF THE CHARTS IS AN AYAKASHI MEDIUM. THEY'RE EXTREMELY RARE.
IF AN AYAKASHI DEVOURS ONE, IT'LL GAIN A BUNCH OF SPIRITUAL POWER.
I DON'T REALLY GET IT...
ドキ
ドキ
BADUM BADUM
BUT IS IT LIKE I'M A SUPER-EXCLUSIVE, EXTREMELY HIGH-CALORIE DESSERT FOR DEMONS?
WHY DO YOU LOOK SO HAPPY?!

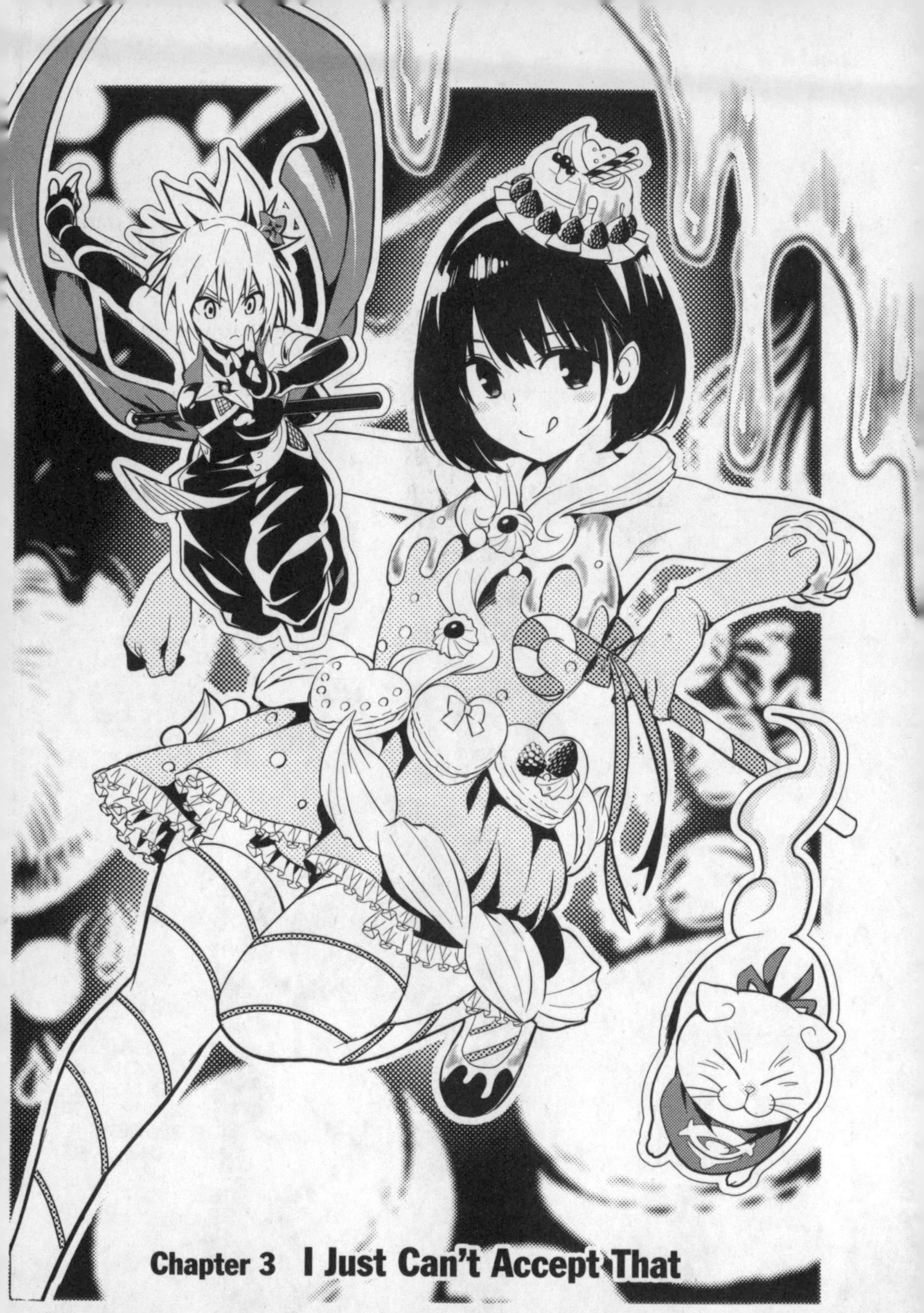

## Chapter 3 I Just Can't Accept That

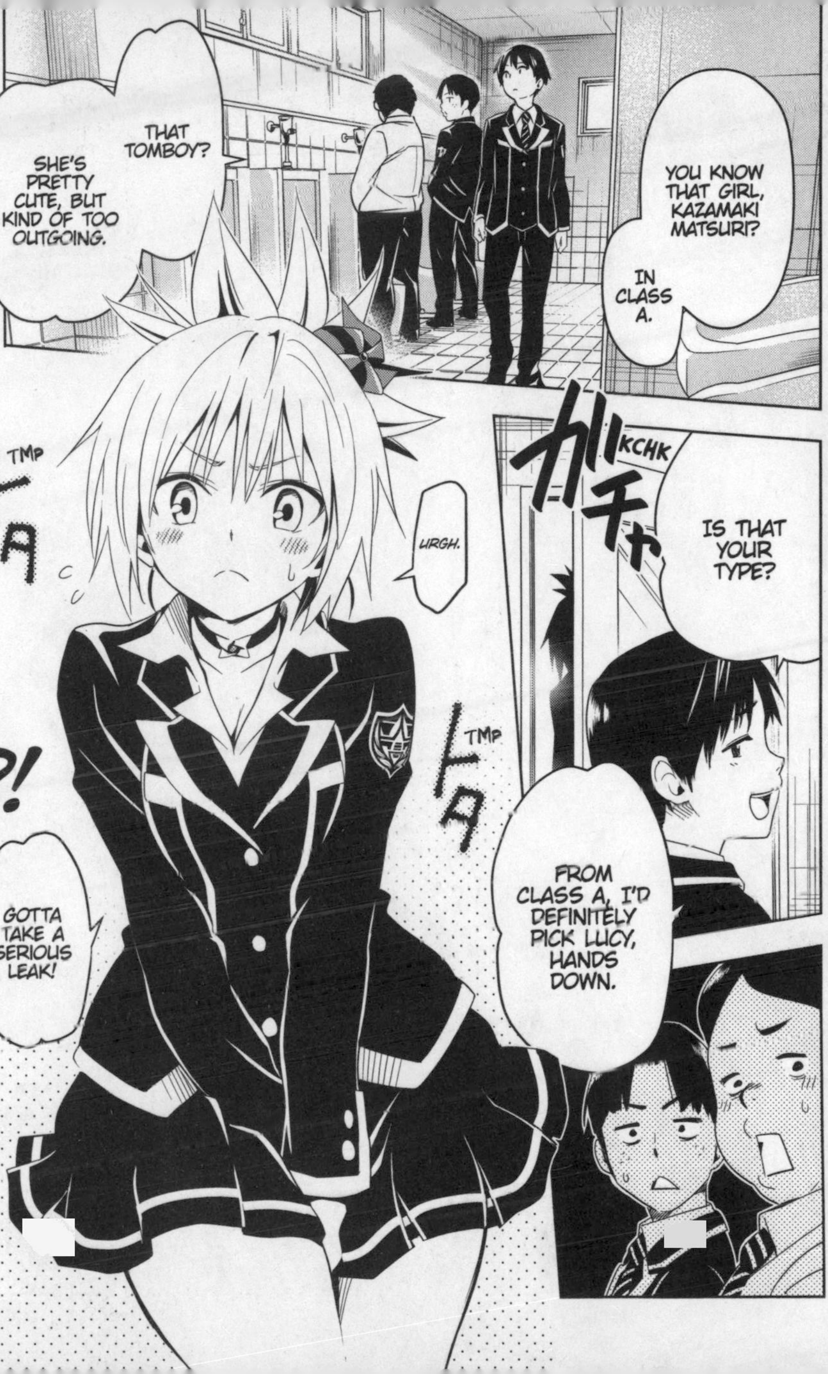
YOU KNOW THAT GIRL, KAZAMAKI MATSURI?
IN CLASS A.
THAT TOMBOY?
SHE'S PRETTY CUTE, BUT KIND OF TOO OUTGOING.
KCHK
IS THAT YOUR TYPE?
FROM CLASS A, I'D DEFINITELY PICK LUCY, HANDS DOWN.
TMP
TMP
URGH.
?!
GOTTA TAKE A SERIOUS LEAK!

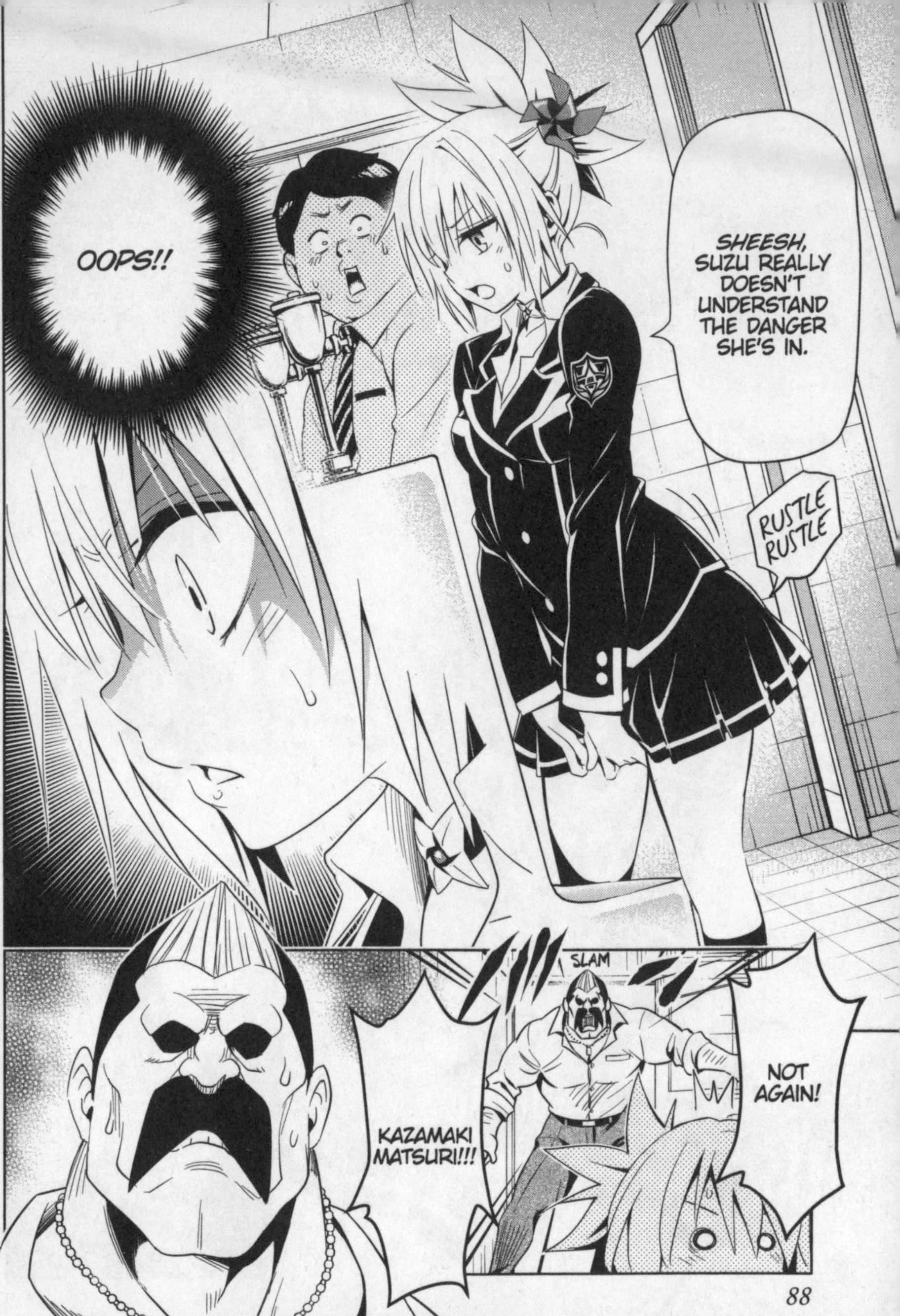
SHEESH, SUZU REALLY DOESN'T UNDERSTAND THE DANGER SHE'S IN.
RUSTLE RUSTLE
OOPS!!
SLAM
NOT AGAIN!
KAZAMAKI MATSURI!!!

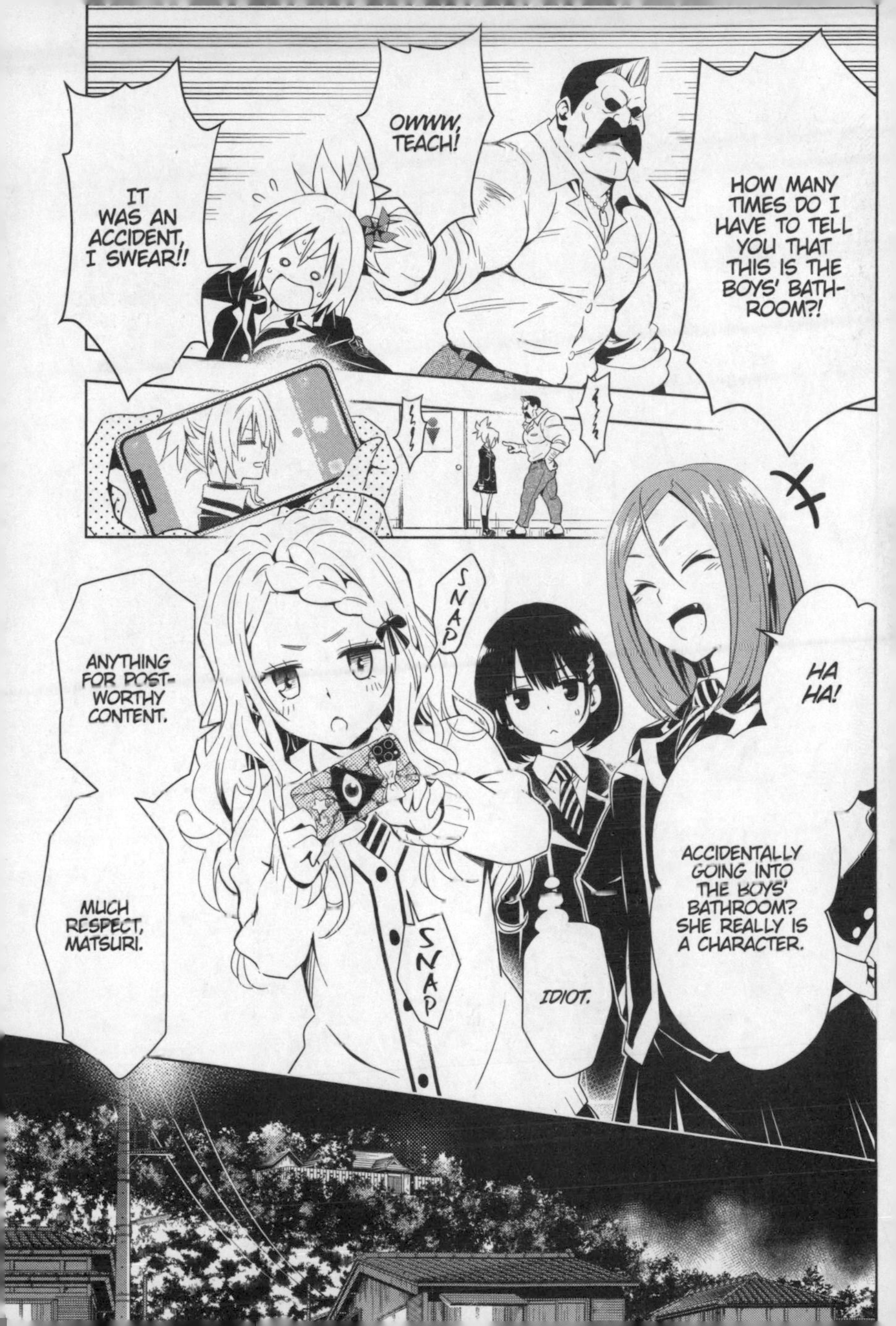
HOW MANY TIMES DO I HAVE TO TELL YOU THAT THIS IS THE BOYS' BATHROOM?!
OWWW, TEACH!
IT WAS AN ACCIDENT, I SWEAR!!
HA HA!
SNAP
ACCIDENTALLY GOING INTO THE BOYS' BATHROOM? SHE REALLY IS A CHARACTER.
ANYTHING FOR POST-WORTHY CONTENT.
IDIOT.
SNAP
MUCH RESPECT, MATSURI.

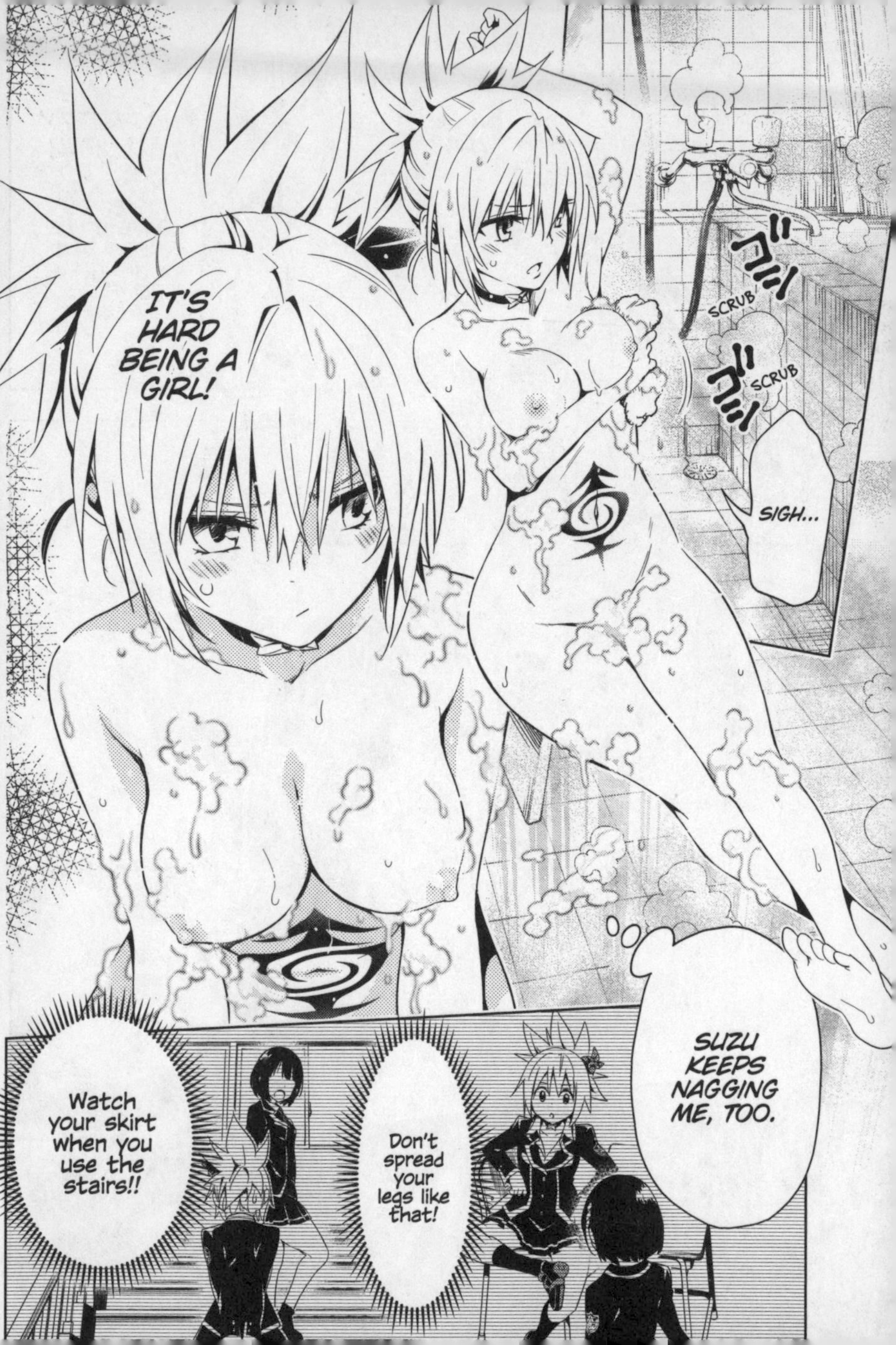
SCRUB
SCRUB
SIGH...
IT'S HARD BEING A GIRL!
SUZU KEEPS NAGGING ME, TOO.
Don't spread your legs like that!
Watch your skirt when you use the stairs!!

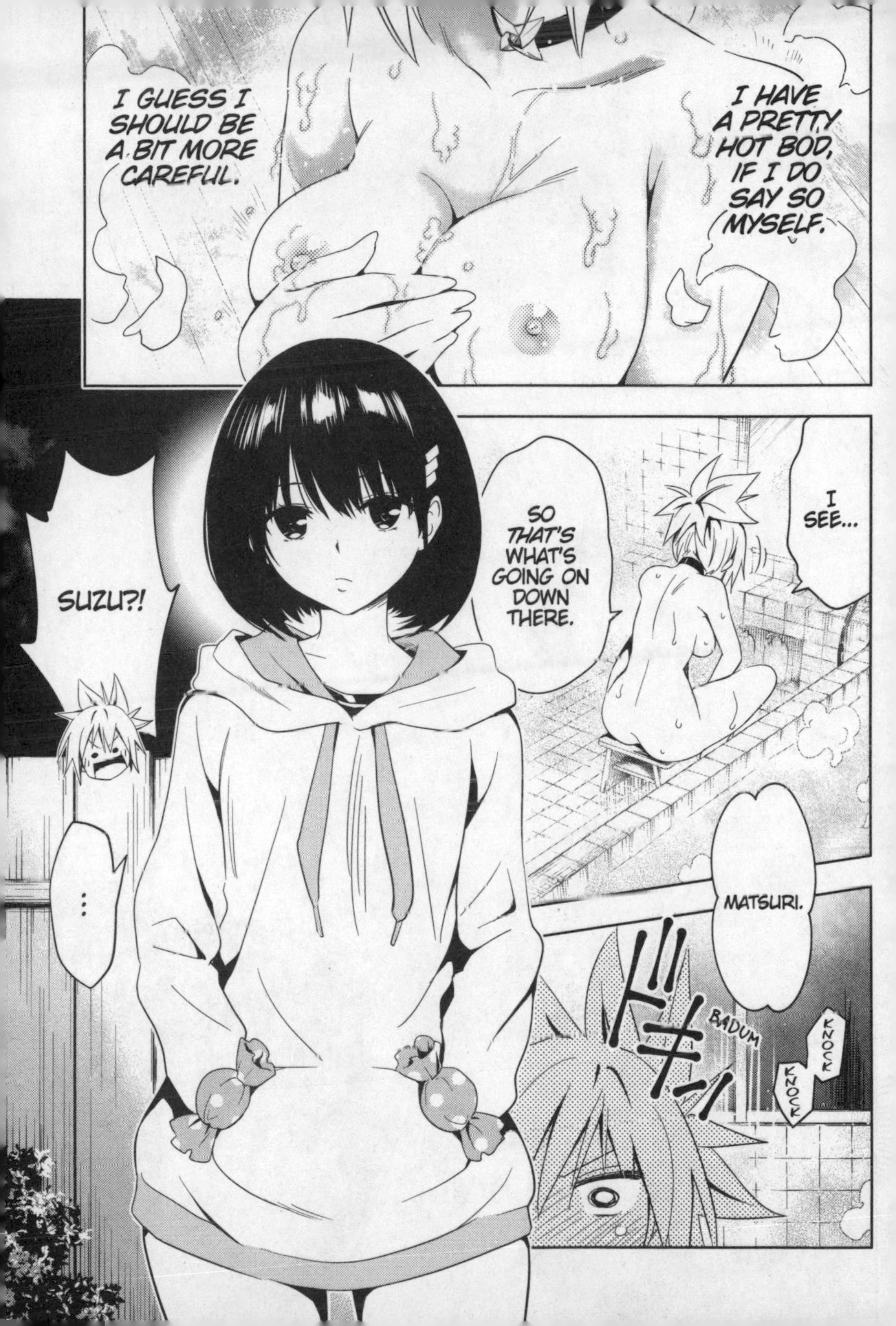
I HAVE A PRETTY HOT BOD, IF I DO SAY SO MYSELF.
I GUESS I SHOULD BE A BIT MORE CAREFUL.
I SEE...
SO THAT'S WHAT'S GOING ON DOWN THERE.
MATSURI.
KNOCK KNOCK
BADUM
SUZU?!
...

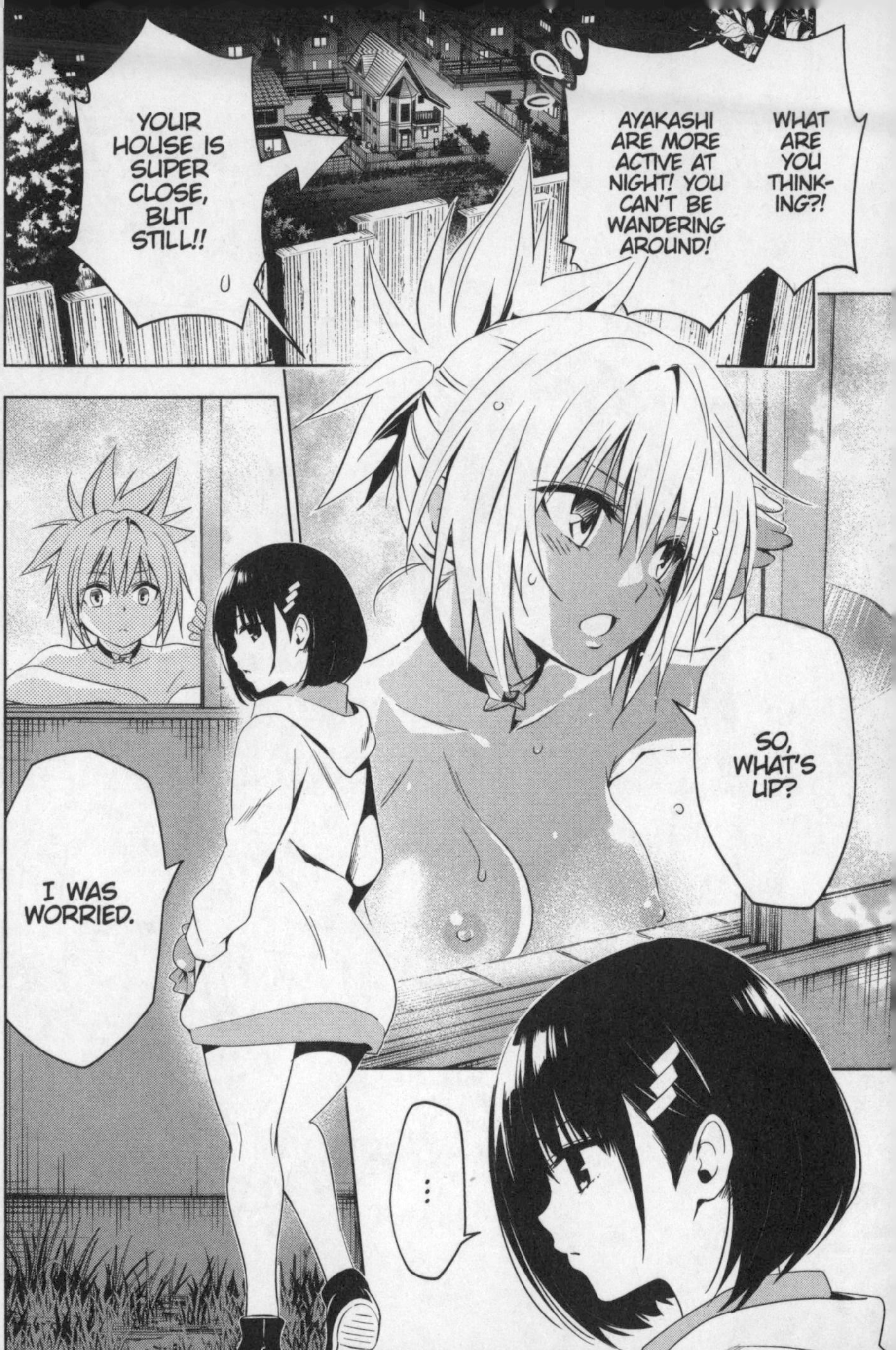
WHAT ARE YOU THINKING?!
AYAKASHI ARE MORE ACTIVE AT NIGHT! YOU CAN'T BE WANDERING AROUND!
YOUR HOUSE IS SUPER CLOSE, BUT STILL!!
SO, WHAT'S UP?
...
I WAS WORRIED.

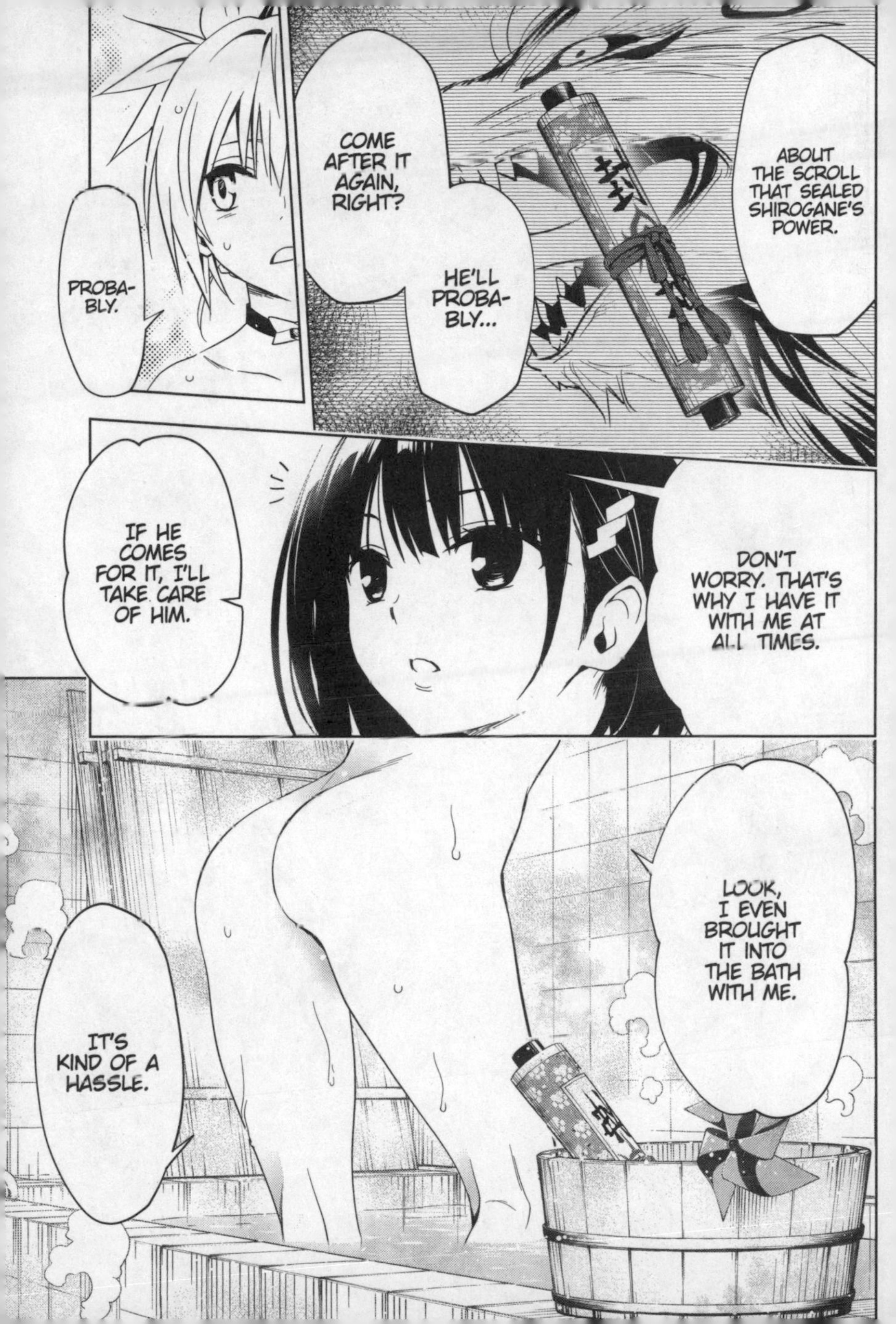
ABOUT THE SCROLL THAT SEALED SHIROGANE'S POWER.
HE'LL PROBABLY...
COME AFTER IT AGAIN, RIGHT?
PROBABLY.
DON'T WORRY. THAT'S WHY I HAVE IT WITH ME AT ALL TIMES.
IF HE COMES FOR IT, I'LL TAKE CARE OF HIM.
LOOK, I EVEN BROUGHT IT INTO THE BATH WITH ME.
IT'S KIND OF A HASSLE.

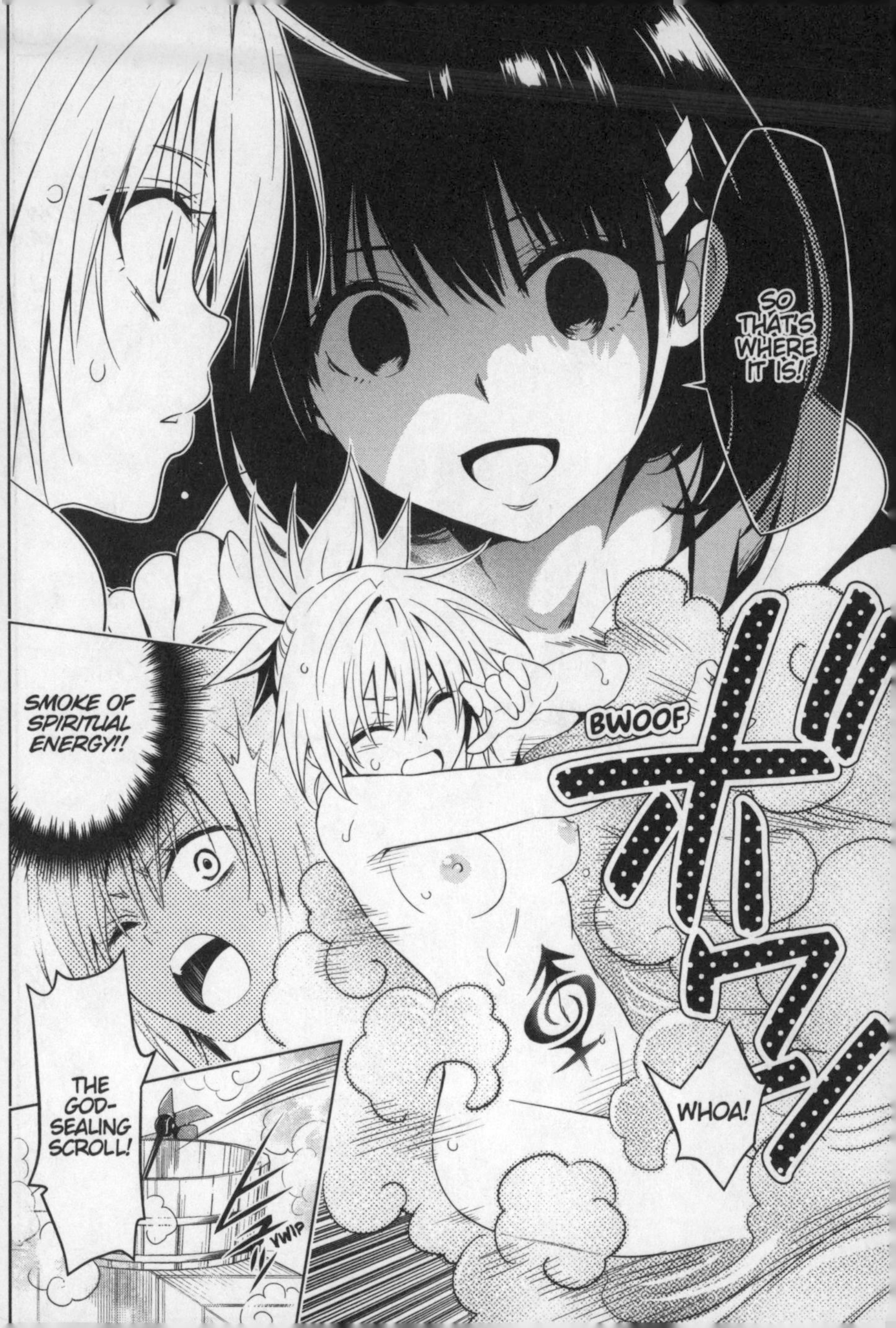
SO THAT'S WHERE IT IS!
BWOOF
WHOA!
SMOKE OF SPIRITUAL ENERGY!!
THE GOD-SEALING SCROLL!
VWIP

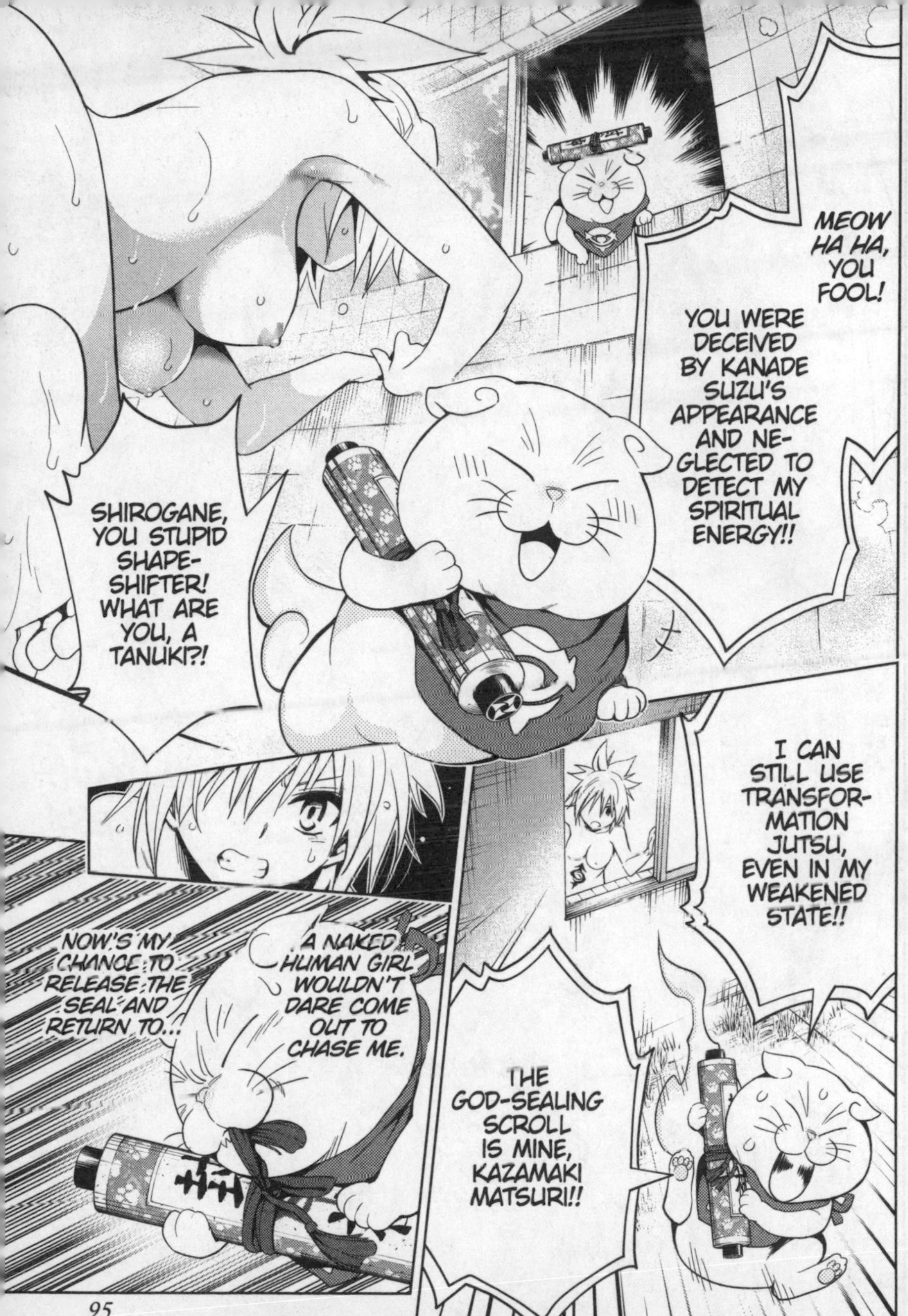
MEOW HA HA, YOU FOOL!
YOU WERE DECEIVED BY KANADE SUZU'S APPEARANCE AND NE-GLECTED TO DETECT MY SPIRITUAL ENERGY!!
SHIROGANE, YOU STUPID SHAPE-SHIFTER! WHAT ARE YOU, A TANUKI?!
I CAN STILL USE TRANSFOR-MATION JUTSU, EVEN IN MY WEAKENED STATE!!
THE GOD-SEALING SCROLL IS MINE, KAZAMAKI MATSURI!!
A NAKED HUMAN GIRL WOULDN'T DARE COME OUT TO CHASE ME.
NOW'S MY CHANCE TO RELEASE THE SEAL AND RETURN TO...

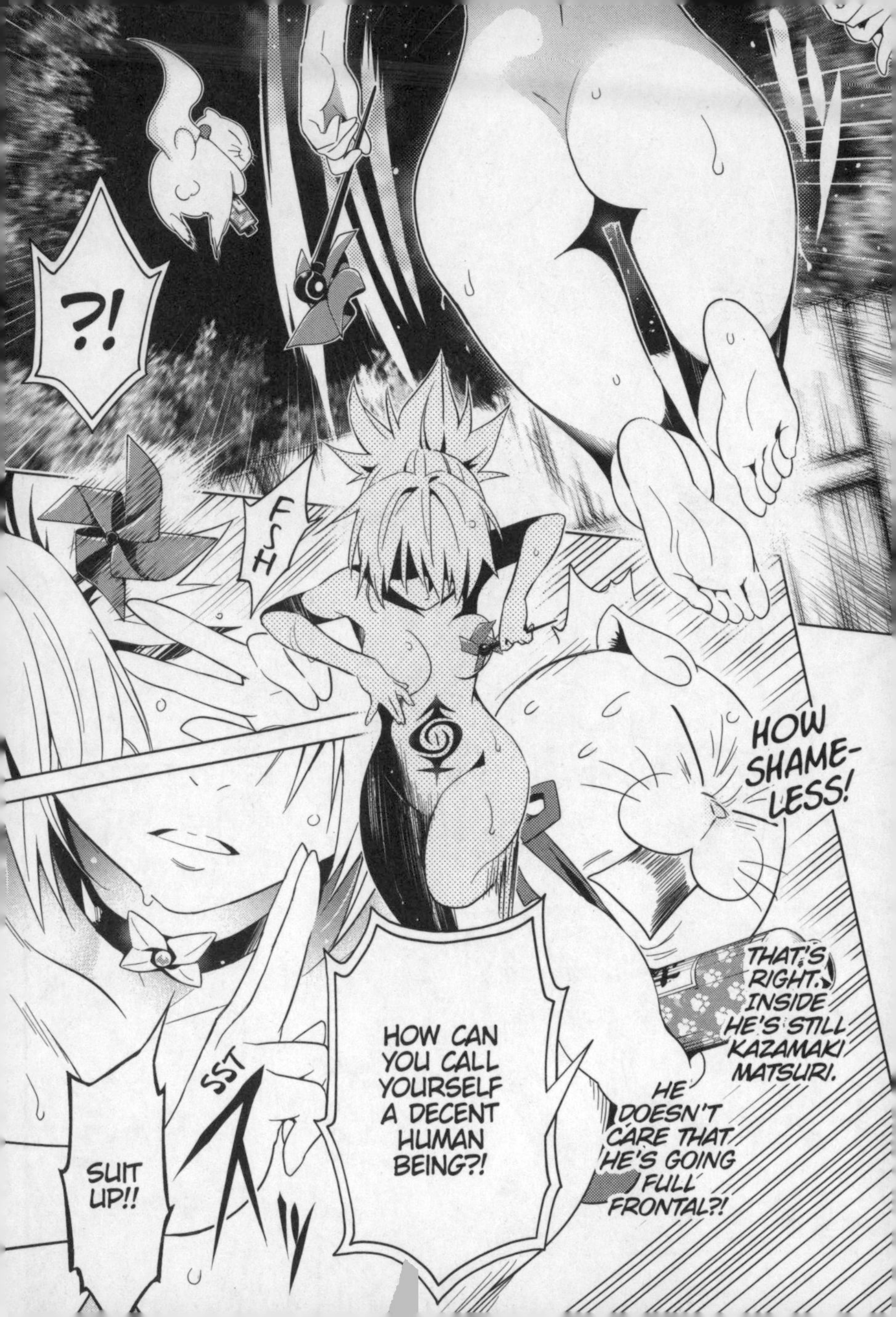
?!
FSH
HOW SHAME-LESS!
THAT'S RIGHT. INSIDE HE'S STILL KAZAMAKI MATSURI.
HE DOESN'T CARE THAT HE'S GOING FULL FRONTAL?!
HOW CAN YOU CALL YOURSELF A DECENT HUMAN BEING?!
SST
SUIT UP!!

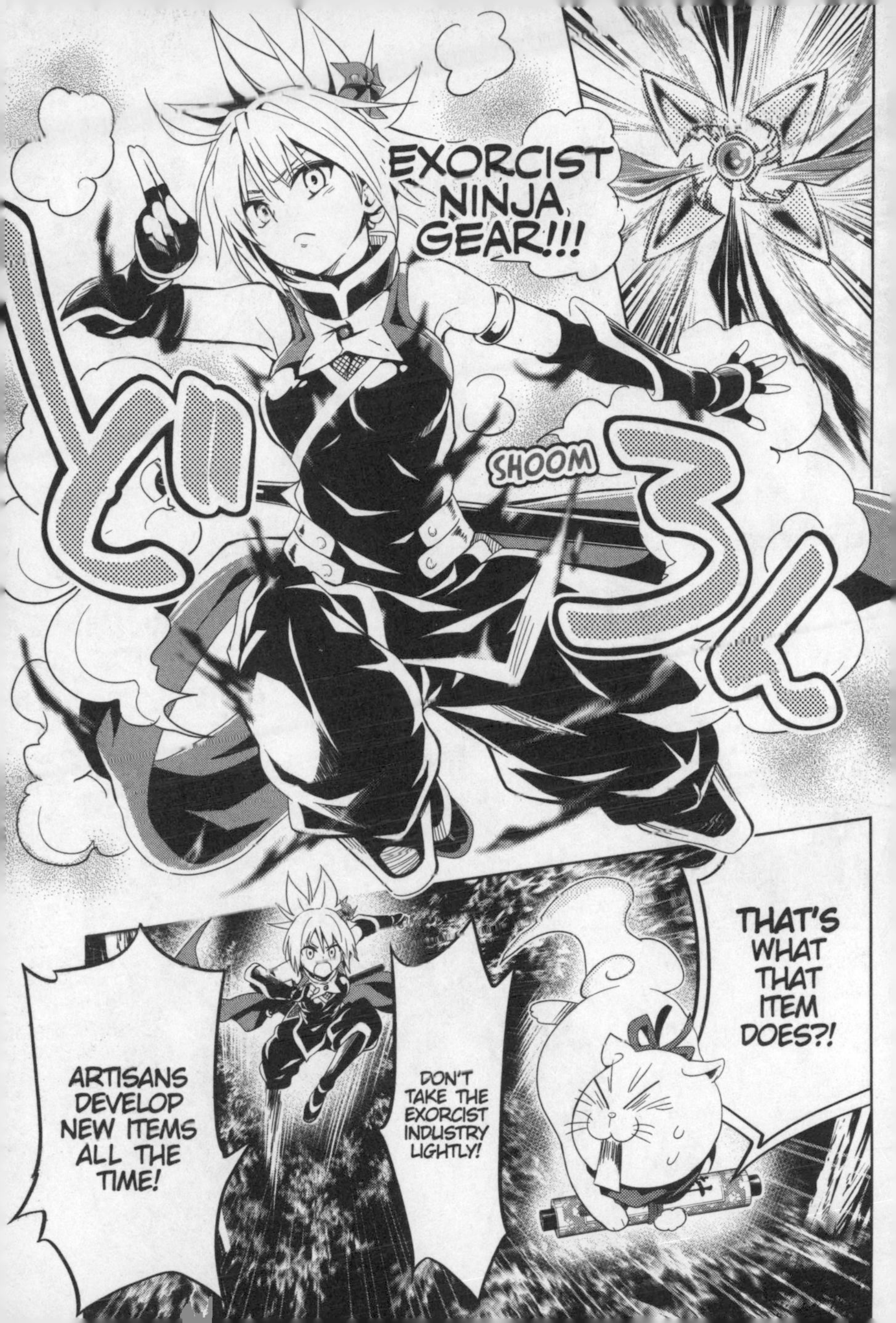
EXORCIST NINJA GEAR!!!
どろん
SHOOM
THAT'S WHAT THAT ITEM DOES?!
DON'T TAKE THE EXORCIST INDUSTRY LIGHTLY!
ARTISANS DEVELOP NEW ITEMS ALL THE TIME!

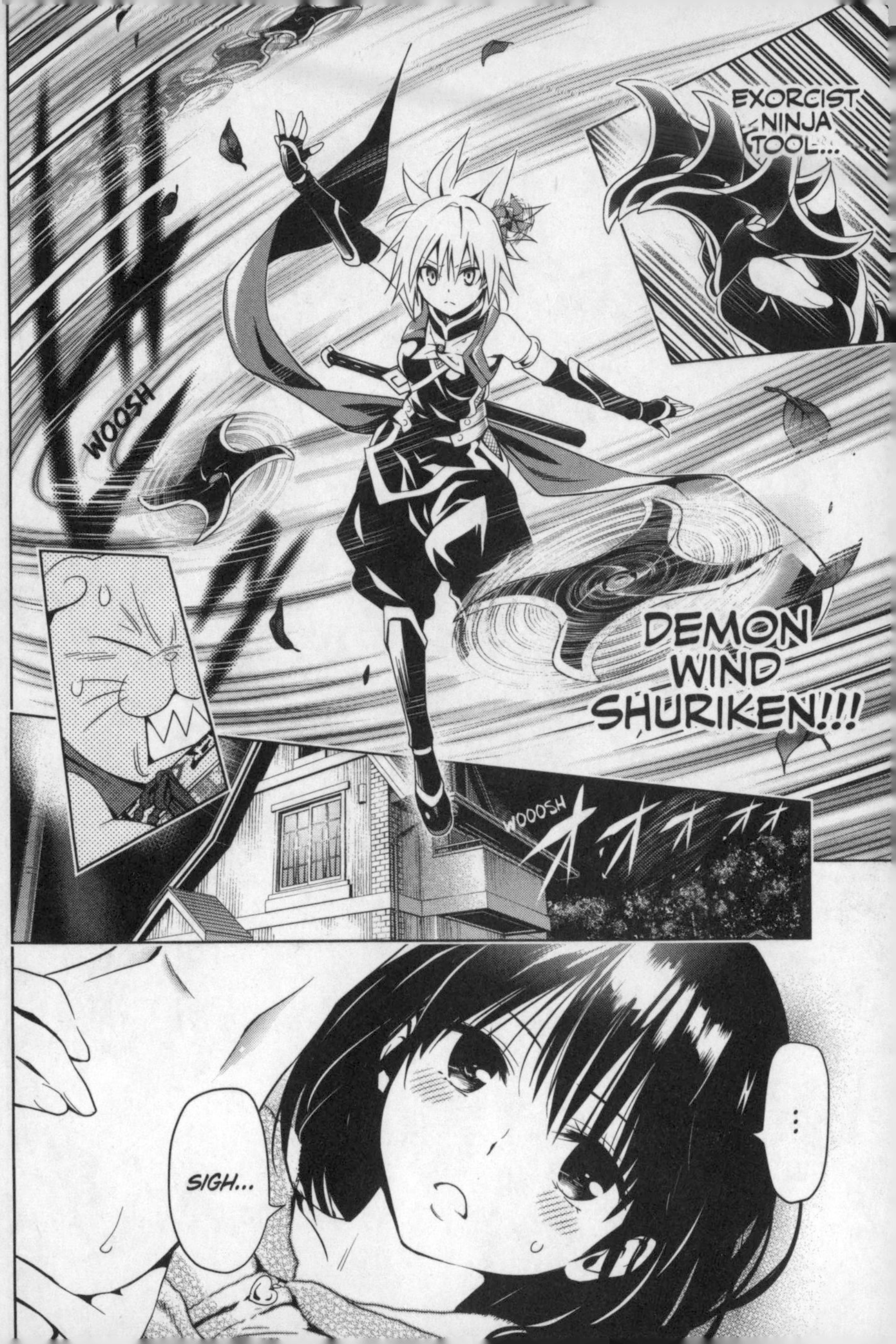
EXORCIST NINJA TOOL...
DEMON WIND SHURIKEN!!!
WOOSH
WOOOSH
...
SIGH...

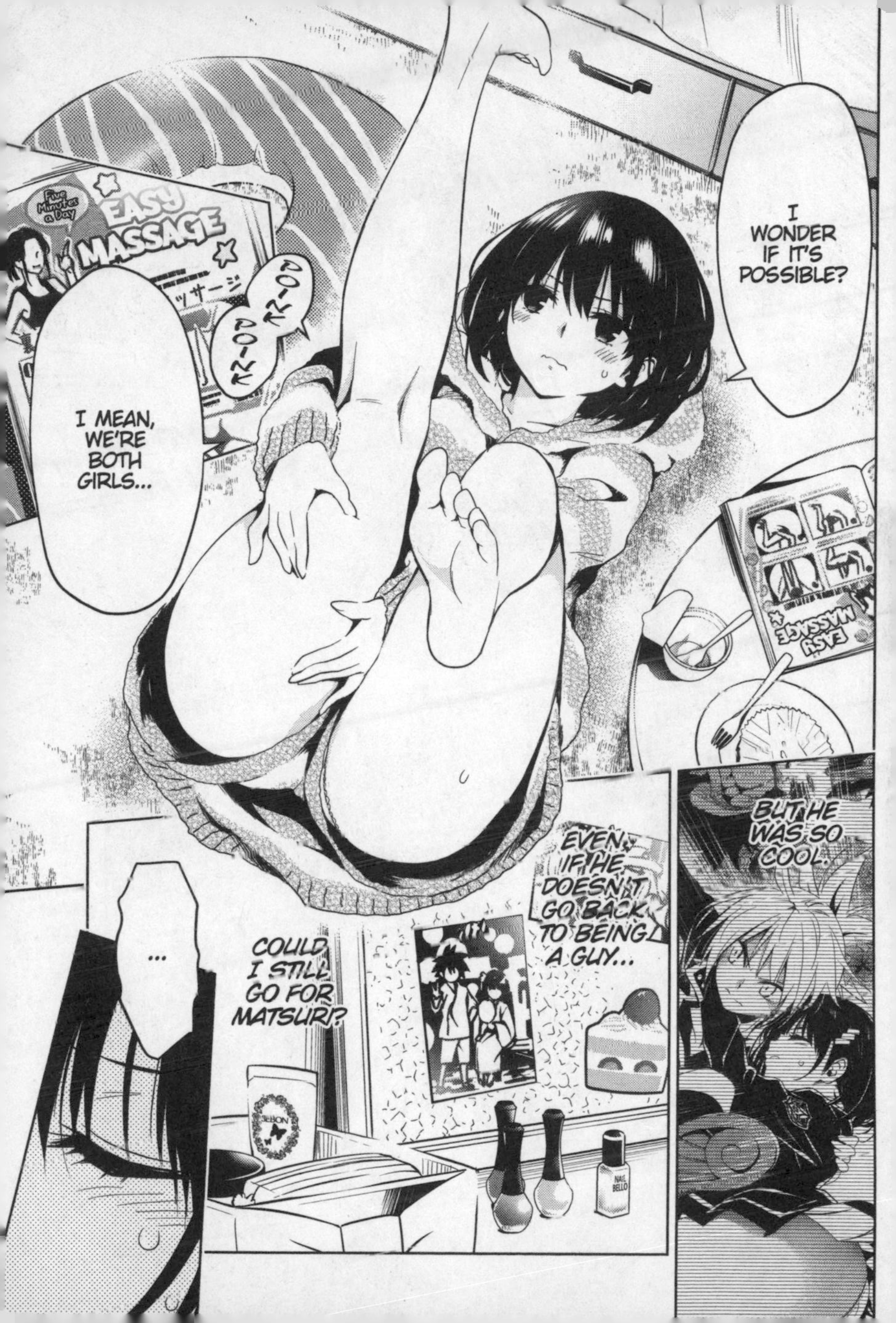
I WONDER IF IT'S POSSIBLE?
POINK POINK
Five Minutes a Day
EASY MASSAGE
I MEAN, WE'RE BOTH GIRLS...
EASY MASSAGE
BUT HE WAS SO COOL.
EVEN IF HE DOESN'T GO BACK TO BEING A GUY...
COULD I STILL GO FOR MATSURI?
NAIL BELLO
...

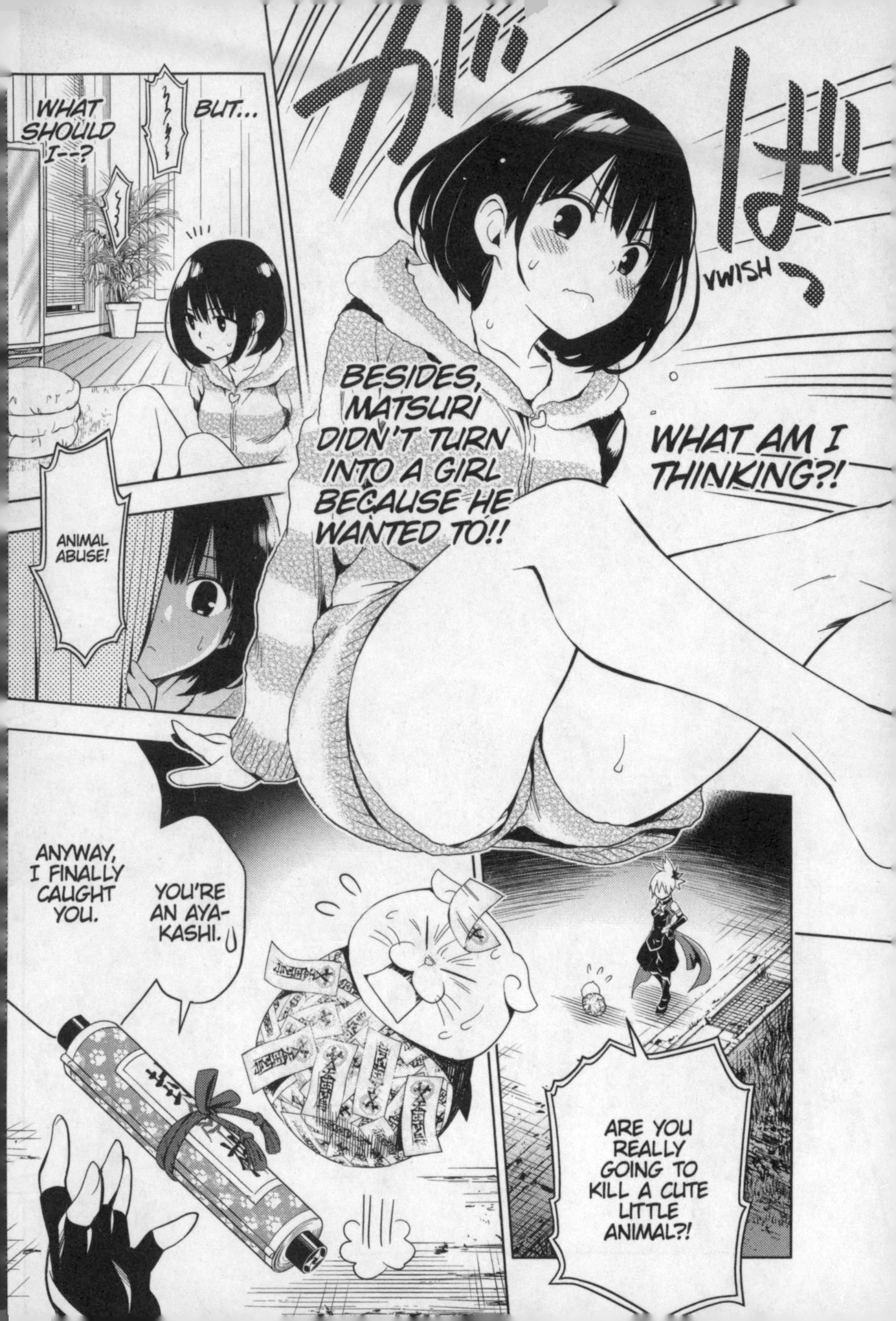

がばっ
VWISH
WHAT AM I THINKING?!
BESIDES, MATSURI DIDN'T TURN INTO A GIRL BECAUSE HE WANTED TO!!
BUT...
WHAT SHOULD I--?
ANIMAL ABUSE!
ARE YOU REALLY GOING TO KILL A CUTE LITTLE ANIMAL?!
YOU'RE AN AYA-KASHI.
ANYWAY, I FINALLY CAUGHT YOU.

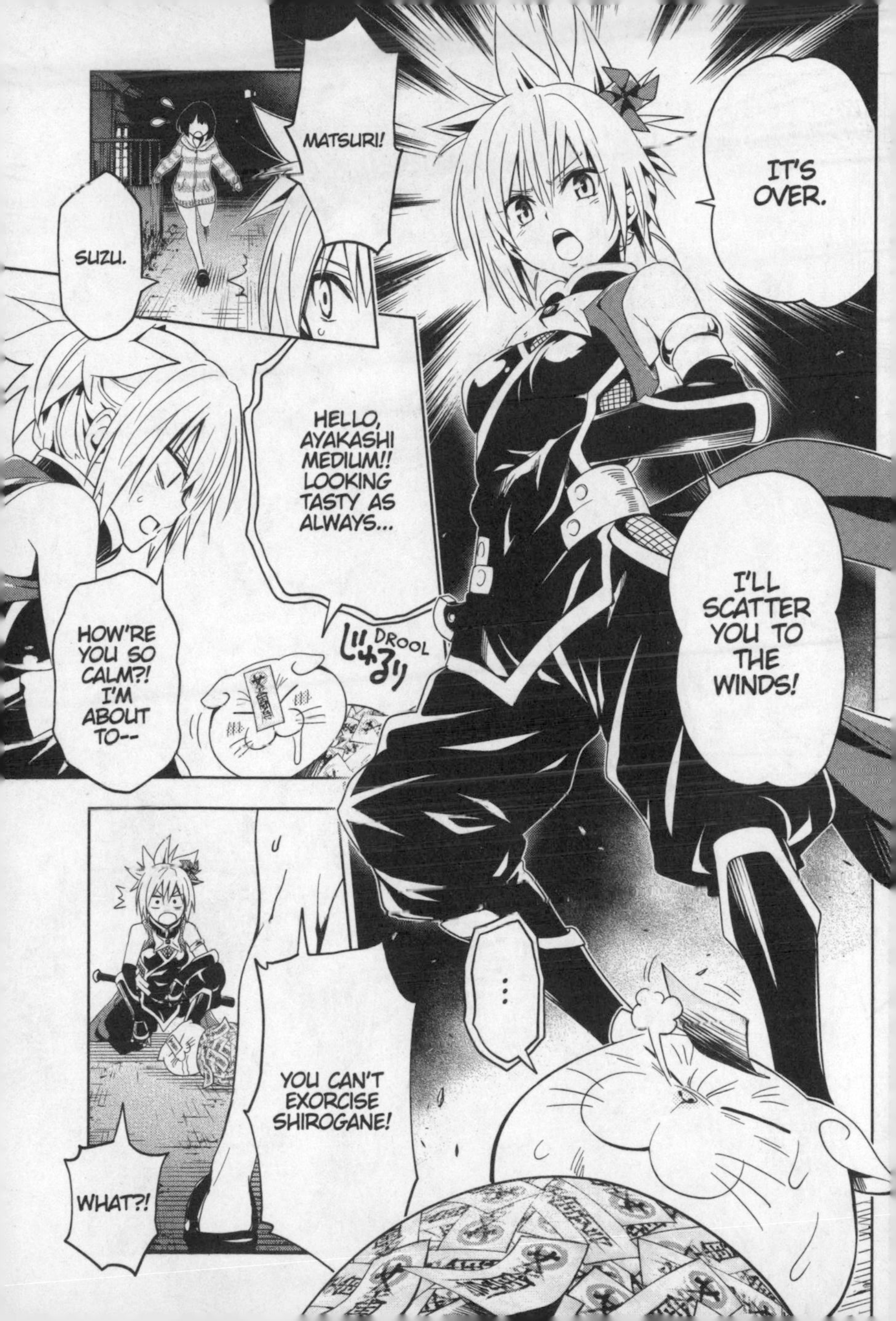
IT'S OVER.
I'LL SCATTER YOU TO THE WINDS!
MATSURI!
SUZU.
HELLO, AYAKASHI MEDIUM!! LOOKING TASTY AS ALWAYS...
じゅるり DROOL
HOW'RE YOU SO CALM?! I'M ABOUT TO--
...
YOU CAN'T EXORCISE SHIROGANE!
WHAT?!

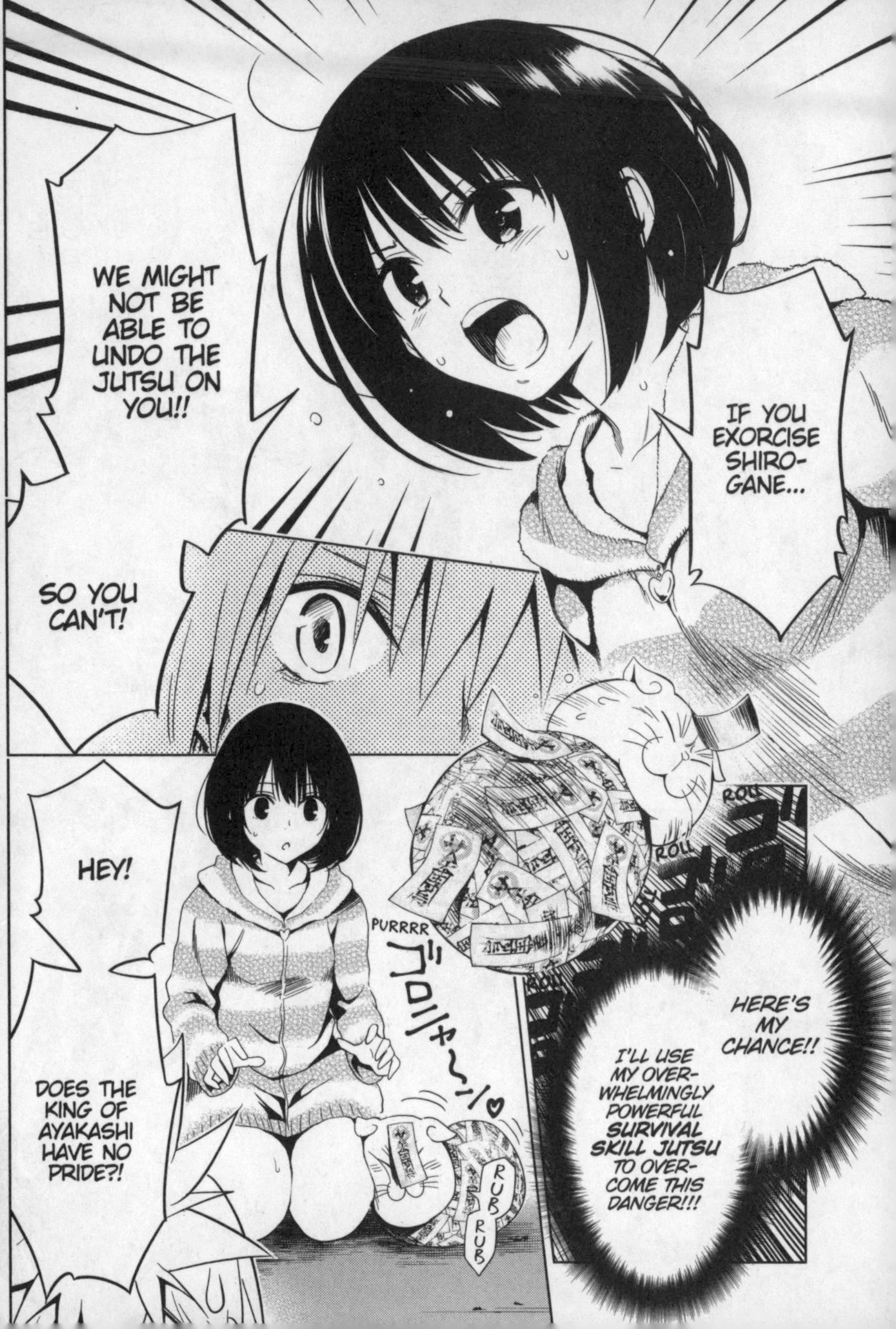
IF YOU EXORCISE SHIRO-GANE...
WE MIGHT NOT BE ABLE TO UNDO THE JUTSU ON YOU!!
SO YOU CAN'T!
ROLL
ROLL
ROLL
HERE'S MY CHANCE!!
I'LL USE MY OVER-WHELMINGLY POWERFUL SURVIVAL SKILL JUTSU TO OVER-COME THIS DANGER!!!
HEY!
PURRRR
RUB
RUB
DOES THE KING OF AYAKASHI HAVE NO PRIDE?!

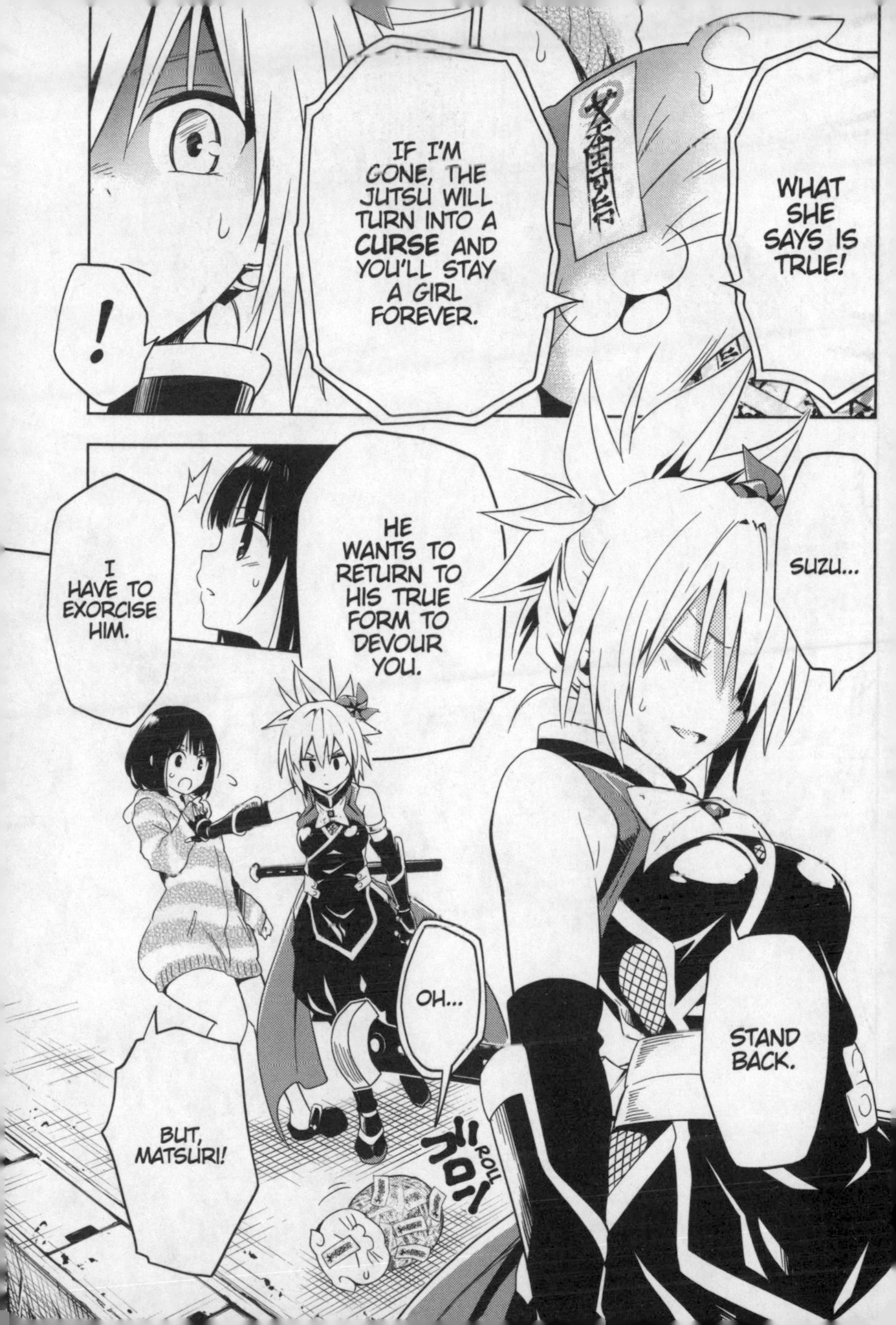
WHAT SHE SAYS IS TRUE!
IF I'M GONE, THE JUTSU WILL TURN INTO A CURSE AND YOU'LL STAY A GIRL FOREVER.
!
SUZU...
HE WANTS TO RETURN TO HIS TRUE FORM TO DEVOUR YOU.
I HAVE TO EXORCISE HIM.
STAND BACK.
OH...
BUT, MATSURI!
ROLL

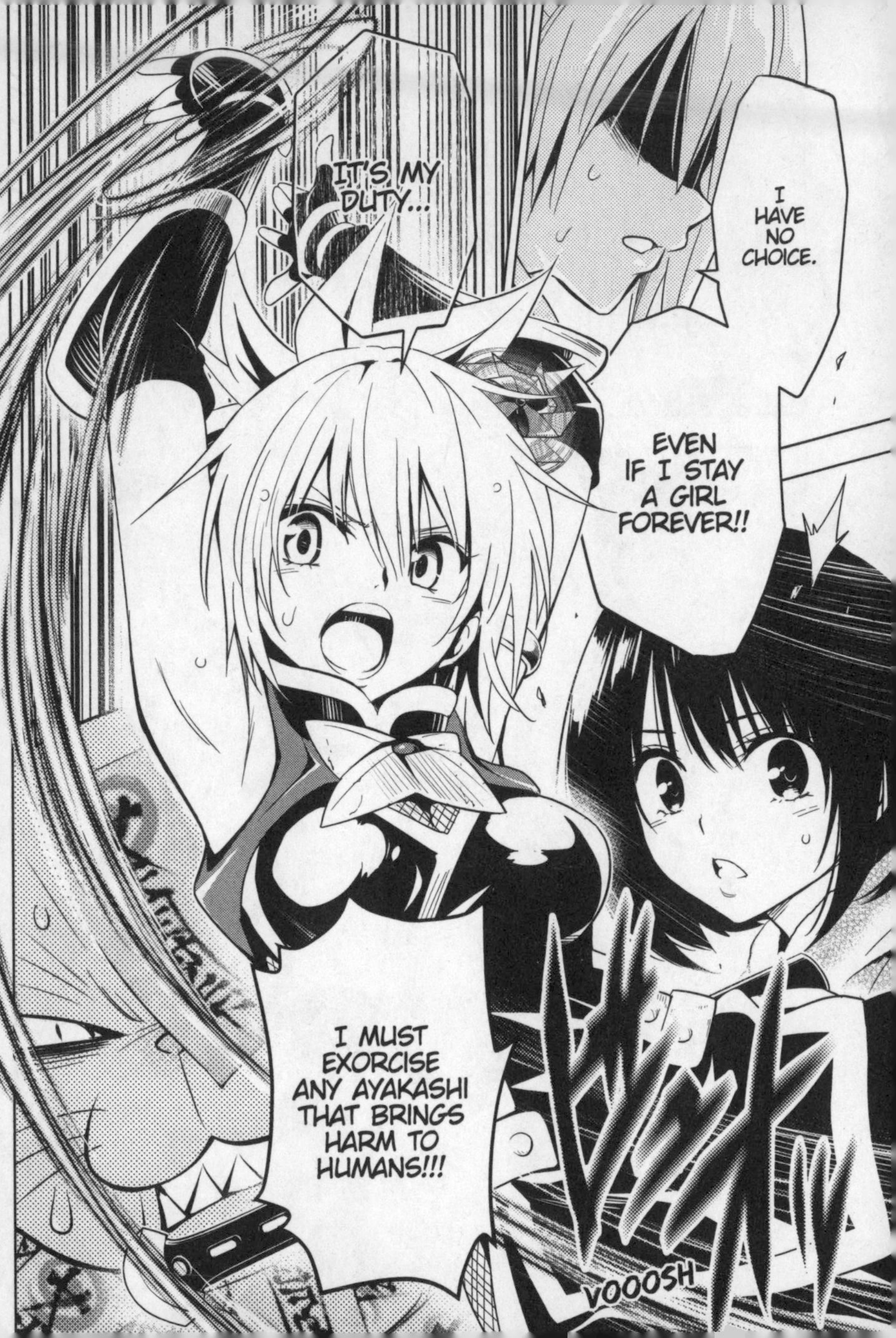
I HAVE NO CHOICE.
IT'S MY DUTY...
EVEN IF I STAY A GIRL FOREVER!!
I MUST EXORCISE ANY AYAKASHI THAT BRINGS HARM TO HUMANS!!!
VOOOSH

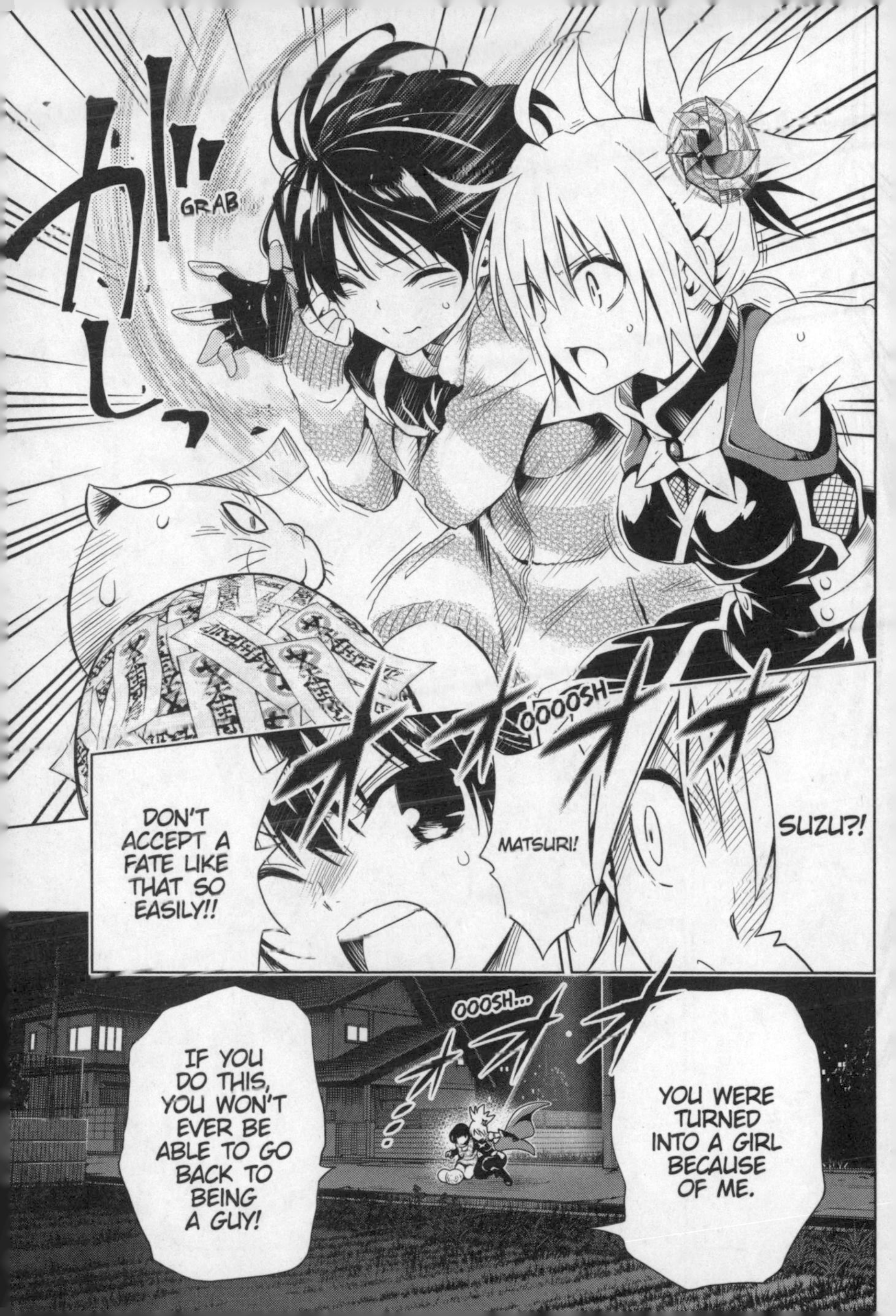
GRAB
OOOOSH
SUZU?!
MATSURI!
DON'T ACCEPT A FATE LIKE THAT SO EASILY!!
OOOSH...
YOU WERE TURNED INTO A GIRL BECAUSE OF ME.
IF YOU DO THIS, YOU WON'T EVER BE ABLE TO GO BACK TO BEING A GUY!

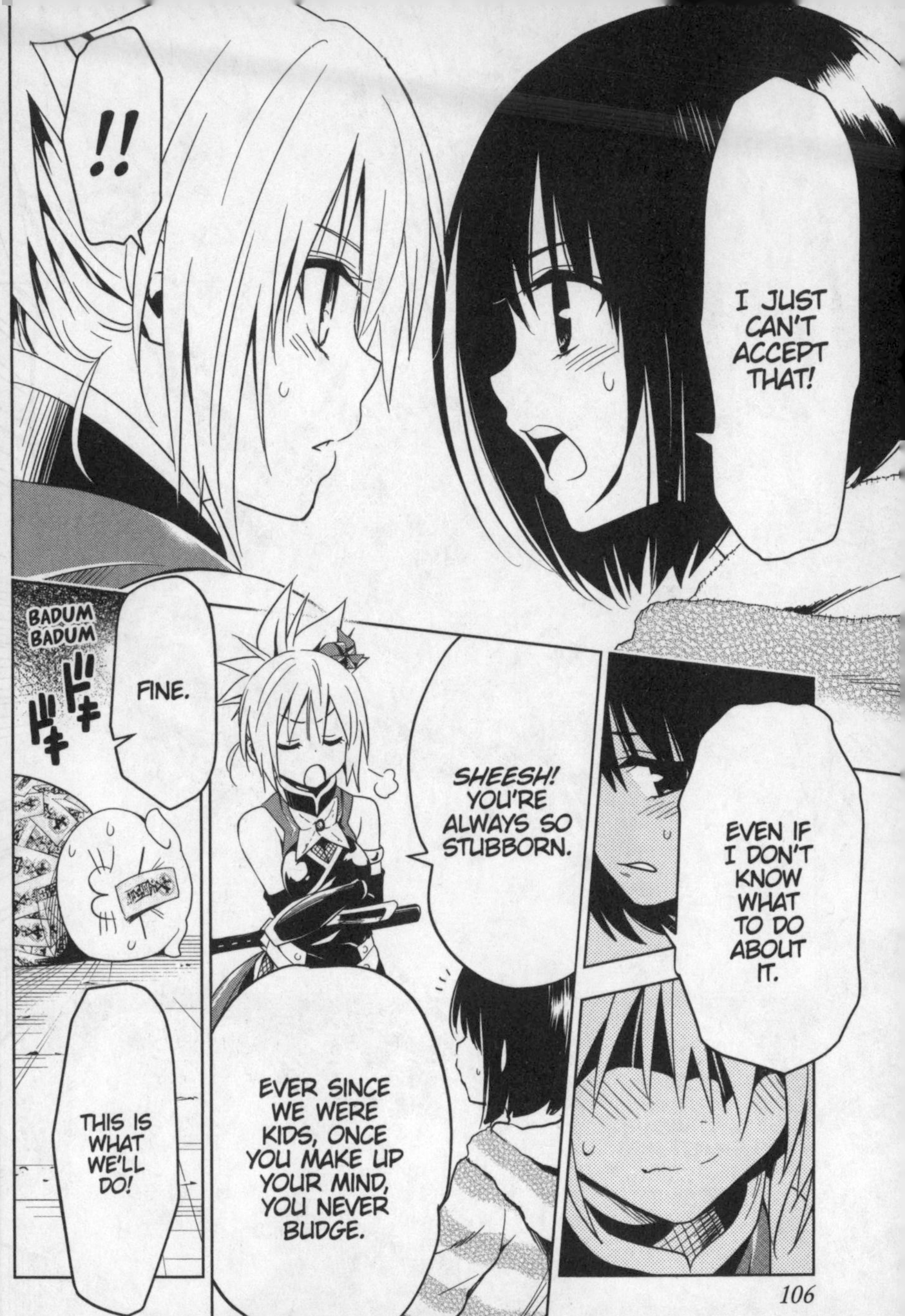
I JUST CAN'T ACCEPT THAT!
!!
EVEN IF I DON'T KNOW WHAT TO DO ABOUT IT.
SHEESH! YOU'RE ALWAYS SO STUBBORN.
EVER SINCE WE WERE KIDS, ONCE YOU MAKE UP YOUR MIND, YOU NEVER BUDGE.
BADUM BADUM
FINE.
THIS IS WHAT WE'LL DO!

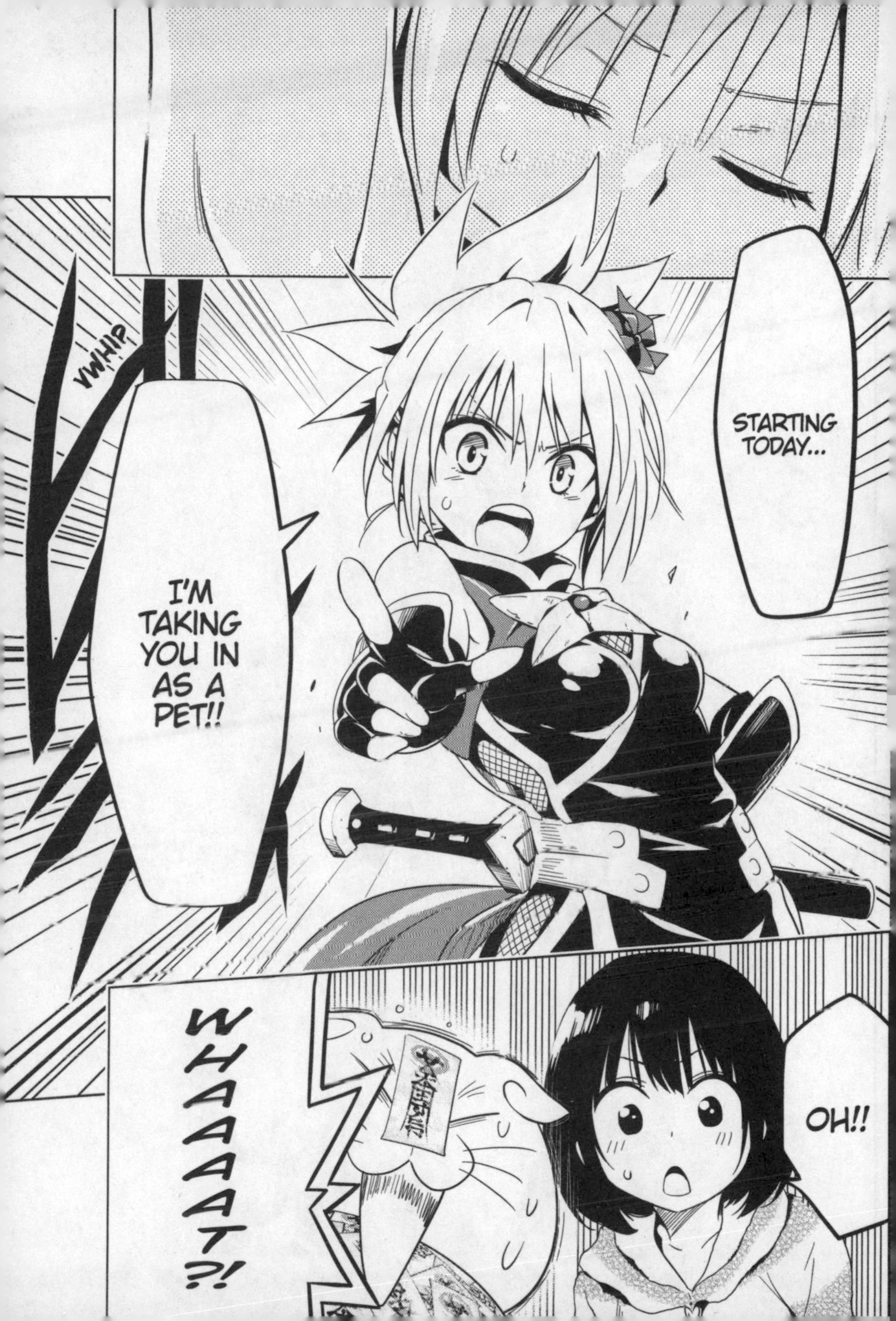
STARTING TODAY...
YWHIP
I'M TAKING YOU IN AS A PET!!
OH!!
WHAAAAAT?!

# Matsuri's Exorcist Ninja Gear Concept Designs

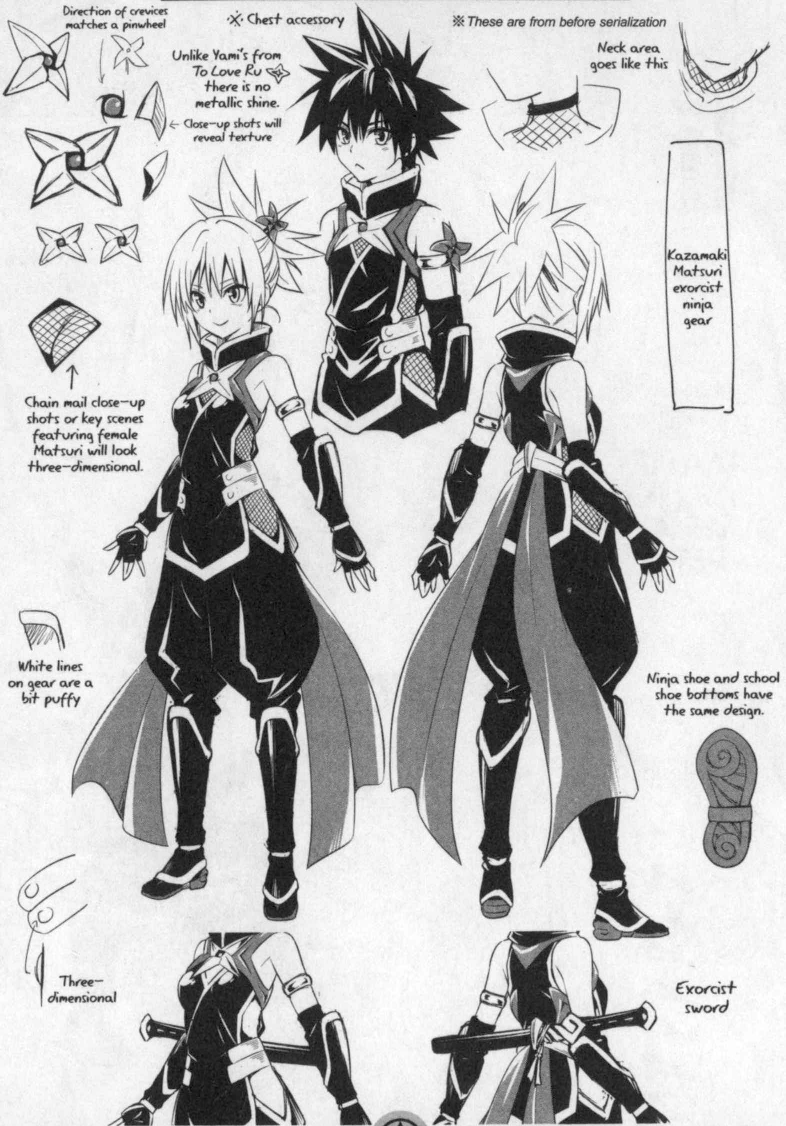
※These are from before serialization
Direction of crevices matches a pinwheel
※Chest accessory
Unlike Yami's from To Love Ru there is no metallic shine.
← Close-up shots will reveal texture
Neck area goes like this
Kazamaki Matsuri exorcist ninja gear
Chain mail close-up shots or key scenes featuring female Matsuri will look three-dimensional.
White lines on gear are a bit puffy
Ninja shoe and school shoe bottoms have the same design.
Three-dimensional
Exorcist sword

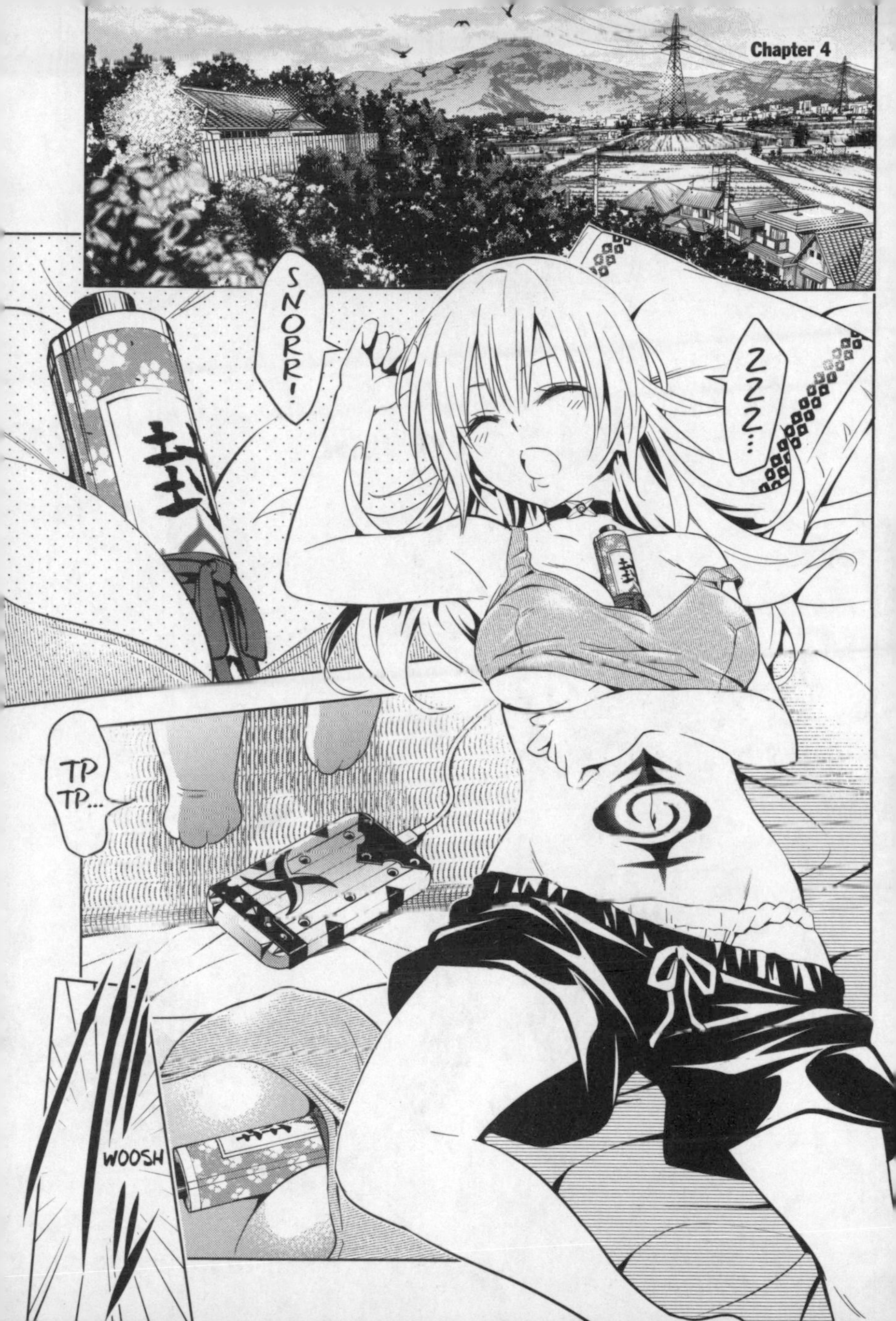
Chapter 4
ZZZ...
SNORR!
TP TP...
WOOSH

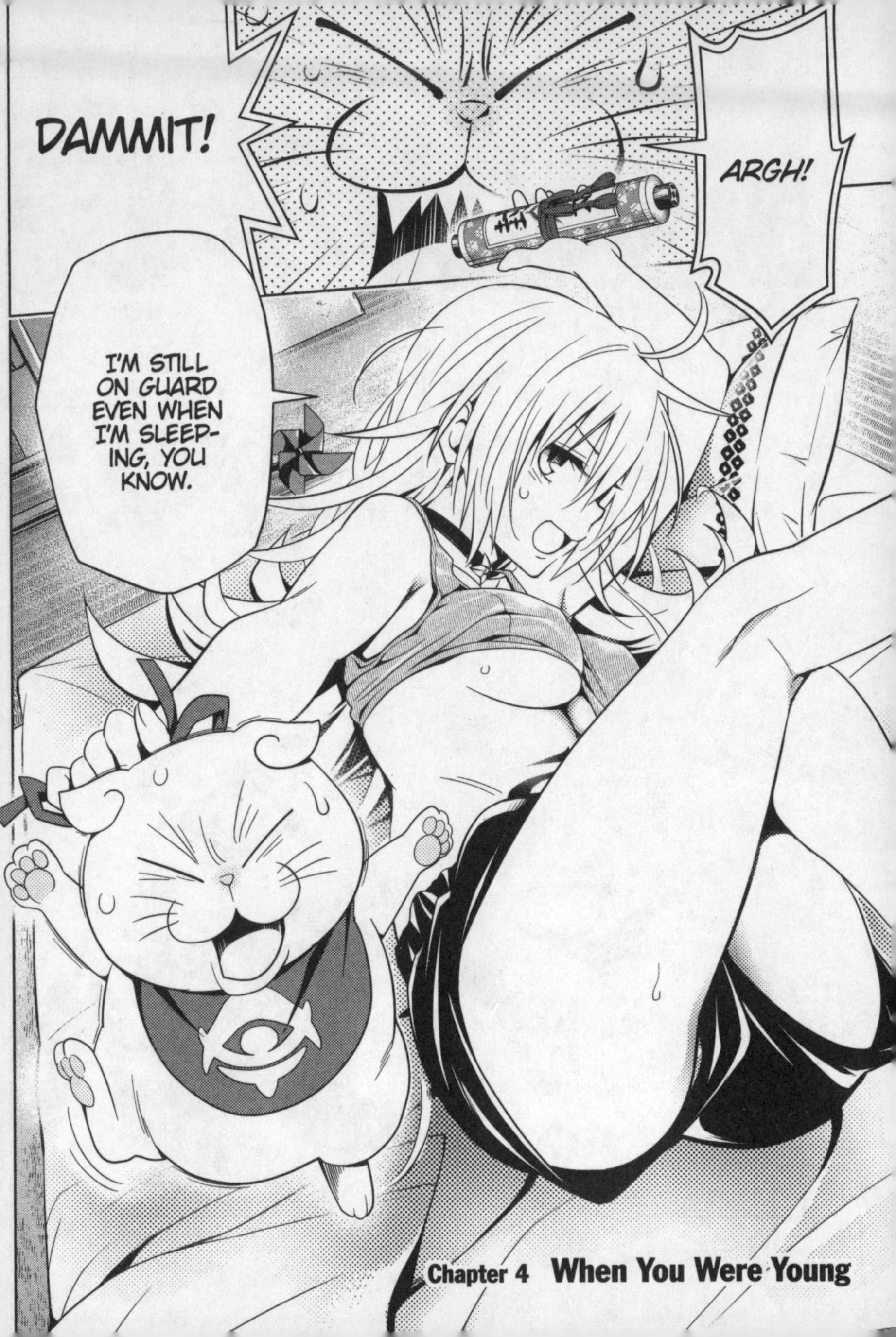
ARGH!
DAMMIT!
I'M STILL ON GUARD EVEN WHEN I'M SLEEPING, YOU KNOW.
Chapter 4 When You Were Young

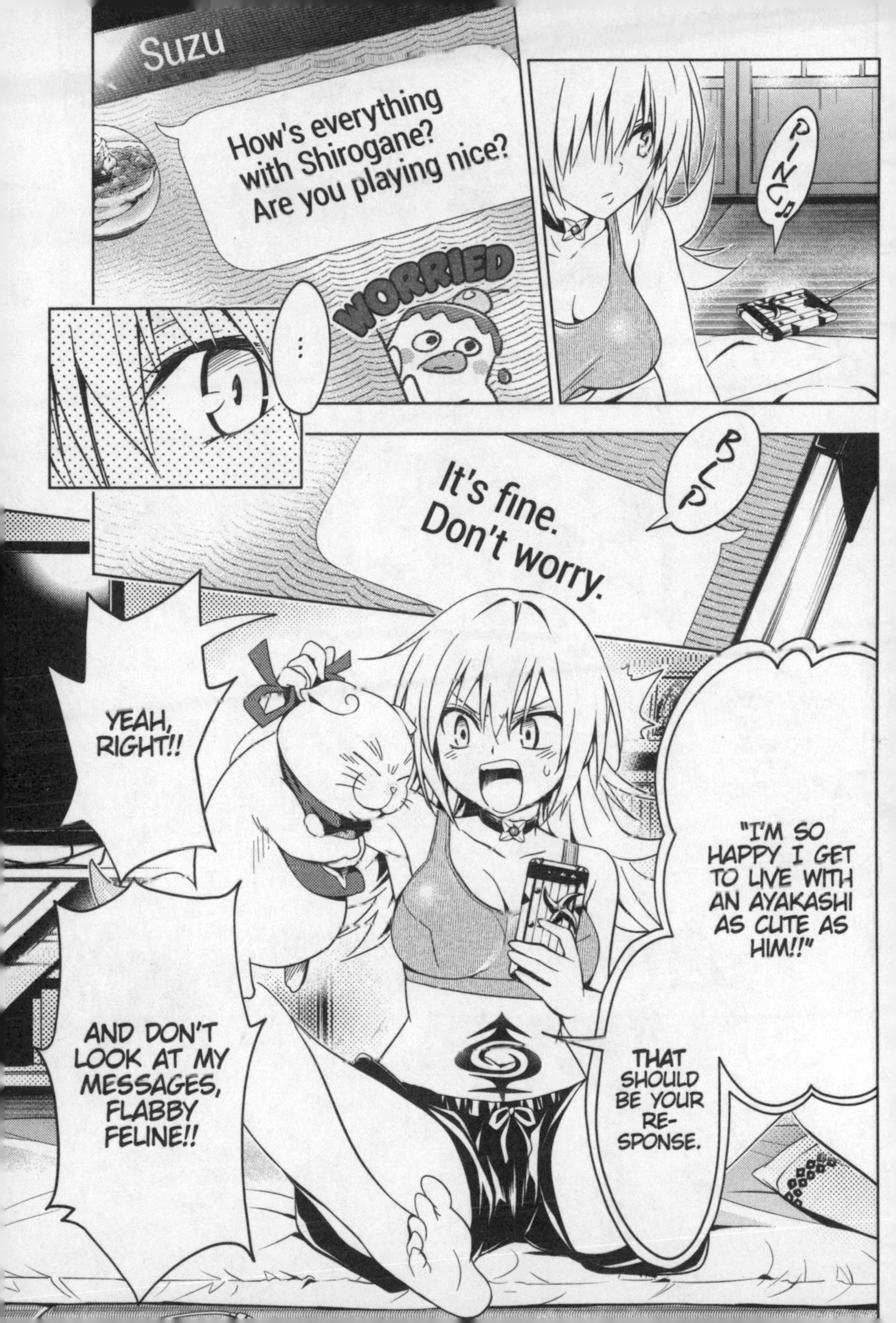
RING♪
Suzu
How's everything with Shirogane? Are you playing nice?
WORRIED
...
BLP
It's fine. Don't worry.
"I'M SO HAPPY I GET TO LIVE WITH AN AYAKASHI AS CUTE AS HIM!!"
THAT SHOULD BE YOUR RE-SPONSE.
YEAH, RIGHT!!
AND DON'T LOOK AT MY MESSAGES, FLABBY FELINE!!

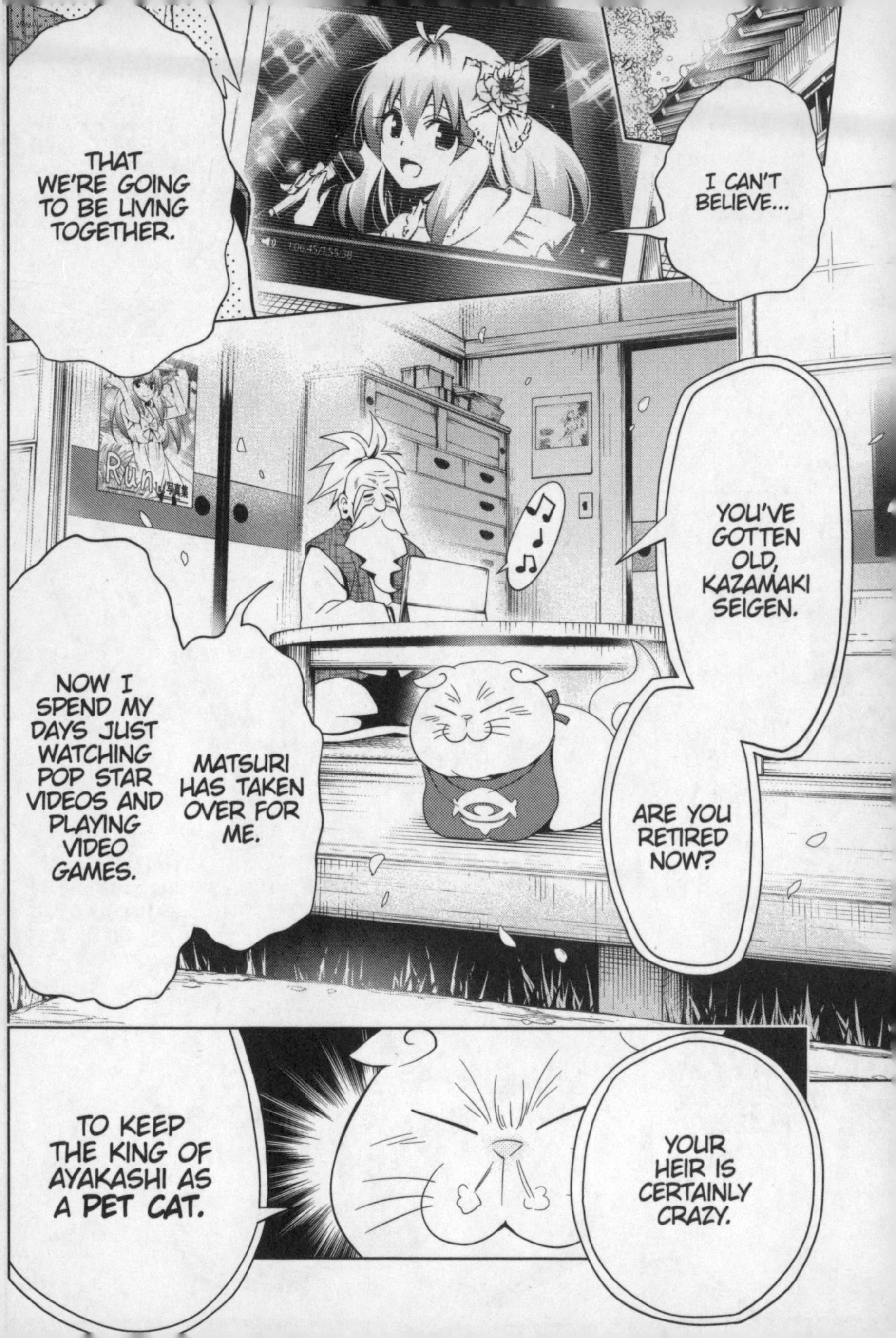
I CAN'T BELIEVE...
THAT WE'RE GOING TO BE LIVING TOGETHER.
YOU'VE GOTTEN OLD, KAZAMAKI SEIGEN.
ARE YOU RETIRED NOW?
MATSURI HAS TAKEN OVER FOR ME.
NOW I SPEND MY DAYS JUST WATCHING POP STAR VIDEOS AND PLAYING VIDEO GAMES.
Run
YOUR HEIR IS CERTAINLY CRAZY.
TO KEEP THE KING OF AYAKASHI AS A PET CAT.

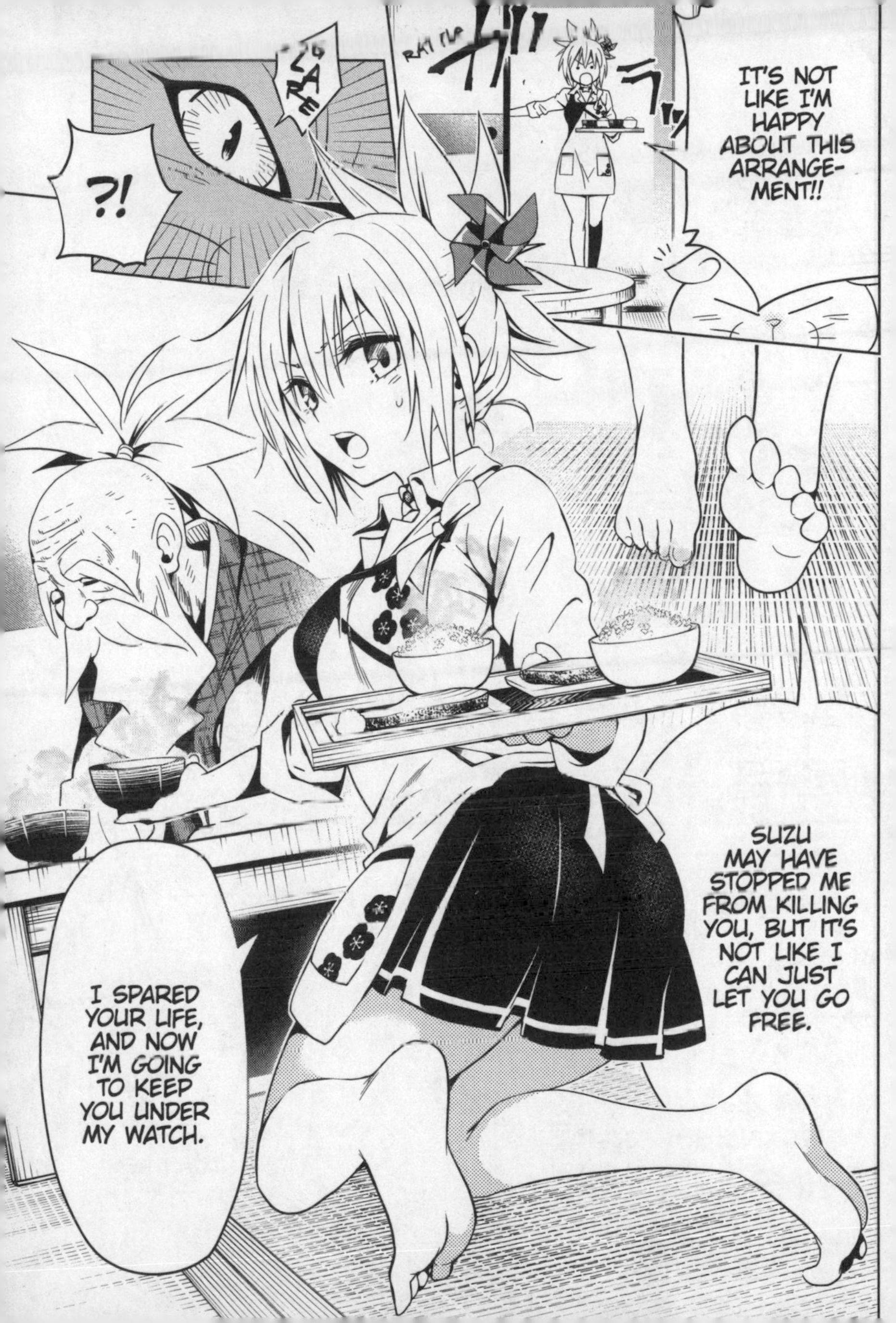

RATTLE
IT'S NOT LIKE I'M HAPPY ABOUT THIS ARRANGE-MENT!!
GLARE
?!
SUZU MAY HAVE STOPPED ME FROM KILLING YOU, BUT IT'S NOT LIKE I CAN JUST LET YOU GO FREE.
I SPARED YOUR LIFE, AND NOW I'M GOING TO KEEP YOU UNDER MY WATCH.

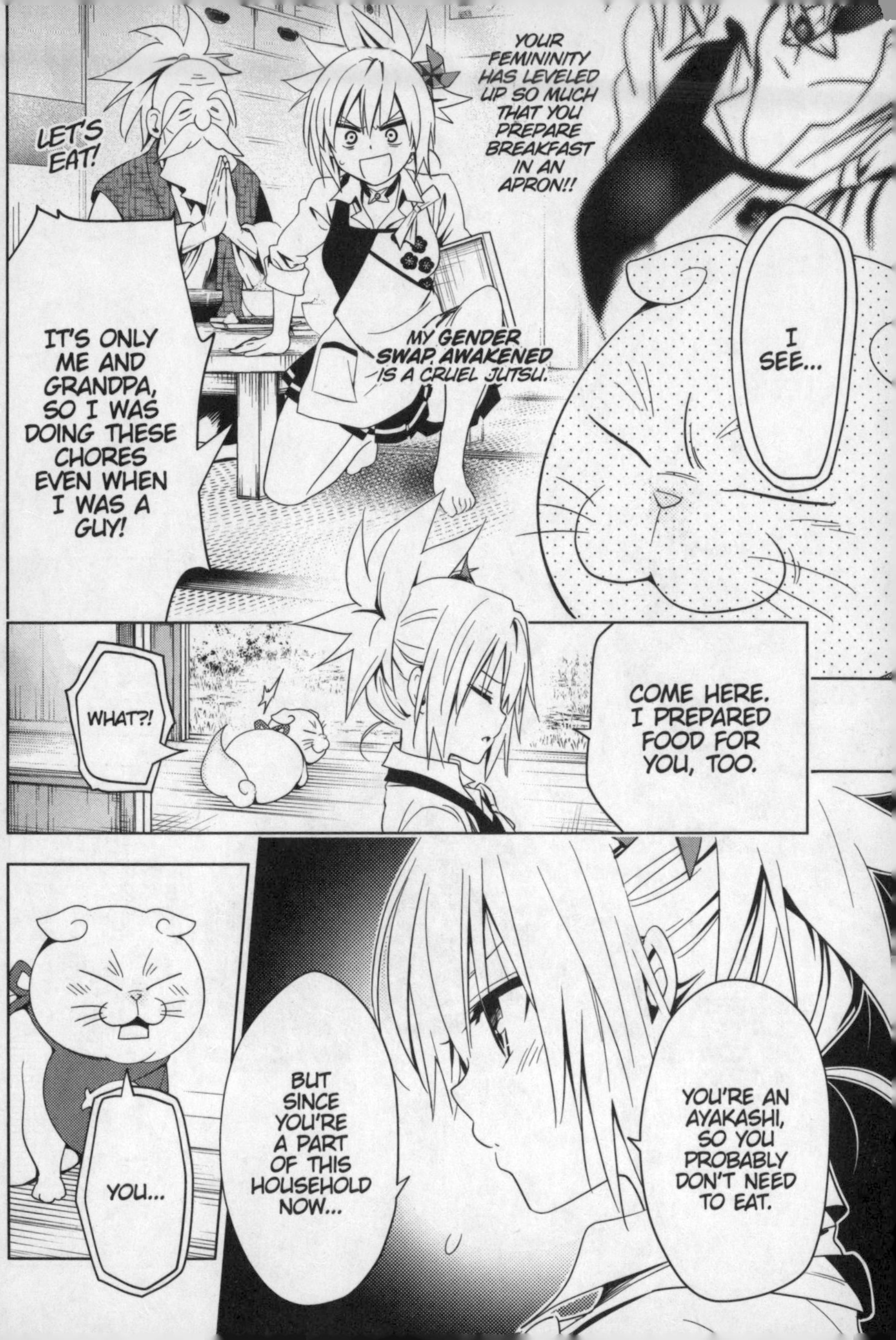
I SEE...
YOUR FEMININITY HAS LEVELED UP SO MUCH THAT YOU PREPARE BREAKFAST IN AN APRON!!
LET'S EAT!
IT'S ONLY ME AND GRANDPA, SO I WAS DOING THESE CHORES EVEN WHEN I WAS A GUY!
MY GENDER SWAP AWAKENED IS A CRUEL JUTSU.
COME HERE. I PREPARED FOOD FOR YOU, TOO.
WHAT?!
YOU'RE AN AYAKASHI, SO YOU PROBABLY DON'T NEED TO EAT.
BUT SINCE YOU'RE A PART OF THIS HOUSEHOLD NOW...
YOU...

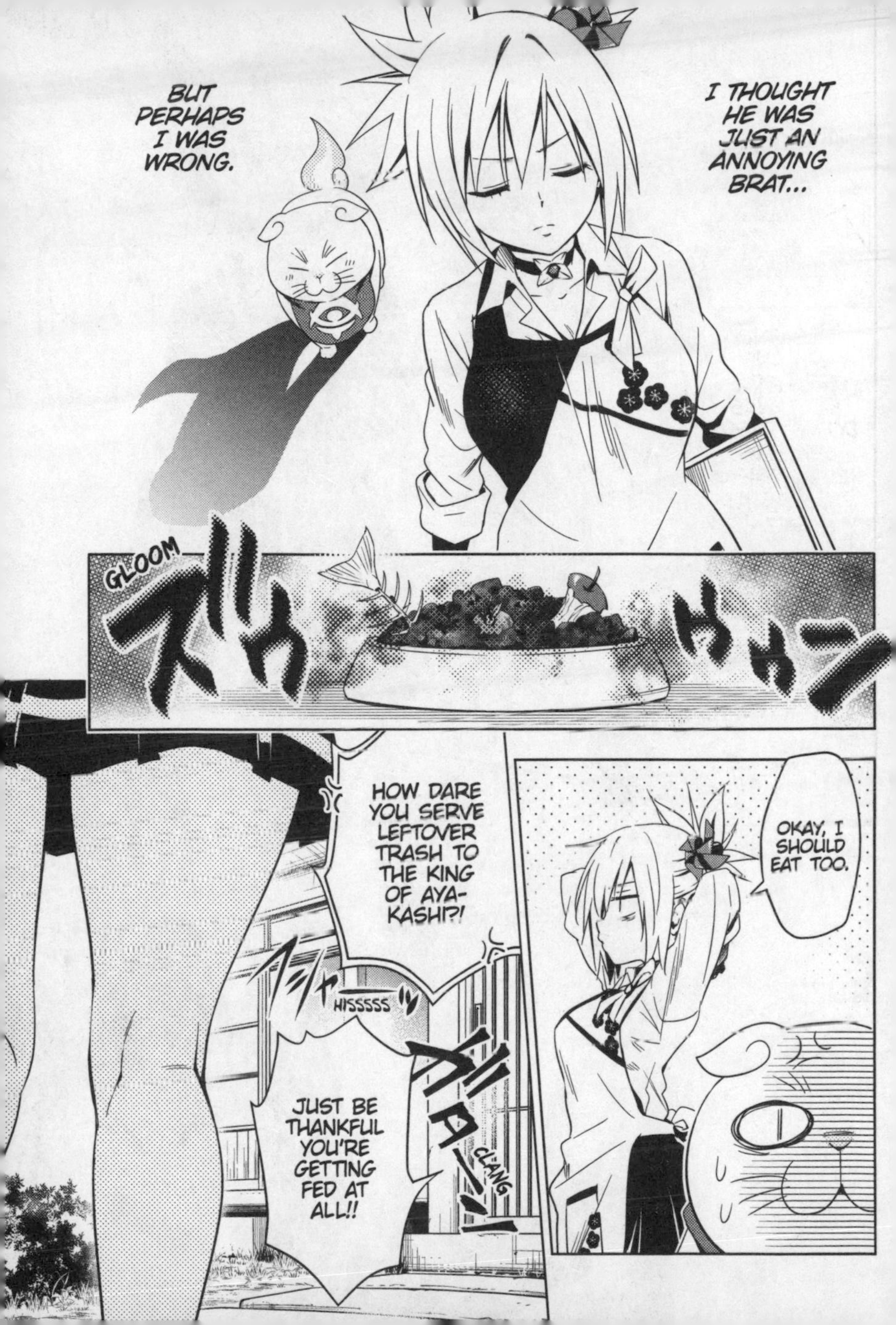
I THOUGHT HE WAS JUST AN ANNOYING BRAT...
BUT PERHAPS I WAS WRONG.
GLOOM
OKAY, I SHOULD EAT TOO.
HOW DARE YOU SERVE LEFTOVER TRASH TO THE KING OF AYA-KASHI?!
HISSSSS
JUST BE THANKFUL YOU'RE GETTING FED AT ALL!!
CLANG

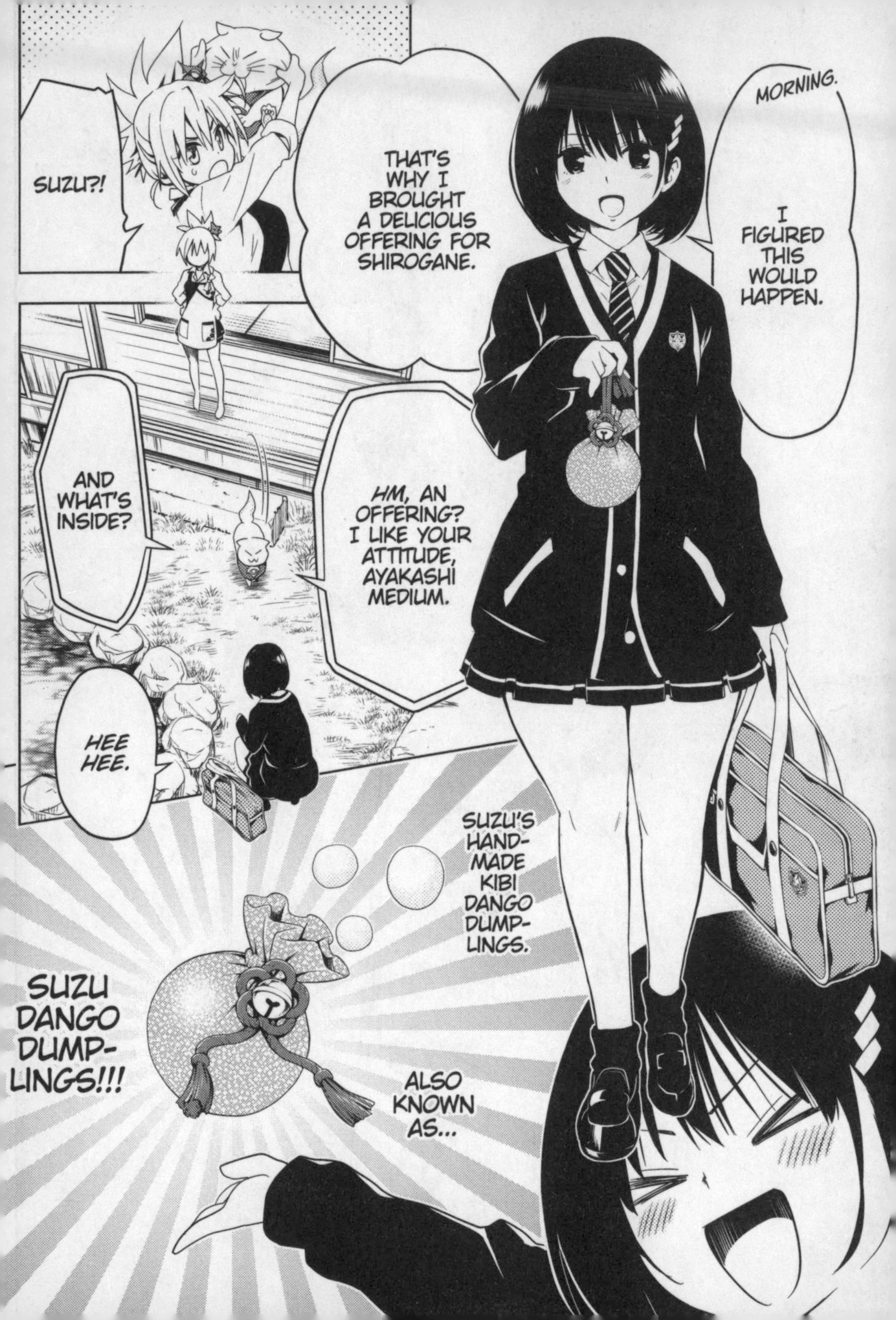
MORNING.
I FIGURED THIS WOULD HAPPEN.
THAT'S WHY I BROUGHT A DELICIOUS OFFERING FOR SHIROGANE.
SUZU?!
*HM*, AN OFFERING? I LIKE YOUR ATTITUDE, AYAKASHI MEDIUM.
AND WHAT'S INSIDE?
*HEE HEE.*
SUZU'S HAND-MADE KIBI DANGO DUMP-LINGS.
ALSO KNOWN AS...
SUZU DANGO DUMP-LINGS!!!

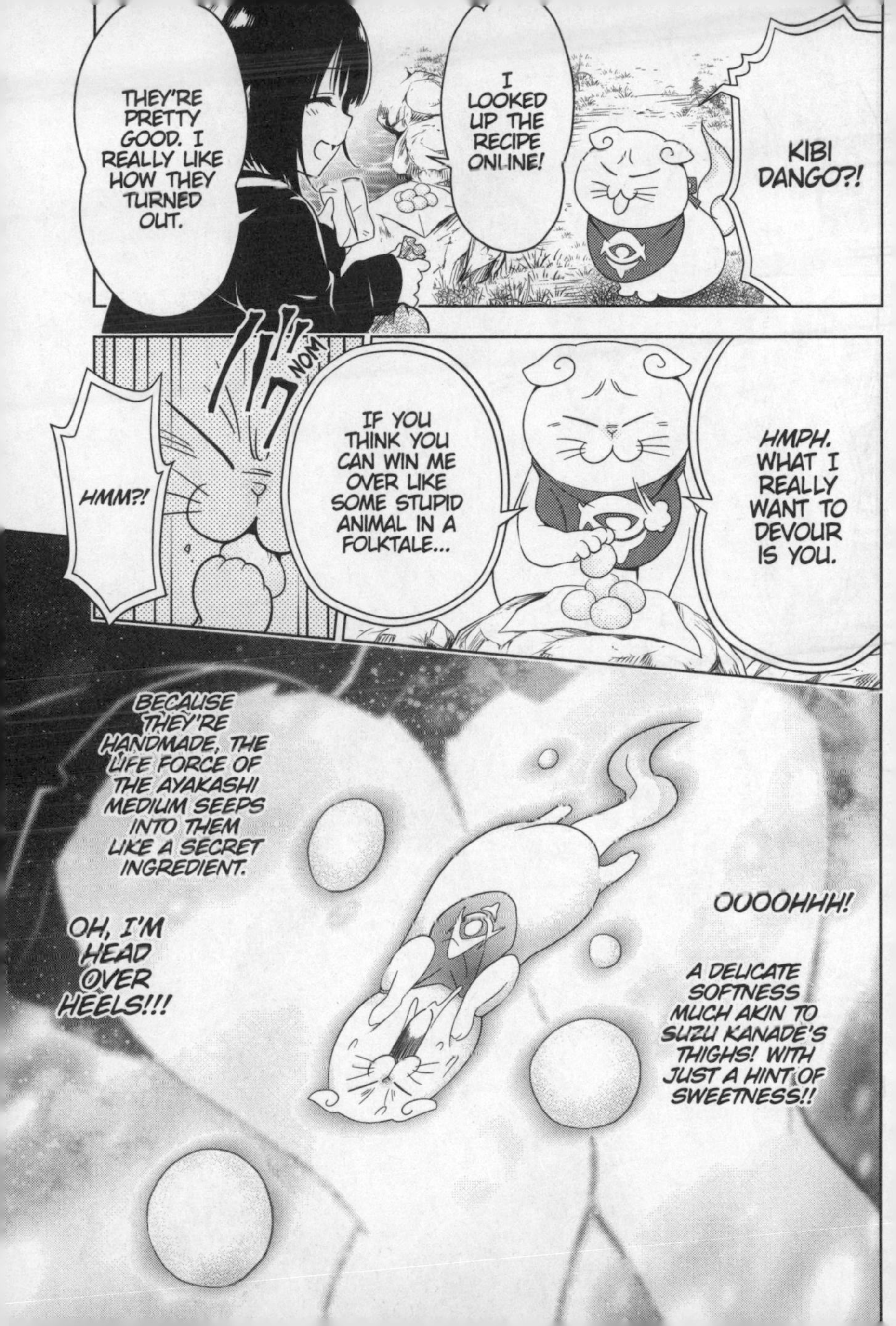
KIBI DANGO?!
I LOOKED UP THE RECIPE ONLINE!
THEY'RE PRETTY GOOD. I REALLY LIKE HOW THEY TURNED OUT.
IF YOU THINK YOU CAN WIN ME OVER LIKE SOME STUPID ANIMAL IN A FOLKTALE...
HMPH. WHAT I REALLY WANT TO DEVOUR IS YOU.
NOM
HMM?!
OUOOHHH!
A DELICATE SOFTNESS MUCH AKIN TO SUZU KANADE'S THIGHS! WITH JUST A HINT OF SWEETNESS!!
BECAUSE THEY'RE HANDMADE, THE LIFE FORCE OF THE AYAKASHI MEDIUM SEEPS INTO THEM LIKE A SECRET INGREDIENT.
OH, I'M HEAD OVER HEELS!!!

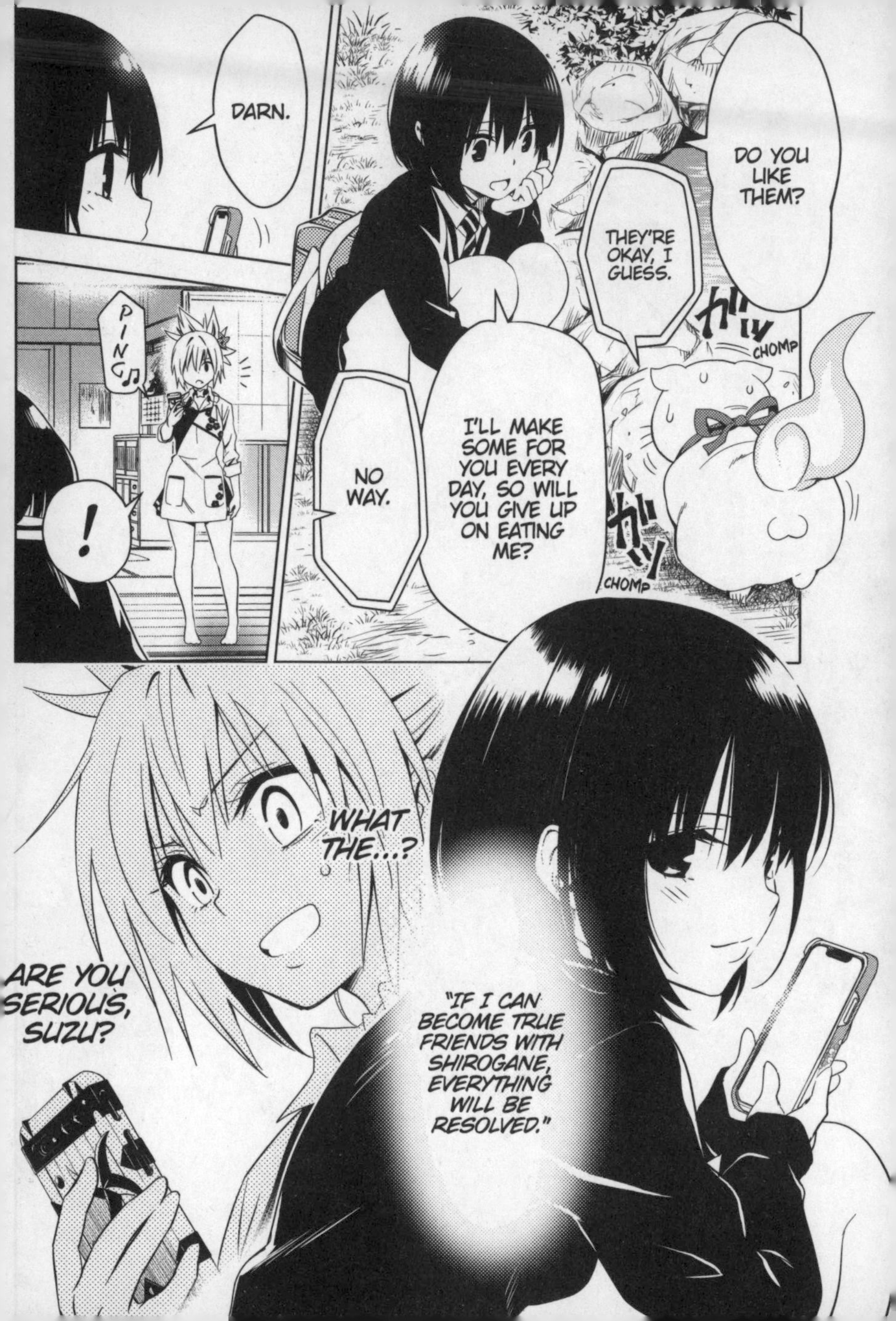
DO YOU LIKE THEM?
THEY'RE OKAY, I GUESS.
CHOMP
I'LL MAKE SOME FOR YOU EVERY DAY, SO WILL YOU GIVE UP ON EATING ME?
NO WAY.
CHOMP
DARN.
PING♫
!
"IF I CAN BECOME TRUE FRIENDS WITH SHIROGANE, EVERYTHING WILL BE RESOLVED."
WHAT THE...?
ARE YOU SERIOUS, SUZU?

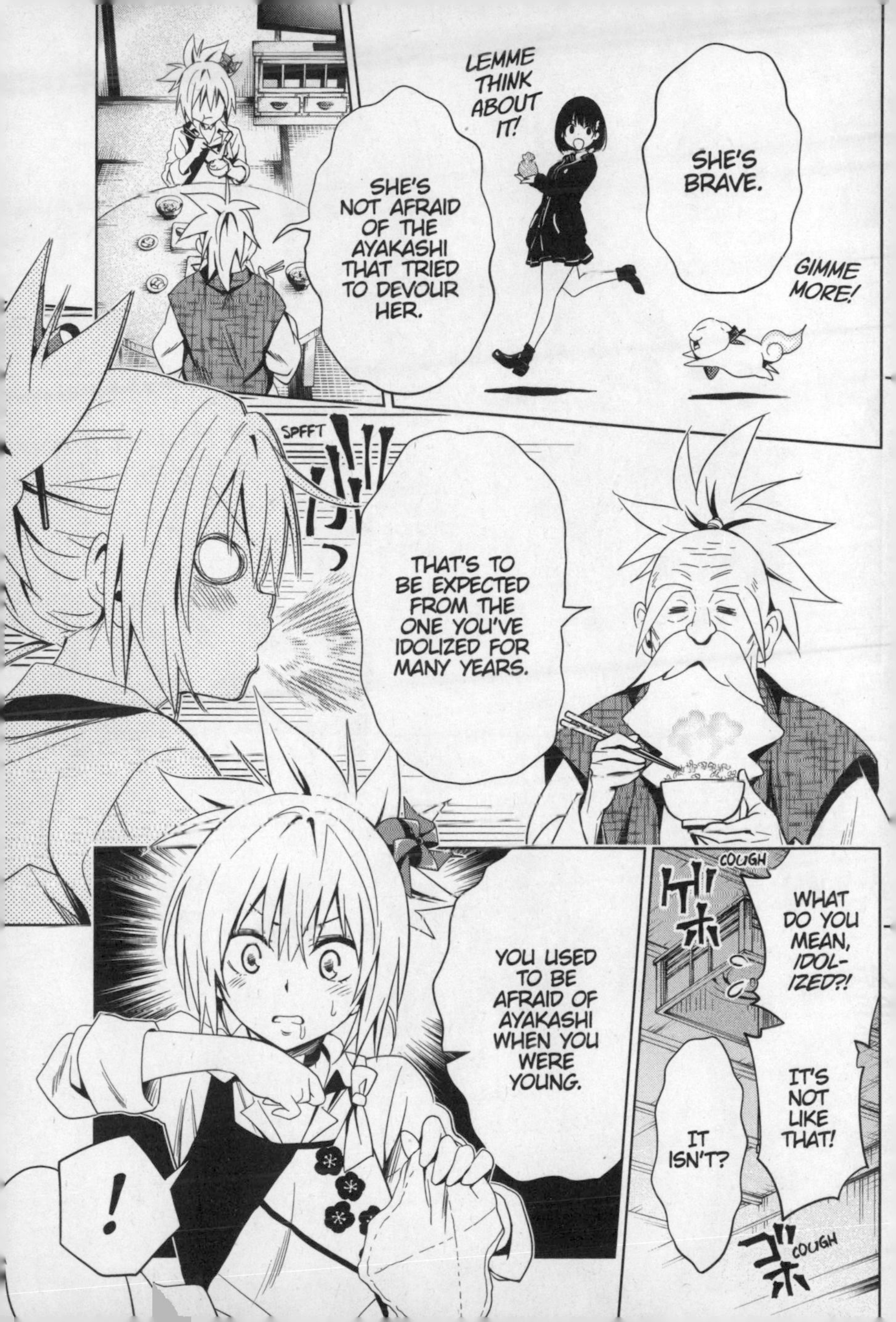
SHE'S BRAVE.
GIMME MORE!
LEMME THINK ABOUT IT!
SHE'S NOT AFRAID OF THE AYAKASHI THAT TRIED TO DEVOUR HER.
THAT'S TO BE EXPECTED FROM THE ONE YOU'VE IDOLIZED FOR MANY YEARS.
SPFFT
COUGH
WHAT DO YOU MEAN, IDOL-IZED?!
IT'S NOT LIKE THAT!
IT ISN'T?
COUGH
YOU USED TO BE AFRAID OF AYAKASHI WHEN YOU WERE YOUNG.
!

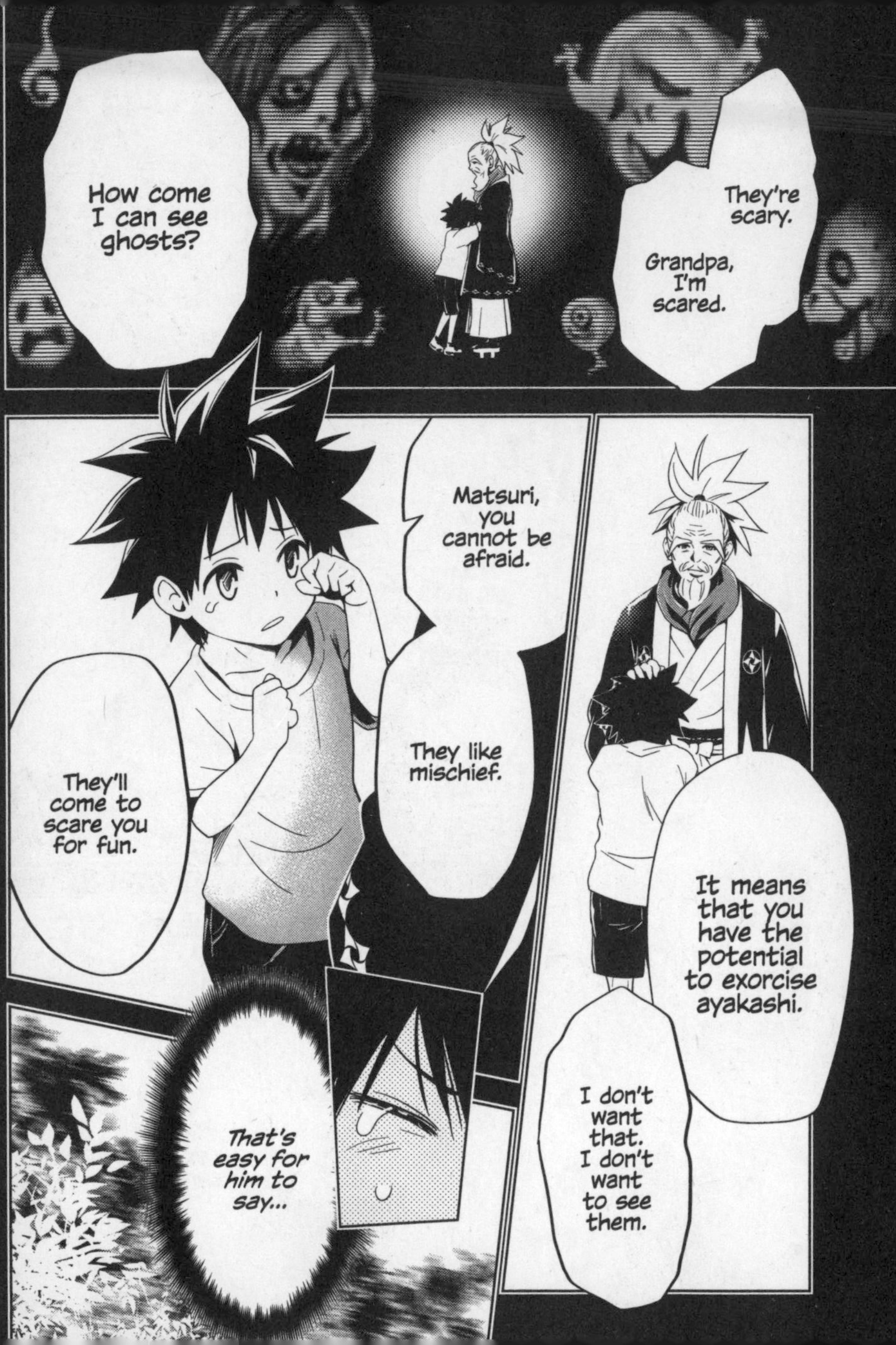
They're scary.
Grandpa, I'm scared.
How come I can see ghosts?
It means that you have the potential to exorcise ayakashi.
I don't want that. I don't want to see them.
Matsuri, you cannot be afraid.
They like mischief.
They'll come to scare you for fun.
That's easy for him to say...

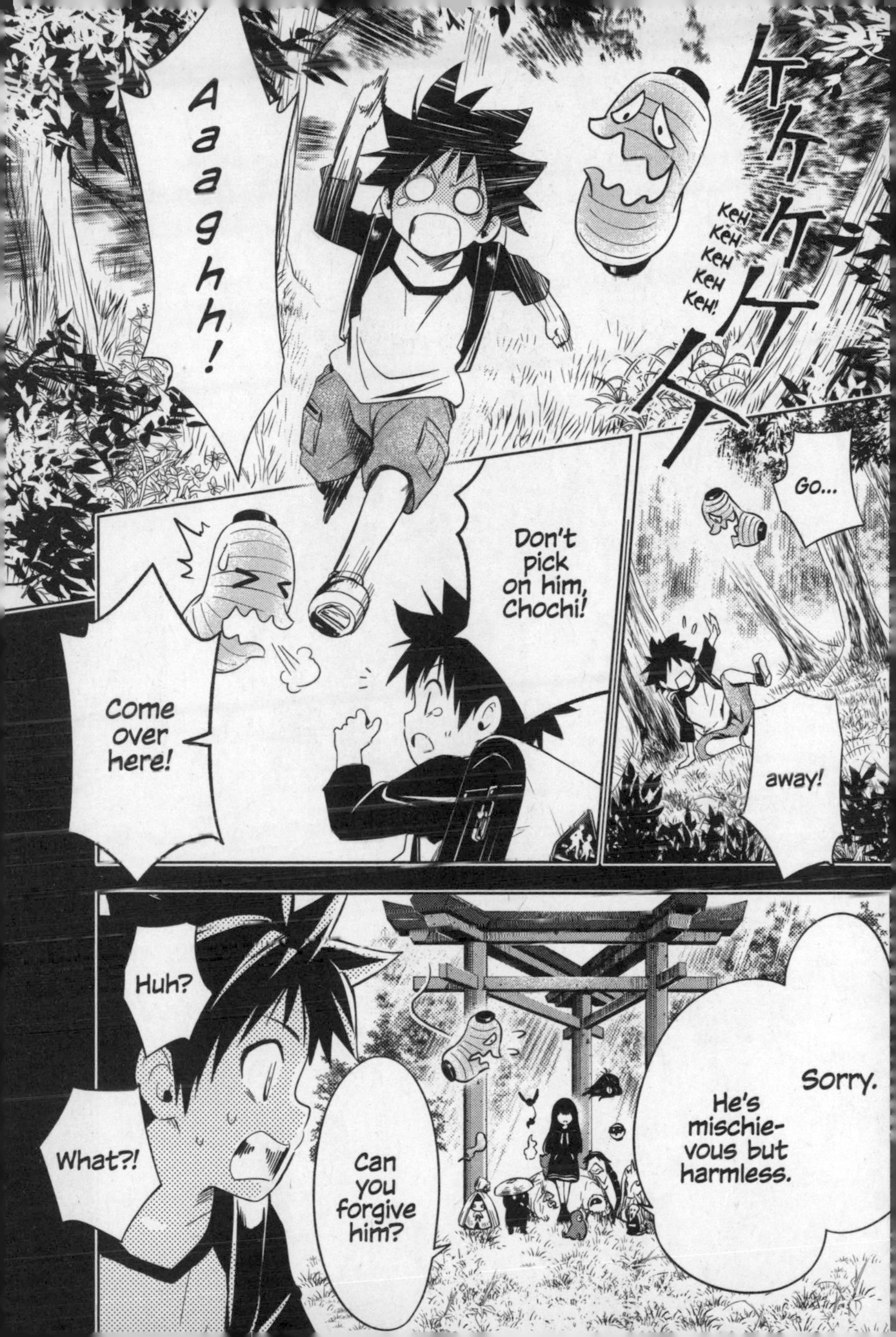
KEH KEH KEH KEH KEH!
Aaaghh!
Go...
away!
Don't pick on him, Chochi!
Come over here!
Sorry.
He's mischie-vous but harmless.
Can you forgive him?
Huh?
What?!

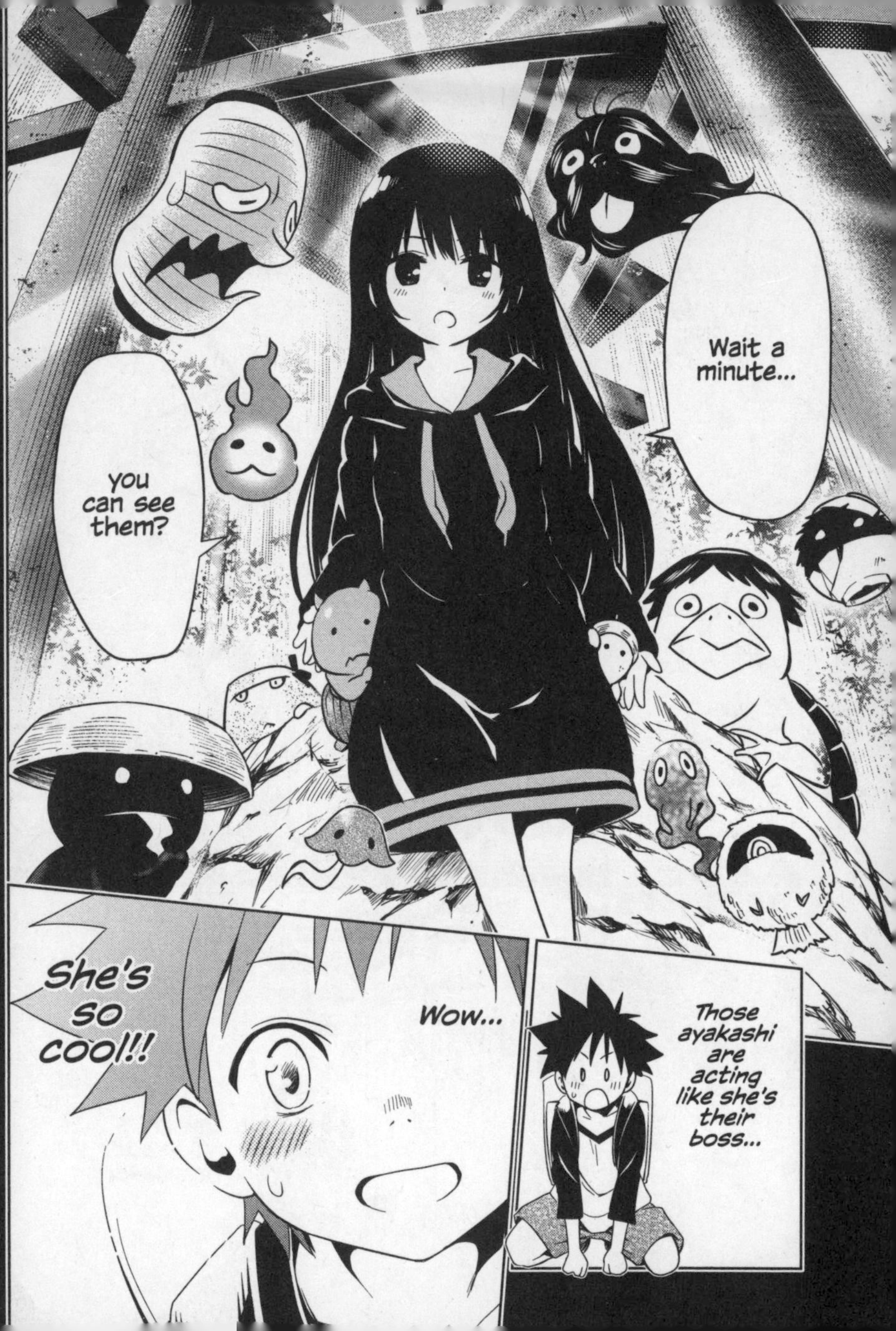
Wait a minute...
you can see them?
Those ayakashi are acting like she's their boss...
Wow...
She's so cool!!

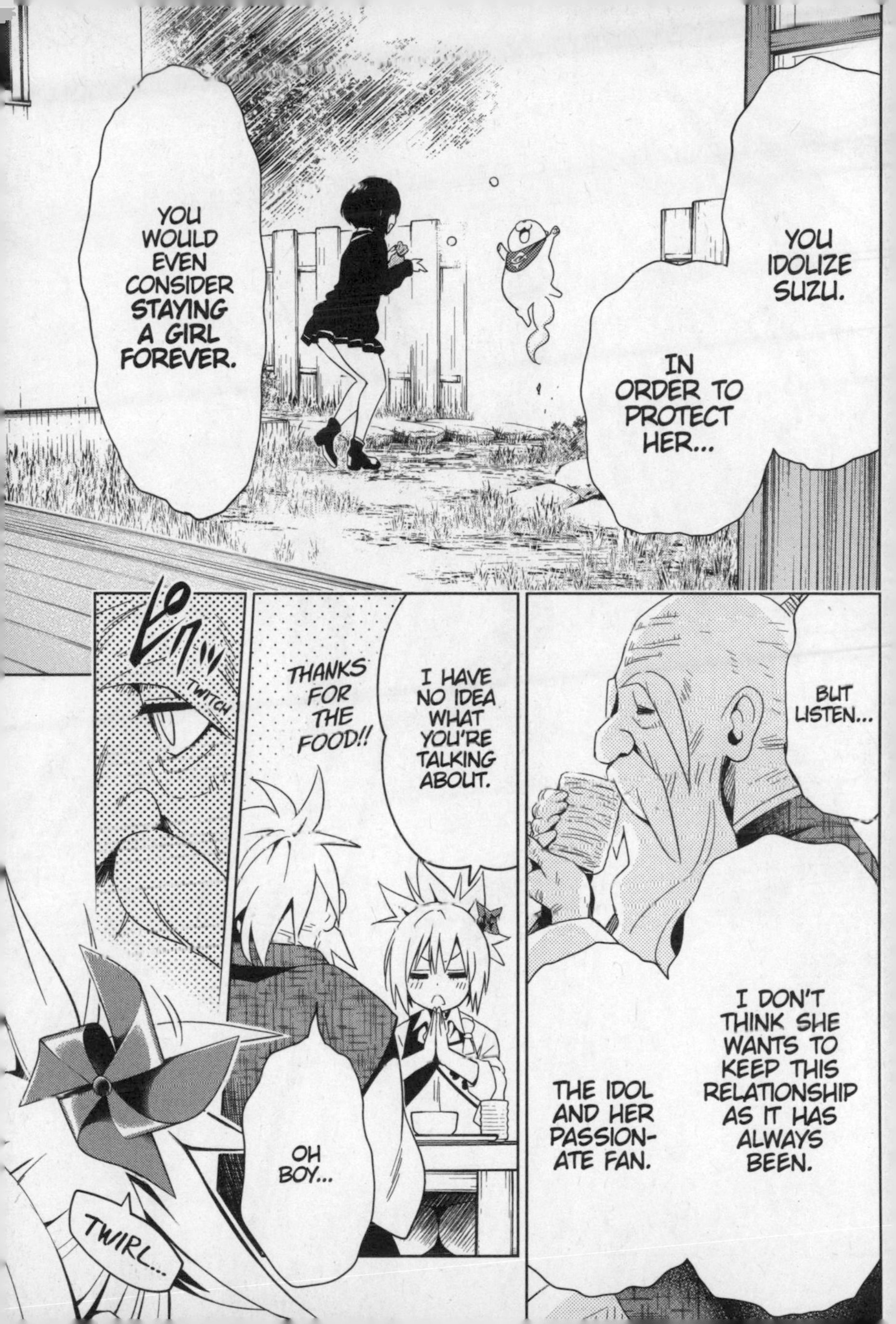
YOU IDOLIZE SUZU.
IN ORDER TO PROTECT HER...
YOU WOULD EVEN CONSIDER STAYING A GIRL FOREVER.
BUT LISTEN...
I DON'T THINK SHE WANTS TO KEEP THIS RELATIONSHIP AS IT HAS ALWAYS BEEN.
THE IDOL AND HER PASSION-ATE FAN.
I HAVE NO IDEA WHAT YOU'RE TALKING ABOUT.
THANKS FOR THE FOOD!!
OH BOY...
TWITCH
TWIRL...

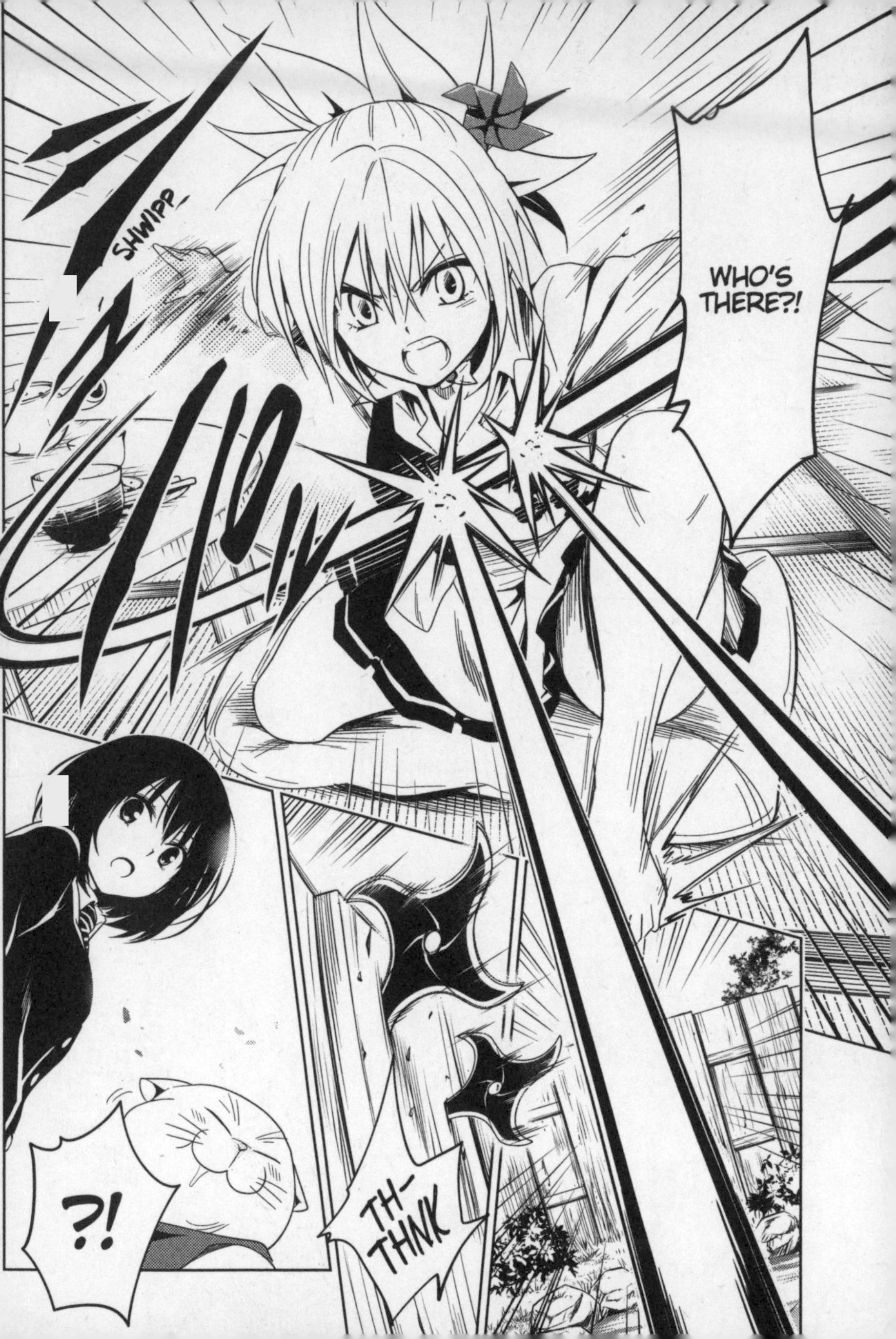
WHO'S THERE?!
SHWIPP
TH-THNK
?!

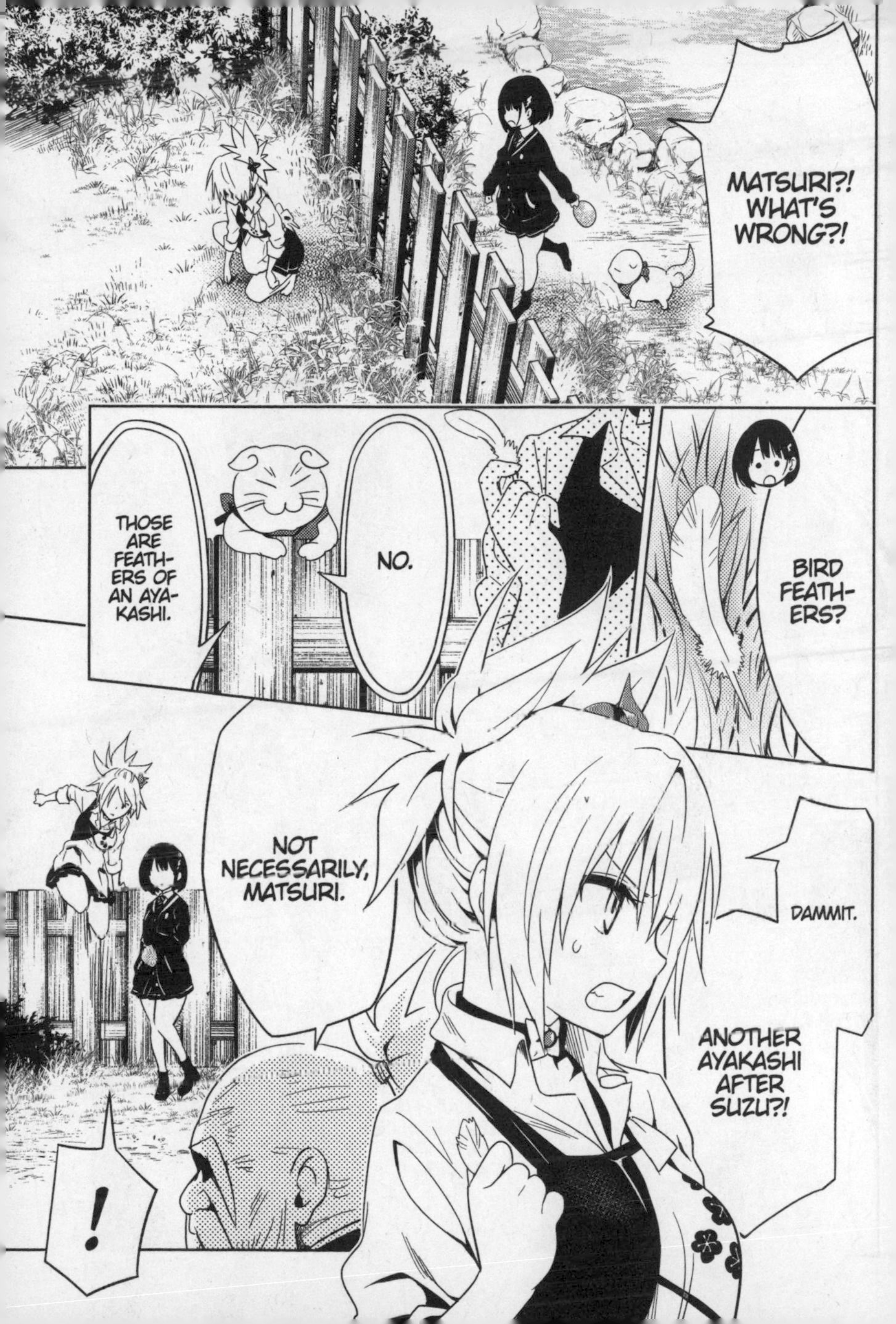
MATSURI?! WHAT'S WRONG?!
BIRD FEATHERS?
NO.
THOSE ARE FEATHERS OF AN AYAKASHI.
DAMMIT.
ANOTHER AYAKASHI AFTER SUZU?!
NOT NECESSARILY, MATSURI.
!

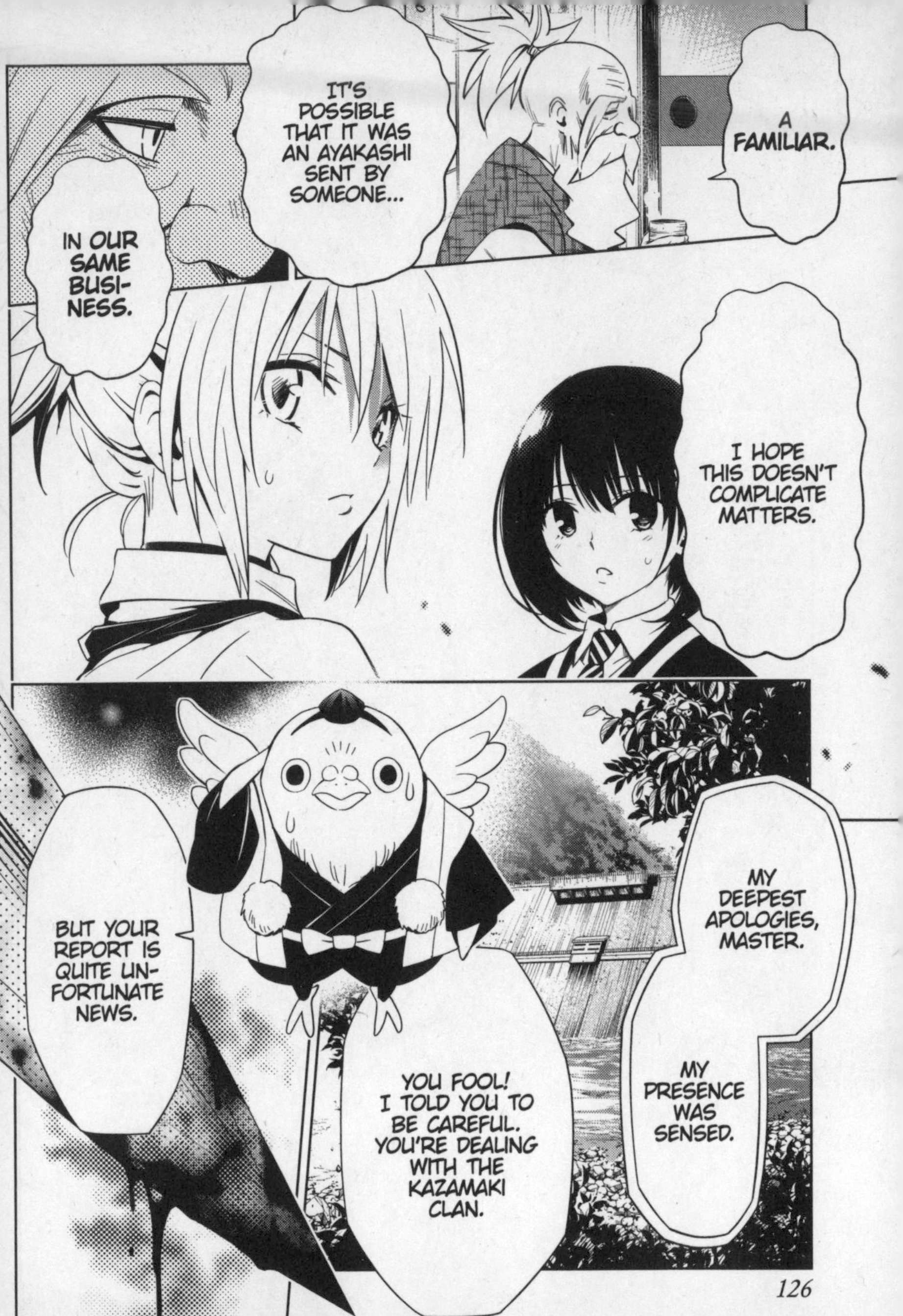
A FAMILIAR.
IT'S POSSIBLE THAT IT WAS AN AYAKASHI SENT BY SOMEONE...
IN OUR SAME BUSI-NESS.
I HOPE THIS DOESN'T COMPLICATE MATTERS.
MY DEEPEST APOLOGIES, MASTER.
MY PRESENCE WAS SENSED.
YOU FOOL! I TOLD YOU TO BE CAREFUL. YOU'RE DEALING WITH THE KAZAMAKI CLAN.
BUT YOUR REPORT IS QUITE UN-FORTUNATE NEWS.

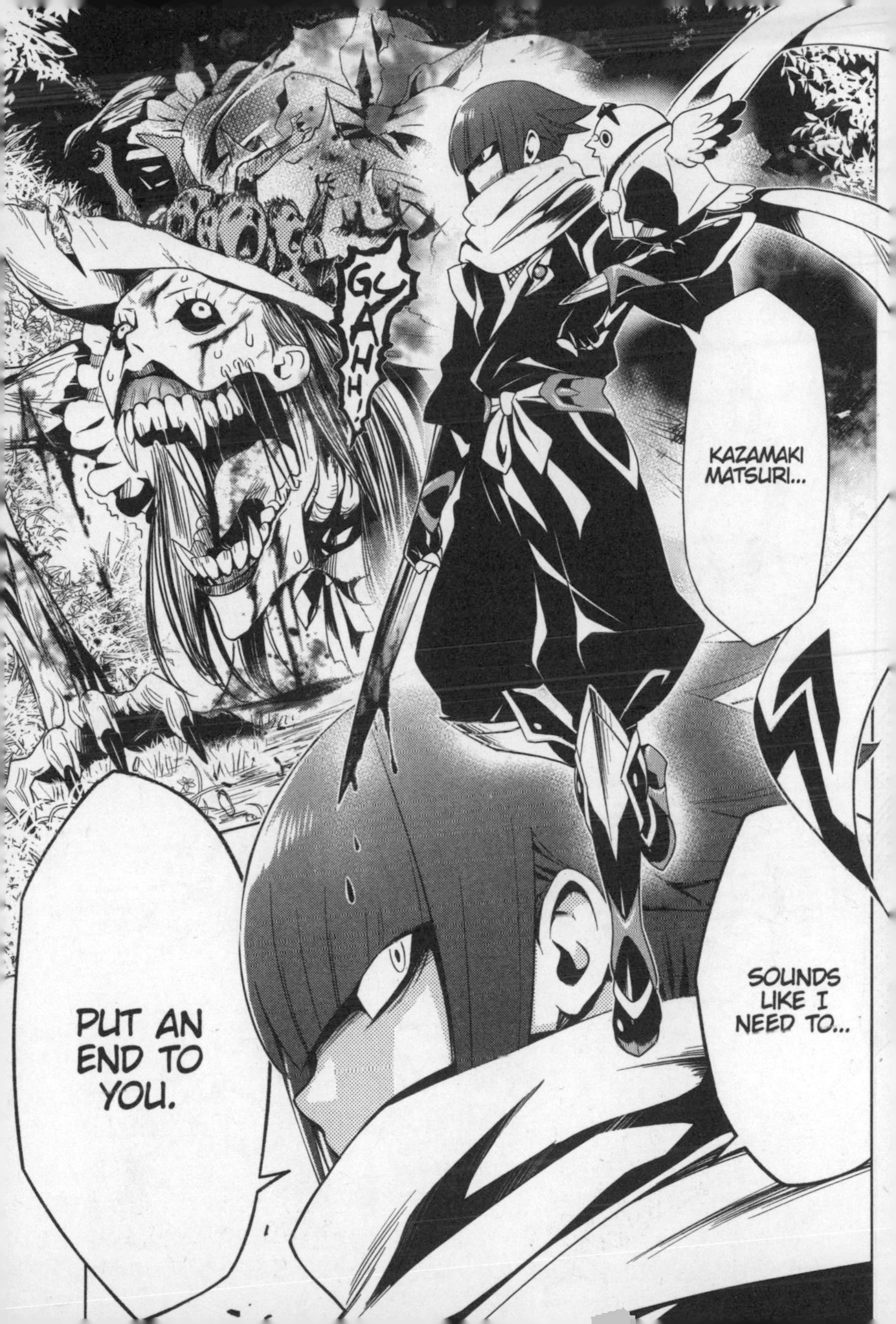
KAZAMAKI MATSURI...
GUAHH!
SOUNDS LIKE I NEED TO...
PUT AN END TO YOU.

## Genba, an Iyo (Human-Faced Spider)

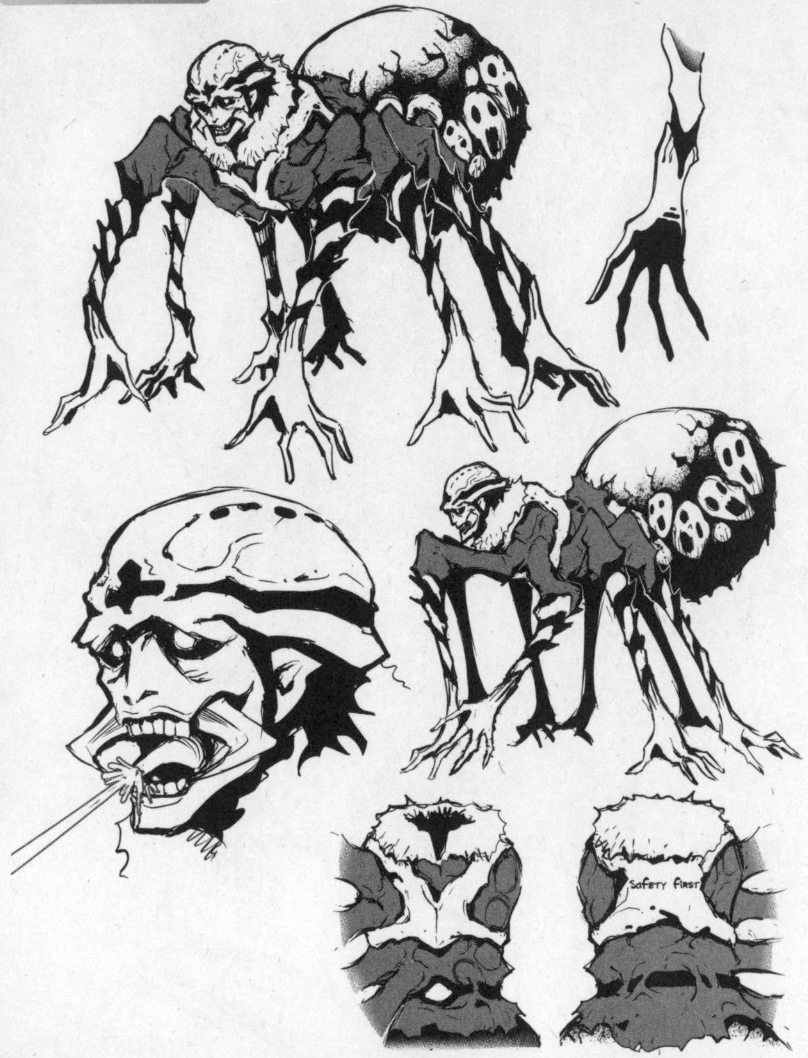
SAFETY FIRST

# Chapter 5 The Lightning-Fast Exorcist Ninja

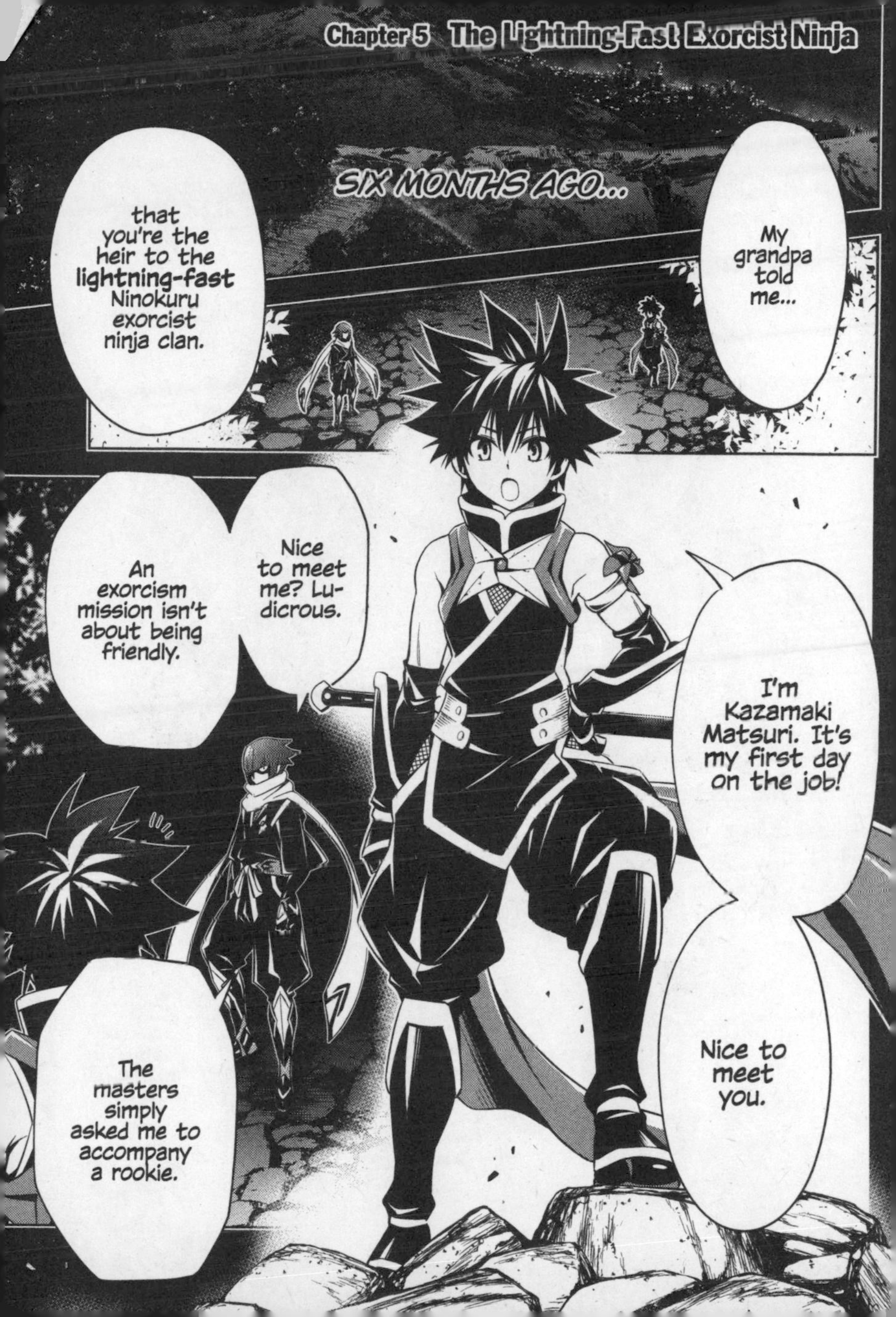

SIX MONTHS AGO...
My grandpa told me...
that you're the heir to the lightning-fast Ninokuru exorcist ninja clan.
I'm Kazamaki Matsuri. It's my first day on the job!
Nice to meet you.
Nice to meet me? Ludicrous.
An exorcism mission isn't about being friendly.
The masters simply asked me to accompany a rookie.

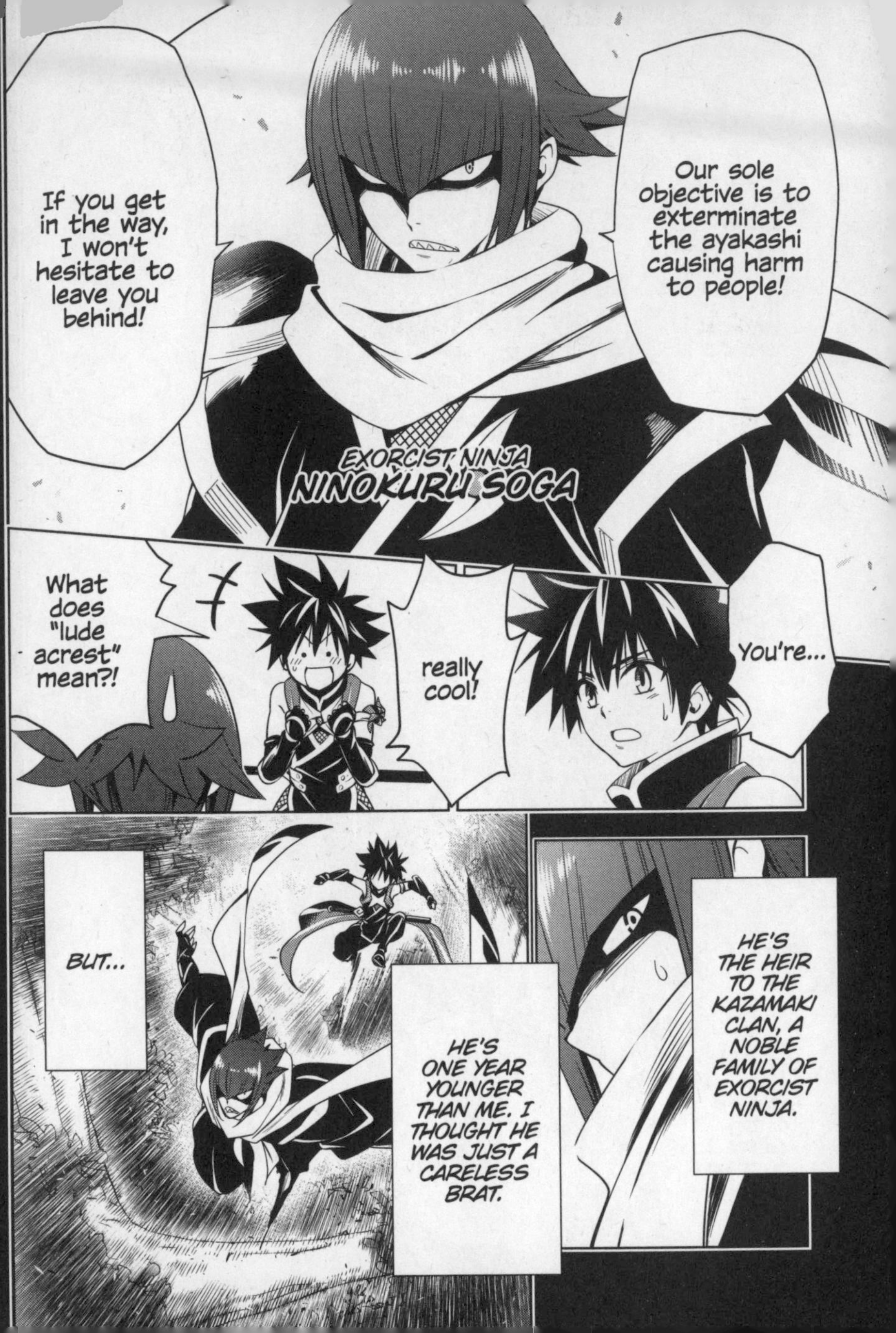
Our sole objective is to exterminate the ayakashi causing harm to people!
If you get in the way, I won't hesitate to leave you behind!
EXORCIST NINJA
NINOKURU SOGA
You're...
really cool!
What does "lude acrest" mean?!
HE'S THE HEIR TO THE KAZAMAKI CLAN, A NOBLE FAMILY OF EXORCIST NINJA.
HE'S ONE YEAR YOUNGER THAN ME. I THOUGHT HE WAS JUST A CARELESS BRAT.
BUT...

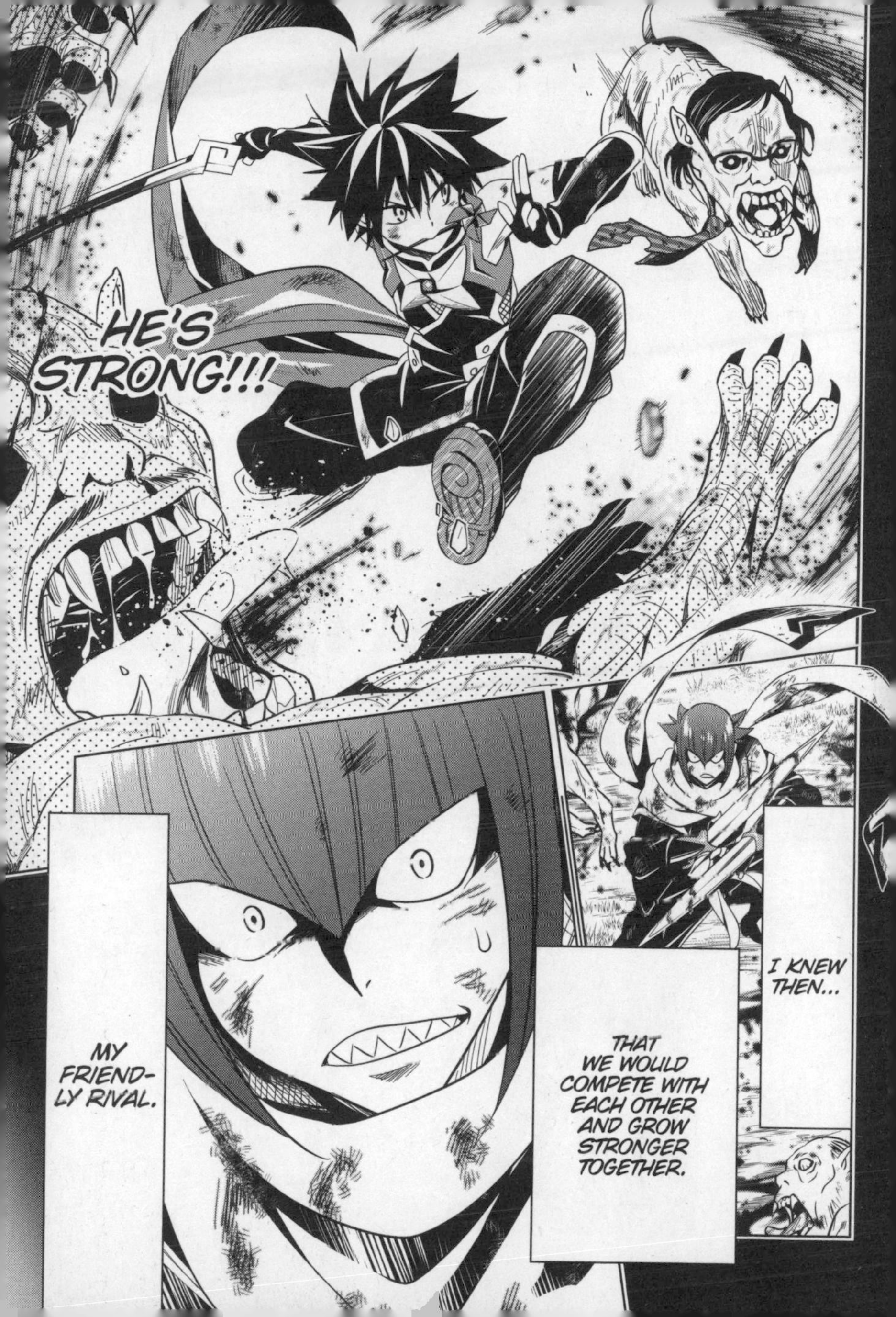
HE'S STRONG!!!
I KNEW THEN...
THAT WE WOULD COMPETE WITH EACH OTHER AND GROW STRONGER TOGETHER.
MY FRIEND-LY RIVAL.

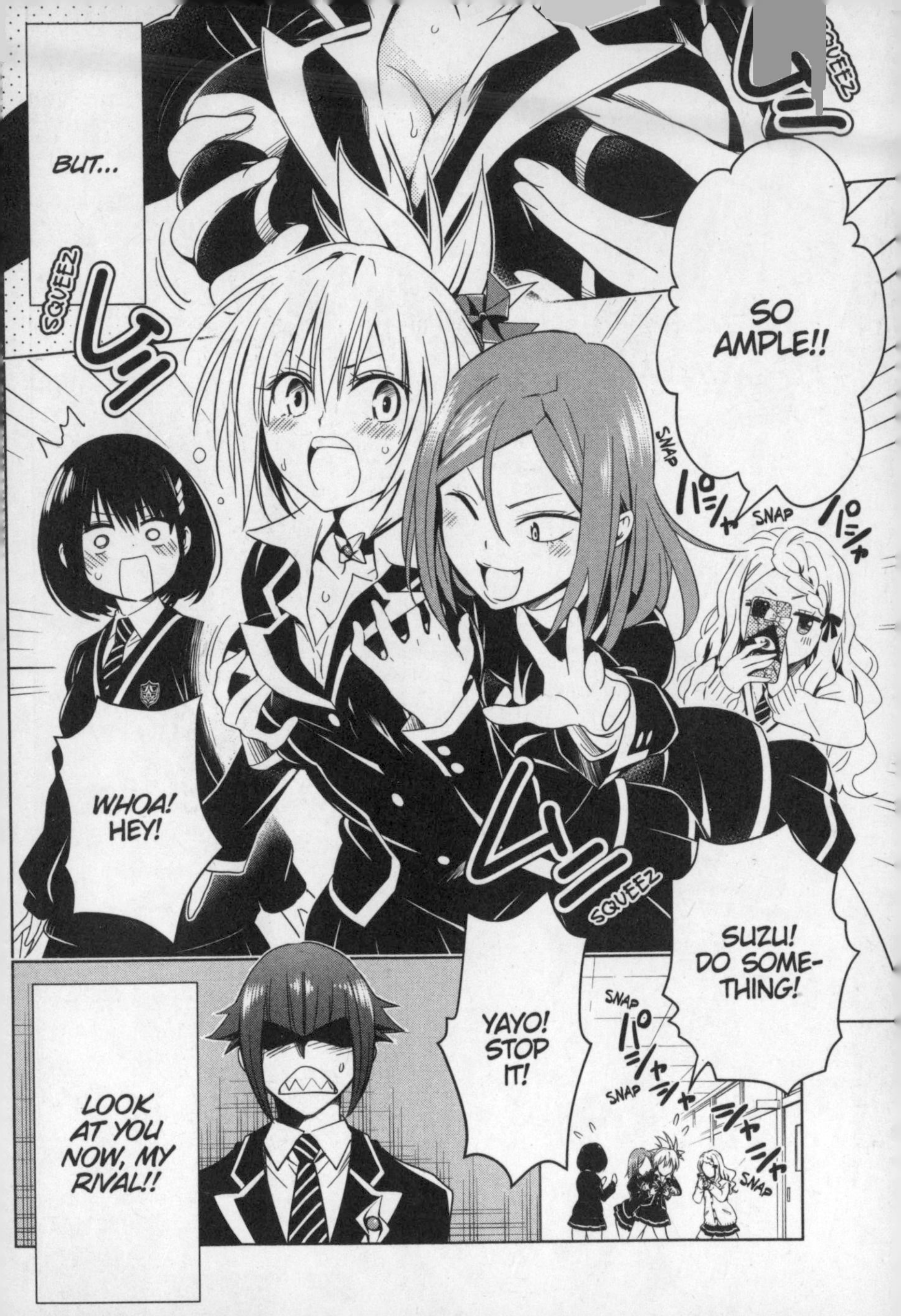
SQUEEZ
SO AMPLE!!
BUT...
SQUEEZ
SNAP
SNAP
WHOA! HEY!
SQUEEZ
SUZU! DO SOME-THING!
YAYO! STOP IT!
SNAP
SNAP
SNAP
LOOK AT YOU NOW, MY RIVAL!!

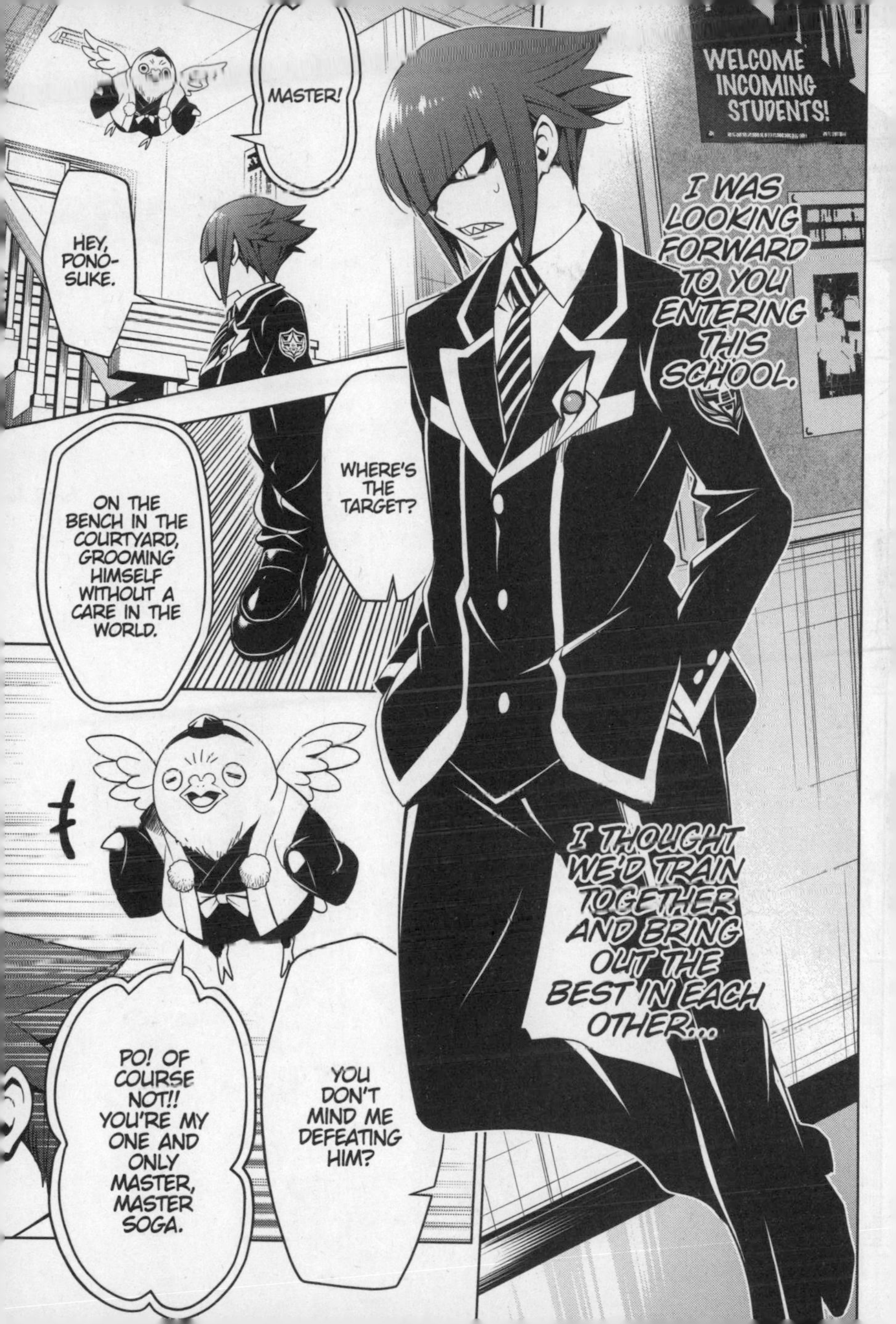
WELCOME INCOMING STUDENTS!
I WAS LOOKING FORWARD TO YOU ENTERING THIS SCHOOL.
I THOUGHT WE'D TRAIN TOGETHER AND BRING OUT THE BEST IN EACH OTHER...
MASTER!
HEY, PONO-SUKE.
WHERE'S THE TARGET?
ON THE BENCH IN THE COURTYARD, GROOMING HIMSELF WITHOUT A CARE IN THE WORLD.
YOU DON'T MIND ME DEFEATING HIM?
PO! OF COURSE NOT!! YOU'RE MY ONE AND ONLY MASTER, MASTER SOGA.

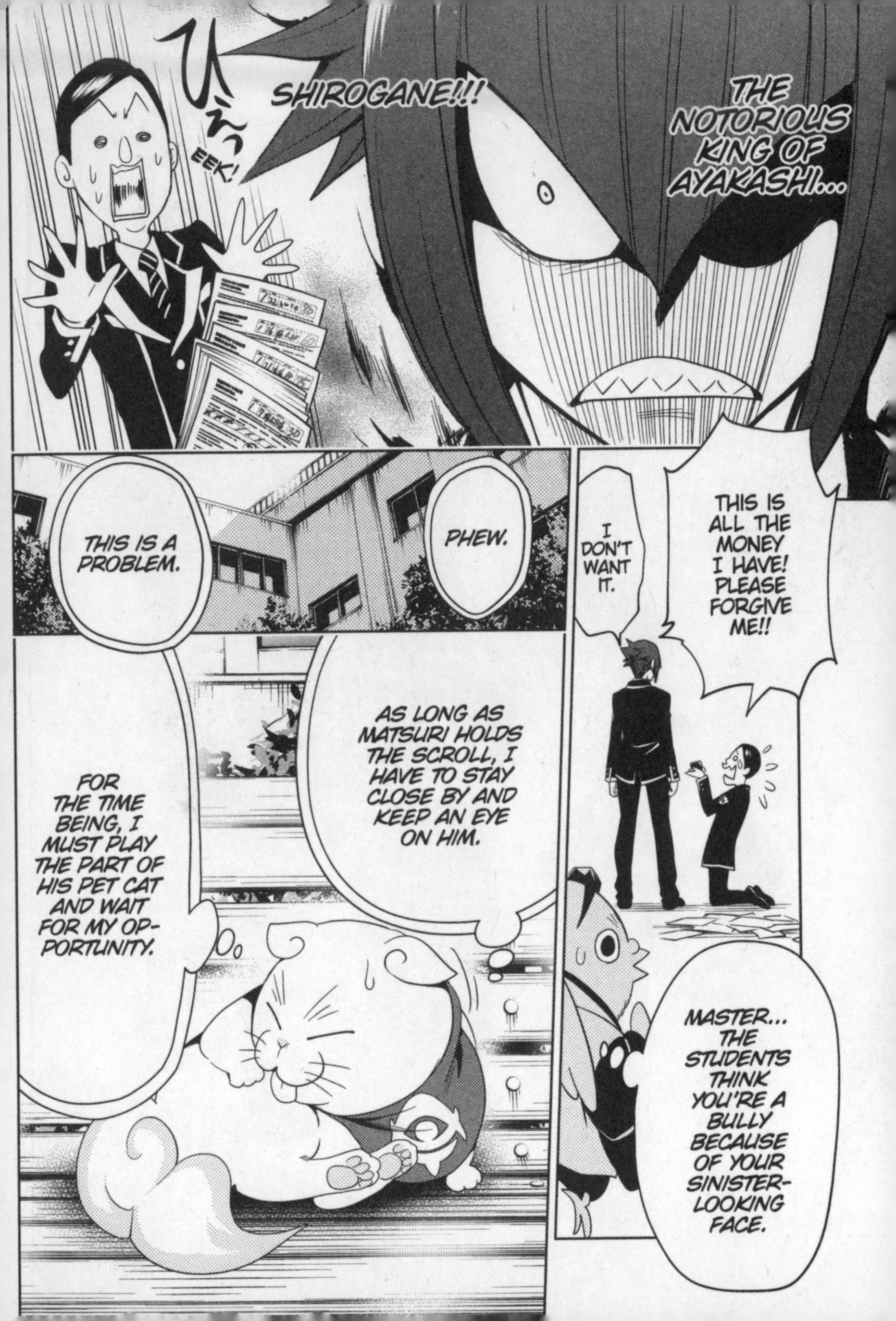
THE NOTORIOUS KING OF AYAKASHI...
SHIROGANE!!!
ひえっ
EEK!
THIS IS ALL THE MONEY I HAVE! PLEASE FORGIVE ME!!
I DON'T WANT IT.
MASTER... THE STUDENTS THINK YOU'RE A BULLY BECAUSE OF YOUR SINISTER-LOOKING FACE.
PHEW.
THIS IS A PROBLEM.
AS LONG AS MATSURI HOLDS THE SCROLL, I HAVE TO STAY CLOSE BY AND KEEP AN EYE ON HIM.
FOR THE TIME BEING, I MUST PLAY THE PART OF HIS PET CAT AND WAIT FOR MY OP-PORTUNITY.

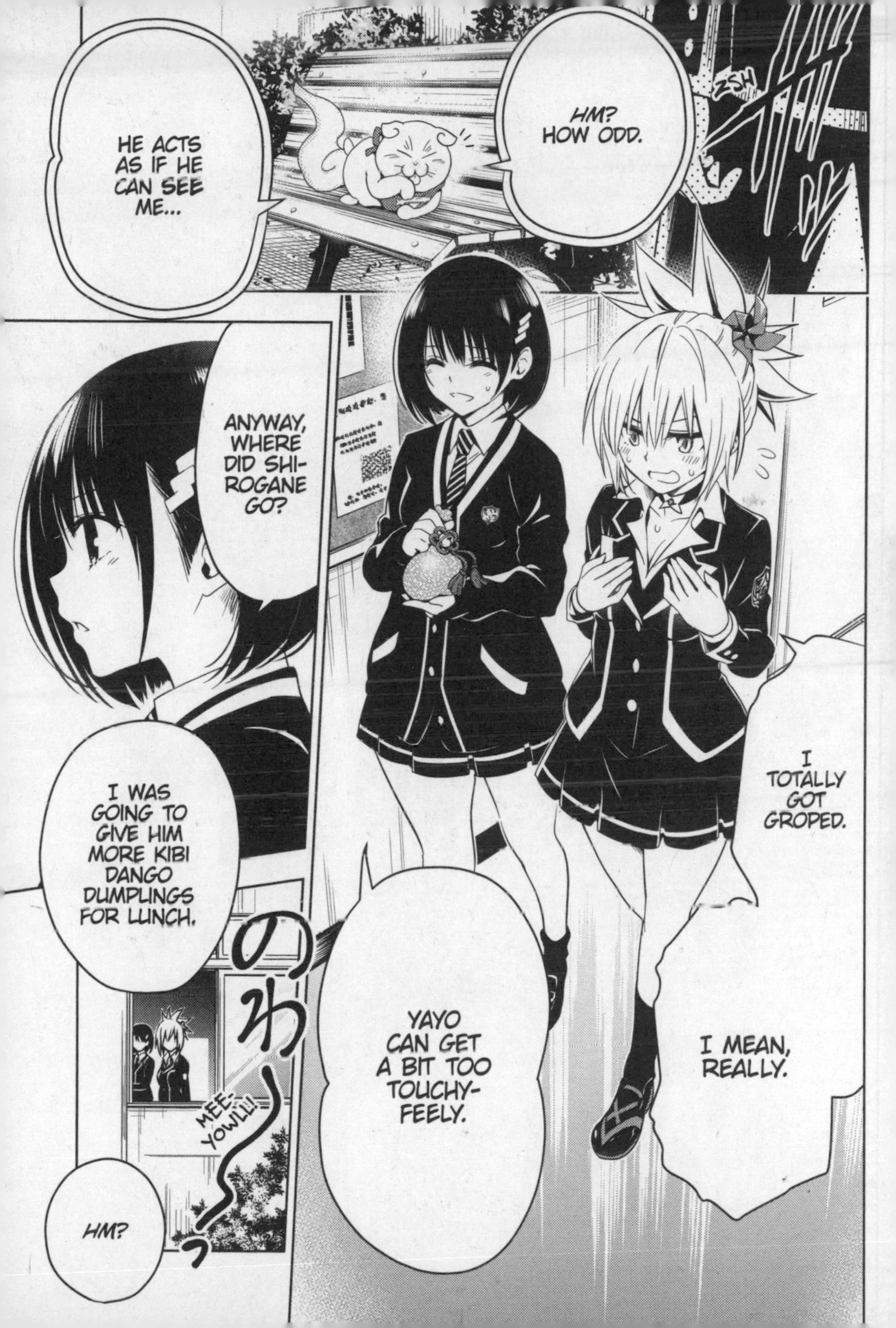
ZSH
HM? HOW ODD.
HE ACTS AS IF HE CAN SEE ME...
I TOTALLY GOT GROPED.
I MEAN, REALLY.
YAYO CAN GET A BIT TOO TOUCHY-FEELY.
ANYWAY, WHERE DID SHIROGANE GO?
I WAS GOING TO GIVE HIM MORE KIBI DANGO DUMPLINGS FOR LUNCH.
のわ～っ
MEE-YOWL!!
HM?

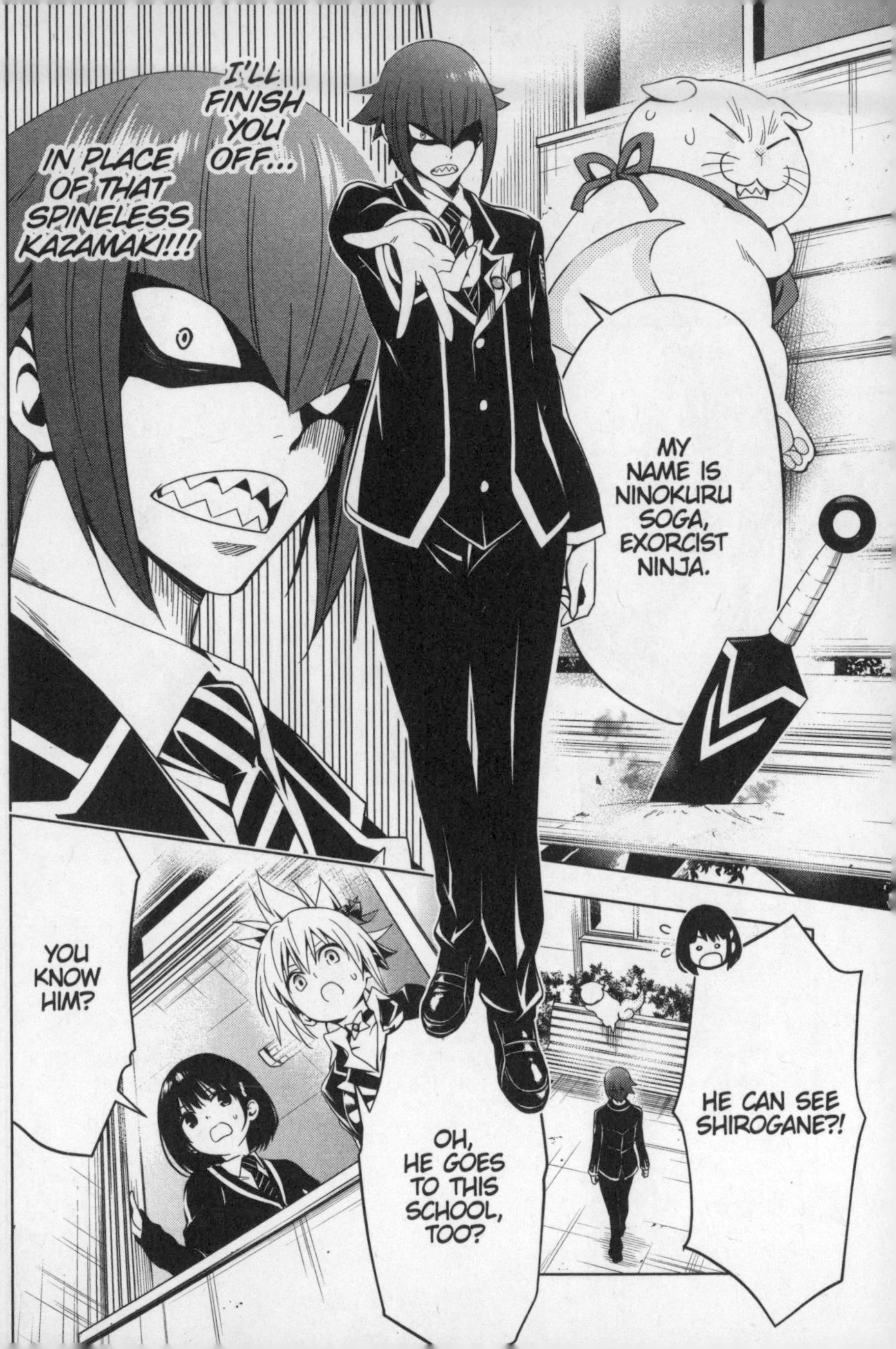
MY NAME IS NINOKURU SOGA, EXORCIST NINJA.
I'LL FINISH YOU OFF...
IN PLACE OF THAT SPINELESS KAZAMAKI!!!
HE CAN SEE SHIROGANE?!
YOU KNOW HIM?
OH, HE GOES TO THIS SCHOOL, TOO?

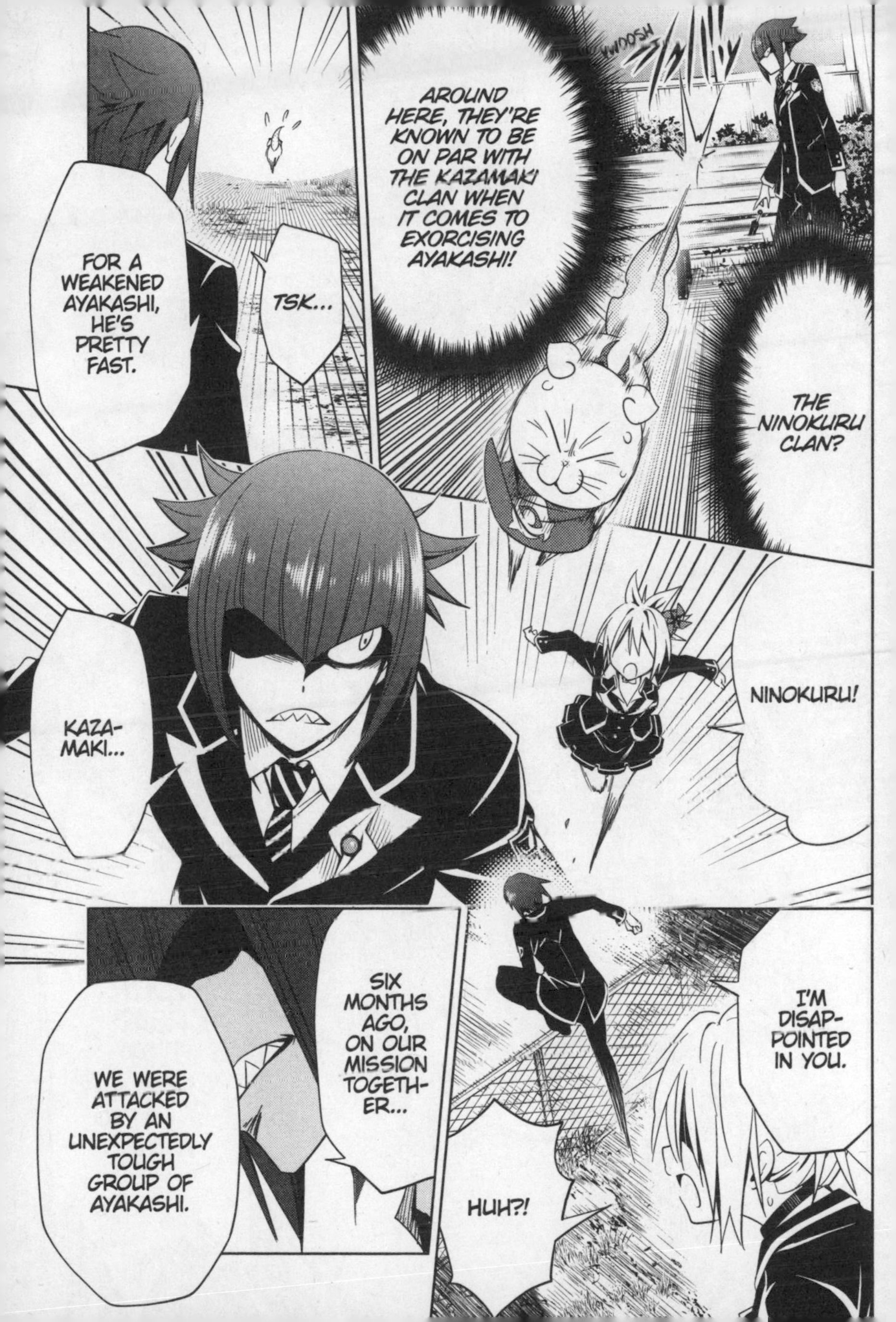
WHOOSH
THE NINOKURU CLAN?
AROUND HERE, THEY'RE KNOWN TO BE ON PAR WITH THE KAZAMAKI CLAN WHEN IT COMES TO EXORCISING AYAKASHI!
TSK...
FOR A WEAKENED AYAKASHI, HE'S PRETTY FAST.
NINOKURU!
KAZA-MAKI...
I'M DISAP-POINTED IN YOU.
HUH?!
SIX MONTHS AGO, ON OUR MISSION TOGETH-ER...
WE WERE ATTACKED BY AN UNEXPECTEDLY TOUGH GROUP OF AYAKASHI.

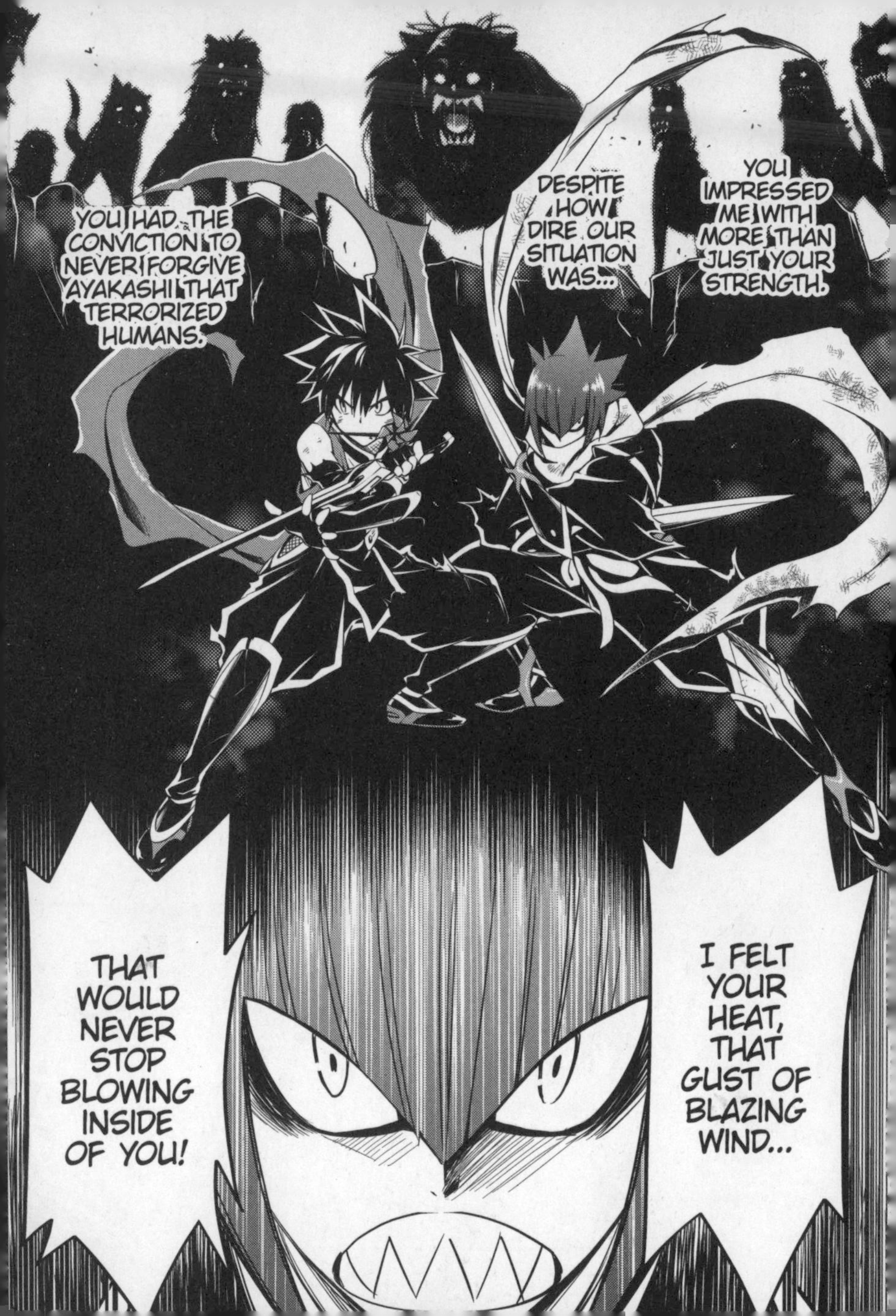
YOU IMPRESSED ME WITH MORE THAN JUST YOUR STRENGTH.
DESPITE HOW DIRE OUR SITUATION WAS...
YOU HAD THE CONVICTION TO NEVER FORGIVE AYAKASHI THAT TERRORIZED HUMANS.
I FELT YOUR HEAT, THAT GUST OF BLAZING WIND...
THAT WOULD NEVER STOP BLOWING INSIDE OF YOU!

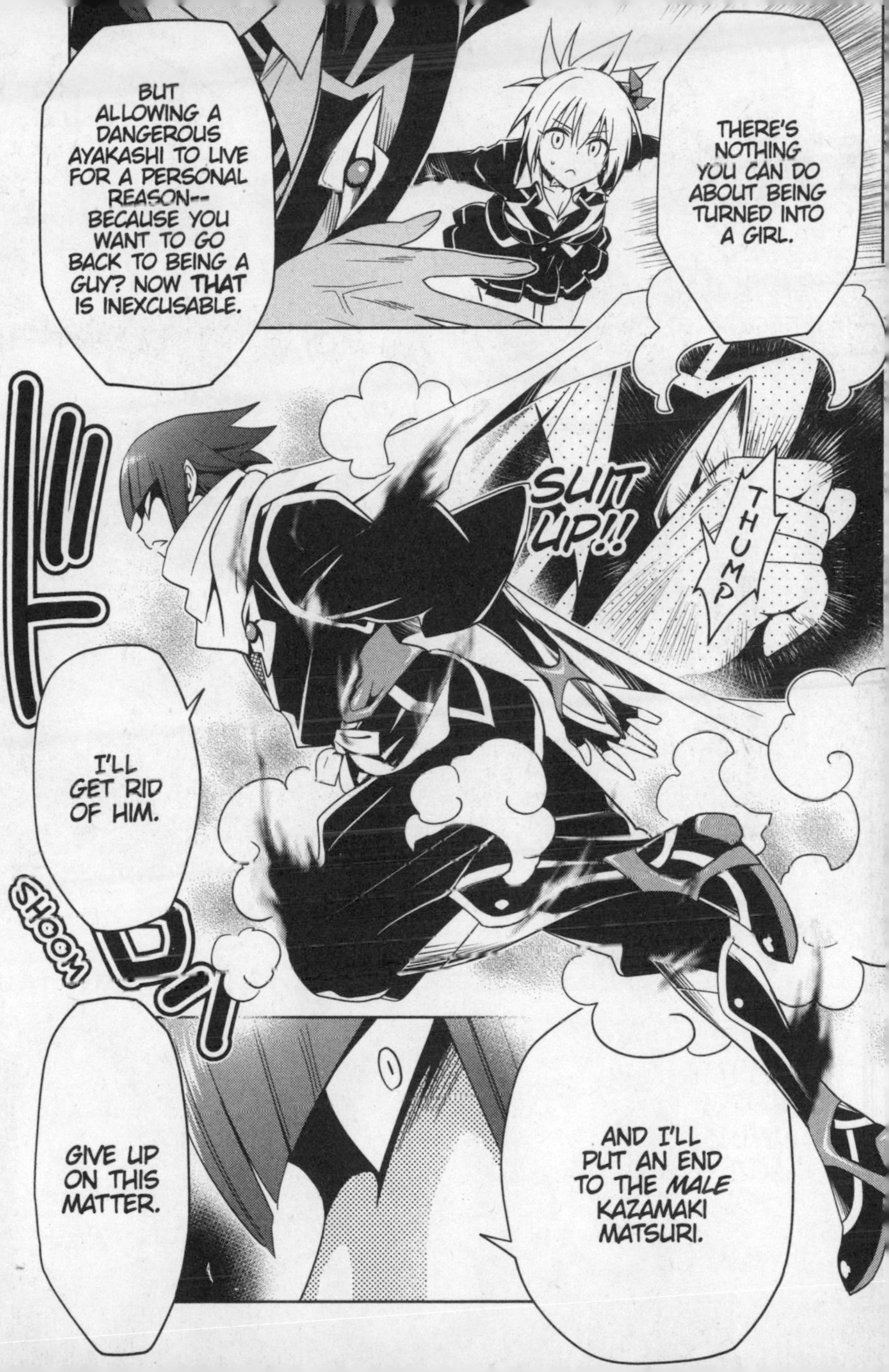
THERE'S NOTHING YOU CAN DO ABOUT BEING TURNED INTO A GIRL.
BUT ALLOWING A DANGEROUS AYAKASHI TO LIVE FOR A PERSONAL REASON--BECAUSE YOU WANT TO GO BACK TO BEING A GUY? NOW THAT IS INEXCUSABLE.
THUMP
SUIT UP!!
I'LL GET RID OF HIM.
SHOOM
AND I'LL PUT AN END TO THE *MALE* KAZAMAKI MATSURI.
GIVE UP ON THIS MATTER.

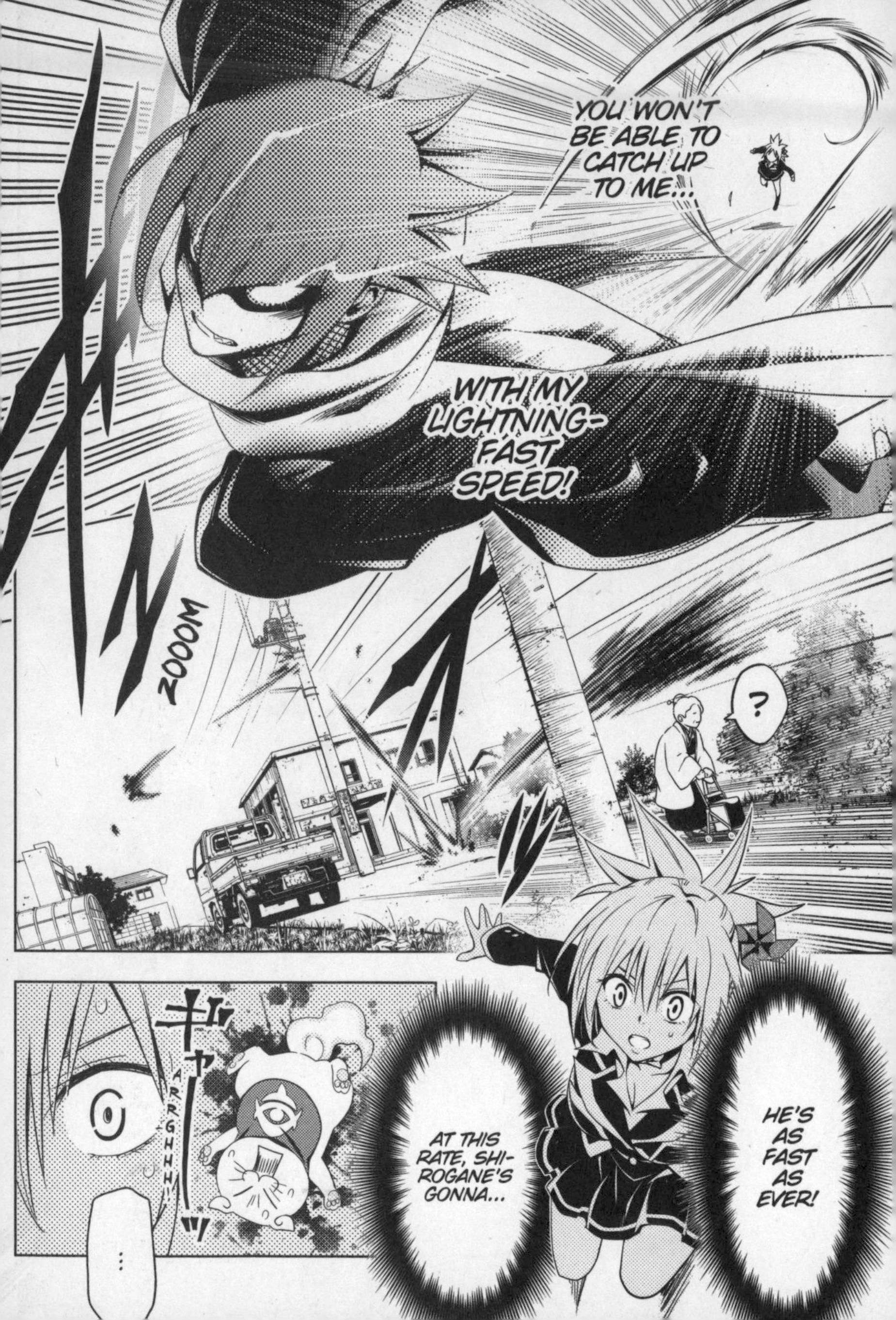
YOU WON'T BE ABLE TO CATCH UP TO ME...
WITH MY LIGHTNING-FAST SPEED!
ZOOOM
?
HE'S AS FAST AS EVER!
AT THIS RATE, SHIROGANE'S GONNA...
ARRGHHH!
...

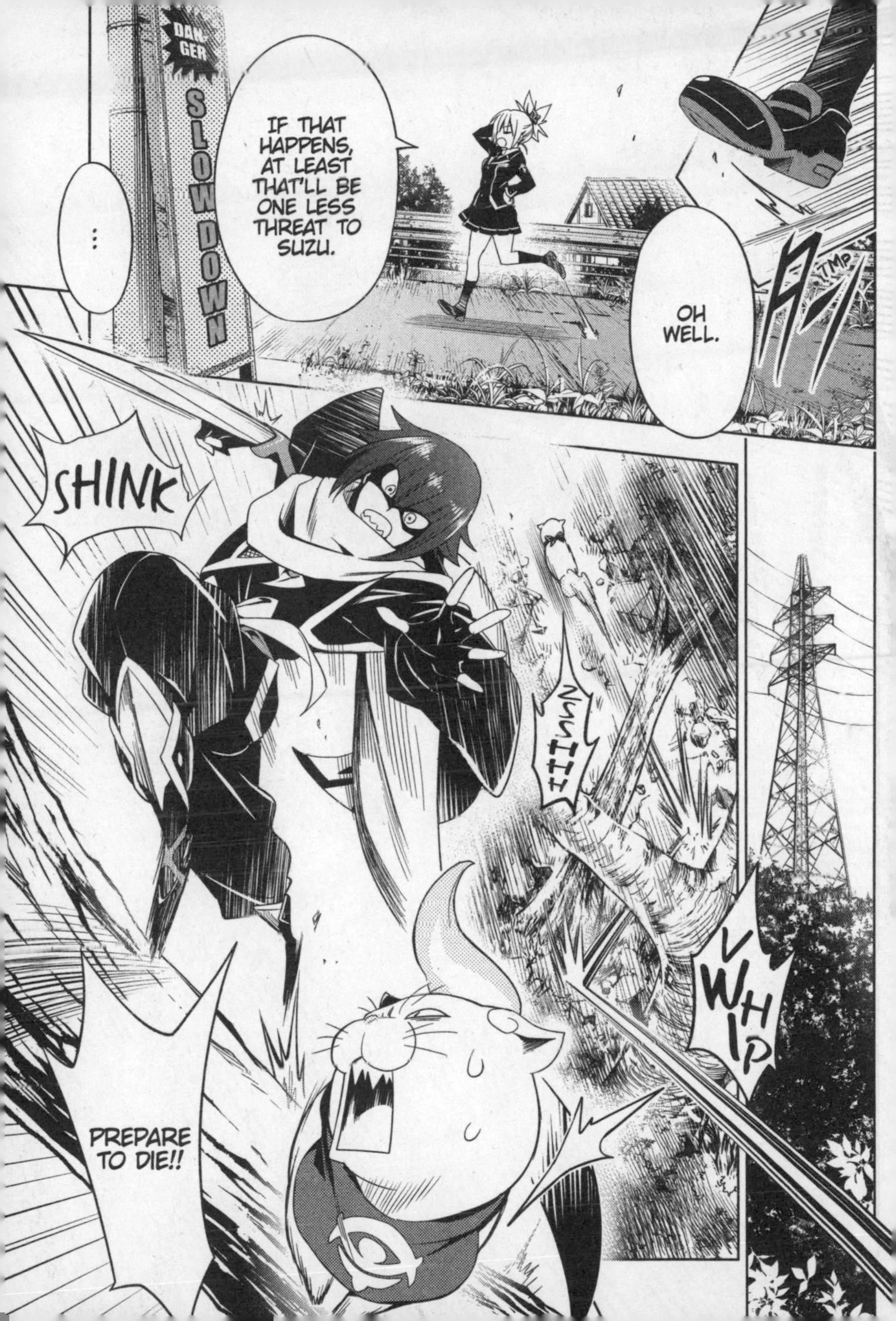
TMP
OH WELL.
IF THAT HAPPENS, AT LEAST THAT'LL BE ONE LESS THREAT TO SUZU.
DANGER
SLOW DOWN
…
WHIP
SSHHHH
SHINK
PREPARE TO DIE!!

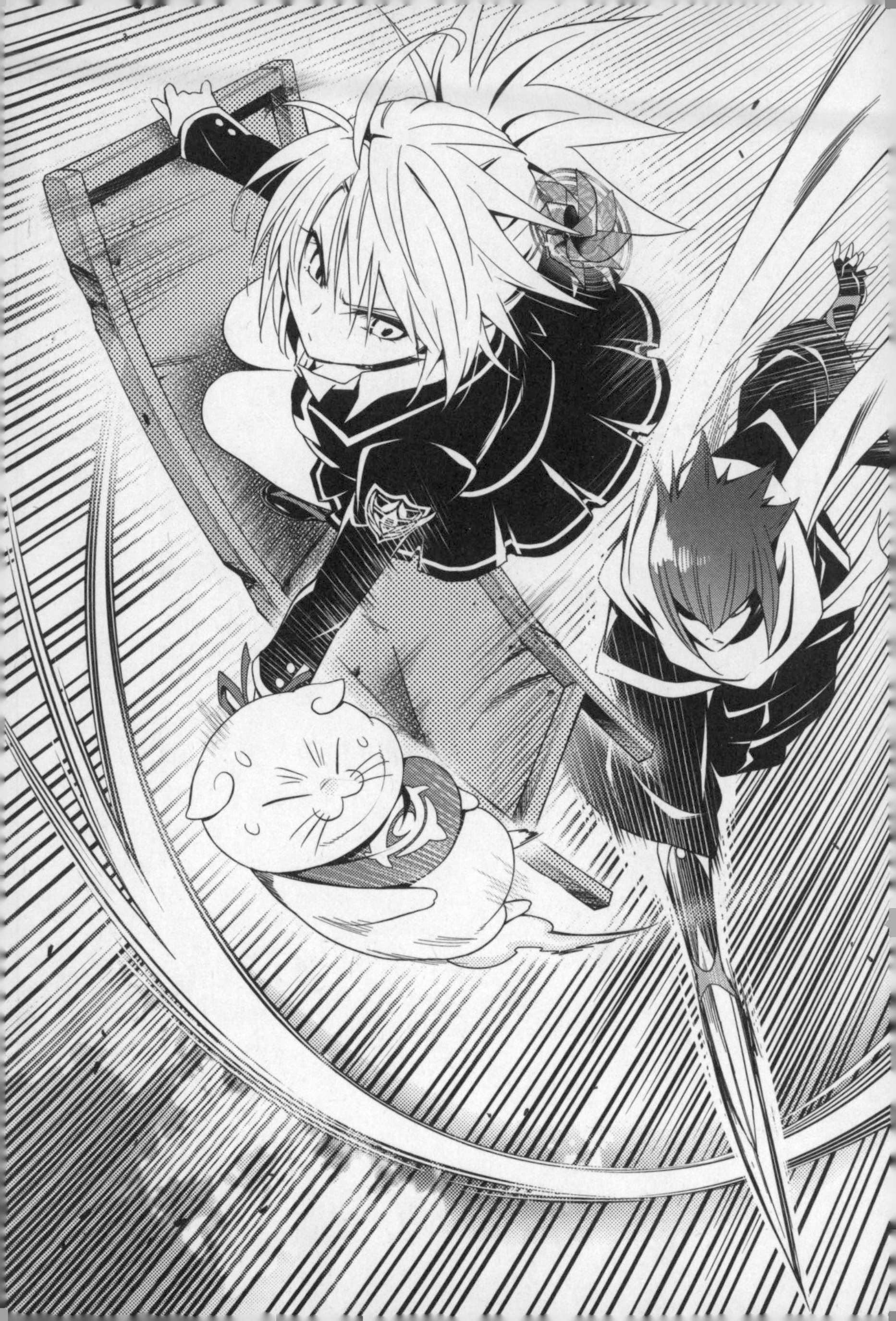

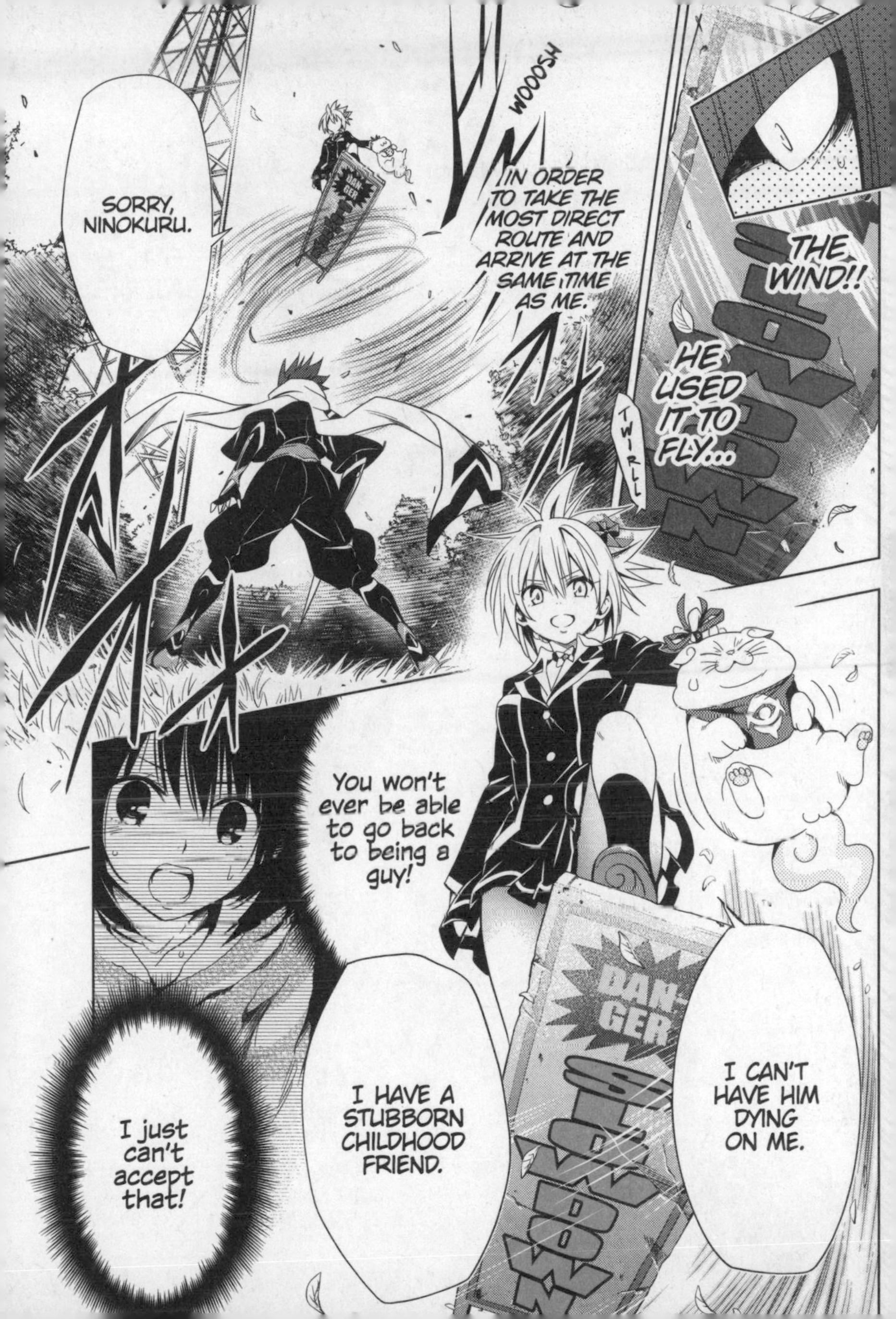
THE WIND!!
SLOW DOWN
HE USED IT TO FLY...
IN ORDER TO TAKE THE MOST DIRECT ROUTE AND ARRIVE AT THE SAME TIME AS ME.
WOOOSH
DAN-GER
TWIRL
SORRY, NINOKURU.
I CAN'T HAVE HIM DYING ON ME.
DAN-GER
SLOW DOWN
I HAVE A STUBBORN CHILDHOOD FRIEND.
You won't ever be able to go back to being a guy!
I just can't accept that!

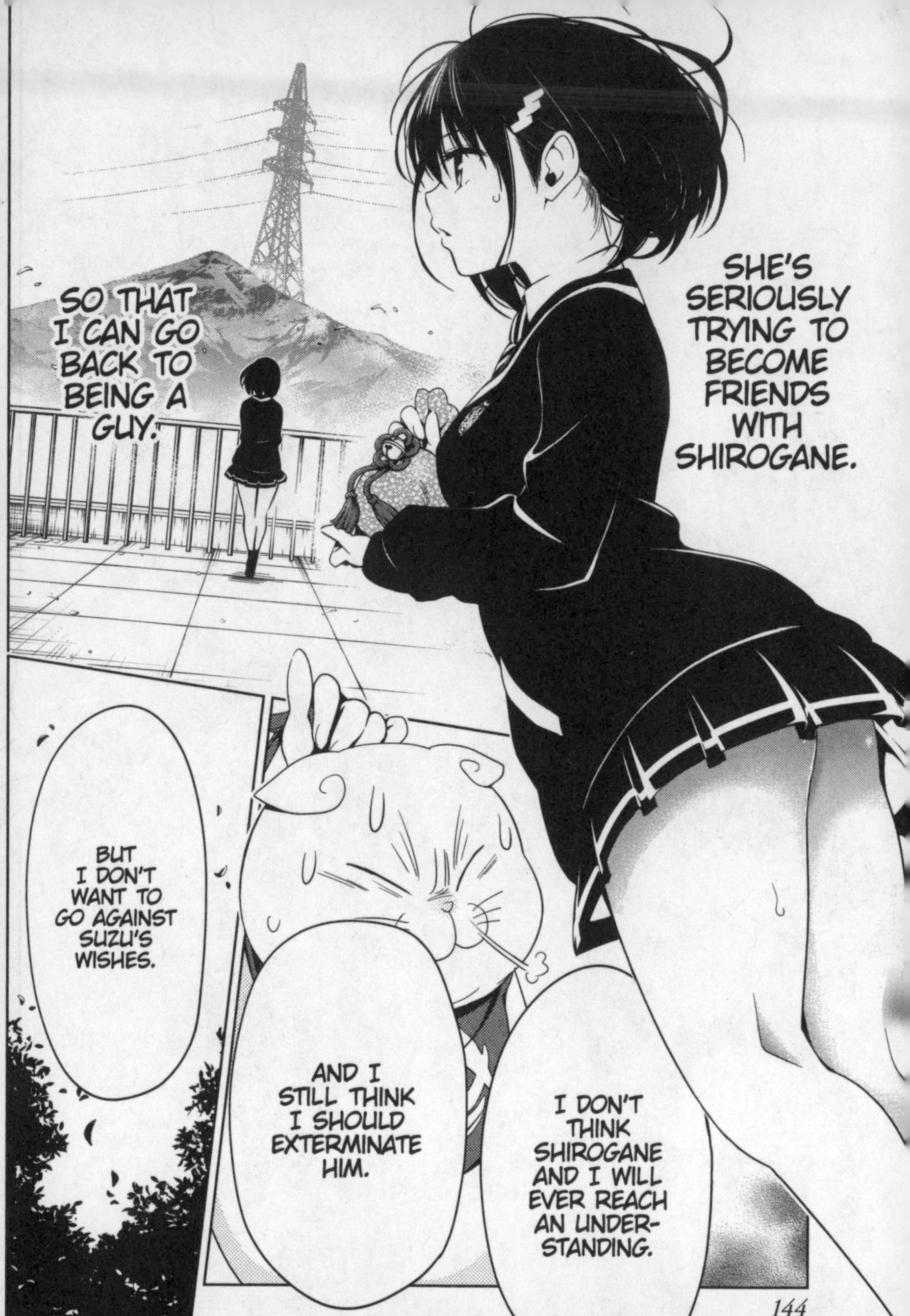
SHE'S SERIOUSLY TRYING TO BECOME FRIENDS WITH SHIROGANE.
SO THAT I CAN GO BACK TO BEING A GUY.
I DON'T THINK SHIROGANE AND I WILL EVER REACH AN UNDER-STANDING.
AND I STILL THINK I SHOULD EXTERMINATE HIM.
BUT I DON'T WANT TO GO AGAINST SUZU'S WISHES.

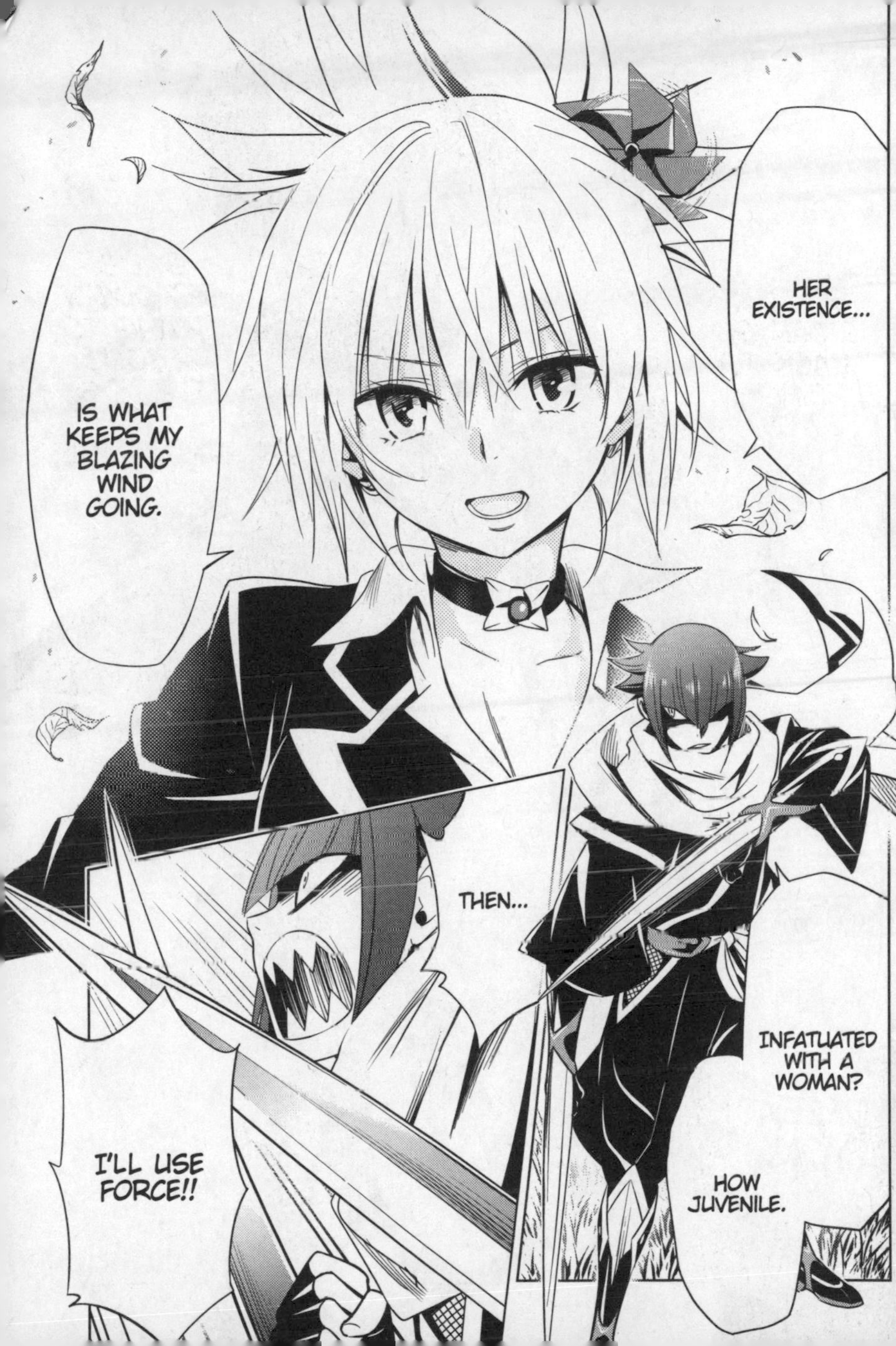
HER EXISTENCE...
IS WHAT KEEPS MY BLAZING WIND GOING.
INFATUATED WITH A WOMAN?
HOW JUVENILE.
THEN...
I'LL USE FORCE!!

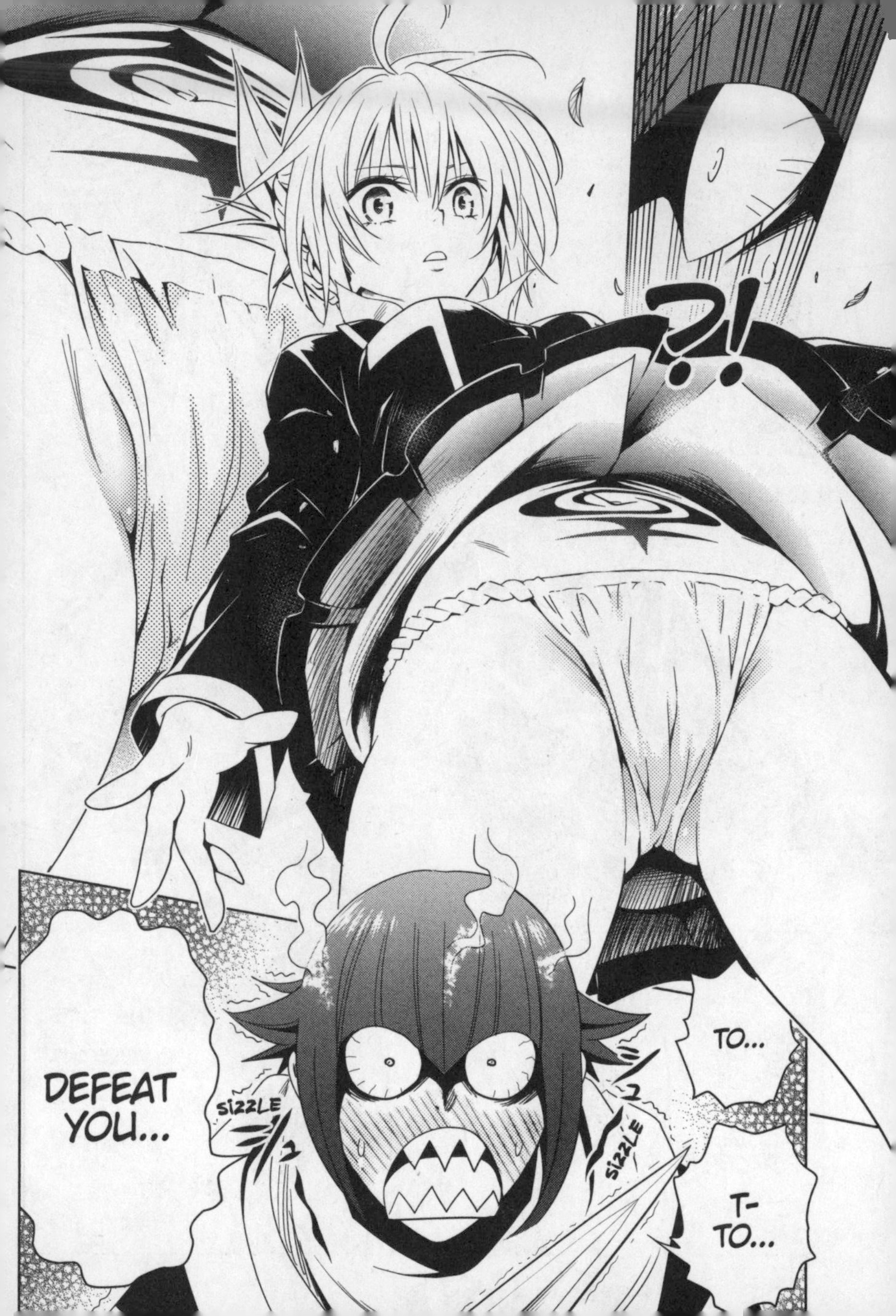
?!
TO...
T- TO...
SIZZLE
SIZZLE
DEFEAT YOU...

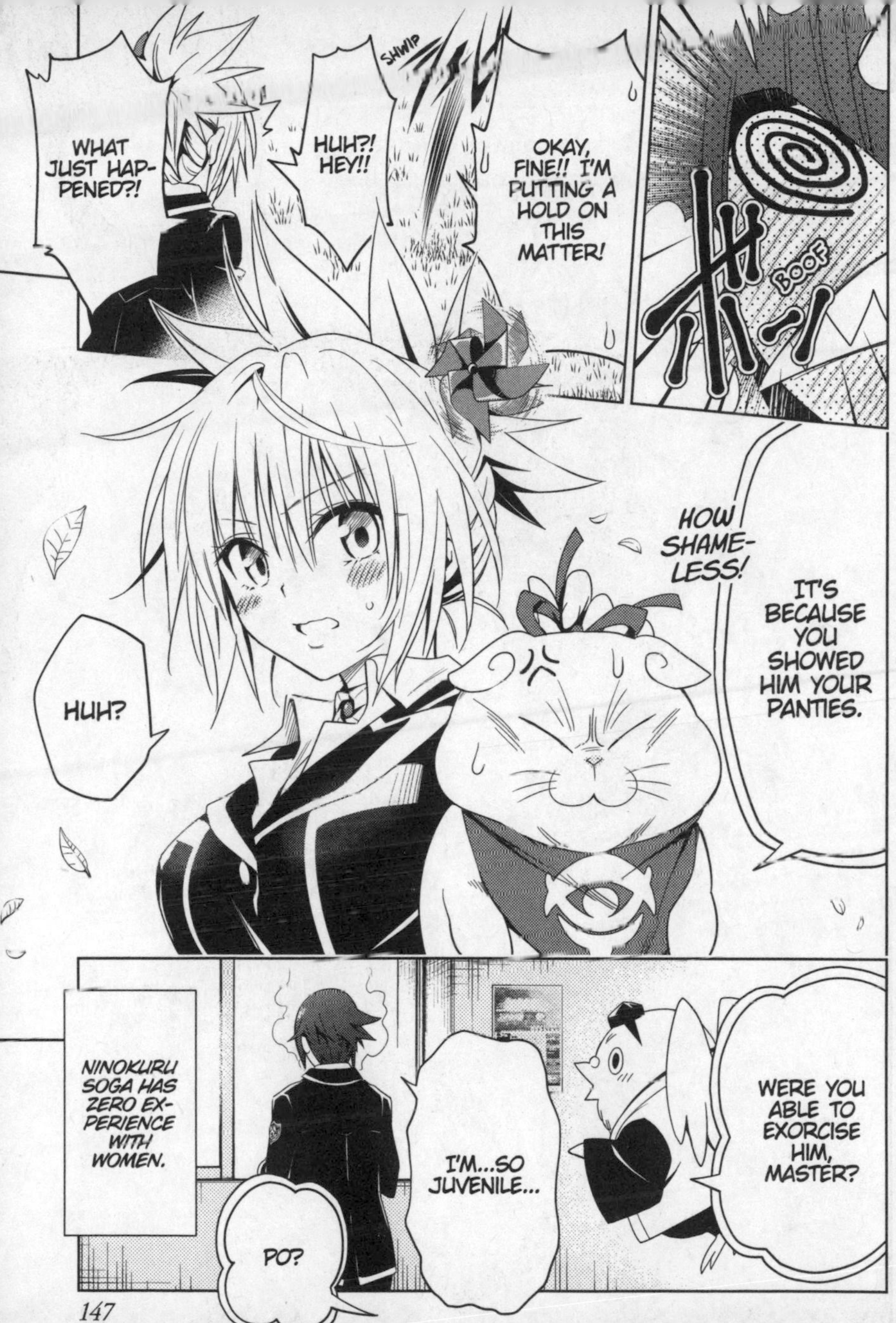
BOOF
OKAY, FINE!! I'M PUTTING A HOLD ON THIS MATTER!
SHWIP
HUH?! HEY!!
WHAT JUST HAP-PENED?!
HOW SHAME-LESS!
IT'S BECAUSE YOU SHOWED HIM YOUR PANTIES.
HUH?
WERE YOU ABLE TO EXORCISE HIM, MASTER?
I'M...SO JUVENILE...
PO?
NINOKURU SOGA HAS ZERO EX-PERIENCE WITH WOMEN.

# Tadare, an Iron-Armed Monk

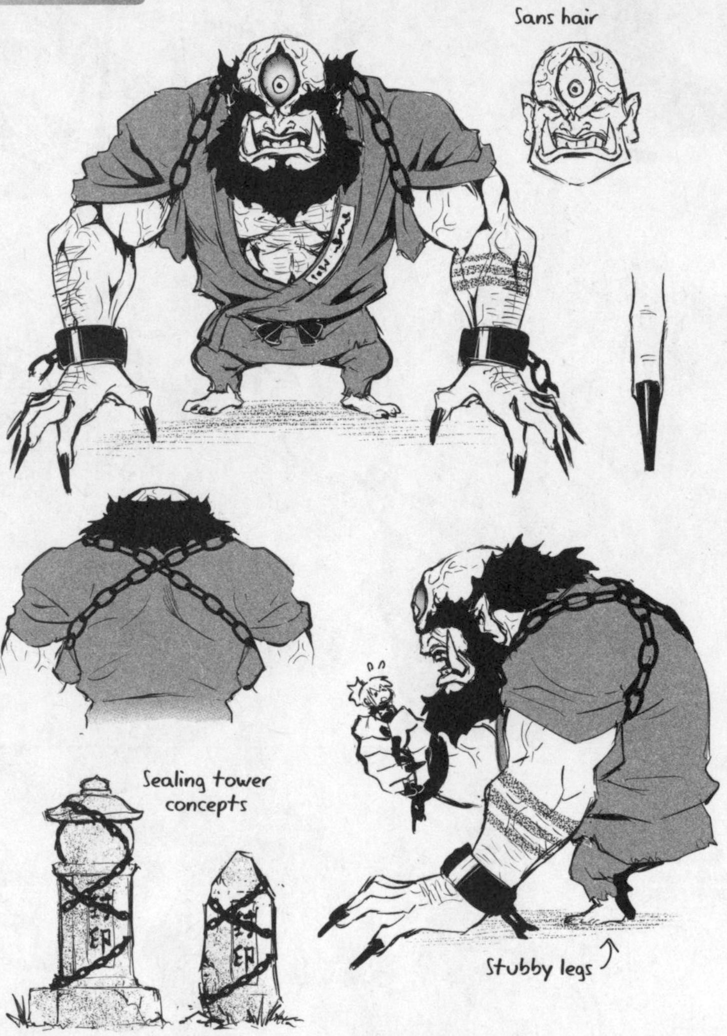
Sans hair
Sealing tower concepts
Stubby legs

## Chapter 6

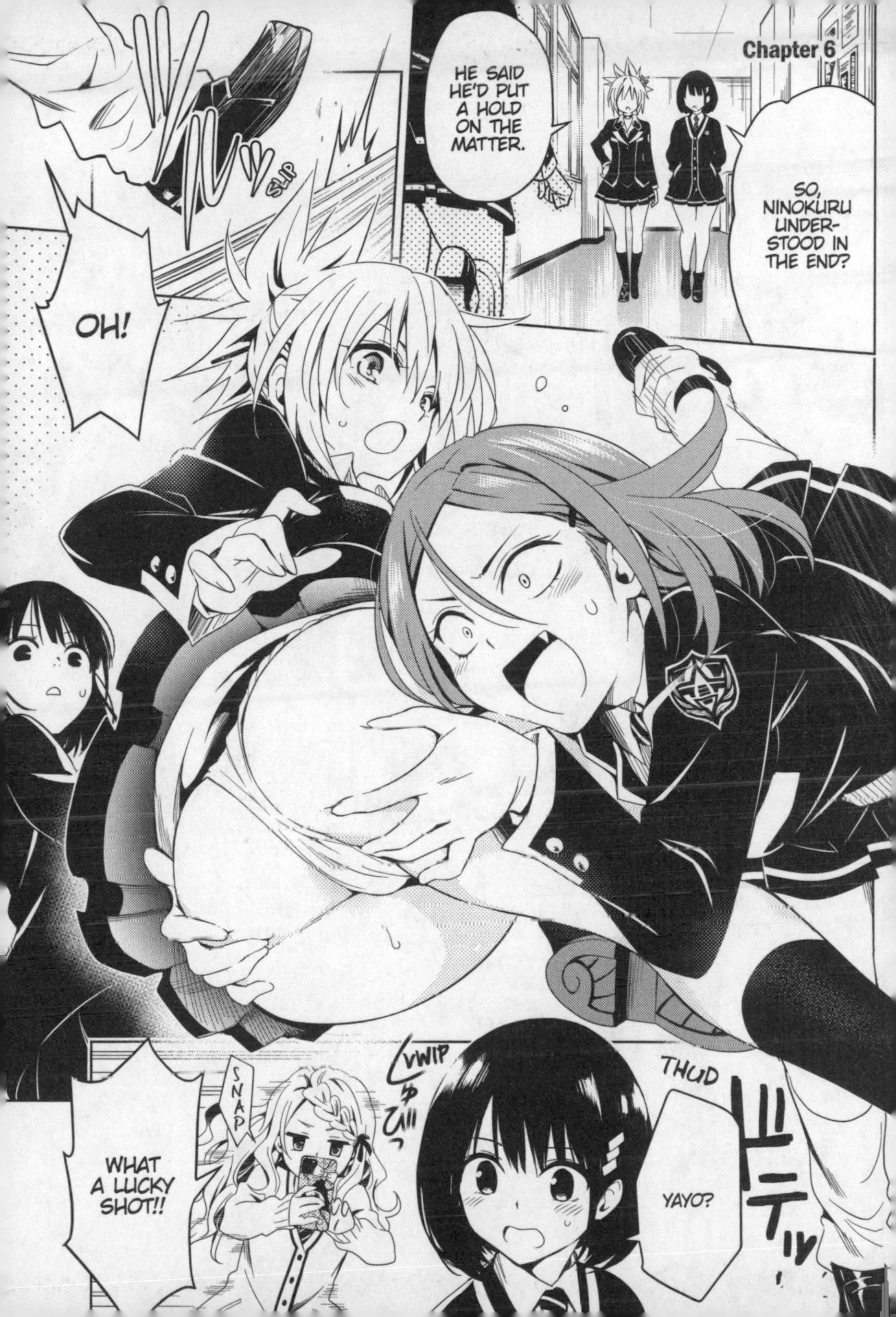
SO, NINOKURU UNDER-STOOD IN THE END?
HE SAID HE'D PUT A HOLD ON THE MATTER.
SLIP
OH!
THUD
YAYO?
VWIP
SNAP
WHAT A LUCKY SHOT!!

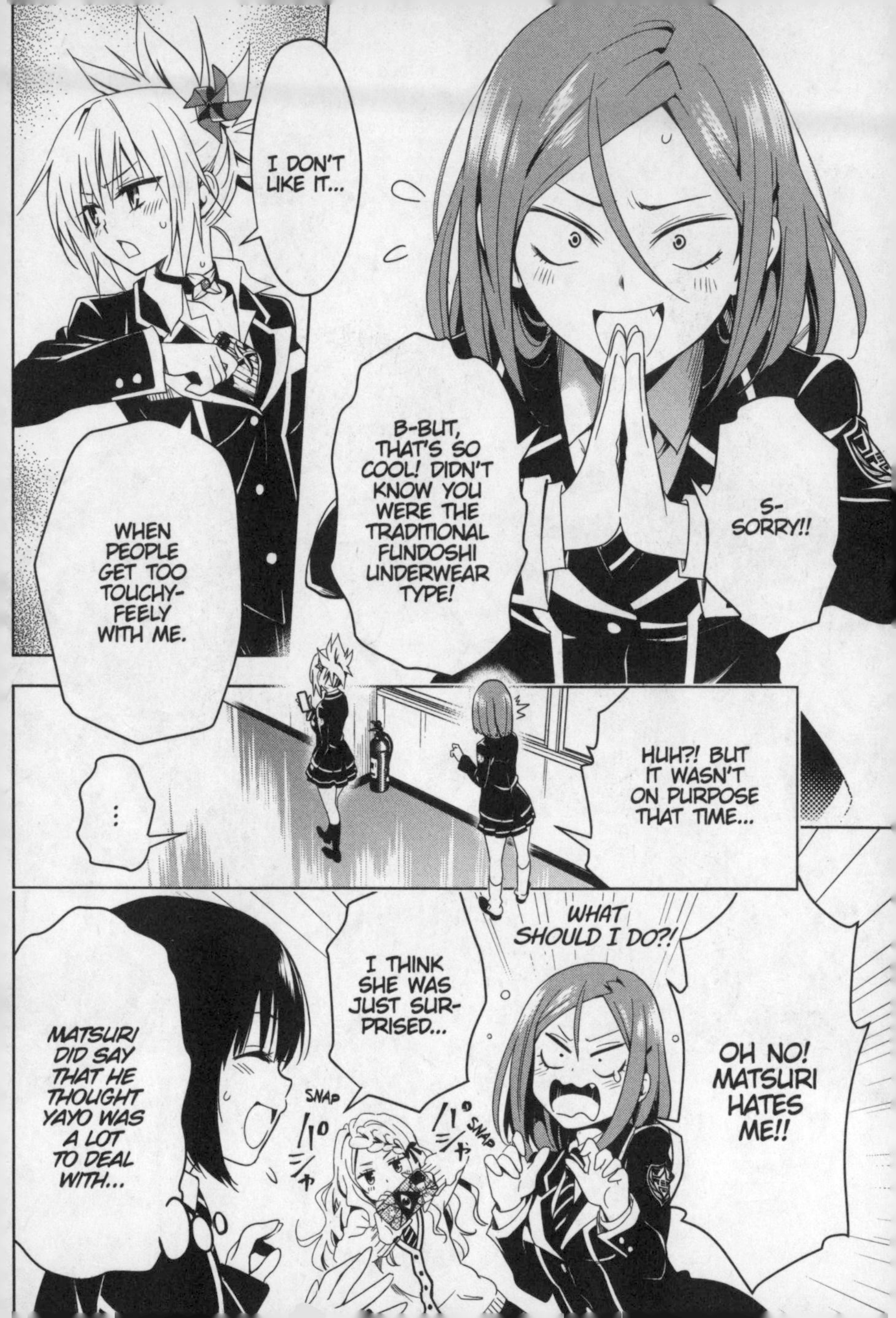
S-SORRY!!
B-BUT, THAT'S SO COOL! DIDN'T KNOW YOU WERE THE TRADITIONAL FUNDOSHI UNDERWEAR TYPE!
I DON'T LIKE IT...
WHEN PEOPLE GET TOO TOUCHY-FEELY WITH ME.
HUH?! BUT IT WASN'T ON PURPOSE THAT TIME...
...
OH NO! MATSURI HATES ME!!
WHAT SHOULD I DO?!
SNAP
I THINK SHE WAS JUST SURPRISED...
SNAP
MATSURI DID SAY THAT HE THOUGHT YAYO WAS A LOT TO DEAL WITH...

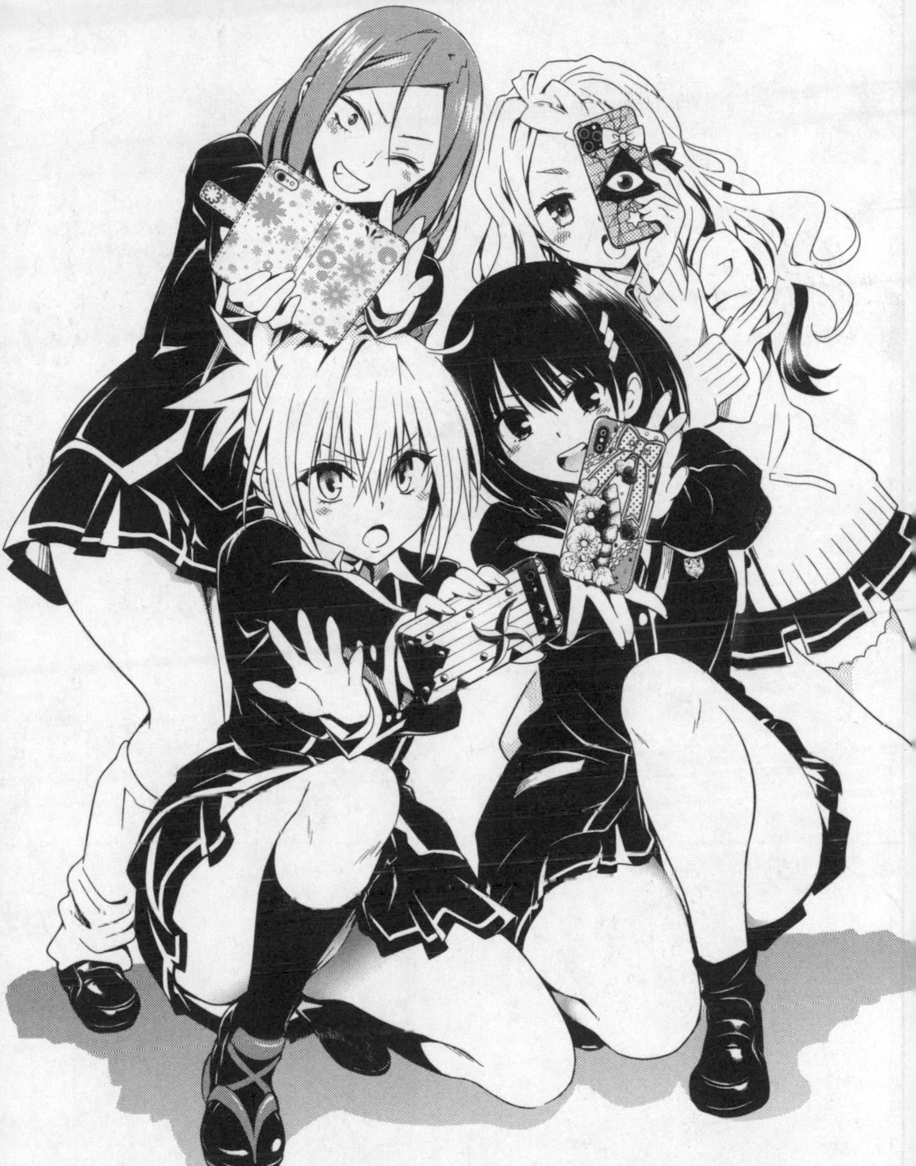

## Chapter 6 Kachofugetsu

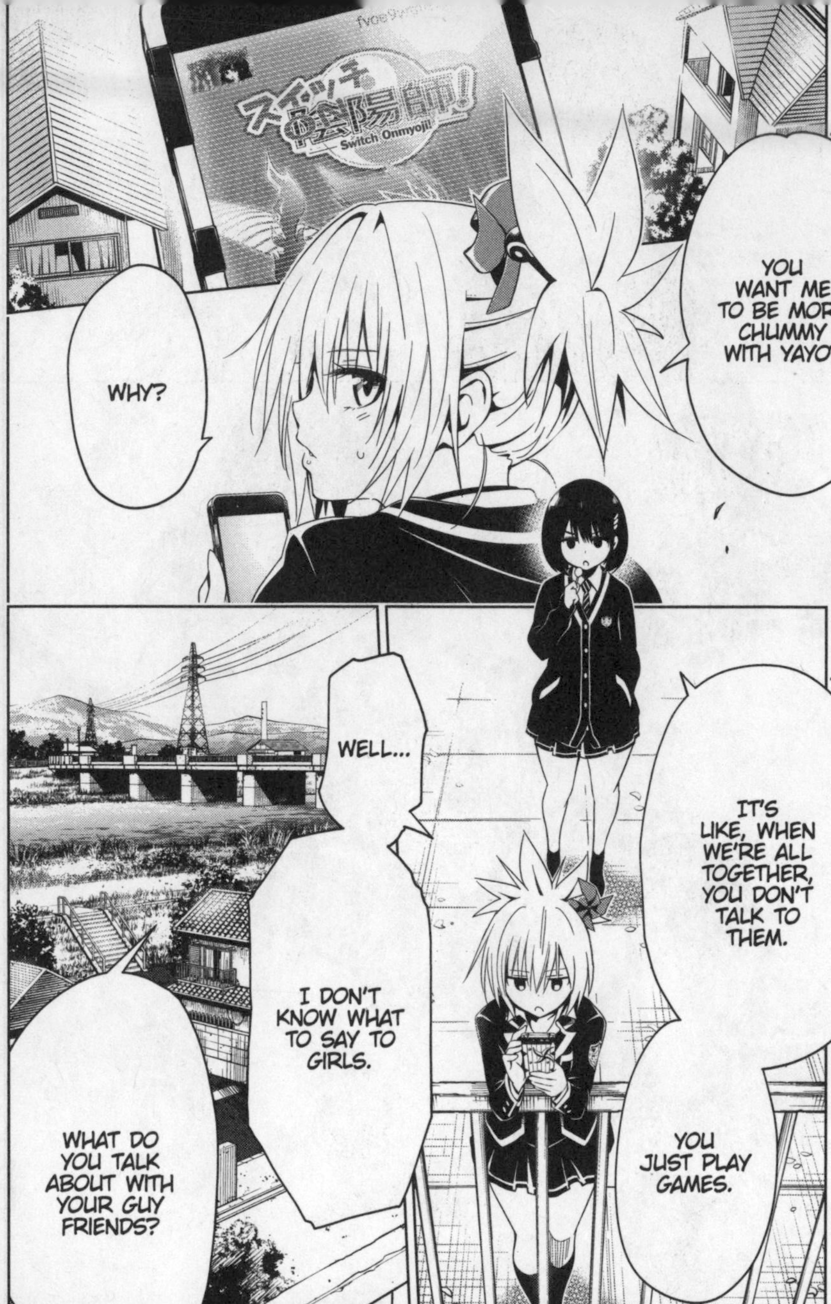
Switch Onmyoji!
YOU WANT ME TO BE MORE CHUMMY WITH YAYO?
WHY?
IT'S LIKE, WHEN WE'RE ALL TOGETHER, YOU DON'T TALK TO THEM.
YOU JUST PLAY GAMES.
WELL...
I DON'T KNOW WHAT TO SAY TO GIRLS.
WHAT DO YOU TALK ABOUT WITH YOUR GUY FRIENDS?

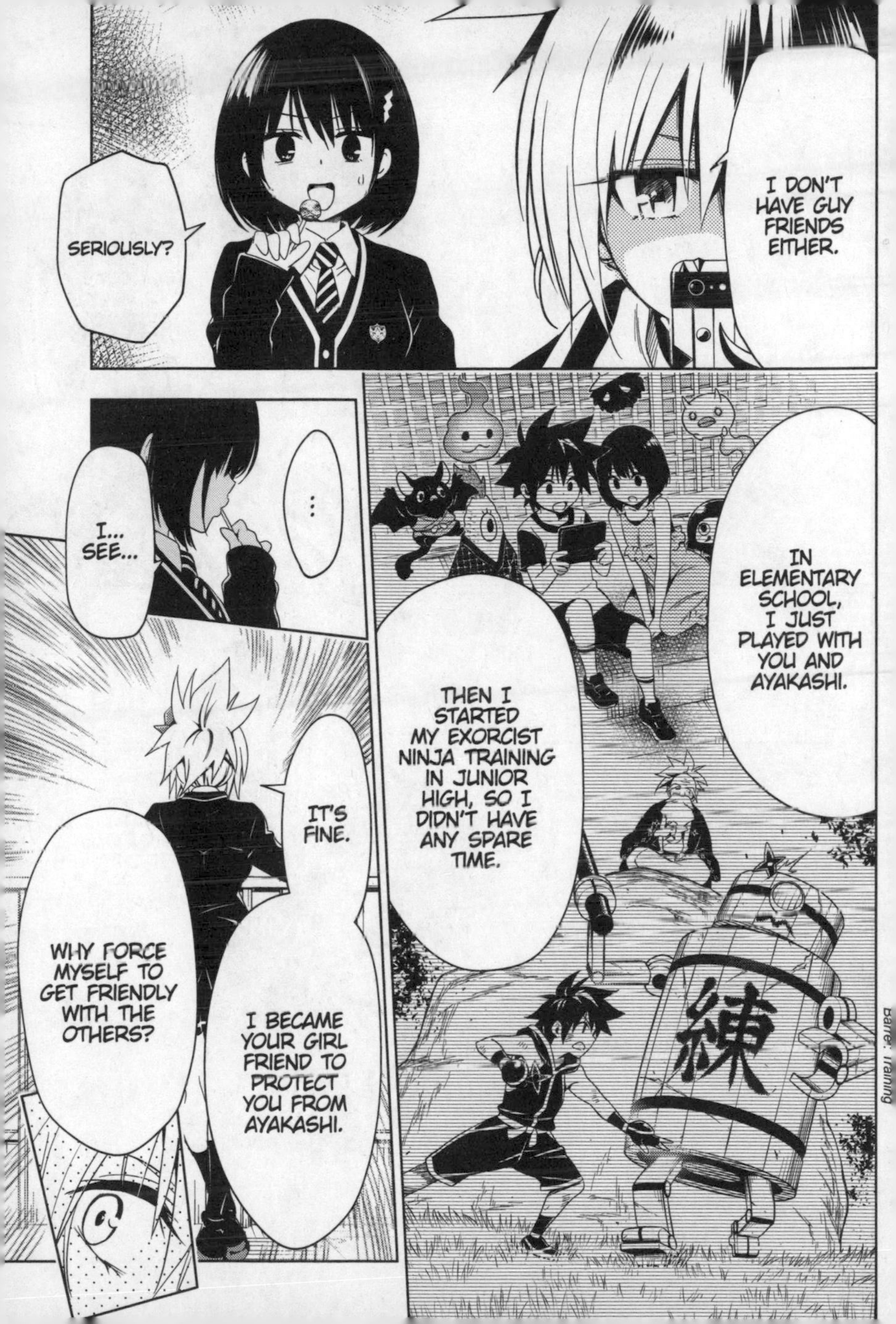
I DON'T HAVE GUY FRIENDS EITHER.
SERIOUSLY?
IN ELEMENTARY SCHOOL, I JUST PLAYED WITH YOU AND AYAKASHI.
THEN I STARTED MY EXORCIST NINJA TRAINING IN JUNIOR HIGH, SO I DIDN'T HAVE ANY SPARE TIME.
練
Barrel: Training
...
I... SEE...
IT'S FINE.
I BECAME YOUR GIRL FRIEND TO PROTECT YOU FROM AYAKASHI.
WHY FORCE MYSELF TO GET FRIENDLY WITH THE OTHERS?

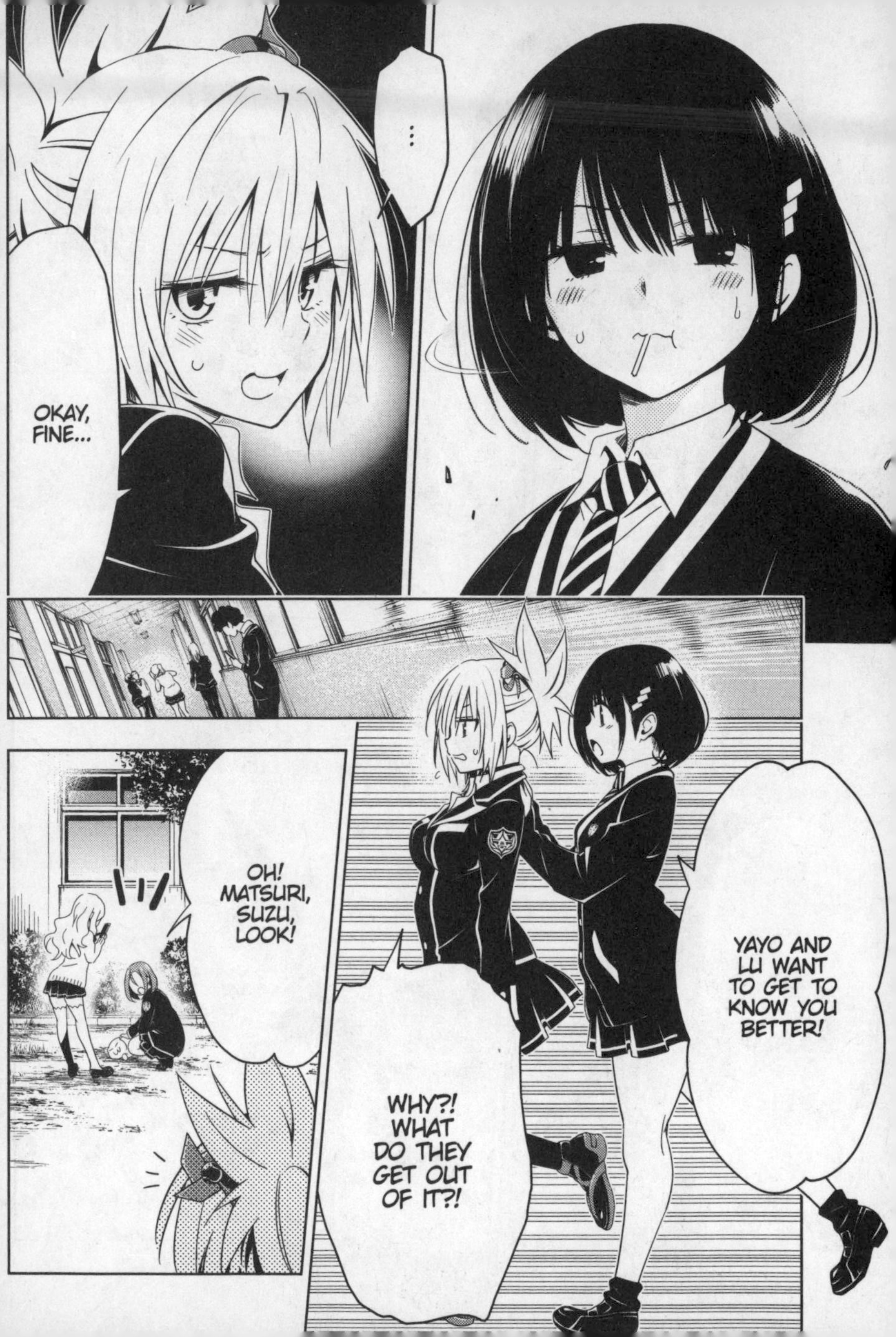
…
OKAY, FINE...
YAYO AND LU WANT TO GET TO KNOW YOU BETTER!
WHY?! WHAT DO THEY GET OUT OF IT?!
OH! MATSURI, SUZU, LOOK!

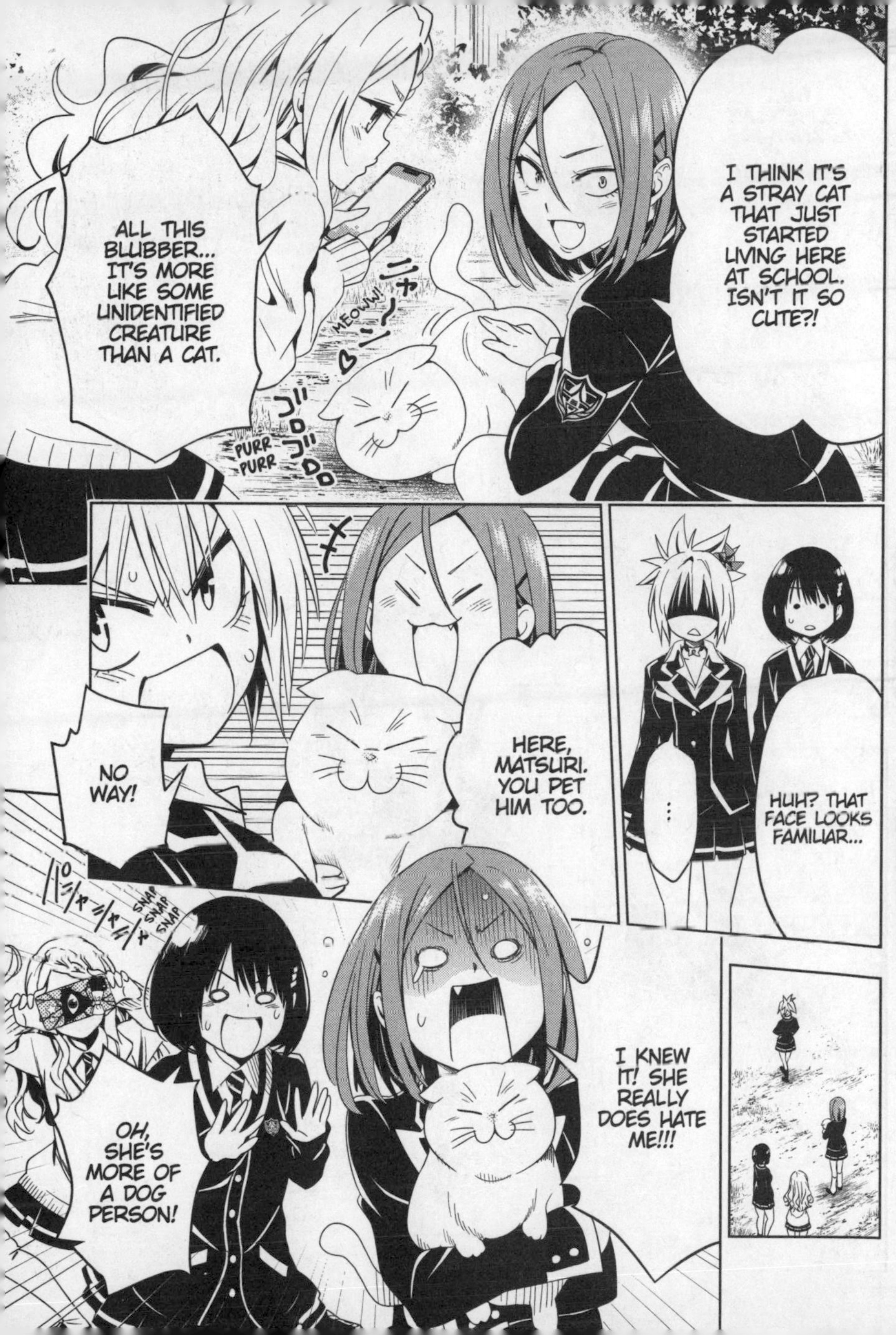
I THINK IT'S A STRAY CAT THAT JUST STARTED LIVING HERE AT SCHOOL. ISN'T IT SO CUTE?!
ニャ～ン♡
MEOWW!
ゴロゴロ
PURR PURR
ALL THIS BLUBBER... IT'S MORE LIKE SOME UNIDENTIFIED CREATURE THAN A CAT.
HUH? THAT FACE LOOKS FAMILIAR...
...
HERE, MATSURI. YOU PET HIM TOO.
NO WAY!
パシャシャシャ
SNAP SNAP SNAP
I KNEW IT! SHE REALLY DOES HATE ME!!!
OH, SHE'S MORE OF A DOG PERSON!

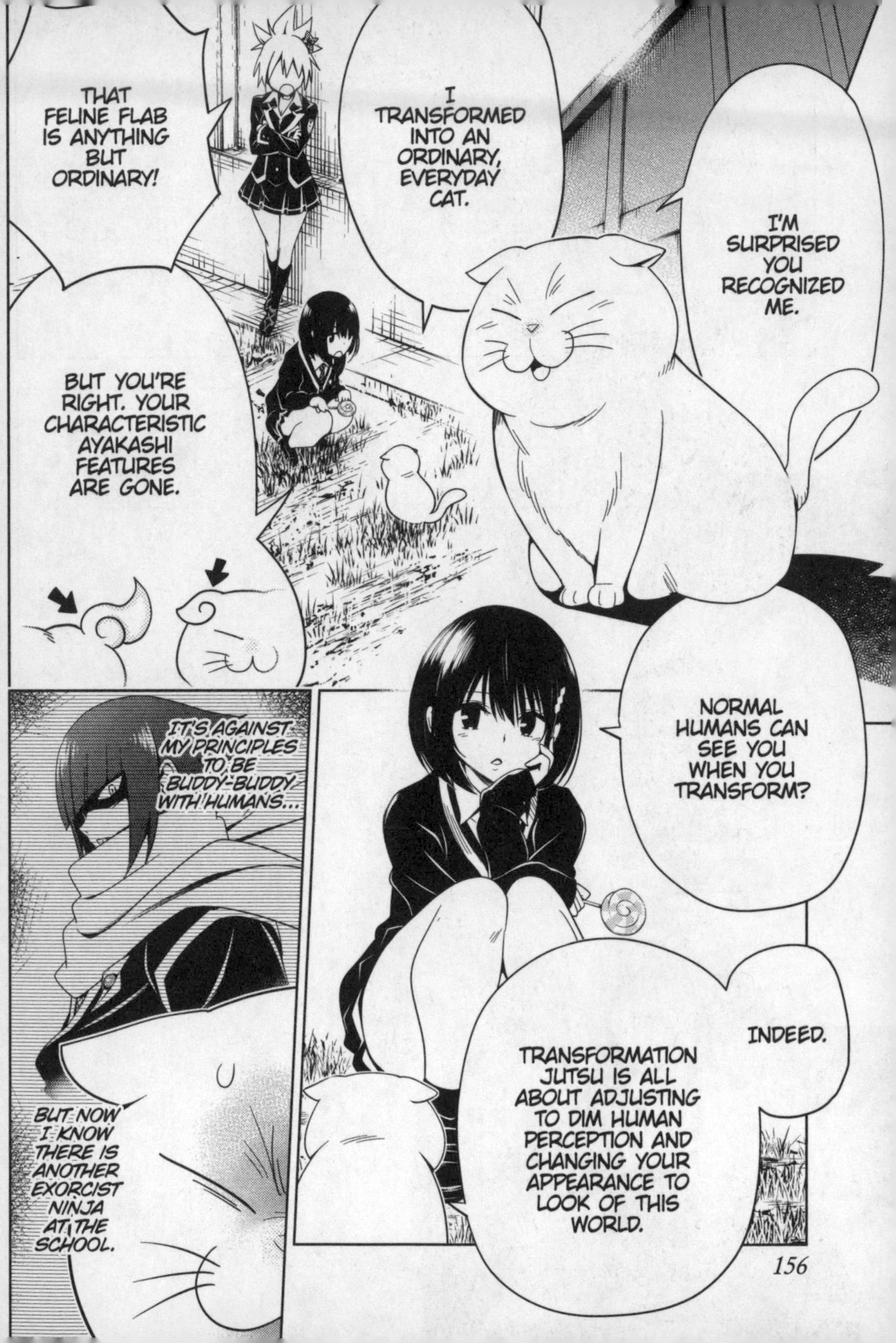

I'M SURPRISED YOU RECOGNIZED ME.
I TRANSFORMED INTO AN ORDINARY, EVERYDAY CAT.
THAT FELINE FLAB IS ANYTHING BUT ORDINARY!
BUT YOU'RE RIGHT. YOUR CHARACTERISTIC AYAKASHI FEATURES ARE GONE.
NORMAL HUMANS CAN SEE YOU WHEN YOU TRANSFORM?
INDEED.
TRANSFORMATION JUTSU IS ALL ABOUT ADJUSTING TO DIM HUMAN PERCEPTION AND CHANGING YOUR APPEARANCE TO LOOK OF THIS WORLD.
IT'S AGAINST MY PRINCIPLES TO BE BUDDY-BUDDY WITH HUMANS...
BUT NOW I KNOW THERE IS ANOTHER EXORCIST NINJA AT THE SCHOOL.

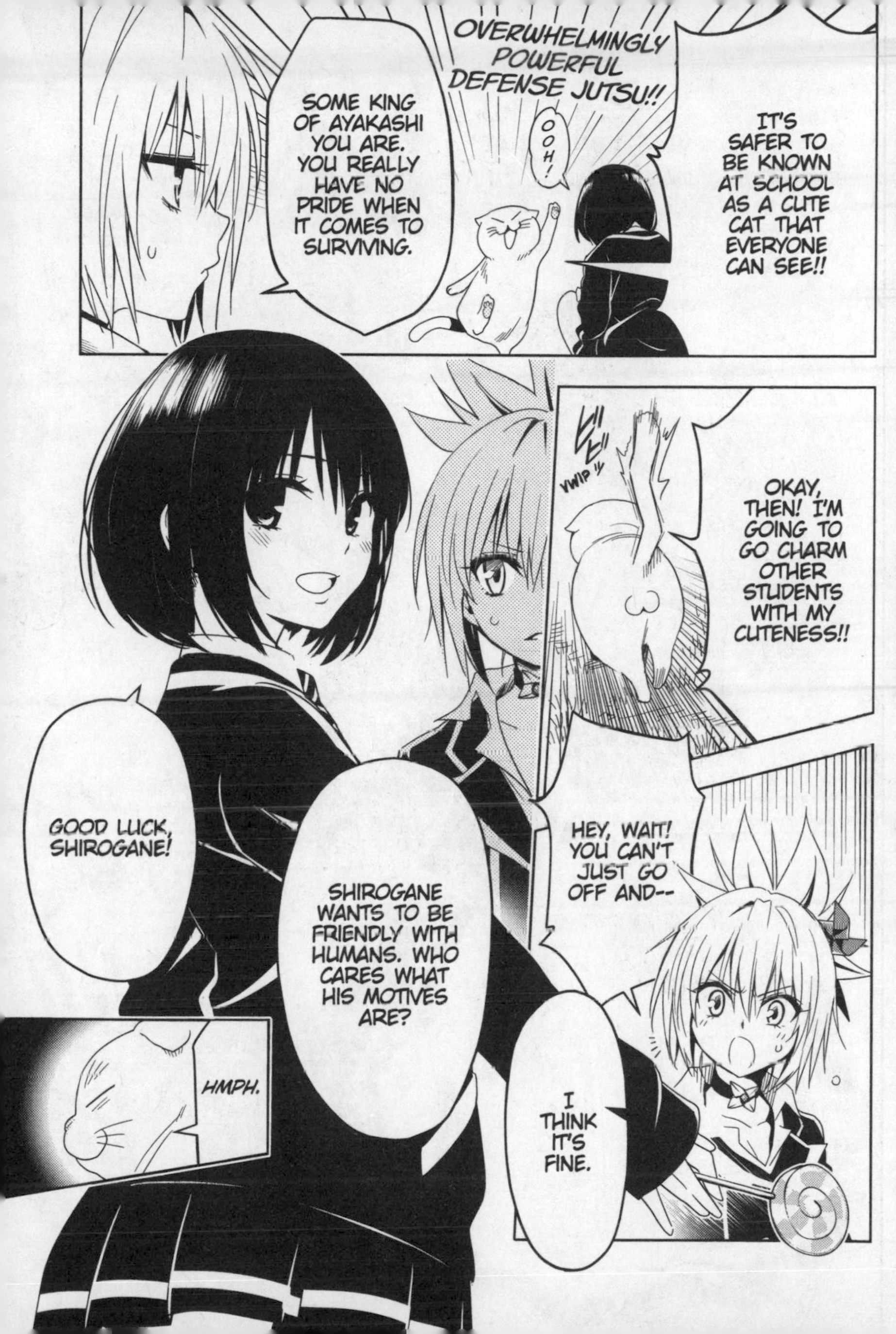
IT'S SAFER TO BE KNOWN AT SCHOOL AS A CUTE CAT THAT EVERYONE CAN SEE!!
OVERWHELMINGLY POWERFUL DEFENSE JUTSU!!
OOH!
SOME KING OF AYAKASHI YOU ARE. YOU REALLY HAVE NO PRIDE WHEN IT COMES TO SURVIVING.
OKAY, THEN! I'M GOING TO GO CHARM OTHER STUDENTS WITH MY CUTENESS!!
VWIP
HEY, WAIT! YOU CAN'T JUST GO OFF AND--
I THINK IT'S FINE.
SHIROGANE WANTS TO BE FRIENDLY WITH HUMANS. WHO CARES WHAT HIS MOTIVES ARE?
GOOD LUCK, SHIROGANE!
HMPH.

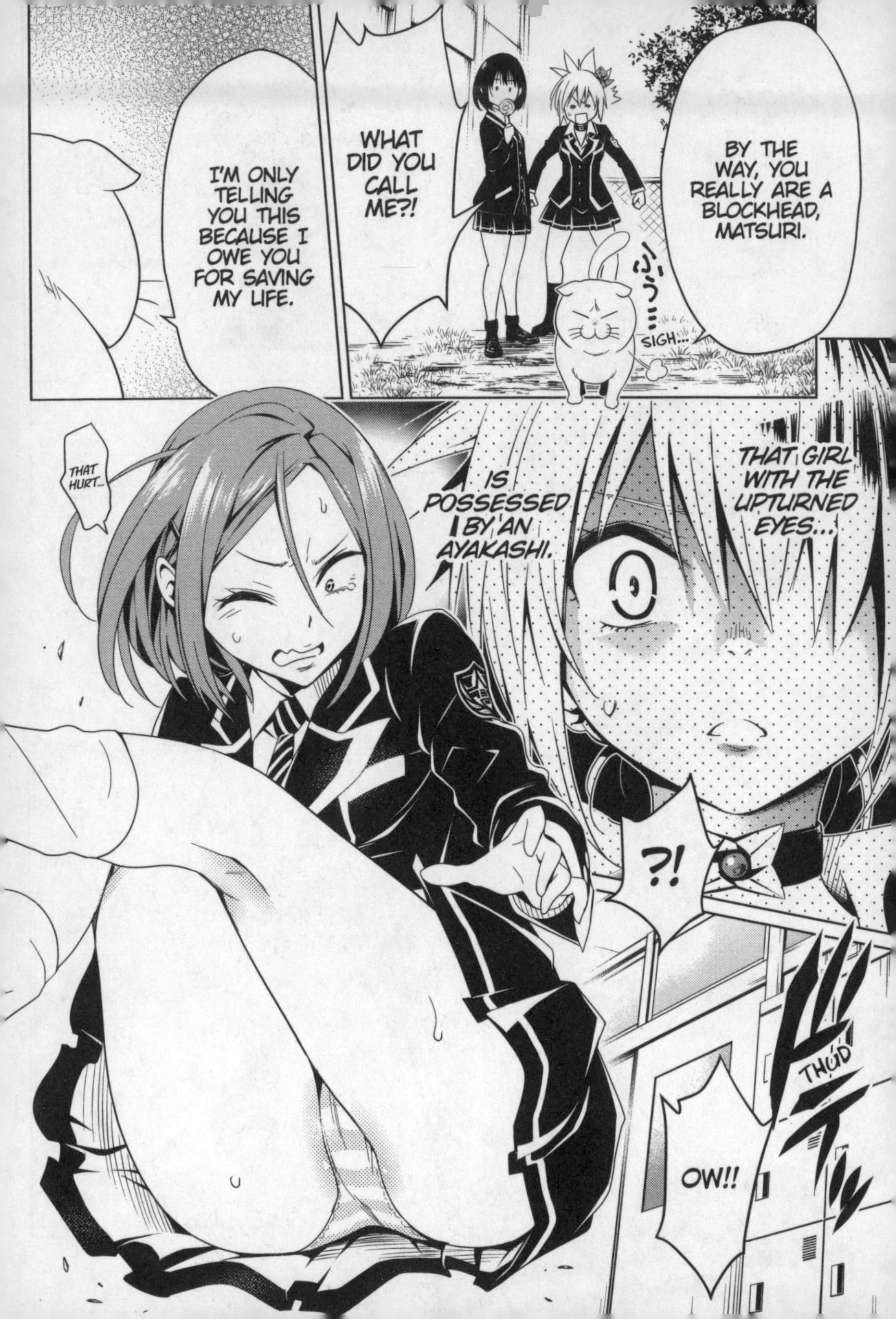
BY THE WAY, YOU REALLY ARE A BLOCKHEAD, MATSURI.
ふぅ…
SIGH...
WHAT DID YOU CALL ME?!
I'M ONLY TELLING YOU THIS BECAUSE I OWE YOU FOR SAVING MY LIFE.
THAT GIRL WITH THE UPTURNED EYES...
IS POSSESSED BY AN AYAKASHI.
?!
THUD
OW!!
THAT HURT...

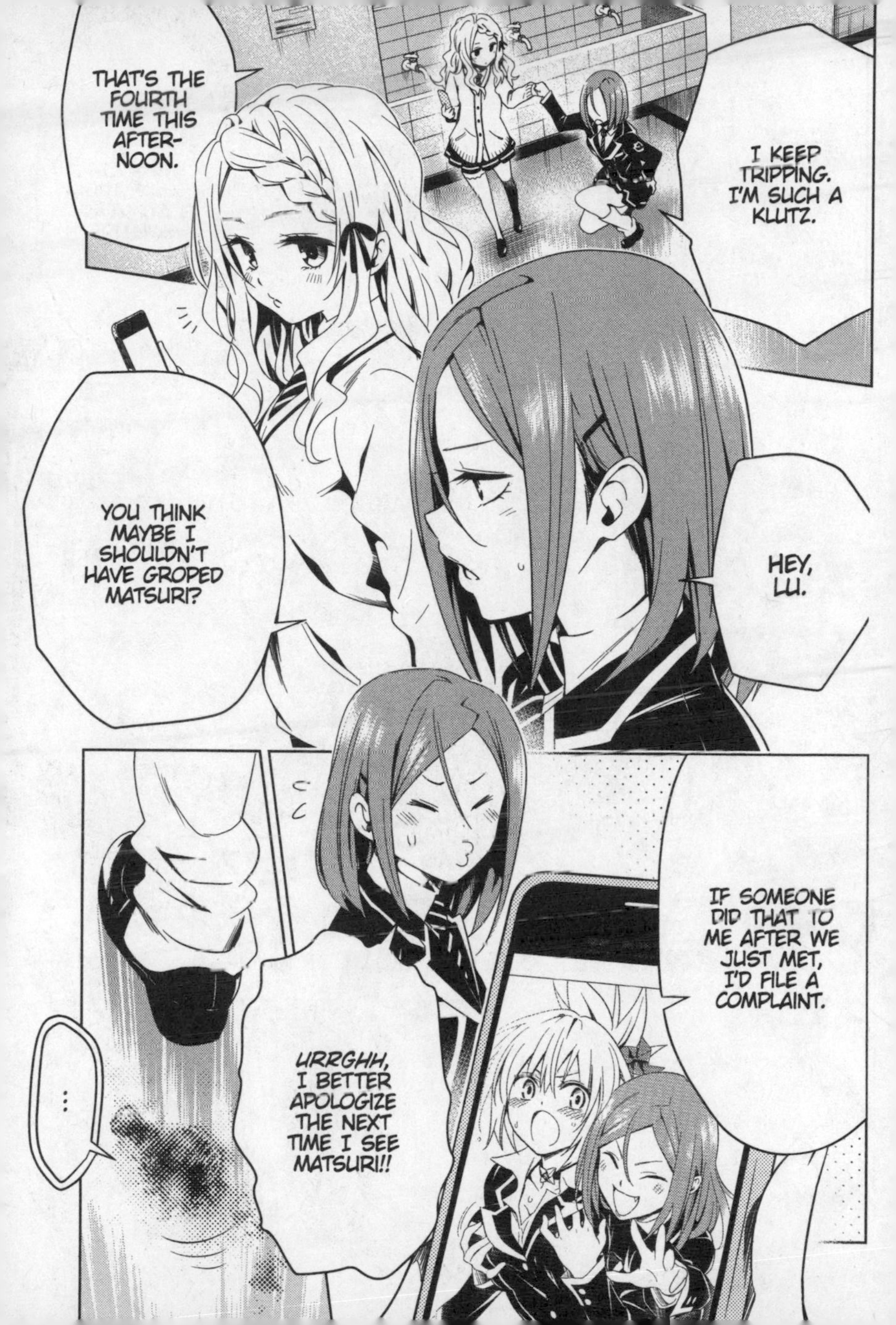
I KEEP TRIPPING. I'M SUCH A KLUTZ.
THAT'S THE FOURTH TIME THIS AFTER-NOON.
HEY, LU.
YOU THINK MAYBE I SHOULDN'T HAVE GROPED MATSURI?
IF SOMEONE DID THAT TO ME AFTER WE JUST MET, I'D FILE A COMPLAINT.
URRGHH, I BETTER APOLOGIZE THE NEXT TIME I SEE MATSURI!!
...

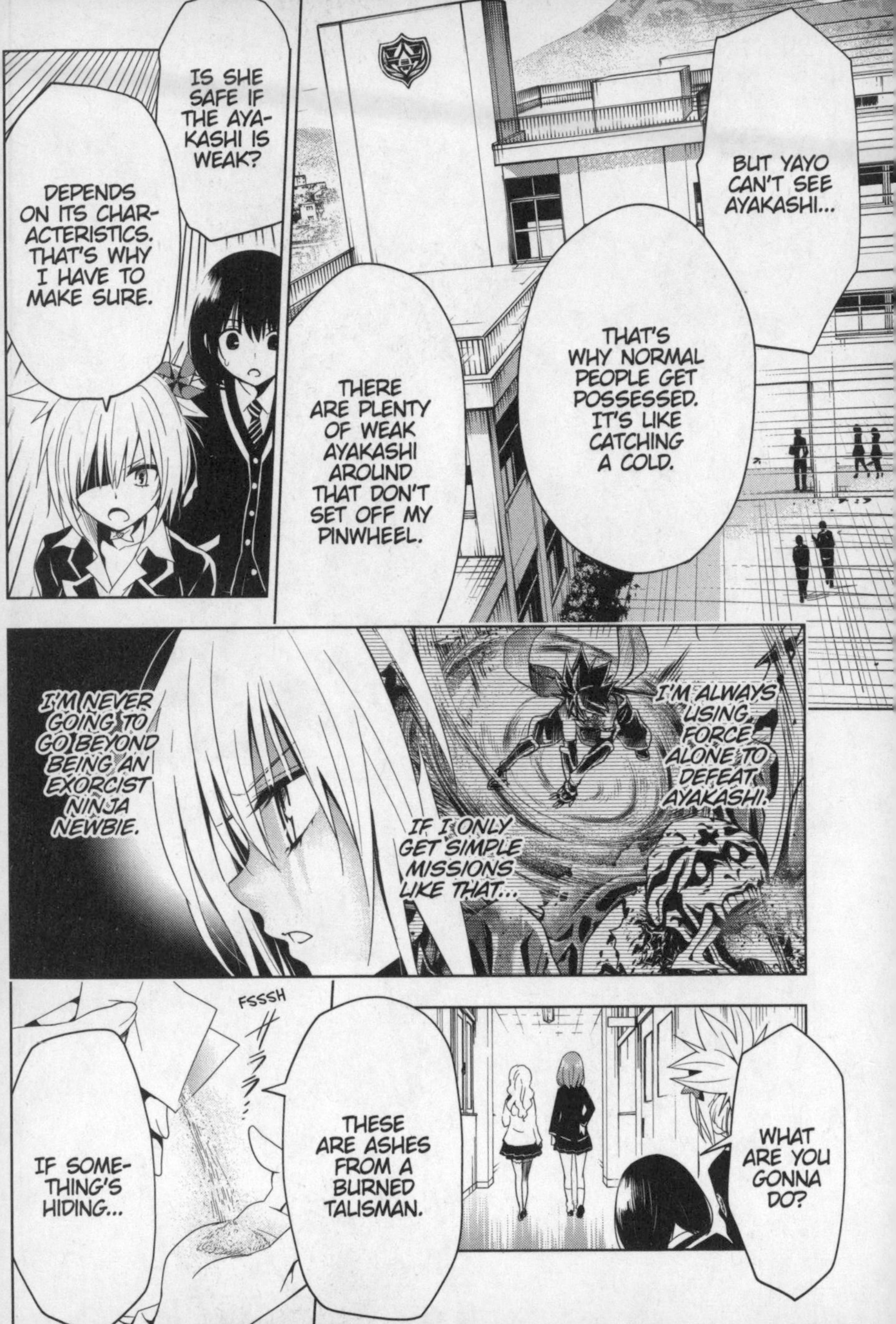

BUT YAYO CAN'T SEE AYAKASHI...
THAT'S WHY NORMAL PEOPLE GET POSSESSED. IT'S LIKE CATCHING A COLD.
THERE ARE PLENTY OF WEAK AYAKASHI AROUND THAT DON'T SET OFF MY PINWHEEL.
IS SHE SAFE IF THE AYAKASHI IS WEAK?
DEPENDS ON ITS CHARACTERISTICS. THAT'S WHY I HAVE TO MAKE SURE.
I'M ALWAYS USING FORCE ALONE TO DEFEAT AYAKASHI.
IF I ONLY GET SIMPLE MISSIONS LIKE THAT...
I'M NEVER GOING TO GO BEYOND BEING AN EXORCIST NINJA NEWBIE.
WHAT ARE YOU GONNA DO?
FSSSH
THESE ARE ASHES FROM A BURNED TALISMAN.
IF SOMETHING'S HIDING...

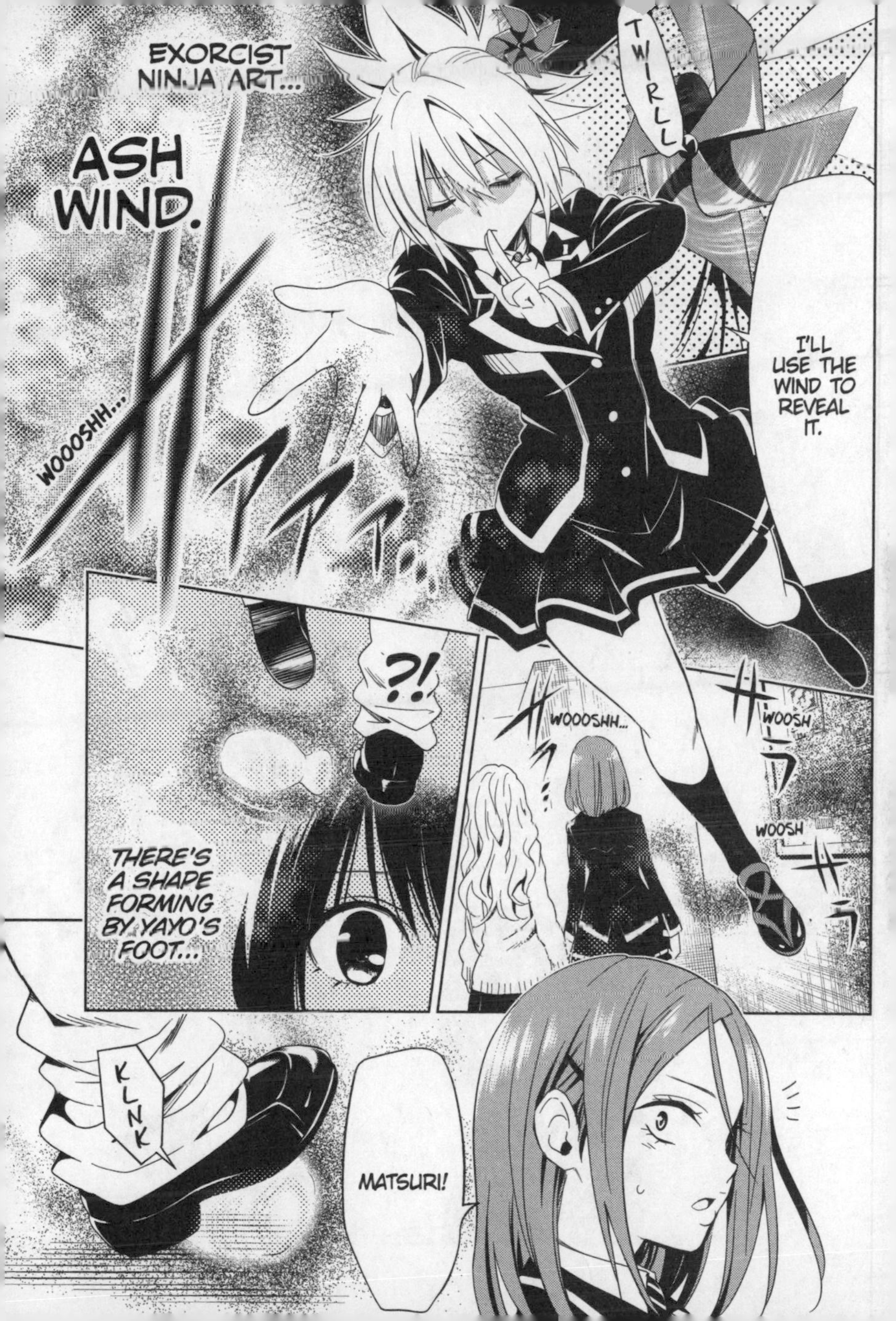
TWIRLL
EXORCIST NINJA ART...
ASH WIND.
I'LL USE THE WIND TO REVEAL IT.
WOOOSHH...
WOOSH
WOOOSHH...
WOOSH
?!
THERE'S A SHAPE FORMING BY YAYO'S FOOT...
MATSURI!
KLNK

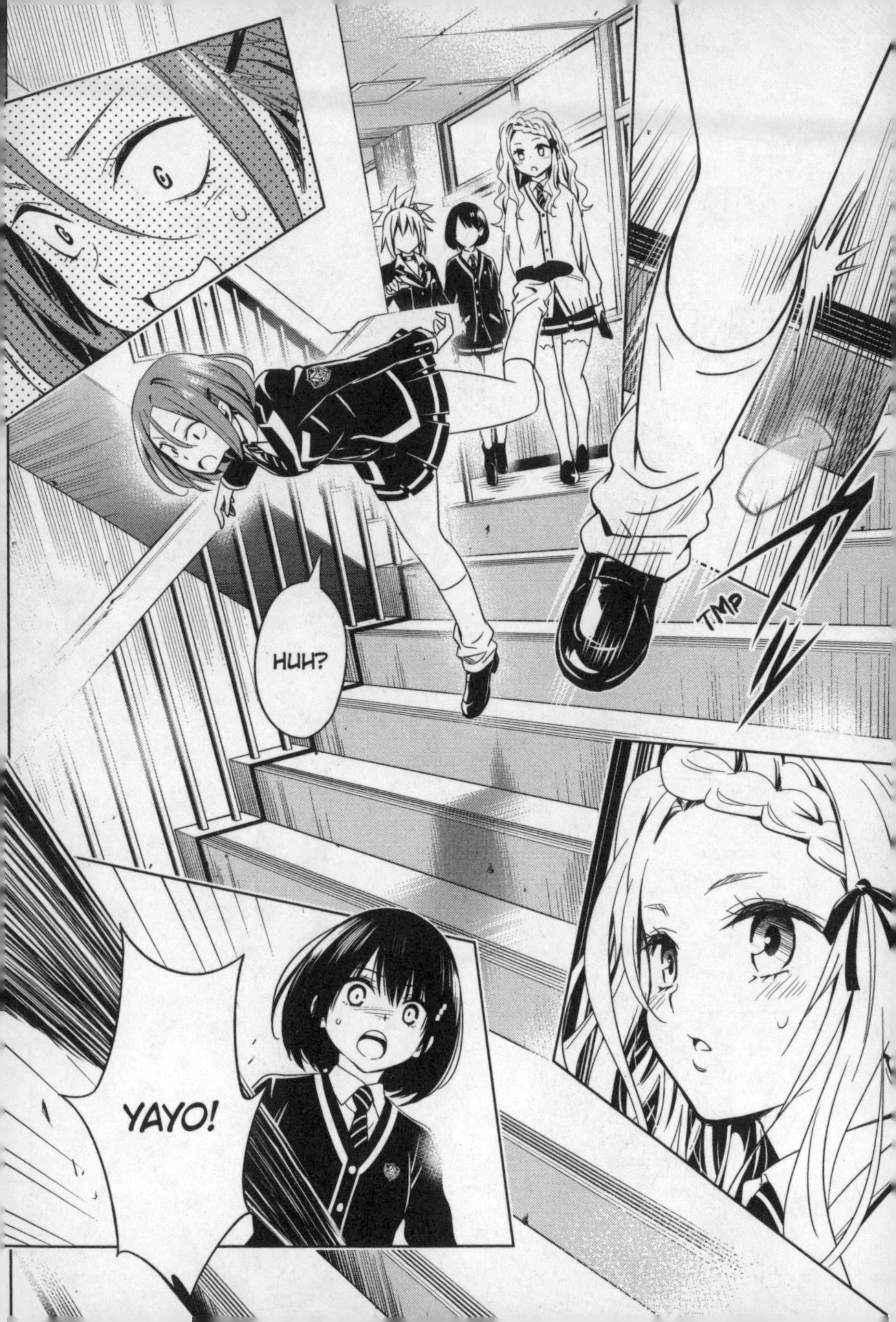

TMP
HUH?
YAYO!

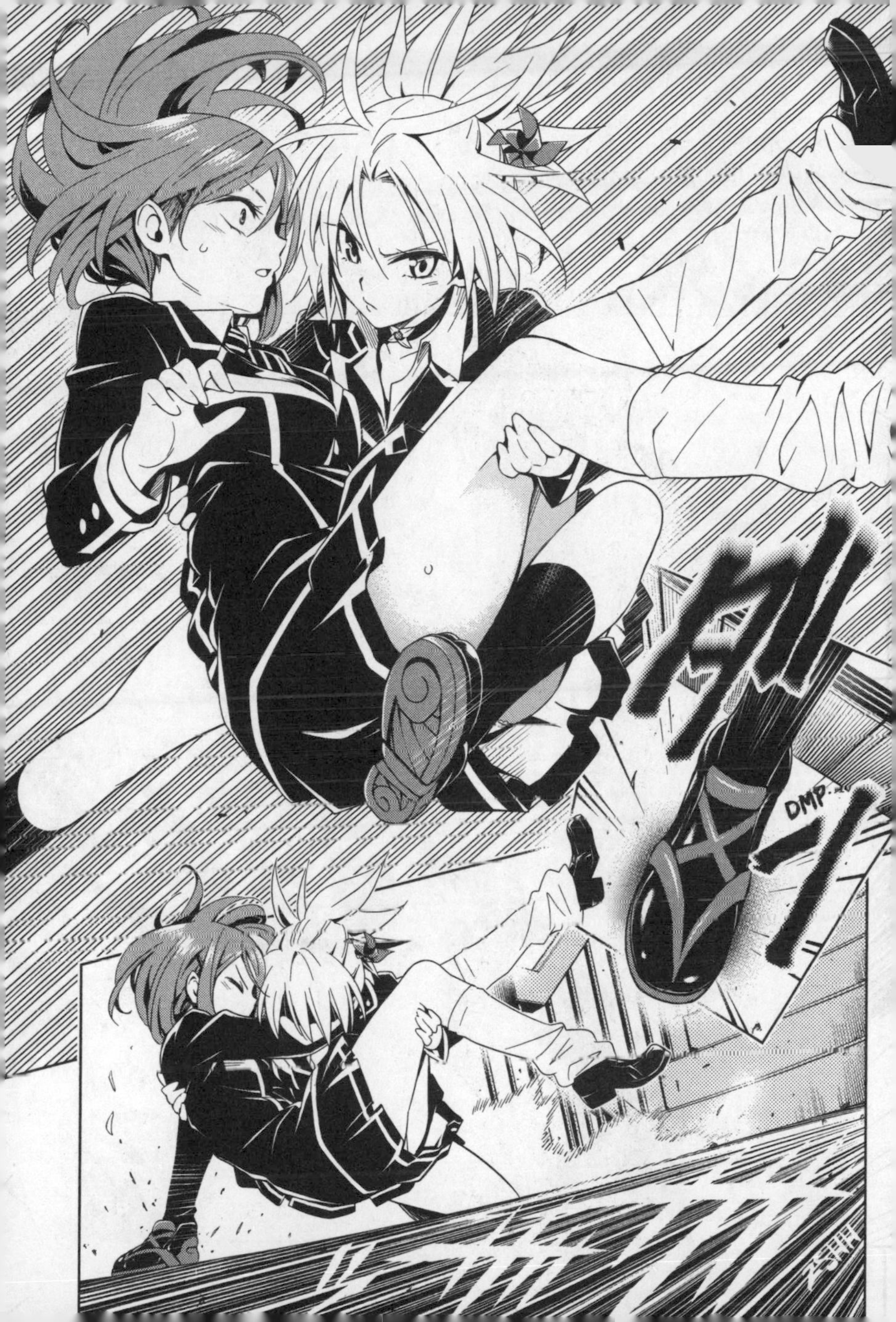
DMP
ZSHH

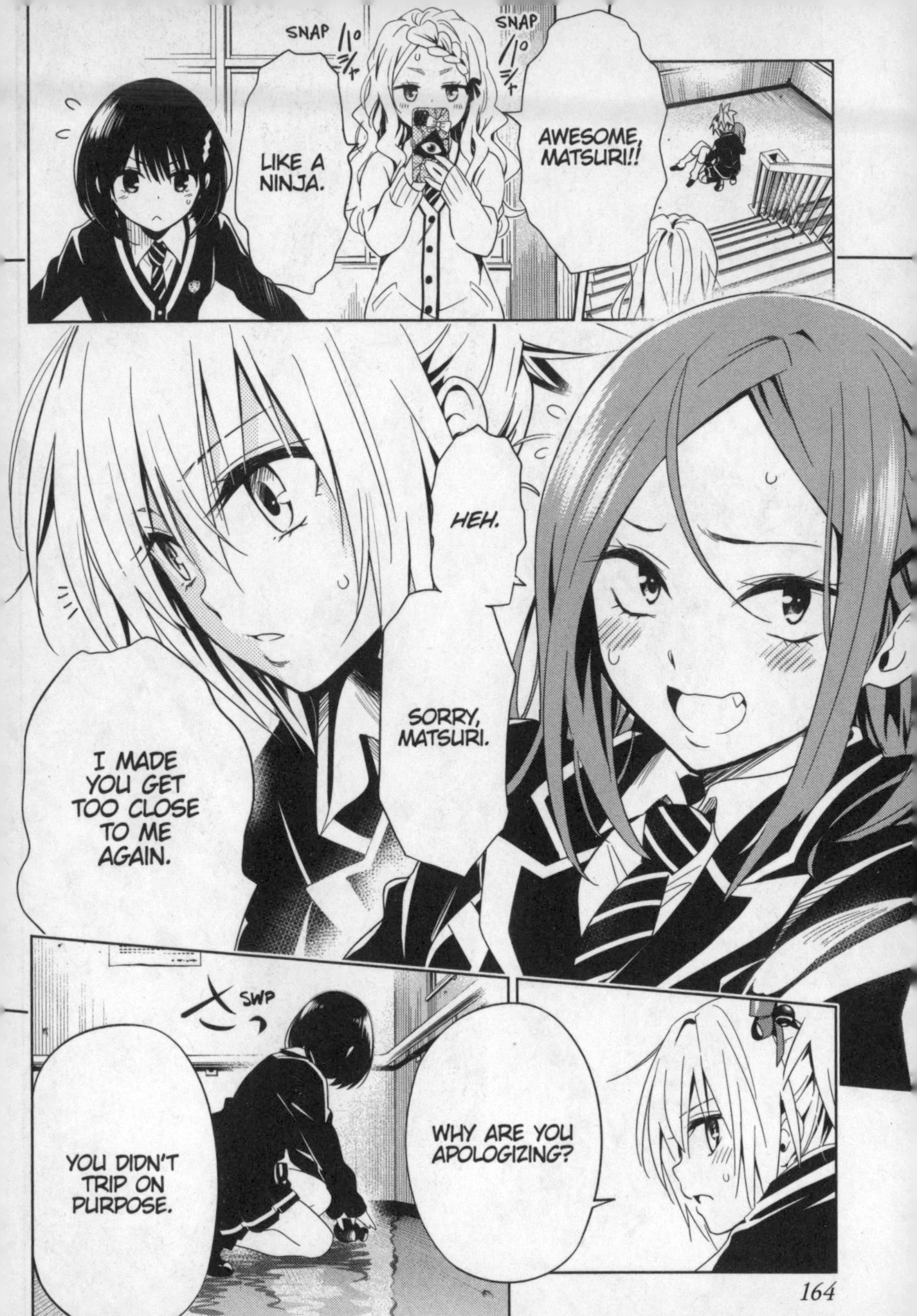
SNAP
AWESOME, MATSURI!!
SNAP
LIKE A NINJA.
HEH.
SORRY, MATSURI.
I MADE YOU GET TOO CLOSE TO ME AGAIN.
WHY ARE YOU APOLOGIZING?
SWP
YOU DIDN'T TRIP ON PURPOSE.

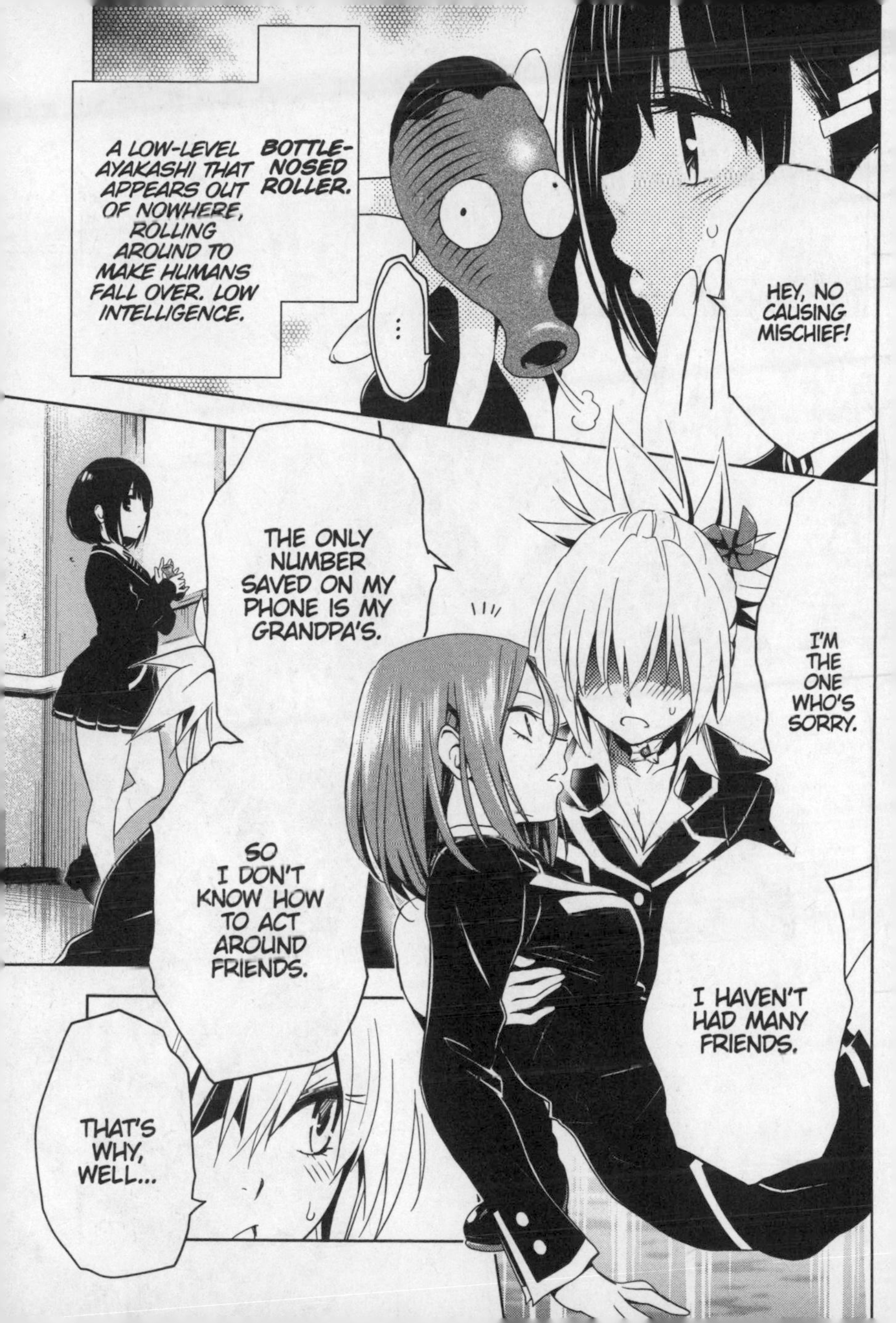
HEY, NO CAUSING MISCHIEF!
BOTTLE-NOSED ROLLER.
A LOW-LEVEL AYAKASHI THAT APPEARS OUT OF NOWHERE, ROLLING AROUND TO MAKE HUMANS FALL OVER. LOW INTELLIGENCE.
I'M THE ONE WHO'S SORRY.
I HAVEN'T HAD MANY FRIENDS.
THE ONLY NUMBER SAVED ON MY PHONE IS MY GRANDPA'S.
SO I DON'T KNOW HOW TO ACT AROUND FRIENDS.
THAT'S WHY, WELL...

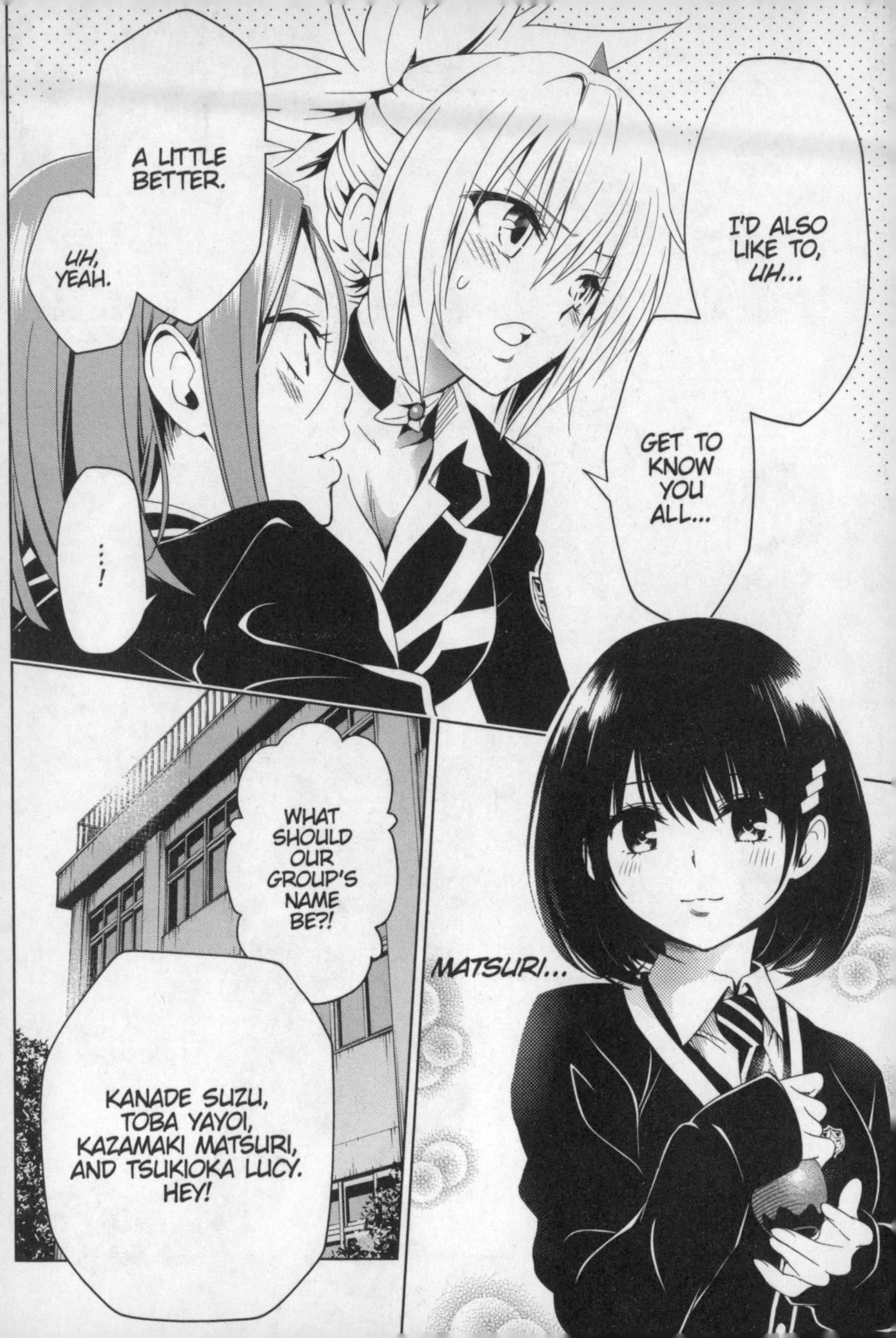
I'D ALSO LIKE TO, UH...
GET TO KNOW YOU ALL...
A LITTLE BETTER.
UH, YEAH.
...!
MATSURI...
WHAT SHOULD OUR GROUP'S NAME BE?!
KANADE SUZU, TOBA YAYOI, KAZAMAKI MATSURI, AND TSUKIOKA LUCY. HEY!

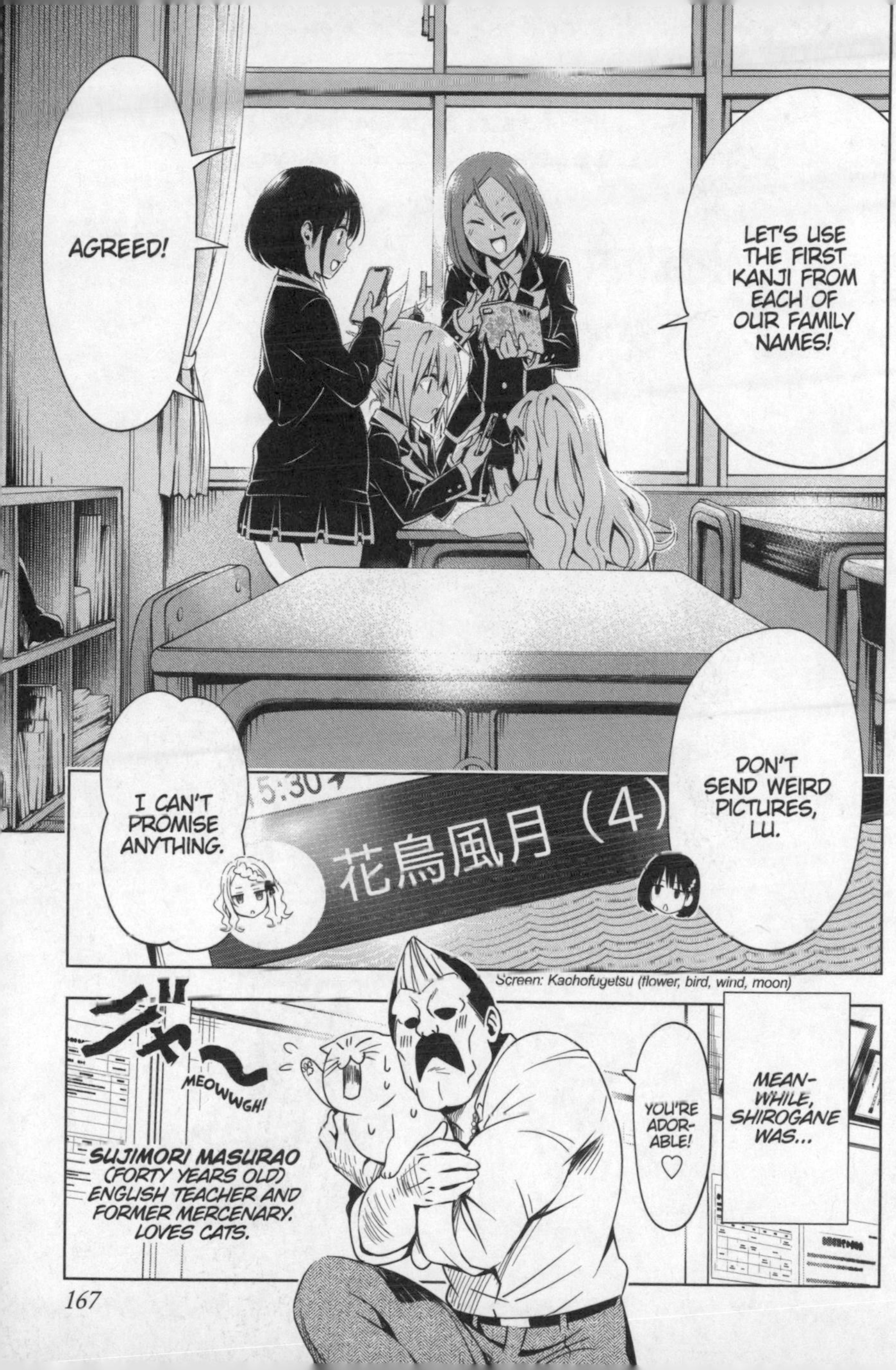
LET'S USE THE FIRST KANJI FROM EACH OF OUR FAMILY NAMES!
AGREED!
DON'T SEND WEIRD PICTURES, LU.
15:30
花鳥風月（4）
I CAN'T PROMISE ANYTHING.
Screen: Kachofugetsu (flower, bird, wind, moon)
MEAN-WHILE, SHIROGANE WAS...
YOU'RE ADOR-ABLE! ♡
ジャ〜
MEOWWGH!
SUJIMORI MASURAO (FORTY YEARS OLD) ENGLISH TEACHER AND FORMER MERCENARY. LOVES CATS.

# Kachofugetsu Smartphones

Matsuri

Suzu

Lucy

Yayoi

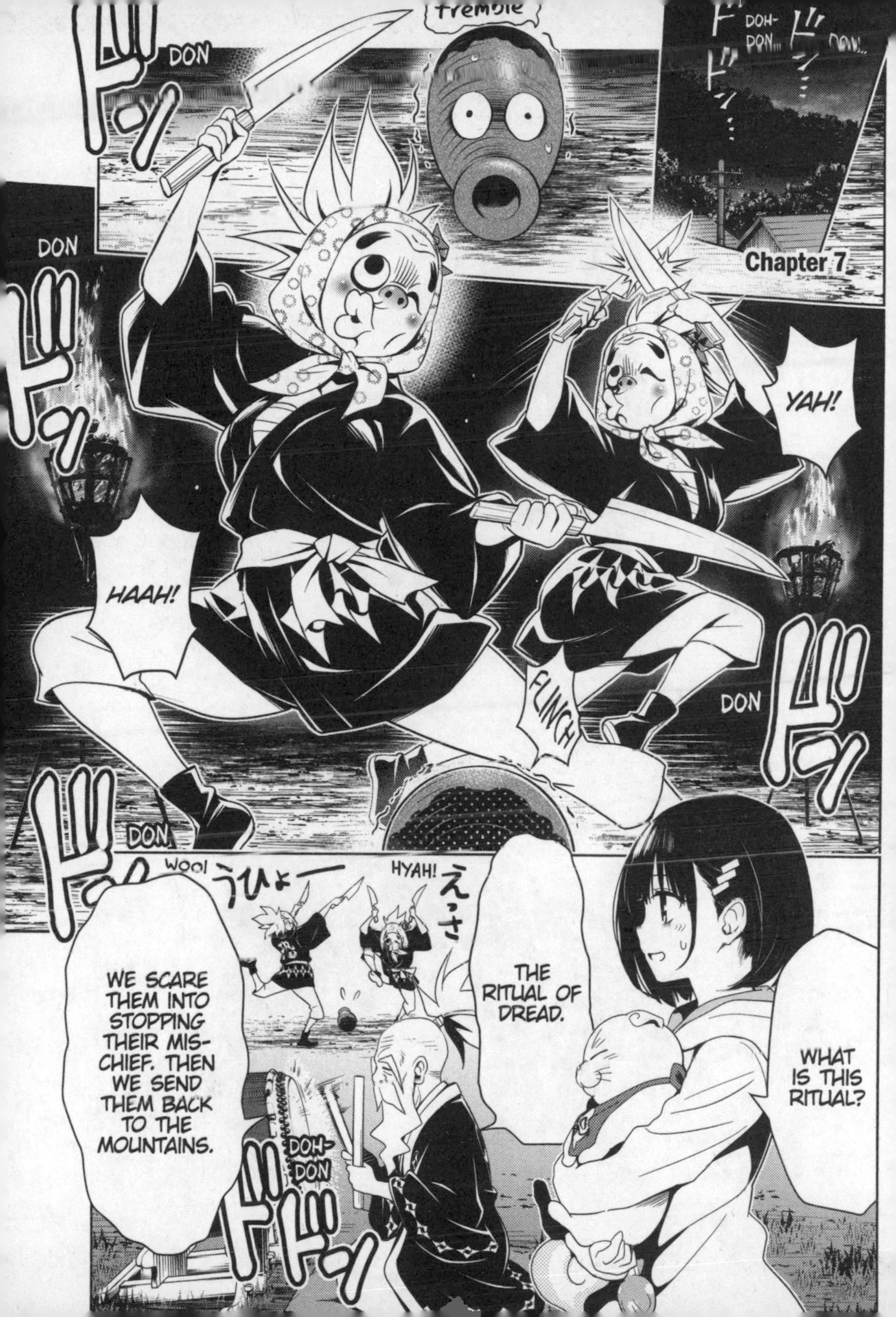

DOH-DON... DON...
Chapter 7
Tremble
DON
DON
YAH!
HAAH!
FLINCH
DON
DON
WHAT IS THIS RITUAL?
THE RITUAL OF DREAD.
WE SCARE THEM INTO STOPPING THEIR MIS-CHIEF. THEN WE SEND THEM BACK TO THE MOUNTAINS.
HYAH!
えっさ
WOO!
うひょー
DOH-DON

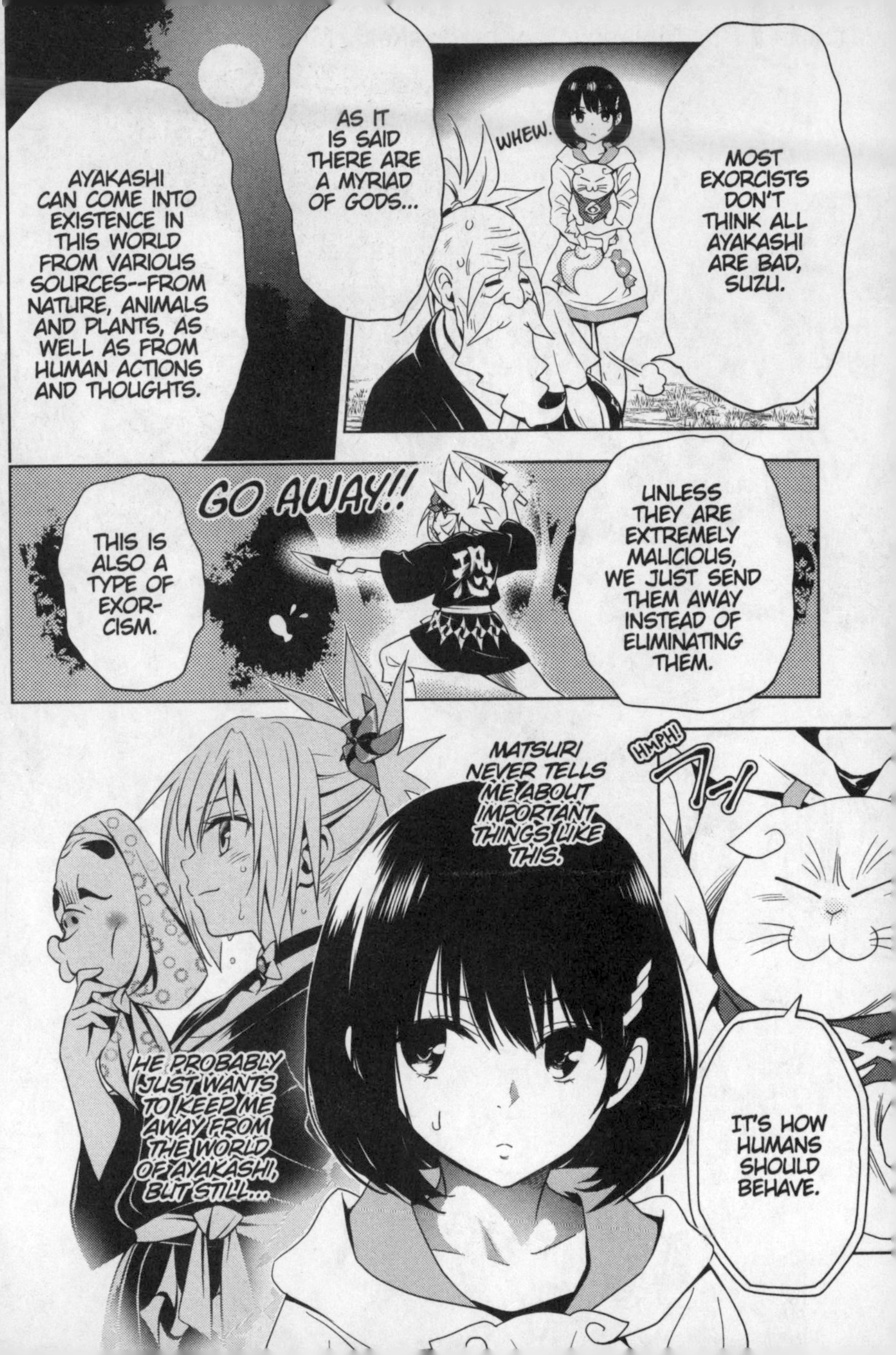
MOST EXORCISTS DON'T THINK ALL AYAKASHI ARE BAD, SUZU.
WHEW.
AS IT IS SAID THERE ARE A MYRIAD OF GODS...
AYAKASHI CAN COME INTO EXISTENCE IN THIS WORLD FROM VARIOUS SOURCES--FROM NATURE, ANIMALS AND PLANTS, AS WELL AS FROM HUMAN ACTIONS AND THOUGHTS.
UNLESS THEY ARE EXTREMELY MALICIOUS, WE JUST SEND THEM AWAY INSTEAD OF ELIMINATING THEM.
GO AWAY!!
THIS IS ALSO A TYPE OF EXOR-CISM.
HMPH!
IT'S HOW HUMANS SHOULD BEHAVE.
MATSURI NEVER TELLS ME ABOUT IMPORTANT THINGS LIKE THIS.
HE PROBABLY JUST WANTS TO KEEP ME AWAY FROM THE WORLD OF AYAKASHI, BUT STILL...

# Chapter 7 The Melancholy of the Ayakashi Medium

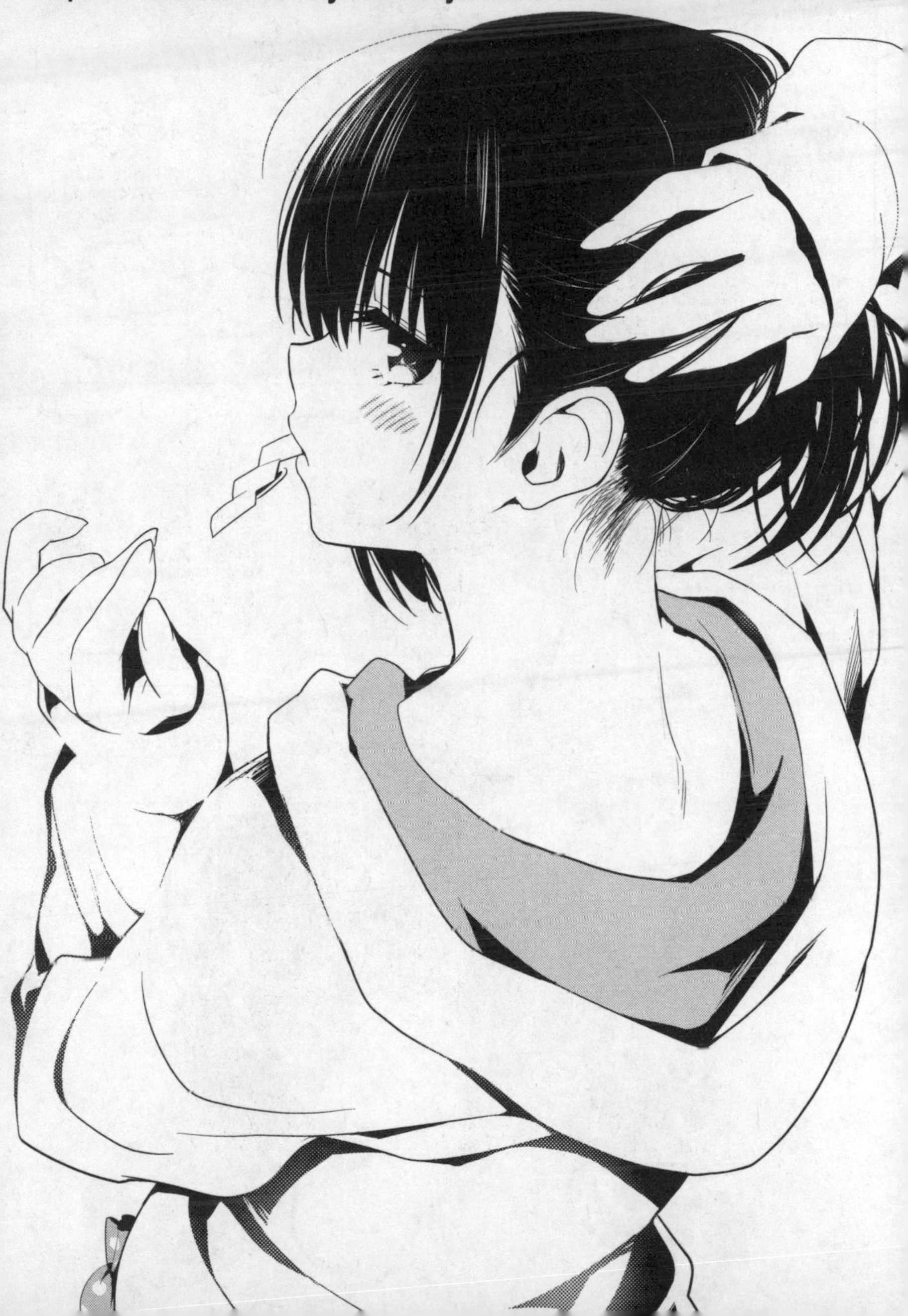

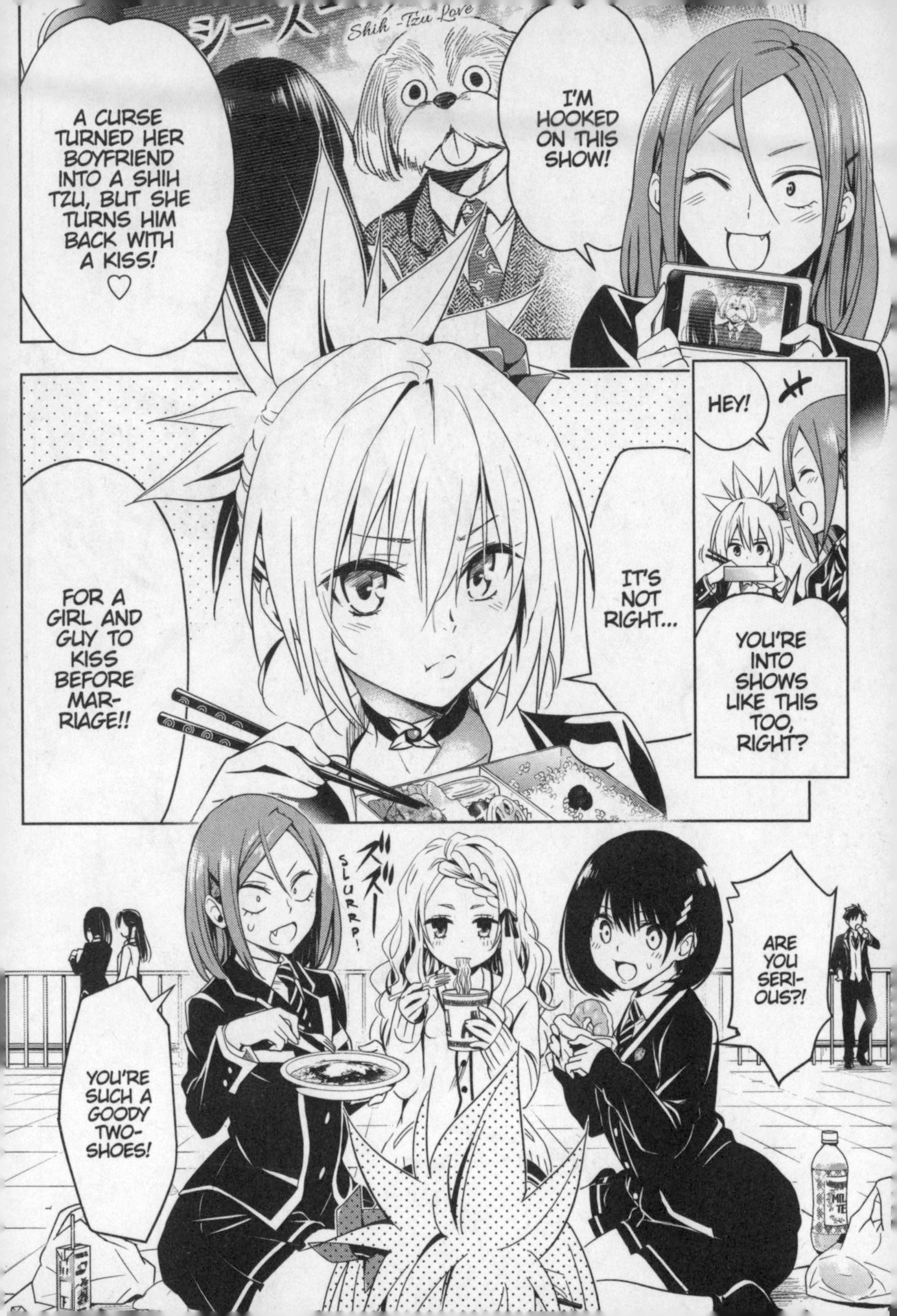
Shih-Tzu Love
I'M HOOKED ON THIS SHOW!
A CURSE TURNED HER BOYFRIEND INTO A SHIH TZU, BUT SHE TURNS HIM BACK WITH A KISS! ♡
HEY!
YOU'RE INTO SHOWS LIKE THIS TOO, RIGHT?
IT'S NOT RIGHT...
FOR A GIRL AND GUY TO KISS BEFORE MAR-RIAGE!!
ARE YOU SERI-OUS?!
SLURRP!
YOU'RE SUCH A GOODY TWO-SHOES!

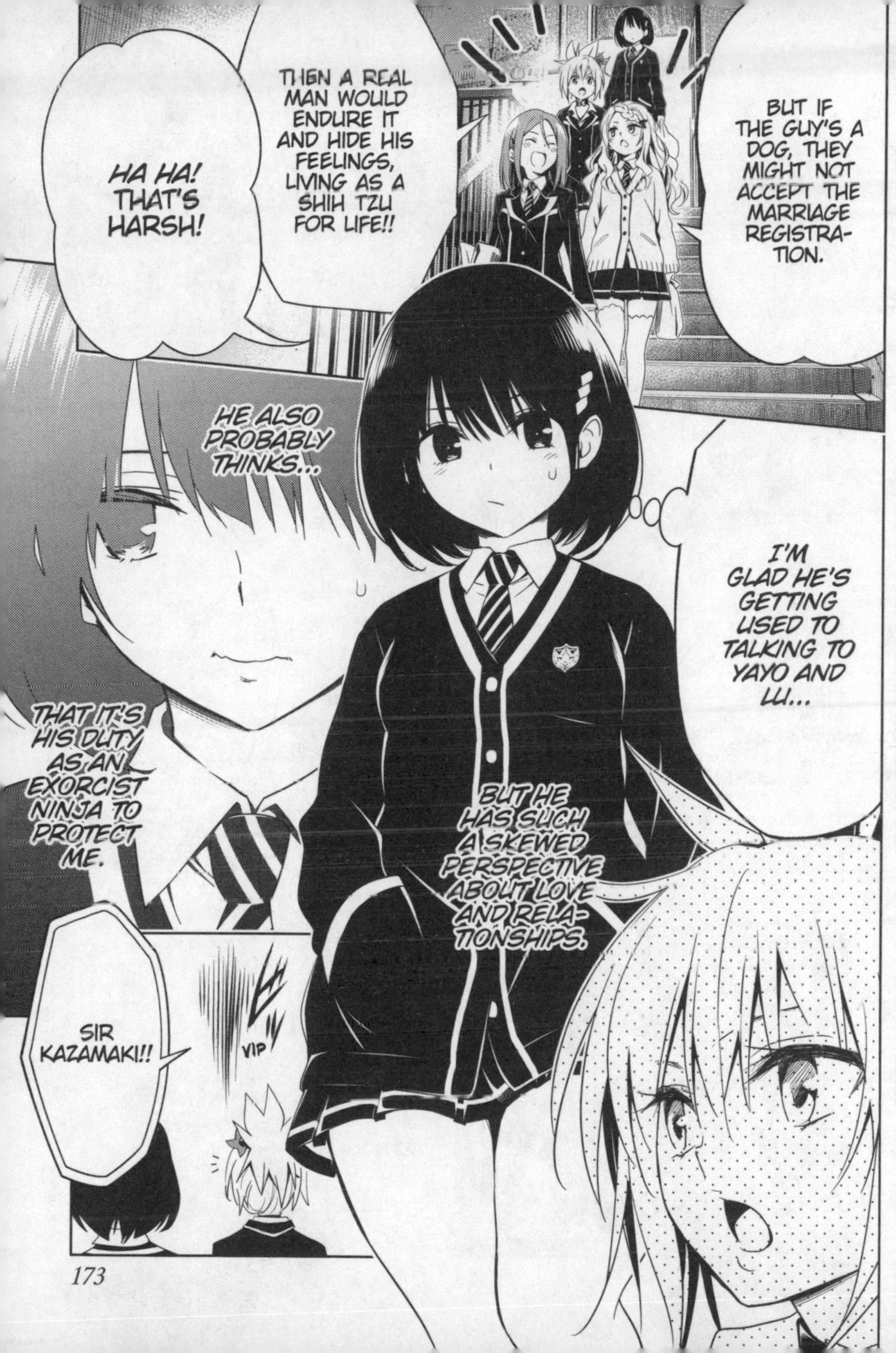
BUT IF THE GUY'S A DOG, THEY MIGHT NOT ACCEPT THE MARRIAGE REGISTRATION.
THEN A REAL MAN WOULD ENDURE IT AND HIDE HIS FEELINGS, LIVING AS A SHIH TZU FOR LIFE!!
HA HA! THAT'S HARSH!
I'M GLAD HE'S GETTING USED TO TALKING TO YAYO AND LU...
BUT HE HAS SUCH A SKEWED PERSPECTIVE ABOUT LOVE AND RELATIONSHIPS.
HE ALSO PROBABLY THINKS...
THAT IT'S HIS DUTY AS AN EXORCIST NINJA TO PROTECT ME.
SIR KAZAMAKI!!
VIP

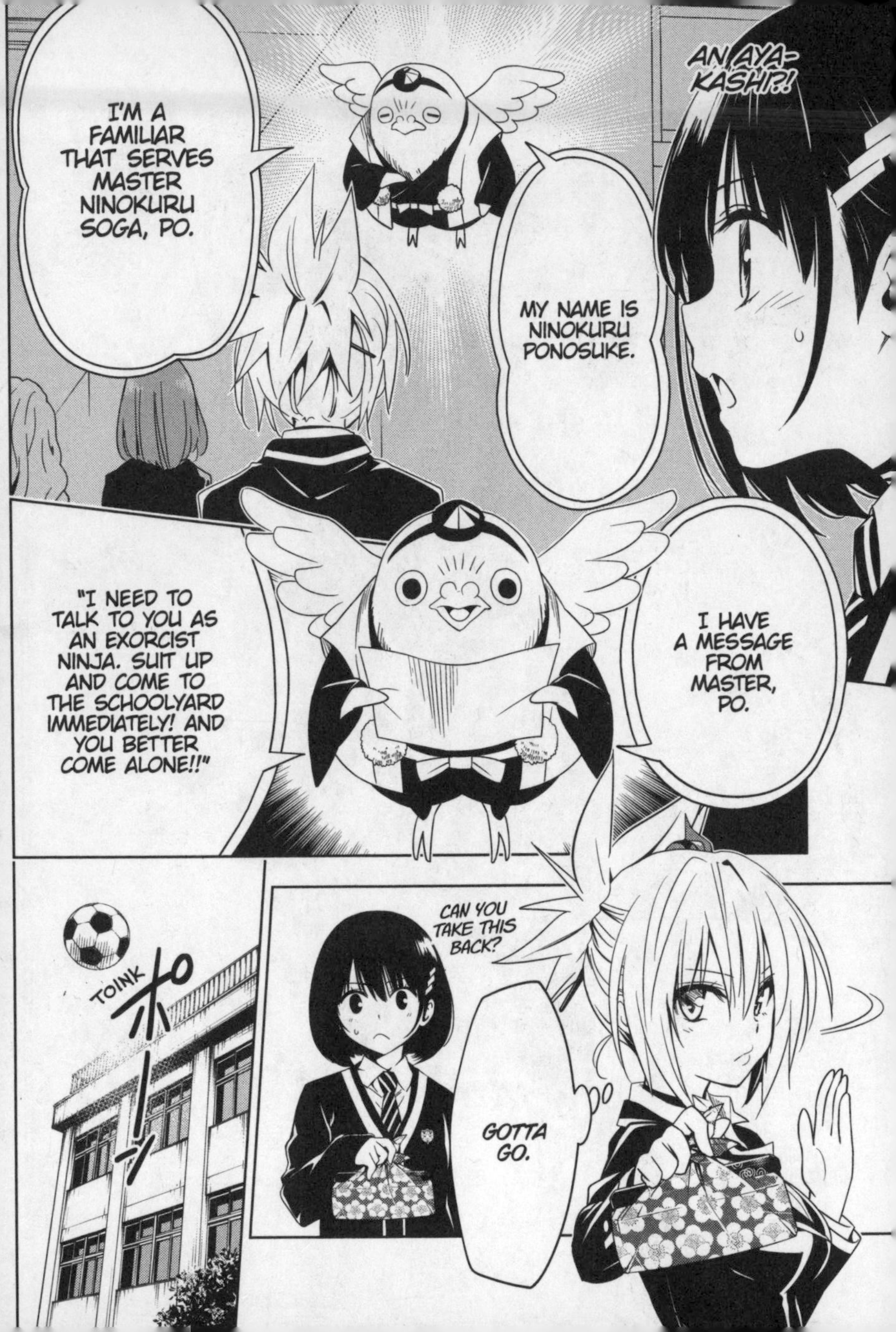
AN AYA-KASHI?!
MY NAME IS NINOKURU PONOSUKE.
I'M A FAMILIAR THAT SERVES MASTER NINOKURU SOGA, PO.
I HAVE A MESSAGE FROM MASTER, PO.
"I NEED TO TALK TO YOU AS AN EXORCIST NINJA. SUIT UP AND COME TO THE SCHOOLYARD IMMEDIATELY! AND YOU BETTER COME ALONE!!"
CAN YOU TAKE THIS BACK?
GOTTA GO.
TOINK

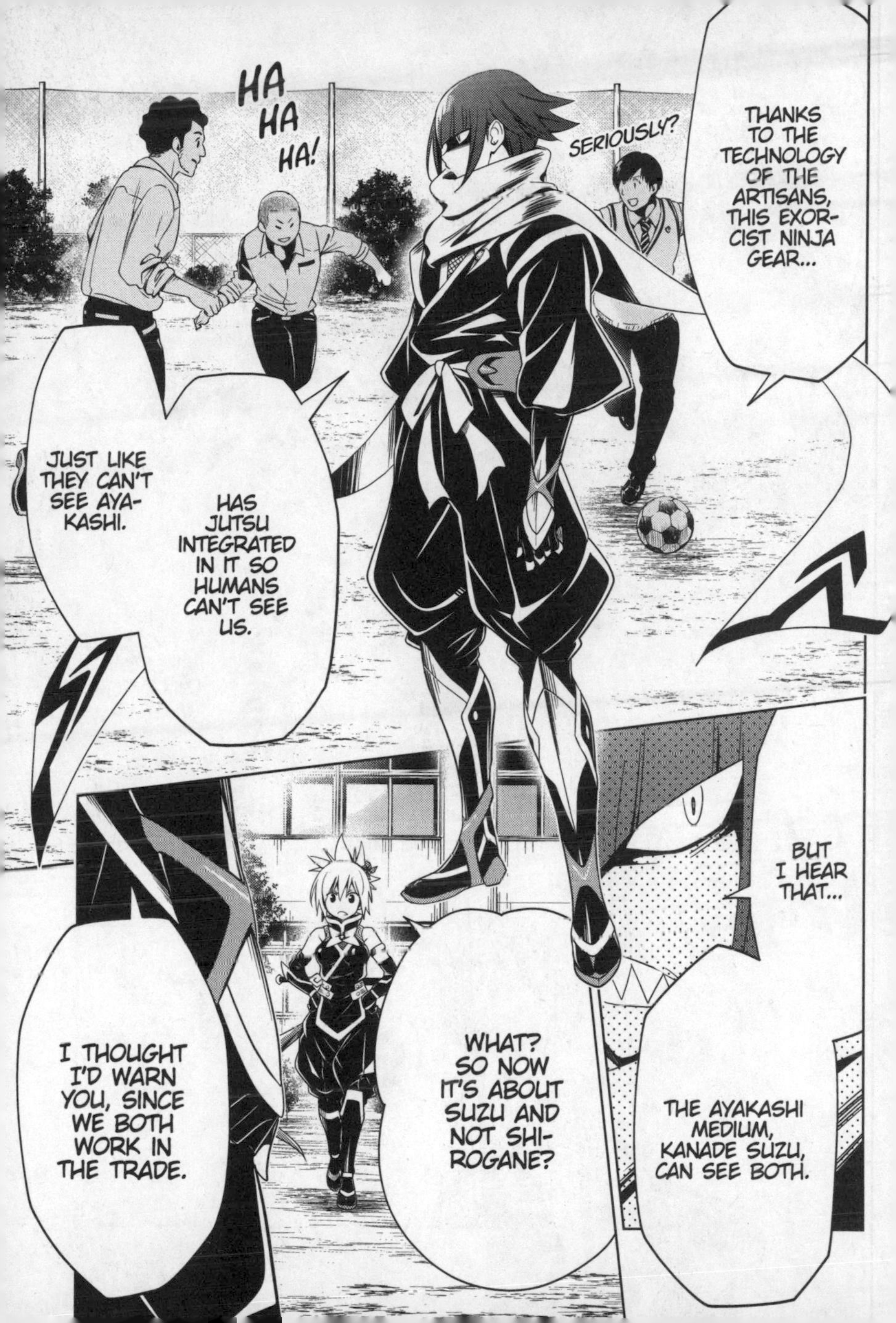
THANKS TO THE TECHNOLOGY OF THE ARTISANS, THIS EXORCIST NINJA GEAR...
SERIOUSLY?
HA HA HA!
HAS JUTSU INTEGRATED IN IT SO HUMANS CAN'T SEE US.
JUST LIKE THEY CAN'T SEE AYAKASHI.
BUT I HEAR THAT...
THE AYAKASHI MEDIUM, KANADE SUZU, CAN SEE BOTH.
WHAT? SO NOW IT'S ABOUT SUZU AND NOT SHIROGANE?
I THOUGHT I'D WARN YOU, SINCE WE BOTH WORK IN THE TRADE.

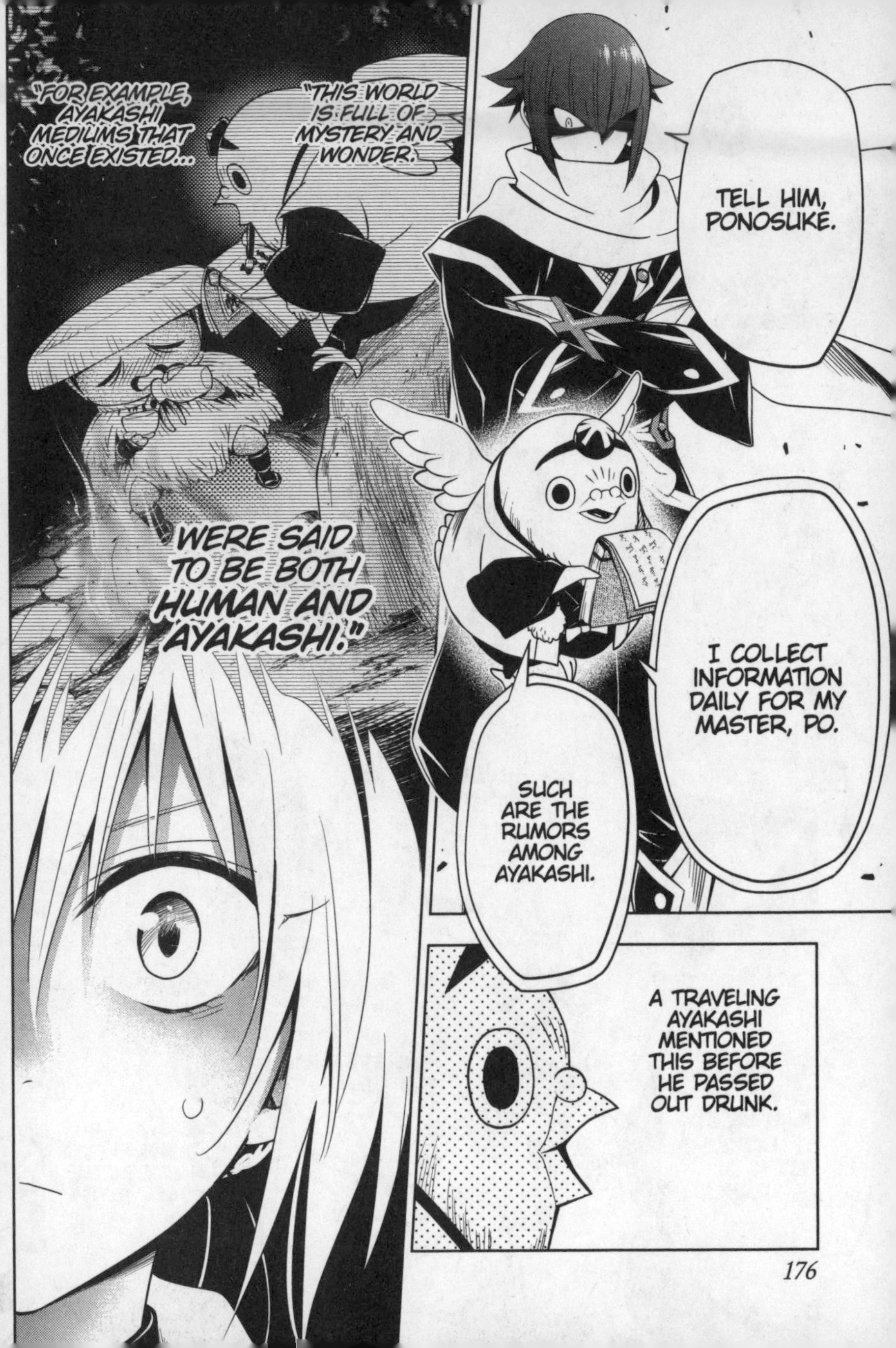
TELL HIM, PONOSUKE.
I COLLECT INFORMATION DAILY FOR MY MASTER, PO.
SUCH ARE THE RUMORS AMONG AYAKASHI.
A TRAVELING AYAKASHI MENTIONED THIS BEFORE HE PASSED OUT DRUNK.
"THIS WORLD IS FULL OF MYSTERY AND WONDER.
"FOR EXAMPLE, AYAKASHI MEDIUMS THAT ONCE EXISTED...
WERE SAID TO BE BOTH HUMAN AND AYAKASHI."

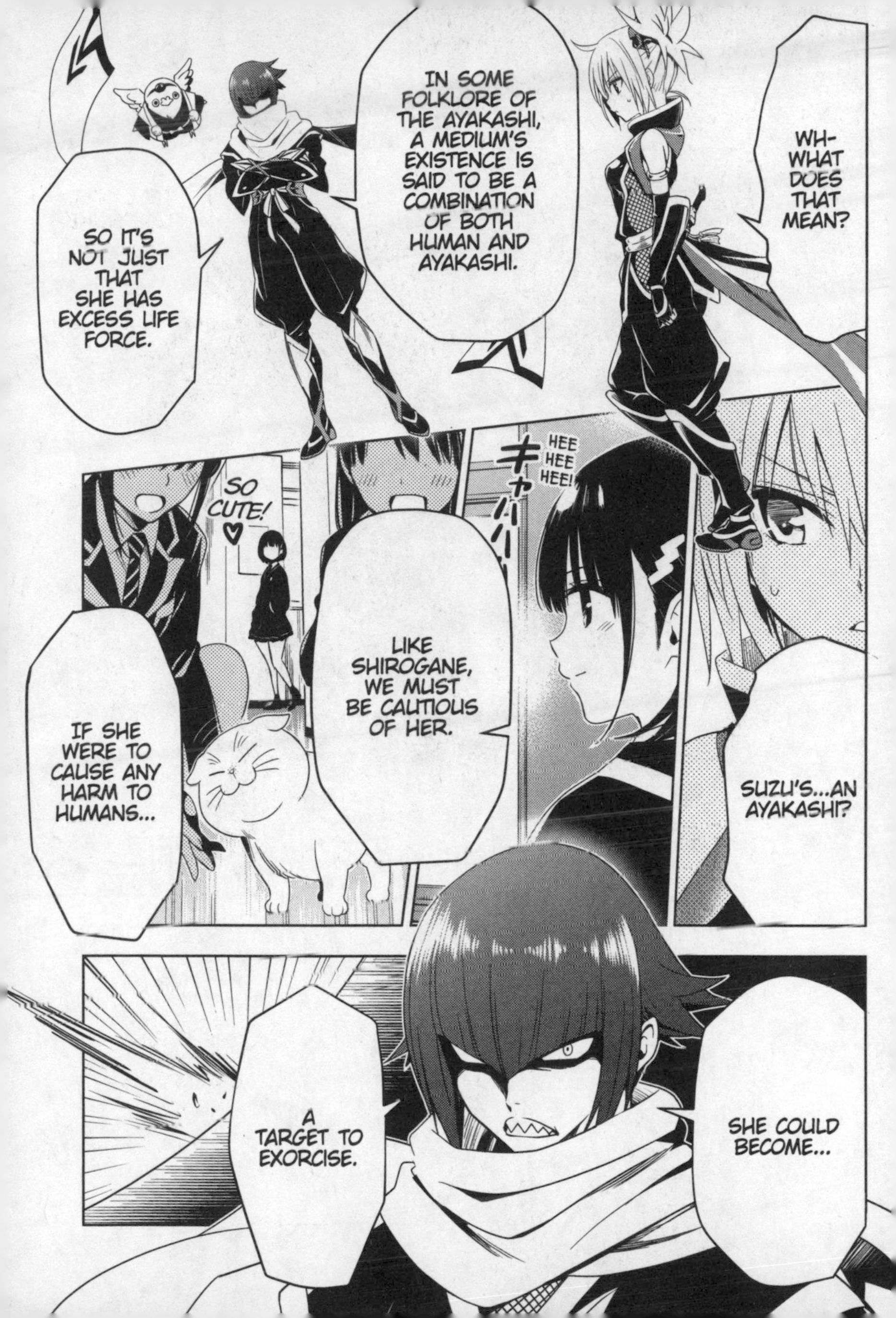
WH- WHAT DOES THAT MEAN?
IN SOME FOLKLORE OF THE AYAKASHI, A MEDIUM'S EXISTENCE IS SAID TO BE A COMBINATION OF BOTH HUMAN AND AYAKASHI.
SO IT'S NOT JUST THAT SHE HAS EXCESS LIFE FORCE.
SUZU'S...AN AYAKASHI?
HEE HEE HEE!
LIKE SHIROGANE, WE MUST BE CAUTIOUS OF HER.
SO CUTE! ♥
IF SHE WERE TO CAUSE ANY HARM TO HUMANS...
SHE COULD BECOME...
A TARGET TO EXORCISE.

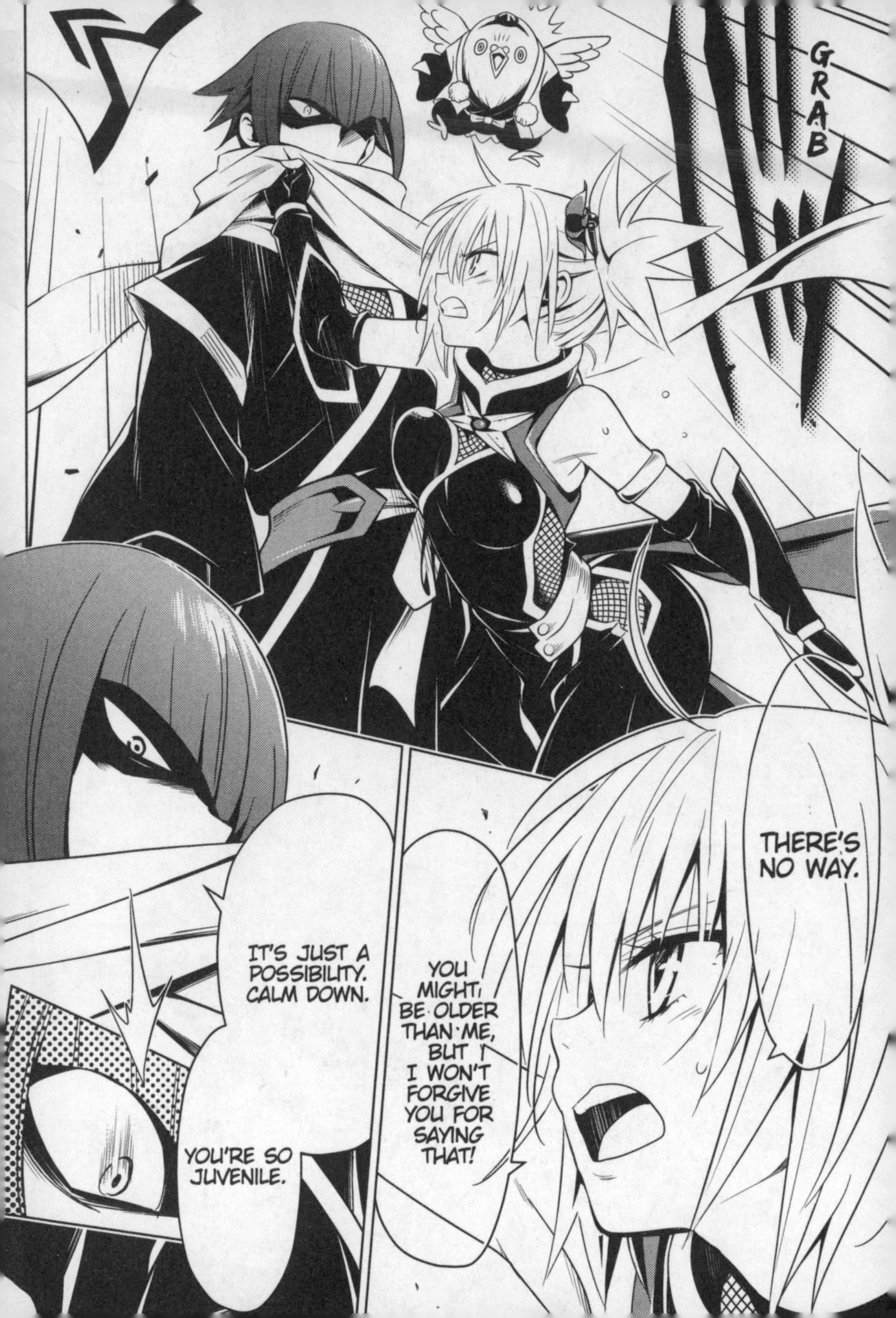
GRAB
THERE'S NO WAY.
YOU MIGHT BE OLDER THAN ME, BUT I WON'T FORGIVE YOU FOR SAYING THAT!
IT'S JUST A POSSIBILITY. CALM DOWN.
YOU'RE SO JUVENILE.

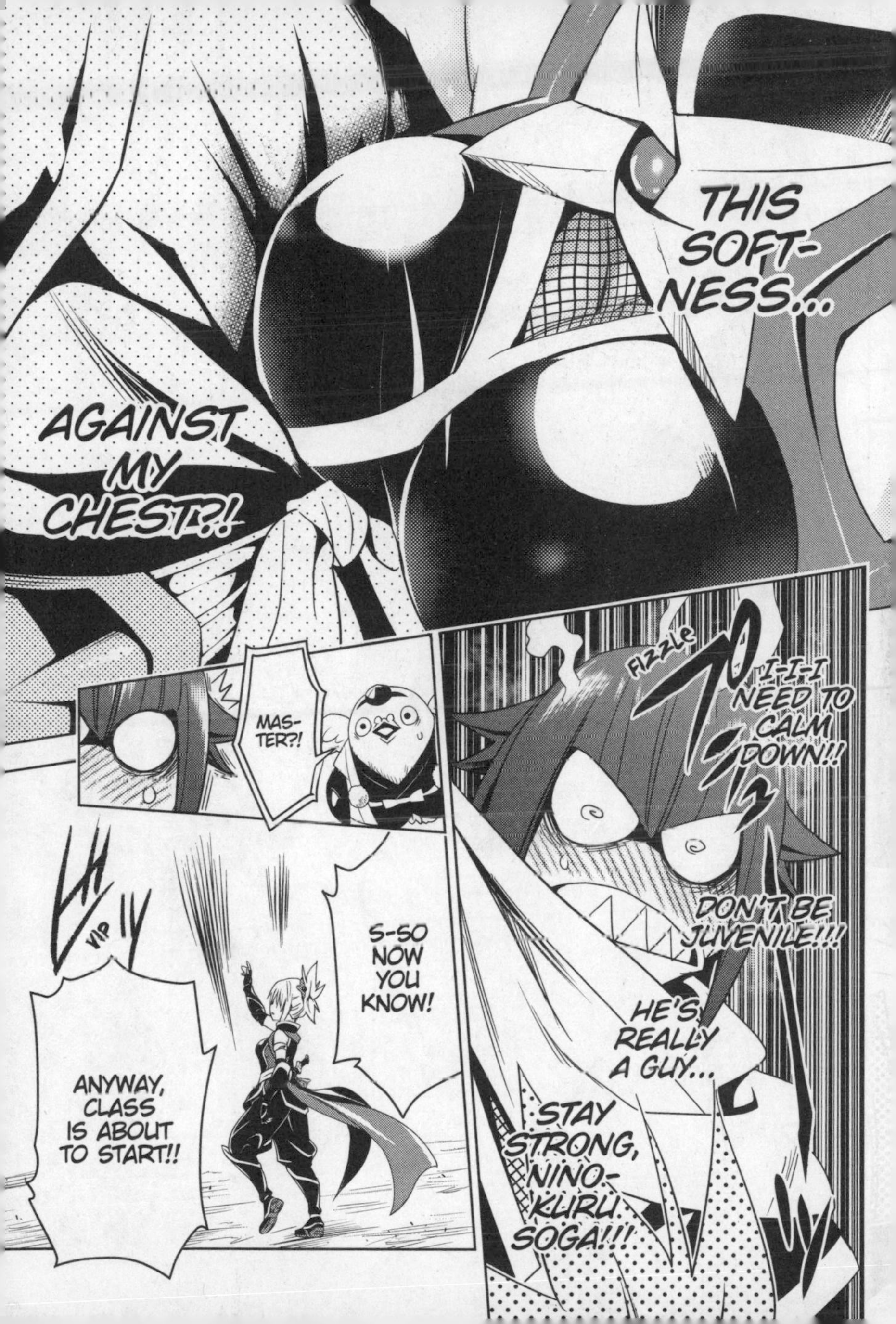
THIS SOFTNESS...
AGAINST MY CHEST?!
Fizzle
I-I-I NEED TO CALM DOWN!!
DON'T BE JUVENILE!!!
HE'S REALLY A GUY...
STAY STRONG, NINOKURU SOGA!!!
MASTER?!
VIP
S-SO NOW YOU KNOW!
ANYWAY, CLASS IS ABOUT TO START!!

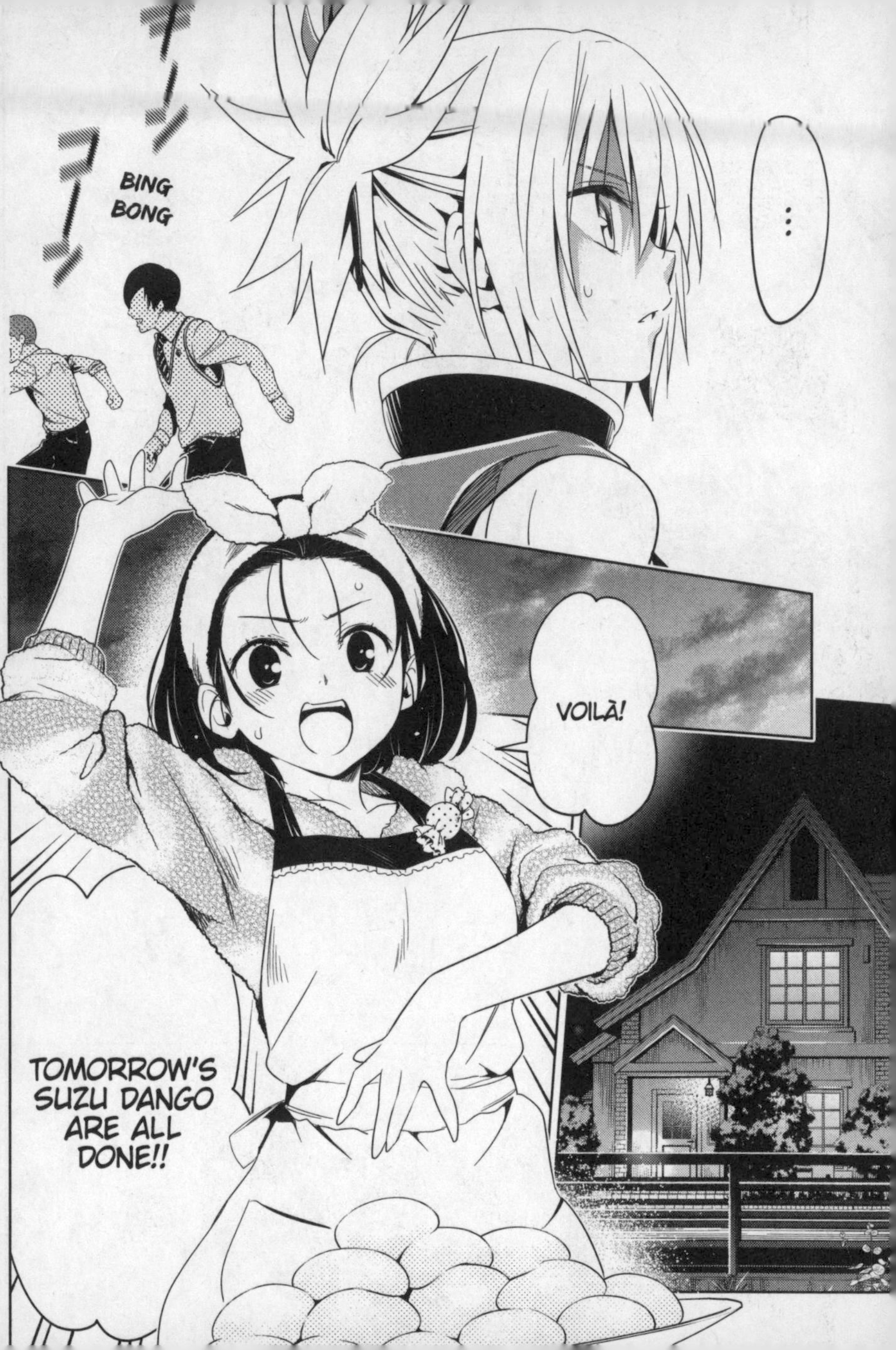
...
BING BONG
VOILÀ!
TOMORROW'S SUZU DANGO ARE ALL DONE!!

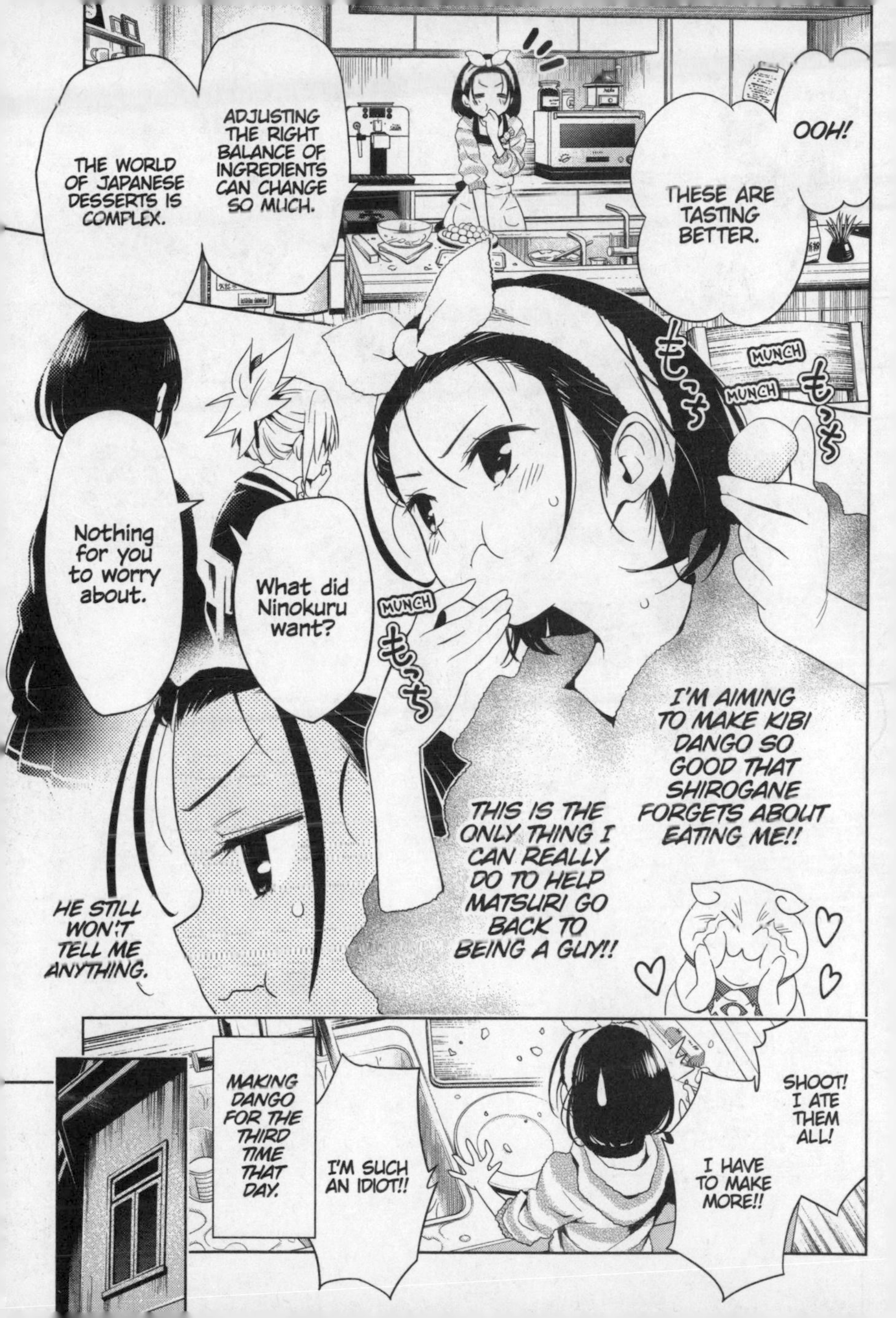
OOH!
THESE ARE TASTING BETTER.
ADJUSTING THE RIGHT BALANCE OF INGREDIENTS CAN CHANGE SO MUCH.
THE WORLD OF JAPANESE DESSERTS IS COMPLEX.
もっち
MUNCH
もっち
MUNCH
What did Ninokuru want?
もっち
MUNCH
Nothing for you to worry about.
I'M AIMING TO MAKE KIBI DANGO SO GOOD THAT SHIROGANE FORGETS ABOUT EATING ME!!
THIS IS THE ONLY THING I CAN REALLY DO TO HELP MATSURI GO BACK TO BEING A GUY!!
HE STILL WON'T TELL ME ANYTHING.
SHOOT! I ATE THEM ALL!
I HAVE TO MAKE MORE!!
I'M SUCH AN IDIOT!!
MAKING DANGO FOR THE THIRD TIME THAT DAY.

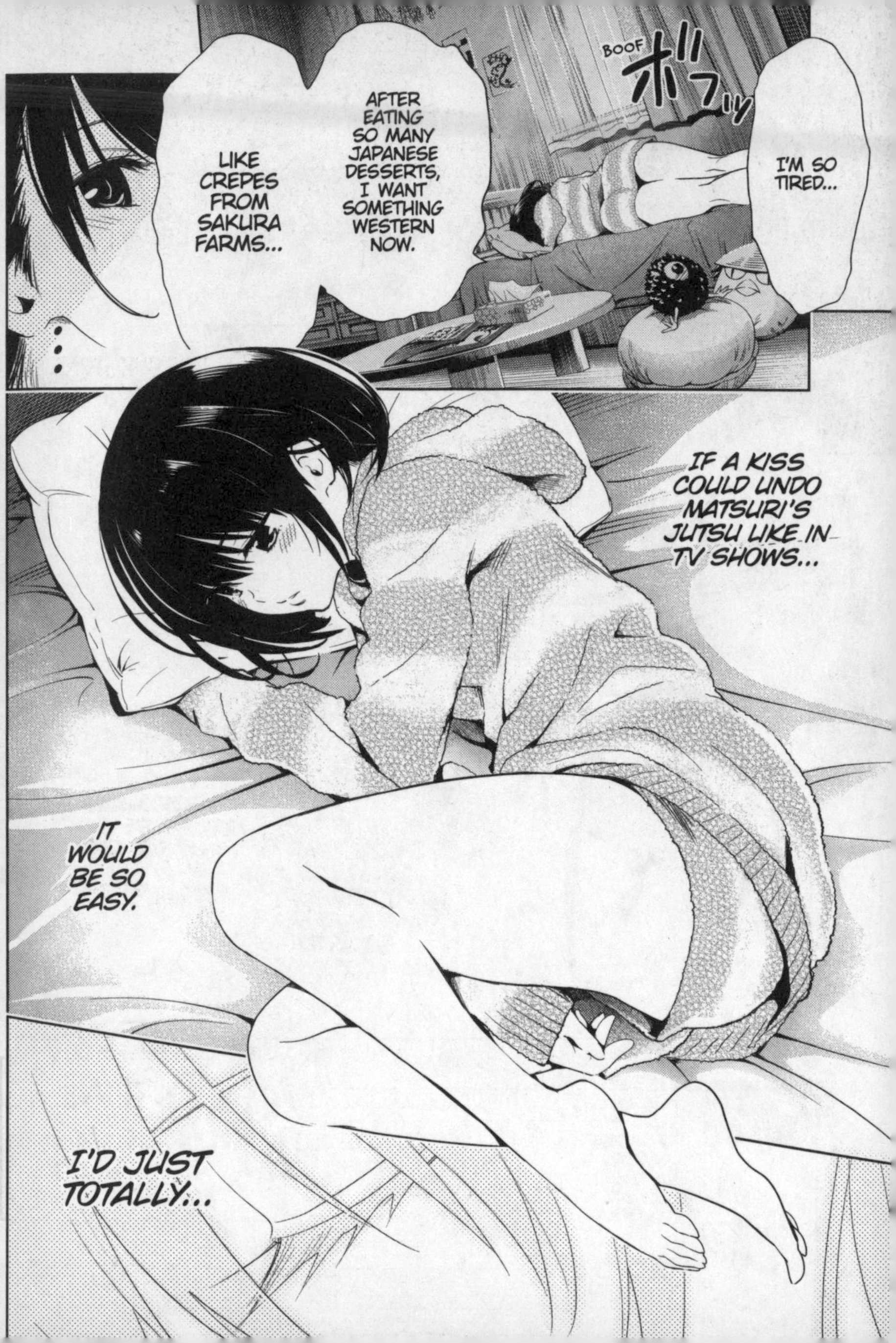
BOOF
ボフッ
I'M SO TIRED...
AFTER EATING SO MANY JAPANESE DESSERTS, I WANT SOMETHING WESTERN NOW.
LIKE CREPES FROM SAKURA FARMS...
...
IF A KISS COULD UNDO MATSURI'S JUTSU LIKE IN TV SHOWS...
IT WOULD BE SO EASY.
I'D JUST TOTALLY...

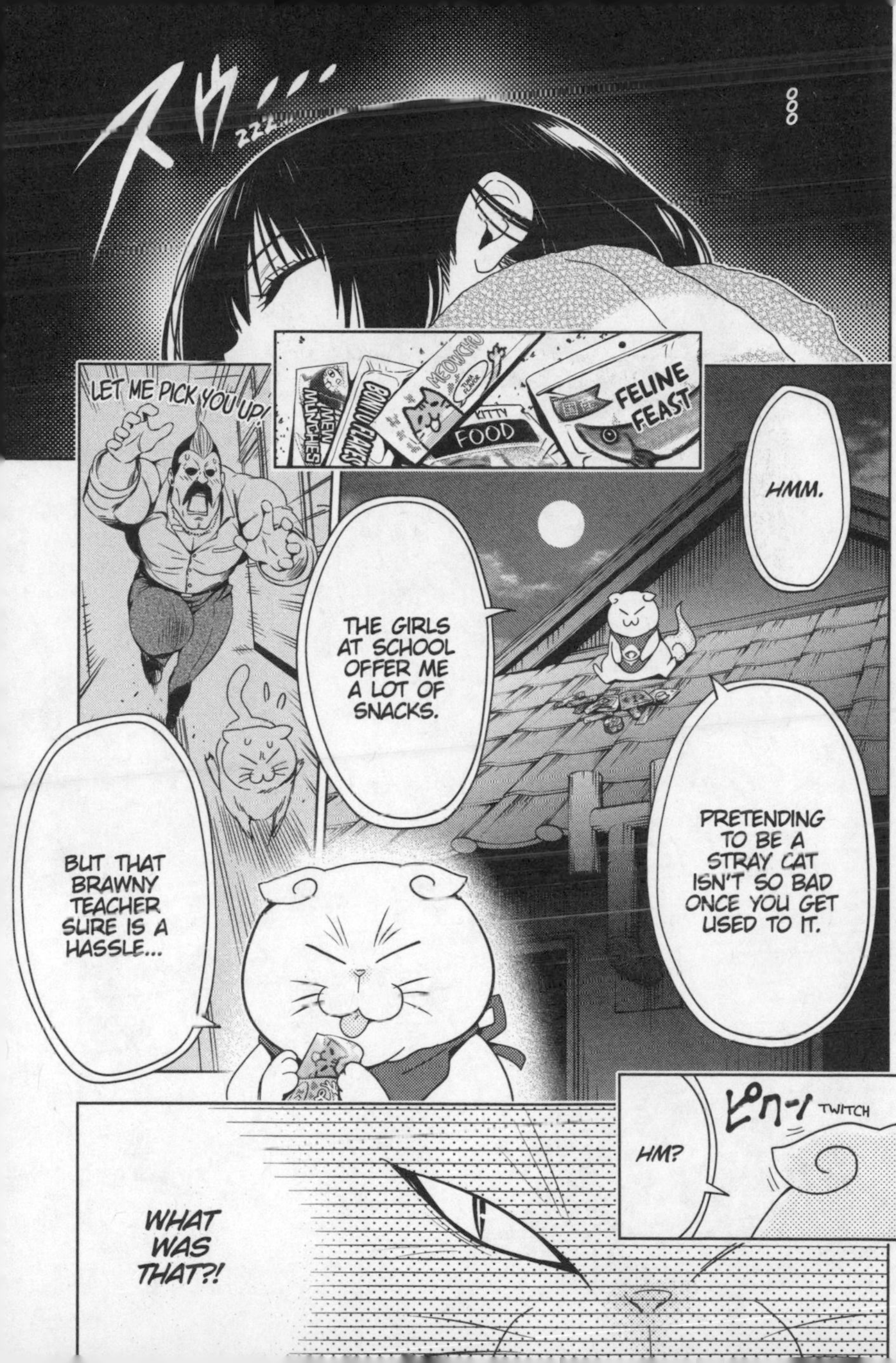
zzz...
FELINE FEAST
KITTY FOOD
MEOWCHU
BONITO FLAKES
MEW MUNCHIES
HMM.
THE GIRLS AT SCHOOL OFFER ME A LOT OF SNACKS.
LET ME PICK YOU UP!
PRETENDING TO BE A STRAY CAT ISN'T SO BAD ONCE YOU GET USED TO IT.
BUT THAT BRAWNY TEACHER SURE IS A HASSLE...
TWITCH
HM?
WHAT WAS THAT?!

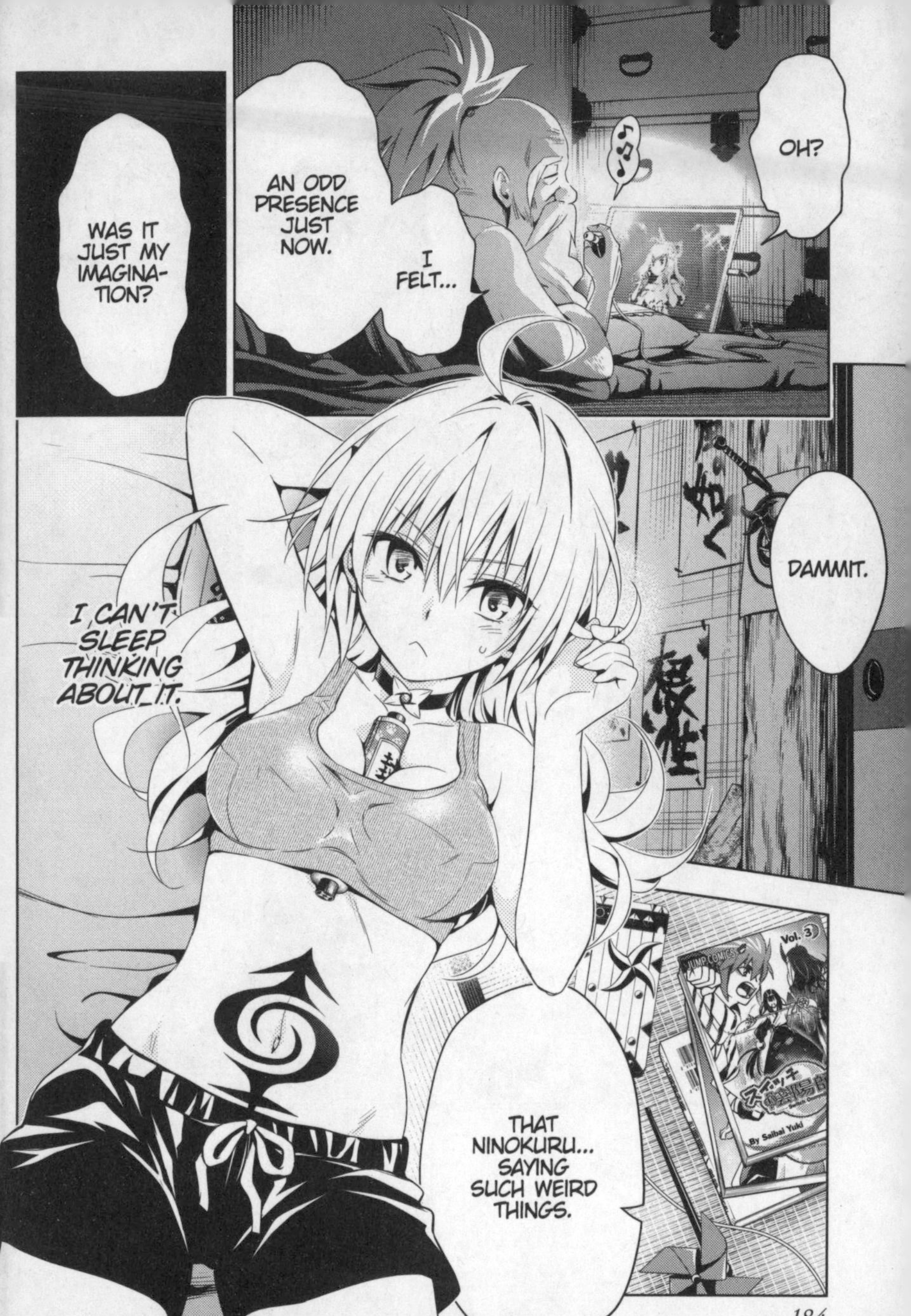
OH?
I FELT...
AN ODD PRESENCE JUST NOW.
WAS IT JUST MY IMAGINATION?
DAMMIT.
I CAN'T SLEEP THINKING ABOUT IT.
THAT NINOKURU... SAYING SUCH WEIRD THINGS.
JUMP COMICS
Vol. 3
By Saibai Yuki

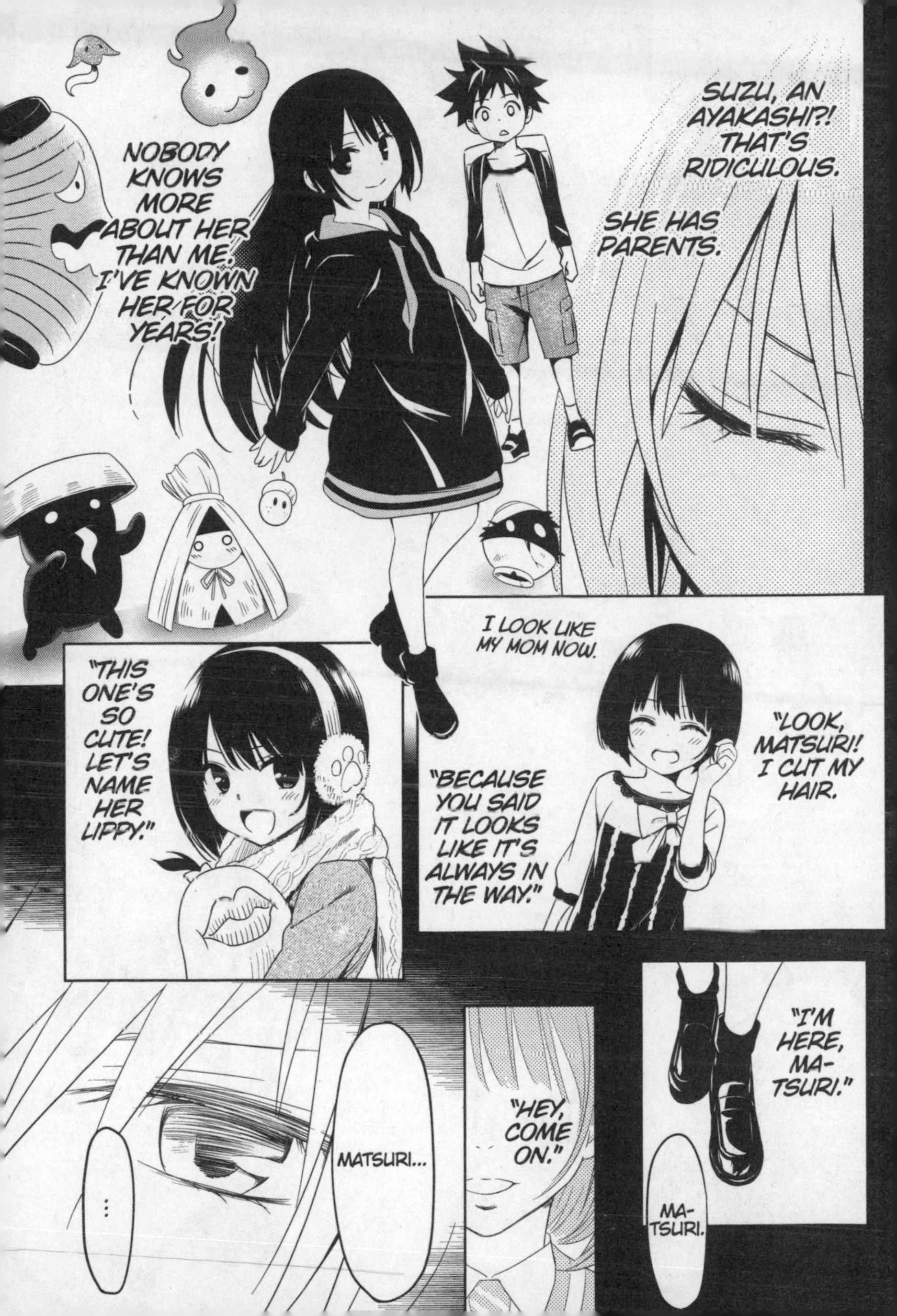
SUZU, AN AYAKASHI?! THAT'S RIDICULOUS.
SHE HAS PARENTS.
NOBODY KNOWS MORE ABOUT HER THAN ME. I'VE KNOWN HER FOR YEARS!
"LOOK, MATSURI! I CUT MY HAIR.
"BECAUSE YOU SAID IT LOOKS LIKE IT'S ALWAYS IN THE WAY."
I LOOK LIKE MY MOM NOW.
"THIS ONE'S SO CUTE! LET'S NAME HER LIPPY."
"I'M HERE, MA-TSURI."
MA-TSURI.
"HEY, COME ON."
MATSURI...
...

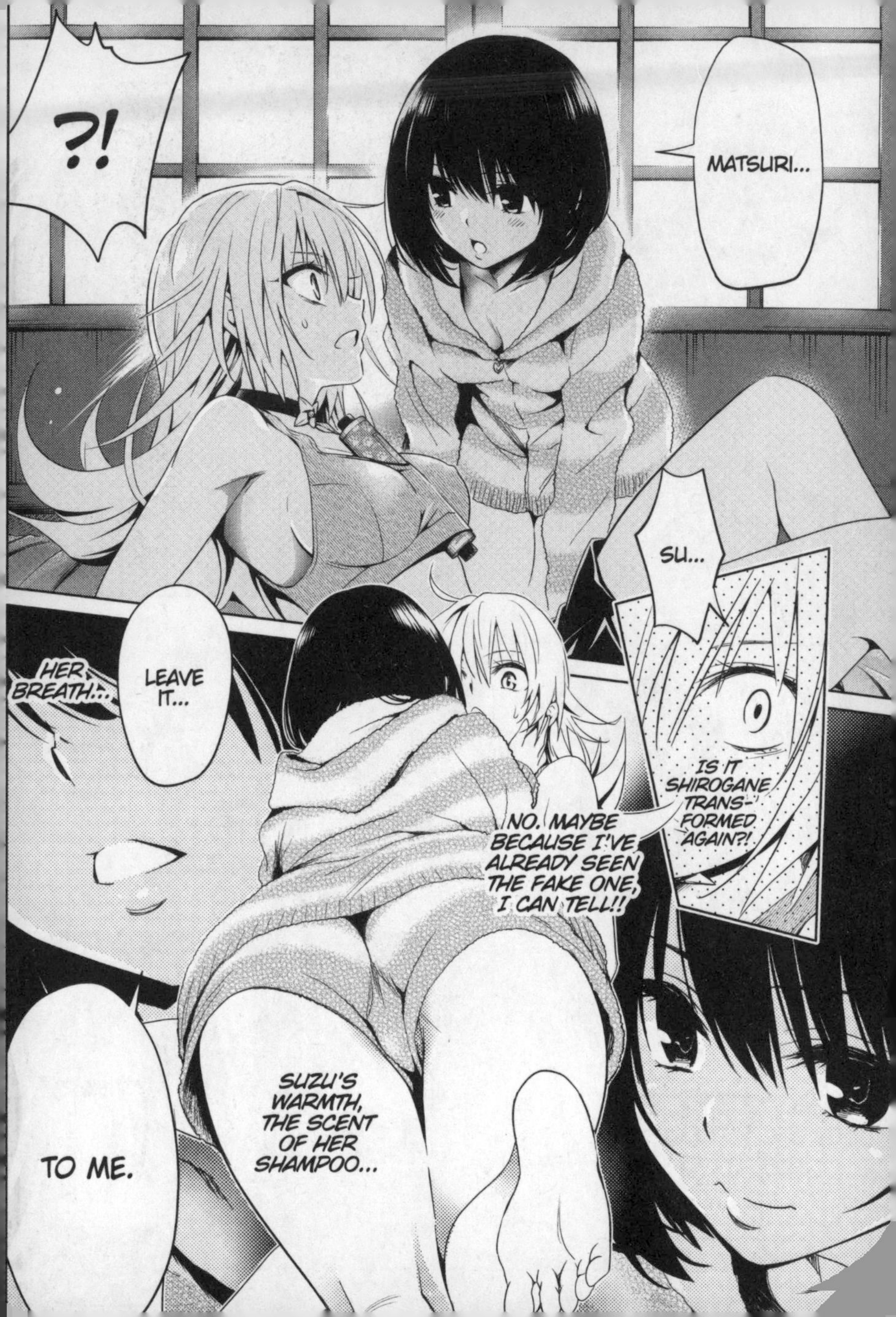
MATSURI...
?!
SU...
IS IT SHIROGANE TRANS-FORMED AGAIN?!
NO. MAYBE BECAUSE I'VE ALREADY SEEN THE FAKE ONE, I CAN TELL!!
LEAVE IT...
HER BREATH...
SUZU'S WARMTH, THE SCENT OF HER SHAMPOO...
TO ME.

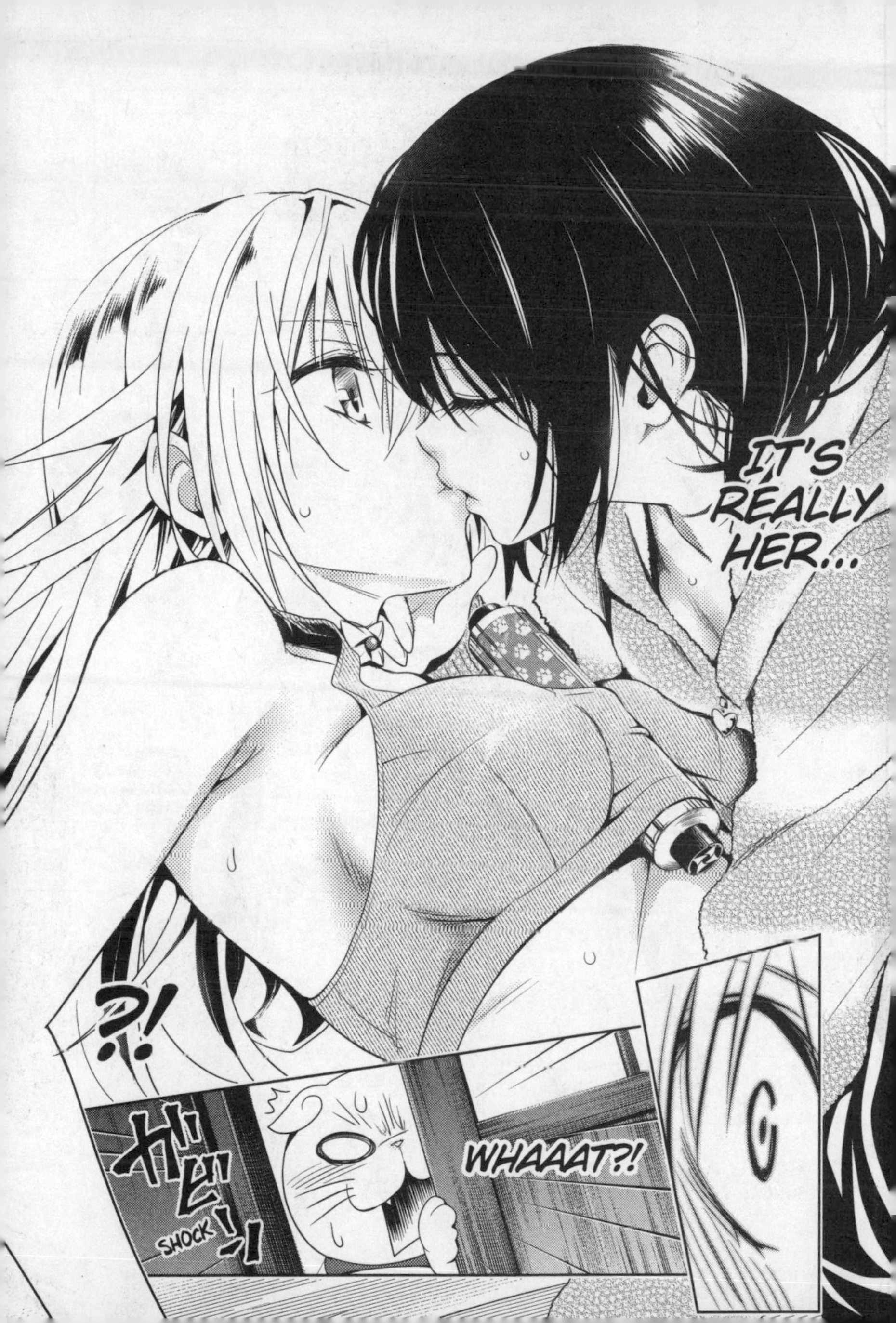
IT'S REALLY HER...
?!
WHAAAT?!
SHOCK

## Bonus Story Matsuri's Undies

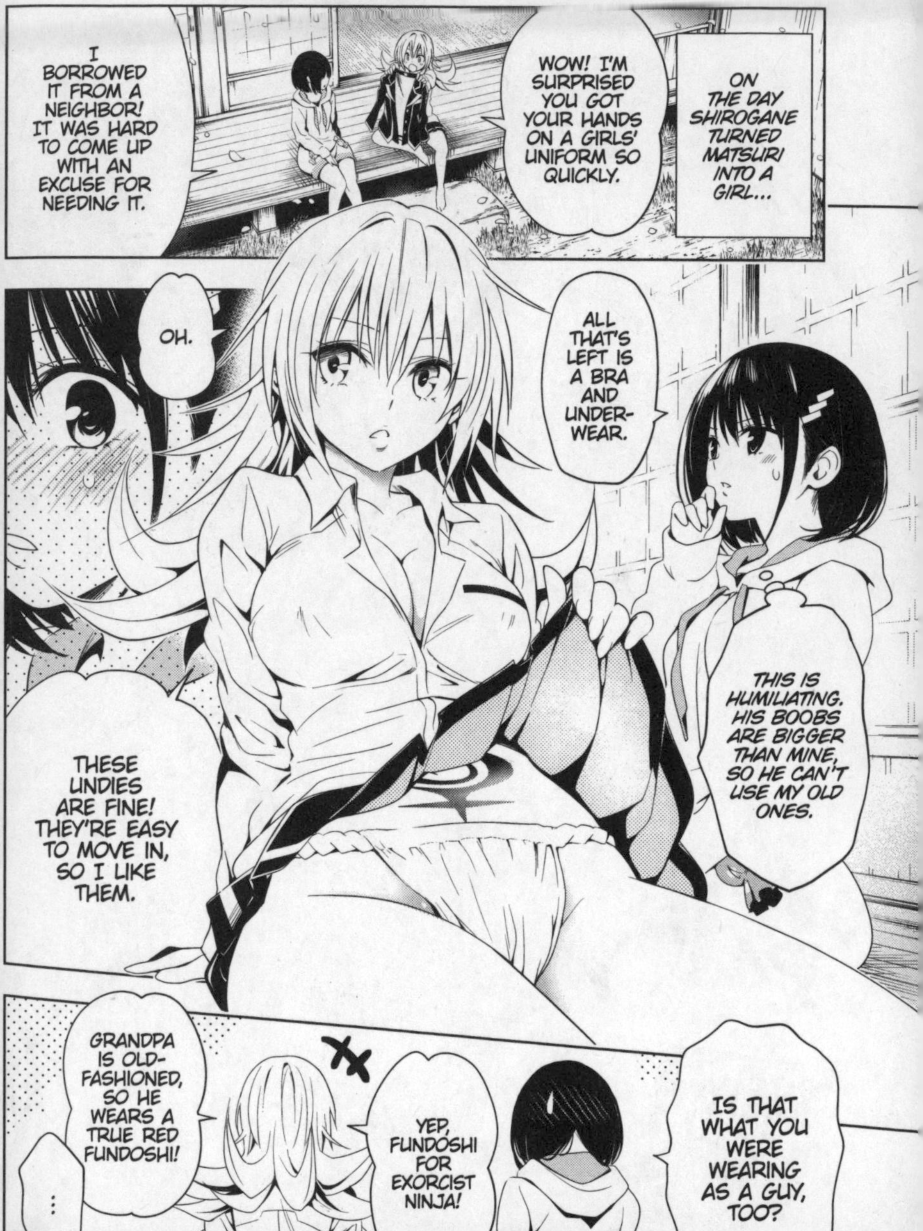

ON THE DAY SHIROGANE TURNED MATSURI INTO A GIRL...
WOW! I'M SURPRISED YOU GOT YOUR HANDS ON A GIRLS' UNIFORM SO QUICKLY.
I BORROWED IT FROM A NEIGHBOR! IT WAS HARD TO COME UP WITH AN EXCUSE FOR NEEDING IT.
ALL THAT'S LEFT IS A BRA AND UNDER-WEAR.
OH.
THIS IS HUMILIATING. HIS BOOBS ARE BIGGER THAN MINE, SO HE CAN'T USE MY OLD ONES.
THESE UNDIES ARE FINE! THEY'RE EASY TO MOVE IN, SO I LIKE THEM.
IS THAT WHAT YOU WERE WEARING AS A GUY, TOO?
YEP, FUNDOSHI FOR EXORCIST NINJA!
GRANDPA IS OLD-FASHIONED, SO HE WEARS A TRUE RED FUNDOSHI!
...


**Volume 1 / End**

# Matsuri's Room Concept Design

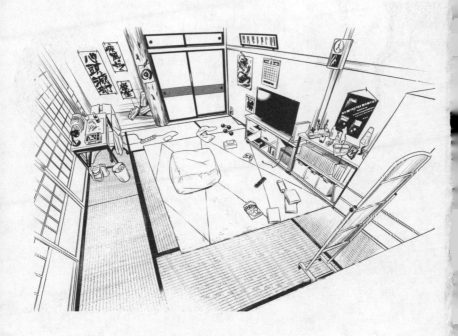

SEVEN SEAS' GHOST SHIP PRESENTS

# AYAKASHI TRIANGLE

story and art by KENTARO YABUKI

VOLUME 1

TRANSLATION
Satsuki Yamashita

LETTERING
Carl Vanstiphout

LOGO DESIGN
George Panella

COVER DESIGN
Nicky Lim

PROOFREADER
Danielle King

COPY EDITOR
B. Lillian Martin

EDITOR
Lark Smith

PRODUCTION DESIGNER
George Panella

PRODUCTION MANAGER
Lissa Pattillo

PREPRESS TECHNICIAN
Melanie Ujimori
Jules Valera

EDITOR-IN-CHIEF
Julie Davis

ASSOCIATE PUBLISHER
Adam Arnold

PUBLISHER
Jason DeAngelis



Seven Seas press and purchase enquiries can be sent to Marketing Manager Lianne Sentar at press@gomanga.com. Information regarding the distribution and purchase of digital editions is available from Digital Manager CK Russell at digital@gomanga.com.



ISBN: 978-1-68579-665-5
Printed in Canada
First Printing: November 2022
10 9 8 7 6 5 4 3 2 1

## READING DIRECTIONS

This book reads from ***right to left***, Japanese style. If this is your first time reading manga, you start reading from the top right panel on each page and take it from there. If you get lost, just follow the numbered diagram here. It may seem backwards at first, but you'll get the hang of it! Have fun!!

1
2
3
4
5
6
7
8
9

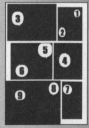